Women and Sexuality in America

a bibliography

G. K. Hall

WOMEN'S STUDIES

Publications

Barbara Haber
Editor

Women and Sexuality in America

a bibliography

NANCY SAHLI

G.K.HALL &CO.

70 LINCOLN STREET, BOSTON, MASS.

Library of Congress Cataloging in Publication Data

Sahli, Nancy Ann.
  Women and sexuality in America

  (A Reference publication in women's studies)
  Includes index.
  1. Women—United States—Sexual behavior—Bibliography.
2. Women—United States—Sexual behavior—History—
Bibliography. I. Title: II. Series.
Z7964.U49S26 1984 [HQ29]   016.3067'088042   84-10751
ISBN 0-8161-8099-7

This publication is printed on permanent/durable acid-free paper
MANUFACTURED IN THE UNITED STATES OF AMERICA

Contents

The Author

Nancy Sahli is on the staff of the National Historical Publications and Records Commission. She graduated from Vassar College and received the Ph.D. from the University of Pennsylvania. She edited the commission's first Directory of Archives and Manuscript Repositories in the United States (1978) and is the author of numerous articles in the fields of archives administration, women's history, and the history of sexuality. Active as a consultant to archival and educational institutions, she is currently writing a history of American women during the first two decades of the twentieth century.

Preface

Women's sexuality, its nature and implications, has been a dominant theme in the development of contemporary feminist theory. The juncture of interest in this subject with the rise of women's history and the history of sexuality as new fields of historical inquiry has generated a need for bibliographic tools to facilitate the researcher's task. This bibliography, to no small extent, has grown out of my own research on women's sexuality and related topics in the late nineteenth and early twentieth centuries, and my realization that existing catalogs, indexes, and other research tools were either too all-encompassing to be used efficiently or, as in the case of many contemporary bibliographies, too ahistorical in their focus to be of much use to scholars seeking to document change over time.

Because of the breadth of the subject and the material available on it, I have had to limit this bibliography in several ways. First, I have chosen to focus primarily on printed materials in the English language--books, pamphlets, and periodical articles--that either were published in the United States during the nineteenth and twentieth centuries or aid in our understanding of women's sexuality in America at that time. Although older items or interpretive writings relating to earlier times have been included occasionally, there was little specific writing about women's sexuality--as opposed to such allied topics as midwifery or woman's overall role--until the early nineteenth century. In fact, many of the sex-related terms we take for granted were not coined until the nineteenth century. It is not surprising that so few historians have chosen to study sexuality and sexual behavior in the colonial period.

I have also chosen to limit the scope of subjects I have included under the rubric "sexuality" to those most directly relating to the definition and behavior of women as sexual beings. The potential for motherhood, for example, plays a role in defining women's sexuality. Child care and birthing practices, for the most part, do not, at least in the literature, and so they have been excluded. Such topics as rape, prostitution, wife battering, and gender role are dealt with in the context of their relationship to woman's innate or acquired sexual identity. Defining sexuality is a difficult task. Increasing scholarship in this field will, it is hoped, lead us to more precise terminology.

Potential entries were initially selected from existing bibliographies relating to sexuality, women's studies, the history of medicine, and allied fields; footnote citations in secondary historical works; and entries in such major multivolume series as the <u>Index-Catalogue of the Library of the Surgeon-General's Office, United States Army</u>, and the printed catalogs of the Institute for Sex Research. Each work was then examined and evaluated in terms of such criteria as its subsequent influence and its significance for gaining an understanding of <u>women's</u> sexuality (many works claiming to discuss people, but that really dealt with men, were thus excluded). Balanced presentation in terms of topics and time periods was also sought. Physical examination of each item alleviated the problem that plagues some bibliographies, that of citing materials that do not exist or are not publicly available.

Literature, popular periodical articles, biographies, and similar works have, with few exceptions, been excluded. My emphasis, therefore, has been on professional literature in such fields as medicine, psychiatry, history, sociology, and women's studies. Maintaining a humanist perspective, however, I have excluded technical works whose specificity or scientific complexity would place them beyond the range of interest of most humanities researchers. Prescriptive literature directed toward popular audiences has, however, been included, as have certain other popular accounts in book form. Over four thousand potential entries were screened for possible inclusion, but, for the reasons outlined above, as well as space limitations, over half of these were excluded from the final product. The bibliography, although it reflects the range of topics and types of publications available in this field, is therefore by no means comprehensive. I can only hope that my selection decisions have been characterized by objective rather than subjective standards. It has, however, simply been impossible to include everything that one might have wanted.

Library locations for books cited in this bibliography may be determined by consulting the <u>National Union Catalog</u>. My own citation is to that edition of the work which I examined, and in most cases, this will be the earliest edition available. Locations of periodicals may be ascertained by consulting the <u>Union List of Serials</u> or the Library of Congress's <u>New Serials Titles</u>. Items not included in one of these union lists, or which are otherwise difficult to locate, have been assigned a library locator symbol as follows: Institute for Sex Research, Indiana University--ISR; Library of Congress--LC; National Library of Medicine--NLM; and the Schlesinger Library, Radcliffe College--SL. Some items are also available as reprints or in microform.

My chapter construction has been guided by major themes in the literature itself. Each chapter begins with a brief introductory statement giving some perspective to the chapter as a whole. Annotated entries are primarily citations to books, whereas the checklists that

follow consist mostly of periodical articles. Citations to works by
Sigmund Freud and Havelock Ellis are to standard editions of these
authors' work rather than to the earliest available American edition.
The author/title index includes citations for authors and works included as entries in the bibliography itself. Authors and works incidentally mentioned in the annotations are included in the subject
index.

Preparation of this bibliography was supported by a grant from
the National Endowment for the Humanities. Research is one of the
great pleasures in my life, and the staffs of several institutions en-
sured that it would be so for this work. They include the National
Library of Medicine, the Library of Congress, the Institute for Sex
Research at Indiana University, the Arthur and Elizabeth Schlesinger
Library on the History of Women in America at Radcliffe College, the
Francis A. Countway Library of Medicine at Harvard University, and the
libraries of the University of Maryland. Other colleagues and friends
uncovered obscure citations, served as sounding boards for my ideas,
and generally cheered me on. To Margaret Child, Linda Henry, Cindy
Todd, and Bill Wallach I am especially grateful. Most of all, I must
thank my research assistant, Carolin B. Head, who waded through what
seemed like endless volumes of crumbling periodicals, straining her
eyes at the fine print of obscure indexes and articles, and who, like
me, wondered if this project would ever end. Well, it has, and here
it is at last.

Introduction

In their recent publication, The Family Book about Sexuality
(entry 859), Mary Steichen Calderone and Eric Johnson define sexuality
as "the whole person, including his or her thoughts, experiences, learn-
ings, ideas, values, and imaginings, as these have to do with his being
male or her being female." In the broadest sense, they are, of course,
correct, and yet such a definition leaves us feeling that sexuality is
almost synonymous with the whole of human life. Other people have at-
tached narrower meanings to the term, focusing on specific sexual ideas,
attitudes, and behavior, such as those related to sexual preference and
identity, but excluding such areas as gender role, pregnancy and childbirth, birth control, and sex discrimination. But even such narrower
definitions leave us asking what is sexual behavior? Is it, as Alfred
C. Kinsey used the term, behavior that can lead ultimately to orgasm?
Or, as many feminists would argue, does this definition impose a male-
oriented model on women, whose sexual feelings and erotic responses
are much more diffuse and less focused on the performance of a particular sequence of actions leading to a specific goal?

Obviously, there are no easy answers to this problem, and if the
definitions of women's sexuality are diverse, so is the literature
that relates to it. Beginning in the early nineteenth century, however, when much of the work in this field began to appear, certain
trends are clearly visible. First, at that time, the dividing line
between professional and popular literature was very thin. Little was
known about human reproductive and sexual physiology, and would-be
scientific writers aiming at an audience of physicians often showed
little difference in either their ideas or manner of presentation from
authors writing for the masses. Hearsay was accepted as fact, and
empirical proof was absent more often than not. And, although this
situation improved as the century progressed, it was not until well
into the twentieth century that truly scientific research into human
sexual behavior would become prevalent. Masters and Johnson's study
of the physiology of human sexual response (entry 580) was not published until 1966.

Obviously, too, much of the material about women was written by men, whose ideas were, in turn, tempered by their own subjective, culturally bound preconceptions of what women's normal sexuality ought to be. There was, however, some difference of opinion, and while writers like William Acton cheerfully denied that women were sexual creatures at all, others warned that women's sexuality could lead them into such dangers as masturbation and nymphomania. Women writers, though in a distinct minority, were not completely free from these dominant strains of thought. Yet, while Elizabeth Blackwell joined with her male colleagues in condemning masturbation, she also called for a recognition of women's sexual nature and of possible differences between the sexuality of women and men.

By the end of the nineteenth century, several new developments were taking place that were reflected in the literature. Sexual variations, or "perversions" as they were then known, were being widely discussed for the first time by European and American sexologists. Close friendships between women, for example, were redefined as examples of lesbian sexuality. The free love movement questioned the rationale of confining heterosexual relationships to conventional marriage, while the social purity movement sought to impose a uniform chastity on unmarried men and women alike. Individuals such as Robert Latou Dickinson and Clelia Duel Mosher started to systematically compile some of the first data on the sexual behavior and attitudes of average women. In Vienna Sigmund Freud initiated work on psychoanalysis, ideas destined to have a major impact on thinking about women's sexuality, while in England Havelock Ellis was writing his Studies in the Psychology of Sex.

In addition to these trends, other patterns in the literature on women's sexuality developed during the early years of the twentieth century. Feminism brought in its wake a rash of studies examining woman's nature and role. And although these synthetic works were often far from objective in their goals, new sociological studies of sexual attitudes and behavior were not. By 1929 when Katharine Bement Davis published Factors in the Sex Life of Twenty-Two Hundred Women (entry 951), knowledge of women's sexuality was light years away from the days of William Acton and Elizabeth Blackwell. Relaxation of censorship codes following World War I plus a liberalization of attitudes regarding permissible sexual behavior increased not only the amount of literature on sex available to the general public but the content of that literature as well.

Although World War II brought a temporary hiatus to much research on sexuality, it had little impact on the work of Alfred C. Kinsey. Funded by grants from the National Research Council, an organization that supported some of the major sex research of that time, he published Sexual Behavior in the Human Female (entry 975) in 1953. While Kinsey was completing his monumental task, William H. Masters was beginning the ground-breaking studies he eventually published, along with colleague Virginia E. Johnson, as Human Sexual Response (entry 580) and Human Sexual Inadequacy (entry 1584).

Feminist theory also experienced a rebirth after World War II, slowly at first with studies such as Simone de Beauvoir's <u>The Second Sex</u> (entry 144) and then in a landslide after the appearance of Betty Friedan's <u>The Feminine Mystique</u> (entry 157). New social science and laboratory research on women's sexuality, such as that conducted by Masters and Johnson, was incorporated into feminist theory. Other developments at this time which contributed substantially to increasing understanding of women's sexuality were the growth of historical research on human sexuality and women's history, the development of new attitudes toward sexual dysfunction and methods for its treatment, and an ever increasing openness toward matters sexual in all areas of American life.

These, then, are some of the patterns in the history and literature of women's sexuality that are documented in this book. Thinking about women's sexuality, while still governed more than we would care to admit by stereotypes and social conditioning, has moved away from folklore, misinformation, and subjective pontificating toward objectivity, rationality, scientific analysis, and a new recognition of women's real concerns and needs. This bibliography may bring its users no closer to a clear definition of women's sexuality than they were at the beginning of this introduction, but if they achieve at least a sense of its historical complexity and diversity, this work will have accomplished its goal.

Bibliography

Bibliography is the cornerstone of sound scholarship, and researchers in female sexuality and related fields have particularly
benefited from the increased availability of specialized bibliographic
materials relating to women resulting from the contemporary feminist
movement. Works such as Patricia K. Ballou's Women: A Bibliography
of Bibliographies (entry 3) and Esther Stineman's Women's Studies: A
Recommended Core Bibliography (entry 33) reflect this trend.

At the same time, many of these bibliographies are comparatively
unhistorical in perspective, making it essential for scholars to delve
deeper into such basic conglomerate tools as the multiple volumes of
the Index-Catalogue of the Library of the Surgeon-General's Office,
United States Army, the Index Medicus, and the many guides to other
popular and professional periodical literature. Not to be overlooked
are the printed catalogs of the holdings of the Institute for Sex
Research, which, because of their subject arrangement, not to mention
their focus on sex-related topics, should form an essential part of the
sexuality researcher's bibliographic vocabulary.

Because most bibliographies do not function as union catalogs,
readers will need to supplement their searches in these volumes with
further consultation of the National Union Catalog, for locations of
books and pamphlets in the United States and Canada, and the Union
List of Serials and the Library of Congress's New Serials Titles for
periodical holdings of libraries. Similar union lists exist for holdings of institutions in certain geographical areas or for specific
subject fields. Some entries may be obsolete because of library dis-
position policies, loss, theft, and related problems, and the comparative rarity of many materials in the field of sex research makes it
essential for the researcher to have a wide array of bibliographic
skills at her or his command. Work with archives, manuscript collections, and similar primary source materials demands equal ingenuity
and perseverance.

1   Abortion Bibliography for 1970–. Troy, N.Y.: Whitston, 1972–.
    This annual, comprehensive bibliography includes materials
from throughout the world. Although medical periodical references
predominate, the bibliographies also include citations to books,
the popular press, and feminist materials. Volumes through 1977
were compiled by Mary K. Floyd.

2   ASTIN, HELEN S., ALICE PARELMAN, and ANNE FISHER. Sex Roles:
    A Research Bibliography. Rockville, Md.: National Institute
    of Mental Health, 1975. 362 pp.
    Materials published between 1960 and 1972 are included in the
456 abstracted citations in this bibliography. About 75 percent of
the listings are journal articles, with the remainder including
books, book chapters, and unpublished papers. Most of the material
is in the English language, and arrangement is alphabetical by
author under broad subject headings. Author and subject indexes
are provided. Only a small number of the citations deal directly
with sexuality or sexual behavior.

3   BALLOU, PATRICIA K. Women: A Bibliography of Bibliographies.
    Boston: G.K. Hall, 1980. 155 pp.
    An important source of bibliographic information for all
areas of women's studies, this compilation includes 557 citations,
most of them from the 1970s.

4   BREWER, JOAN SCHERER, and ROD W. WRIGHT. Sex Research:
    Bibliographies from the Institute for Sex Research. Phoenix:
    Oryx Press, 1979. 212 pp.
    Brewer and Wright have prepared a list of bibliographies
most frequently requested by researchers from the Information
Service at the Institute for Sex Research. The compilers' definition of bibliography is somewhat flexible. For example, some articles and books are cited that contain only extensive footnote
citations to useful materials, rather than formal bibliographies.
The citations are grouped under broad subject categories, and
there is an emphasis on current rather than historical works. In
addition to the citations, a section lists sources of sex research
information in the United States and gives names and addresses of
relevant periodicals and organizations. There are also author and
subject indexes.

5   CAREY, EMILY A. Women: Sexuality, Psychology and Psychotherapy:
    A Bibliography. Boston: Womanspace, 1976. 29 pp. SL.
    This short bibliography consists of two sections, one of
general citations in the field and the second of references relating more specifically to female sexuality. The quality of the
entries is uneven, and too often the information given is incomplete
("Gavron, D. and R. Shekelle, 'Mood, presonality [sic], and the
menstrual cycle,' unpub. data, 1969"). Entries are arranged al-
phabetically by author and are not annotated.

6   DOLLEN, CHARLES. Abortion in Context: A Select Bibliography. Metuchen, N.J.: Scarecrow Press, 1970. 150 pp.
Approximately 1,400 entries, including materials on female sexuality, marriage, and related fields are found here. Listed are English-language books and articles focusing on the years 1967-69, with some older material. Medical, legal, religious, and popular literature are cited. The arrangement is alphabetical by author and title. A subject index is provided, as is a list of periodicals and publishers serving as the source of citations.

7   INDIANA UNIVERSITY, INSTITUTE FOR SEX RESEARCH, LIBRARY. Catalog of Periodical Literature in the Social and Behavioral Sciences Section, Library of the Institute for Sex Research, Indiana University Including Supplement to Monographs 1973-1975. 4 vols. Boston: G.K. Hall, 1976.
This catalog, which is a reprint of catalog cards created at the Institute for Sex Research, is an essential resource for researchers into all aspects of sexuality in the post-World War II era. Each entry, with the exception of the monograph update entries (supplementing the institute's published monograph catalog), provides complete bibliographic information on an individual article, including those in compilations. Because each article is listed in three different ways--by author, title, and subject-- users have a variety of access points to citations. Although some popular magazines (MS., Redbook, etc.) are included, the majority of the entries are from professional journals in the fields of medicine, psychiatry, psychology, law, and sociology. Newspapers are not included. Although a few pre-World War II citations can be found, researchers should consult other sources, such as the Index Medicus and the Surgeon General's Library catalog index for early references.

8   _____. Catalog of the Social and Behavioral Sciences, Monograph Section. 4 vols. Boston: G.K. Hall, 1974.
In this reproduction of the institute's card catalog, Western nineteenth- and twentieth-century materials predominate. Included are historical materials relating to sexual behavior, covering such topics as the history of early sex education, marriage, abortion, contraception, women's rights, sex ethics, religion, sex laws, venereal disease, and prostitution, as well as contemporary research in sexual behavior and attitudes. The institute's collection of erotic art and literature is not included, but bibliographies on the subject and censorship studies are.

9   PERKINS, BARBARA BRIDGMAN. Adolescent Birth Planning and Sexuality: Abstracts of the Literature. Washington, D.C.: Consortium on Early Childbearing and Childrearing, Child Welfare League of America, 1974. 75 pp.
Surveying literature published between 1965 and 1973, this bibliography includes a section of twenty-five detailed abstracts of books and periodicals published during these years in the area

of adolescent sexual behavior and sexuality. It is useful for obtaining a quick overview of research done during that period.

10 RITCHIE, MAUREEN. Women's Studies: A Checklist of
    Bibliographies. London: Mansell, 1980. 107 pp.
    This bibliography includes 452 citations in the main text, plus 37 others in an appendix. Most of the references relating to sexuality are found in a 35-item section on "sex roles," somewhat of a misnomer for materials ranging from lesbians to rape. Ritchie includes only bibliographies that have been issued as discrete entities; she excludes those that have appeared in the backs of books or as part of textual articles, thereby limiting the scope of her work severely. The entries, which are arranged by subject, are not annotated, but Ritchie does include useful information on ordering and purchase procedures, although not in all cases where it might be desirable. Scholars will probably want to supplement their use of Ritchie with other materials.

11 ROBERTS, J.R. Black Lesbians: An Annotated Bibliography.
    Tallahassee, Fla.: Naiad Press, 1981. 93 pp.
    Because black lesbians have been largely neglected by researchers, the black lesbian experience has been denied and invalidated. To remedy this void in our knowledge and to correct the attitude of neglect that currently exists, J.R. Roberts has prepared this first bibliography in the field. Focusing on materials relating to the United States, she incorporates references to literature, music, political activism, research, and other topics. Both periodicals and monographs are included, and most entries are annotated. Entries are arranged topically and thereunder alphabetically. There is an author/subject index, a directory of black gay/lesbian organizations, and some unique photo illustrations. Roberts has selected most of her citations from publications of the 1970s, with an emphasis on the feminist press. Much relevant nonfeminist research, for example, studies of prison populations, is not included.

12 SEIDEN, ANNE M. "Overview: Research on the Psychology of
    Women. I. Gender Differences and Sexual and Reproductive
    Life." American Journal of Psychiatry 133, no. 9 (September
    1976):995-1007.
    Written in the context of feminism and the growth of women's studies as an academic discipline, this review article critiques materials from psychiatry, sociology, psychology, and other fields, including popular works as well as unpublished materials. Fields covered, among others, are menstruation and the menstrual cycle, menopause, coitus, and sex therapy. Noticeably absent are such topics as lesbianism, sexual variation, and adolescent sexuality, although the first of these is dealt with in part 2 (see entry 13). Seiden calls on researchers to be aware of the many variables involved in understanding women's sexuality and other aspects of their lives. There is a 132-item bibliography, arranged in order of citation in the text.

13 _____. "Overview: Research on the Psychology of Women. II. Women in Families, Work, and Psychotherapy." American Journal of Psychiatry 133, no. 10 (October 1976):1111-23.

This is a continuation of Seiden's significant review article on current research trends in the psychology of women. One section deals with lesbianism, not as a type of pathological condition, but as a form of social bonding relationship. Seiden decries the paucity of research literature on lesbians and the profession's neglect of the research that is available. Other topics covered include family structure, child rearing, clinical treatment, the impact of the therapist's and researcher's gender on final outcomes, and the psychology of women as a conceptual framework. The bibliography section includes 122 citations arranged in the sequence in which they are referred to in the text.

14 SERUYA, FLORA C., SUSAN LOSHER, and ALBERT ELLIS. Sex and Sex Education: A Bibliography. New York: R.R. Bowker, 1972. 336 pp.

Over two thousand titles are represented in this bibliography, which includes both recent research and older works. References are drawn primarily from psychological and sociological literature. Citations for books, pamphlets, and newspapers are organized topically. Journal articles, however, are not included. Although there are only occasional annotations, this is still an excellent source of bibliographic information.

15 Sex in Contemporary Society: A Catalog of Dissertations. Ann Arbor, Mich.: Xerox University Microfilms, 1973. 14 pp. LC: uncataloged, on reference shelf in microfilm reading room.

This compilation of microfilm titles relating to sex is a valuable reference tool for the sexuality researcher. Titles, which span the period 1938-73, reflect a much wider chronological and subject range than might be expected from the catalog's title. They are arranged topically, and thereunder by author's name. Some of the topics: religion and sex, sex in literature and cinema, and sex education. Although many titles have found their way into print as monographs, many have not.

16 SHERMAN, JULIA A. On the Psychology of Women: A Survey of Empirical Studies. Springfield, Ill.: Charles C. Thomas, 1971. 304 pp.

In this review of empirical studies in the psychology of women, Sherman emphasizes the biology of sex differences. Her overall thesis is that despite the influence Freud's theory of female development has had, it is not supported by adequate empirical evidence. Chapter 8 focuses specifically on female sexuality, while other relevant materials may be found throughout the book. There is also an extensive bibliography of books and periodical articles.

17 WALKER, MARCIA J. Toward the Prevention of Rape: A Partially

Annotated Bibliography. Report no. 27, Center for Correctional
Psychology. University: University of Alabama, Department of
Psychology, Center for Correctional Psychology, 1975. 101 pp.
ISR.

Walker annotates 150 books and articles relating to rape,
its prevention, the treatment of victims, and other topics. She
addresses especially the ways in which psychology, sociology, and
other behavioral sciences examine rape problems. Although rape is
primarily a question of power, violence, and male attitudes toward
women, the question of the victim's sexual role in the assault is
frequently raised, especially in court, making this indeed an issue
relating to women's sexuality and how it is perceived by society.
Sources from outside the United States are included. There is a
separate, unannotated listing following the main text of additional
books and articles.

18 WEINBERG, MARTIN S., and ALAN P. BELL. Homosexuality: An
    Annotated Bibliography. New York: Harper and Row, 1972. 550
    pp.

    Prepared at the Institute for Sex Research, this bibliography
lists materials published between 1940 and 1968, too early to include citations to most works appearing as part of the contemporary
women's movement or as part of the post-Masters and Johnson spate
of sex research. There are 1,263 citations, only 98 of which per-
tain specifically to lesbians, although lesbian material could
probably be gleaned from some of the general citations. Belles-
lettres (biography and literary works), popular magazines, and
newspaper articles are excluded. Each entry is annotated, and
there are author and subject indexes.

19 WELBORN, TERESA. Human Sexuality: A Current Bibliography.
    San Francisco: Multi Media Resource Center, 1974. 71 pp.

    This general bibliography covering all areas of human sexu-
ality includes only monograph literature arranged in alphabetical
order by author, although a separate list of periodicals is included. Searching is aided by lists of titles by subject, such
as women's sexuality, lesbianism, children's and adolescent sexuality, and sex research. Most items are from the 1960s and 1970s,
although some earlier citations are included. Each entry is
briefly annotated, and the annotation usually includes a value
judgment on the material's worth. This bibliography is far from
comprehensive and tends to omit authors with whose biases Welborn
and the center disagree.

20 ZUKERMAN, ELYSE. Changing Directions in the Treatment of Women:
    A Mental Health Bibliography. DHEW Publication no. (ADM) 79-749.
    Rockville, Md.: National Institute of Mental Health, 1979.
    494 pp.

    Compiled to reflect the growth of treatment literature re-
sulting from questioning of traditional mental health treatment
for women, this bibliography includes material from the period

1960-77. Also listed is earlier literature that had an impact on psychotherapy for women. "The literature selected for inclusion goes beyond psychotherapy to include all efforts to help women grow and develop, cope with the crises that women experience, and deal with the pain and problems created by their social situation in our culture." A substantial number of entries relate to sexuality, including such topics as sexual dysfunction, orgasm, sex therapy, and masturbation. The book is arranged in six sections: theoretical literature, criticism of the treatment of women, research response to criticism, theory and research in new therapy approaches, treatment for specific problems and populations, and alternatives to traditional psychotherapy. All 407 entries are abstracted in detail, and there are author and subject indexes.

21 BARNES, DOROTHY L. Rape: A Bibliography, 1965-1975. Troy, N.Y.: Whitston, 1977. 154 pp.

22 BULLOUGH, VERN, et al. A Bibliography of Prostitution. New York: Garland, 1977. 419 pp.

23 CONSTANTINE, LARRY L., and JOAN M. CONSTANTINE. "Group and Multilateral Marriage: Definitional Notes, Glossary, and Annotated Bibliography." Family Process 10, no. 2 (June 1971): 157-76.

24 DAMON, GENE, JAN WATSON, and ROBIN JORDAN. The Lesbian in Literature: A Bibliography. 2d ed. Reno, Nev.: Ladder, 1975. 96 pp.

25 EVANS, HANNAH I., and NICOLE B. SPEREKAS. Sexual Assault Bibliography: 1920-1975. JSAS Document MS 1368. Washington, D.C.: American Psychological Association, 1976. 60 pp.

26 HOCHSCHIELD, ARLIE RUSSELL. "A Review of Sex Role Research." American Journal of Sociology 78, no. 4 (January 1973):1011-29.

27 HUGHES, MARIJA MATICH. The Sexual Barrier: Legal, Medical, Economic and Social Aspects of Sex Discrimination. Washington, D.C.: Hughes Press, 1977. 843 pp.

28 JACOBS, SUE-ELLEN. Women in Perspective: A Guide for Cross-Cultural Studies. Urbana: University of Illinois Press, 1974. 299 pp.

29 KEMMER, ELIZABETH JANE. Rape and Rape-related Issues: An Annotated Bibliography. New York: Garland, 1977. 174 pp.

30 MEDNICK, MARTHA T.S., and HILDA J. WEISSMAN. "The Psychology of Women: Selected Topics." Annual Review of Psychology 26 (1975):1-18.

31   The Rape Bibliography: A Collection of Abstracts. St. Louis:
     St. Louis Feminist Research Project, 1976. 93 pp.

32   STEWART, KAREN ROBB. Adolescent Sexuality and Teenage Pregnancy:
     A Selected, Annotated Bibliography with Summary Forewords.
     Chapel Hill: Carolina Population Center, University of North
     Carolina, 1976. 43 pp.

33   STINEMAN, ESTHER. Women's Studies: A Recommended Core
     Bibliography. Littleton, Colo.: Libraries Unlimited, 1979.
     670 pp.

Historical Interpretations

The rise of the new social history and women's history as fields of historical inquiry, the contemporary search for the roots of women's oppression as well as continuity in feminist philosophy, and a heightened awareness and availability of research resources have, in the past fifteen years, led to increased interest in the interpretation of the history of female sexuality. Because sex was so long tabooed and neglected as a subject of legitimate research, however, historians in this field have had to face several barriers.

One of the most obvious, of course, is the lack of an established historiographical tradition and methodology other than that used in the writing of more conventional social and intellectual history. As historians of women so rightly point out, traditional bases of periodization simply do not apply to many questions of women's lives and sexuality. Attempts to relate sexual attitudes and behavior to broader issues of economic, political and social concern have only just begun and are often hampered by the sheer breadth of material relating to the sexual realm. Even defining what is meant by sexuality and whether the same parameters outline men's and women's lives is an unresolved issue.

The nineteenth century, or the "Victorian period," as some would call it, has exerted a special fascination for historians of women's sexuality in America. From G.J. Barker-Benfield's writings on sexual surgery (entries 36, 37) to Carroll Smith-Rosenberg's now classic interpretation of women's relationships (entry 82), scholars have examined such questions as dominant themes in prescriptive literature and the relation of prescriptive ideology to actual behavior. The colonial era has not been served nearly as well (indeed, hardly at all). Many twentieth-century developments, such as the rise of the behavior survey and laboratory-based sex research have yet to be adequately evaluated, although the work of such scholars as James H. Jones (entry 55) is a good beginning.

Some historians, like some theoretical writers on women's sexuality, have a penchant for leaping from specific cases to broad generalizations that may or may not accurately reflect the reality of the past. Another danger to which some fall prey is the use of a rather narrow range of types of source materials. Jonathan Katz's pioneering documentary compilation, Gay American History (entry 56), demonstrates how truly diverse the sources for studying the history of human sexuality can be.

Users of this bibliography may wish to compare the topics covered by the books and articles listed in this section with the subjects covered in the other sections. Additional clues for further research may come from the index entries. Historians have only begun to produce solid work in this field, and their conclusions should be subjected to careful appraisal in the light of new resources and possibilities for interpretative revision. The feminist/nonfeminist/quasi-feminist debate over evaluation of similar events and ideas in the past is but one arena in which historians of women's sexuality will find themselves in years to come.

34   ABERLE, SOPHIE D., and GEORGE W. CORNER. Twenty-five Years of Sex Research: History of the National Research Council Committee for Research in Problems of Sex 1922-1947. Philadelphia: W.B. Saunders, 1953. 248 pp.

Although there is not much material relating specifically to women in this book, it is essential for understanding the historical background of sex research in the United States. Particularly useful is the information on funding priorities and research networks. Numerous lists and charts are also included.

35   BARKER-BENFIELD, GRAHAM JOHN [Ben Barker-Benfield]. "The Spermatic Economy: A Nineteenth-century View of Sexuality." Feminist Studies 1, no. 1 (1972):45-74.

Presenting in concise form much of the same material covered in The Horrors of the Half-known Life (entry 36), Barker-Benfield offers an overview of nineteenth-century conceptions of human sexuality, including the development of economic metaphors for sexual behavior. He hypothesizes that two contrasting views of woman-- as sexless saint and as dangerously sensuous animal--led to a materialistic conception of gynecological surgery as a means of controlling women's sexuality as well as mental disturbances supposedly caused by pathological conditions involving women's sex organs.

36   BARKER-BENFIELD, G[RAHAM] J[OHN]. The Horrors of the Half-known Life: Male Attitudes toward Women and Sexuality in Nineteenth-century America. New York: Harper and Row, 1976. 366 pp.

Despite its title, this book is primarily a discussion of the writings and careers of physicians J. Marion Sims and Augustus Kinsley Gardner, and the Reverend John Todd. Although Barker-Benfield's primary thesis, that nineteenth-century American men manipulated female sexuality to serve nationalistic goals of control and dominance, is certainly plausible, his supporting evidence is taken too much out of context to be convincing. Moreover, he fails to correlate rhetoric with real behavior of women. For example, his claims about the rapacity of nineteenth-century sexual surgery and the butchery of nascent American gynecological specialists are not backed up by any solid statistics or other evidence proving that this was, indeed, the case. Barker-Benfield also seems to have an underlying belief that nineteenth-century American women were manipulable, controllable, gullible, and totally at the mercy of unscrupulous practitioners. Gynecological and sexual surgery need to be analyzed historically, but this work leaves much to be desired in objectively satisfying that need.

37 BRECHER, EDWARD M. The Sex Researchers. Boston: Little, Brown, 1969. 354 pp.

Brecher is a science writer who, with his wife, has also written An Analysis of Human Sexual Response. One chapter of The Sex Researchers is devoted to women theorists, but Brecher's selections--Elizabeth Blackwell, Leah Schaefer, Niles Newton, Helena Wright, and Mary Jane Sherfey--are rather eclectic. This eclecticism prevails throughout the book, as the author acknowledges in his introduction: "Studies which failed to arouse my interest are here dismissed in a paragraph or a sentence, or are ignored altogether." Use with caution, for this is a popular account with some errors both of fact and interpretation.

38 BULLOUGH, VERN L., and BONNIE BULLOUGH. "Lesbianism in the 1920's and 1930's: A Newfound Study." Signs 2, no. 4 (Summer 1977):895-904.

In this article Vern and Bonnie Bullough summarize material from an unpublished manuscript describing lesbians and male homosexuals in Salt Lake City during the 1930s. This is an especially welcome addition to the literature because most material relating to lesbians at that time is found either in pejorative case studies and prescriptive literature or in largely inaccessible archives and manuscript collections. Researchers should note that the Bulloughs do not indicate whether the original manuscript has been placed in a public repository, thereby facilitating firsthand and perhaps more detailed analysis than is presented here, or whether it remains in their sole possession.

39 BURNHAM, JOHN. "The Progressive Era Revolution in American Attitudes toward Sex." Journal of American History 59, no. 4 (March 1973):885-908.

Burnham focuses here on venereal disease and the purity movement. Unfortunately, he seems to be unaware of knowledge about venereal disease that existed much earlier in the nineteenth-century. He has let periodization dictate his sources and his interpretation of them, rather than letting his topic develop organically and chronologically.

40   COOK, BLANCHE WIESEN. "The Historical Denial of Lesbianism."
     Radical History Review 20 (Spring-Summer 1979):60-65.
         This is a critique of Miss Marks and Miss Woolley, Anna Mary
     Wells's 1978 biography of Mary Woolley, a president of Mt. Holyoke
     College, and her friend, lover, and colleague Jeannette Marks.
     Cook discusses the persistent historical refusal to acknowledge the
     variety, intensity, and validity of women's emotional and erotic
     experiences with one another, and she criticizes Wells's book for
     denying the lesbian identity of its subjects. She outlines the
     history of Wells's use of the Woolley papers at Mt. Holyoke, call-
     ing for a re-examination of this collection and the two women's
     lives that will take into account all the dimensions of their ex-
     istence, as well as a redefinition of what it means to be a lesbian.

41   COTT, NANCY F. "Passionlessness: An Interpretation of Victorian
     Sexual Ideology, 1790-1850." Signs 4, no. 2 (Winter 1978):219-
     36.
         A major change in views of women's sexuality took place be-
     tween the seventeenth and nineteenth centuries. Nancy Cott main-
     tains that during this period a dominant Anglo-American definition
     of women as particularly sexual beings was transformed into the
     view that women's sexual appetites were much smaller than those
     of men. Examining British and American sources, she links the rise
     of passionlessness to the rise of evangelical religion between the
     1790s and the 1830s. Thus, a concept that became part of much
     medical ideology in the mid-nineteenth century had its origins in
     moralistic and religious thought of an earlier era. Cott sees
     passionlessness as a positive force, which replaced sexual deter-
     minism with a new view of woman emphasizing her moral character as
     her chief motivating force.

42   DEGLER, CARL N. "What Ought to Be and What Was: Women's
     Sexuality in the Nineteenth Century." American Historical Review
     79, no. 5 (December 1974):1467-90.
         In the first part of this article, Degler summarizes the view
     of many twentieth-century historians--that nineteenth-century women
     were sexually repressed. These historians, he argues, have derived
     this idea not from research on actual behavior, but from reading
     the prescriptions of certain writers (Acton, Kellogg, et al.) who
     were trying to convey a particular sexual ideology. Degler offers
     evidence from other authorities to show that there were diverse
     schools of thought regarding "normal" female sexuality throughout
     the nineteenth century. In the second part of the article, Degler
     presents information on female sexual behavior gathered from forty-
     five women by Dr. Clelia Mosher of Stanford University. This data
     demonstrates that at least some women had active sex lives and
     feelings and that prescriptive arguments favoring women's sexual
     repression were not always echoed in actual behavior.

43   DELANEY, JANICE; MARY JANE LUPTON, and EMILY TOTH. The Curse:
     A Cultural History of Menstruation. New York: Dutton, 1976.
     276 pp.

Menstruation is perhaps even more of a given for women than childbirth and motherhood. Delaney, Lupton, and Toth discuss the taboos, attitudes, and social constructs that surround the history and current status of this biological fact of woman's existence. Among these are taboos restricting sexual activity with menstruating women, and the authors devote one chapter to this subject. In other sections of the book, slang expressions, jokes, and literary references to the menstrual sex taboo can be found. Other subjects dealt with include sexual intercourse as a supposed cause of menstruation, and sexuality and menopause. Researchers will find the footnote citations, which include an extremely wide range of sources, of particular interest.

44 DITZION, SIDNEY. Marriage, Morals, and Sex in America: A History of Ideas. Expanded ed., with a new chapter by the author. New York: W.W. Norton, 1978. 460 pp.

Originally published in 1953, this overview of American sexual attitudes has subsequently appeared in several other editions. It continues to provide a useful summary of ideas, although, as research into the history of sexuality continues, this will not indefinitely be the case. Ditzion's approach, moreover, is an eclectic one. While Puritans are totally neglected, an entire chapter (and there are only twelve of them in all) is devoted to free love. Such selectivity, however, enables the author to focus on his chief theme, the unity and interdependency of social reform movements, which, subtly or overtly, include sexual ideology as an integral part of their overall philosophy. Although there are no footnotes (except for the "new" chapter) and only a sparse, outdated bibliography, the book includes many textual references to books, periodicals, and other publications.

45 DUFFY, JOHN. "Masturbation and Clitoridectomy: A Nineteenth Century View." Journal of the American Medical Association 186, no. 3 (October 1963):246-48.

In this summary of nineteenth-century views on clitoridectomy as a "cure" for excessive masturbation, Duffy contends that well-publicized excesses by British surgeon Isaac Baker Brown led most English and American physicians to dismiss the operation as a means of treatment. He points out, however, that there was a brief revival of interest in the latter years of the century.

46 ENGLEHARDT, H. TRISTAM, Jr. "The Disease of Masturbation: Values and the Concept of Disease." Bulletin of the History of Medicine 48, no. 2 (Summer 1974):234-48.

Obviously influenced by the ideas of Thomas Szasz, Englehardt offers some interesting observations on the impact of social values and concepts of perfection and reality on the formulation of definitions of disease.

47 FADERMAN, LILLIAN. Surpassing the Love of Men: Romantic Friendship and Love between Women from the Renaissance to the

Present. New York: William Morrow, 1981. 496 pp.
This cultural history of romantic friendship and love traces
patterns of women's erotic relationships from the sixteenth century
to the present. Faderman finds, as have other scholars before her,
that a change in attitude, from acceptance to condemnation, occurred in the late nineteenth century. This change, which drastically
altered the emotional options available to women, was a result of
medical and psychiatric ideas, the pejorative identification of
women's love relationships with feminism and independence, and the
negative portrayal of female same-sex relationships in literature
written by men.
Utilizing literary sources, correspondence, and similar materials, Faderman suggests that expectations for same-sex relationships are culturally determined, changing over time: "Throughout
most of the twentieth century, . . . the enriching romantic friendship that was common in earlier eras is thought to be impossible,
since love necessarily means sex and sex between women means lesbian and lesbian means sick." At times her denial of conscious
sexuality and genital expression in pre-twentieth-century relationships seems strained, especially given the paucity of clear evidence
of a nonliterary origin. Readers should not miss the larger point,
however: that male-dominated culture has the power to define what
is "normal" and "permissible" where women's relationships are concerned. This is an important study, and although historians familiar with nonliterary sources may disagree with some of Faderman's
conclusions and theses, her work provides an essential link in the
chain of women's history.

48   FASSLER, BARBARA. "Theories of Homosexuality as Sources of
     Bloomsbury's Androgyny." Signs 5, no. 2 (Winter 1979):237-51.
     Fassler discusses how writings of early twentieth-century
sex theorists influenced and were used by Bloomsbury writers.
This is an important article because it demonstrates a direct link
between theory and actual behavior as well as the impact of theory
on the writers' work.

49   FOSTER, JEANNETTE H. Sex Variant Women in Literature.
     Baltimore: Diana Press, 1975. 420 pp.
     When this book first appeared in 1956, it was because
Jeannette Foster used her own money for its publication and distribution through Vantage Press, a vanity press. By the 1970s, the
social climate and attitudes toward lesbianism had so dramatically
changed that commercial republication by one of the new women's
presses was enthusiastically welcomed. Like Jonathan Katz's Gay
American History (entry 56), Sex Variant Women in Literature is a
tour de force of research and compilation of often obscure materials.
In Foster's case, her purpose is to present a summary discussion of
lesbians in the Western literary tradition, both as authors and as
subjects. At times her choice of subjects to discuss may seem to
be based more on variations in gender roles than in actual sexuality, but researchers studying all aspects of female-female

14

interpersonal relationships will appreciate Foster's broad base of selection. This pioneering work has had a significant influence on more recent studies, such as Bettie Wysor's The Lesbian Myth (entry 1360) and Lillian Faderman's Surpassing the Love of Men (entry 47), and should remain a standard for many years to come.

50   GORDON, LINDA. Woman's Body, Woman's Right: A Social History
      of Birth Control in America. New York: Grossman, 1976. 479 pp.
           Woman's Body, Woman's Right views birth control as a politi-
      cal issue, a question of female power, and analyzes the history of
      the movement from a Marxist, class-oriented perspective. This ap-
      proach is only partially successful, not only because of Gordon's
      loose application of the term class, but also because, as she cau-
      tions early on, "the economic roles of women in capitalist society
      cannot always be fitted into class categories based on men's work."
           Gordon traces the folklore and history of contraception, di-
      viding the modern movement into three stages: voluntary mother-
      hood (late nineteenth century), birth control (1910-20), and planned
      parenthood (1920 to date), each of which she believes expressed the
      interests of different classes of women. There is useful informa-
      tion on various aspects of the relationship of birth control to
      broader sexual attitudes and behavior, and on such topics as the
      provision of modern contraception to black people and the supposed
      link between contraception and abortion.

51   GORDON, MICHAEL, and PENELOPE J. SHANKWEILER. "Different Equals
      Less: Female Sexuality in Recent Marriage Manuals." Journal of
      Marriage and the Family 33, no. 3 (August 1971):459-66.
           Examining eighteen best-selling marriage (sex) manuals writ-
      ten between 1930 and 1970 and drawing on their knowledge of earlier
      literature, sociologists Gordon and Shankweiler conclude that few
      changes in the depiction of female sexuality occurred, despite the
      ever-increasing body of empirical research available. They attri-
      bute the perpetuation of these stereotypes to the male "experts"
      who wrote the books and their desire to maintain patriarchal, sex-
      ist perceptions of women's sexuality, regardless of whether their
      conception related to the reality of female physiology and emotion-
      al health.

52   HALE, NATHAN G., Jr. Freud and the Americans: The Beginnings
      of Psychoanalysis in the United States, 1876-1917. New York:
      Oxford University Press, 1971. 574 pp.
           This meticulously researched monograph provides essential
      background for understanding developments in psychological theory
      as well as changes in prescriptive literature in the late nineteenth
      and early twentieth centuries.

53   HALLER, JOHN S., Jr., and ROBIN M. HALLER. The Physician and
      Sexuality in Victorian America. Urbana: University of Illinois
      Press, 1974. 331 pp.
           Chapters three and four of this somewhat diffuse book deal

in part with female sexuality. The Hallers strive to present a range of both popular and professional medical opinion; their main concern is with prescription rather than actual behavior. Some of the Hallers' observations on real behavior, such as those on the predominance of frigidity and lack of sexual satisfaction among married women, have been challenged by such scholars as Carl N. Degler, and their lack of tangible evidence to support their assertions does little to instill confidence in their ability to make the transition from prescription to real life. Read in conjunction with other studies, however, this book can play a useful role in introducing readers to nineteenth-century prescriptive literature. In addition to sexuality, these chapters include material on such topics as contraception, motherhood, and tight lacing. There is a bibliography as well as detailed footnotes.

54   HOFFMAN, FRANK. "Prolegomena to a Study of Traditional Elements in the Erotic Film." Journal of American Folklore 78, no. 308 (April-June 1965):143-48.
      Using about four hundred reels of film from the collection of the Institute for Sex Research, Hoffman outlines the principal components of erotic films, which he defines as "thoroughly illegal pornographic productions usually known as 'stag films.'" He analyzes them in terms of three time periods: the mid-1920s, the years just before World War II, and the 1960s, in regard to plot and situation components. Hoffman does not differentiate between American and foreign productions, apparently feeling that sexual motifs of this type are part of a universal, folkloristic language not bound by the limits of specific cultural contexts.

55   JONES, JAMES H. "The Origins of the Institute for Sex Research: A History." Ph.D. dissertation, Indiana University, 1972. 303 pp. ISR, LC.
      This study examines the role of funding agencies in supporting the early development (to 1947) of the Institute for Sex Research and the research of its founder, Alfred C. Kinsey. It includes information on the policies of such organizations as the Committee for Research in Problems of Sex of the National Research Council, the Bureau of Social Hygiene, the Rockefeller Foundation, and Indiana University, where the institute is located. It also contains material on the roles of key individuals, such as Robert M. Yerkes and Alan Gregg, and on the early survey and interview work of Kinsey and the institute staff.

56   KATZ, JONATHAN. Gay American History: Lesbians and Gay Men in the U.S.A. New York: Crowell, 1976. 690 pp.
      Jonathan Katz must surely qualify as one of the premier historical detectives of all time. His decision to assemble this exciting collection of original documents rather than simply writing a conventional monograph has only made his presentation that more fascinating and useful to the reader and researcher. Material on lesbians is included throughout the book and one chapter,

"Passing Women: 1782-1920," is exclusively about cross dressing among women. Katz has culled his sources from a wide range of materials, including medical literature, unpublished manuscripts, photographs, and oral interviews created specially for this volume. In addition to the document texts, Katz has included extensive introductory notes, a detailed index, and references to additional sources. This is an essential work for all students of sexuality and history and serves as a model for similar documentary compilations in other fields.

57   KEATING, WALTER S. [HENRIETTA ROSENBERG, pseud.]. Sex Studies
     from Freud to Kinsey. New York: Stravon, 1949. 92 pp.
         Sex Studies digests Freud, Ellis, the Kinsey male volume,
     and several marriage manuals.

58   KENNEDY, DAVID M. Birth Control in America: The Career of
     Margaret Sanger. New Haven: Yale University Press, 1970. 320
     pp.
         As part of this study of Margaret Sanger's role in the development of the birth control movement in the United States between 1914 and the beginning of World War II, David Kennedy includes information on Sanger's attitudes toward women's sexuality, as well as on the context of legal, medical, and religious opinion at the time. No doubt some of his generalizations ("Nineteenth-century Americans first met the modern problem of sex by officially denying sexuality") would have been different had his knowledge of that century's thought on sexuality been more extensive. Indeed, the book is strongest when he is describing the specific incidents involved in making birth control a viable political and social movement, rather than when he attempts to provide an intellectual framework for such activity. Sanger's being influenced by Ellis and Freud is emphasized.
         Kennedy, whose evaluation is tempered by Roman Catholic attitudes toward contraception, sees his subject as almost a throwback to an earlier point of view: "When she apotheosized motherhood and dwelt on the centrality of sexual expression to feminine fulfillment, Mrs. Sanger seemed merely to dress out in new language nineteenth-century ideas about woman's sacredness and sexual uniqueness." There is especially interesting material on eugenics, the role of Robert Latou Dickinson in fostering the involvement of the medical profession in the movement, and the unevenness of anti-birth control legislation in the states. Kennedy's bibliographic documentation, while dated, is nonetheless useful.

59   KERN, LOUIS J. An Ordered Love: Sex Roles and Sexuality in
     Victorian Utopias--the Shakers, the Mormons, and the Oneida
     Community. Chapel Hill: University of North Carolina Press,
     1981. 430 pp.
         This is a study of sex roles and sexuality in three nineteenth-century communities, those of the Shakers, the Mormons, and the followers of John Humphrey Noyes at Oneida. Kern finds that

although sexual behavior and roles in these groups varied widely
from the conventional practices of the time, they nevertheless
were predicated on an ideology of women's inferiority and male
dominance. Although Kern's footnotes will prove useful in leading
researchers to additional materials, it seems strange that a work
dealing in large part with the Mormons should not even mention materials in the LDS Church Historical Department in Salt Lake City.
This may be a result of Kern's heavy dependence on printed sources,
but should not be overlooked when evaluating the definitiveness of
this work.

60   KRICH, ARON M. "Before Kinsey: Continuity in American Sex
     Research." Psychoanalytic Review 53 (Summer 1966):233-54.
     Krich's survey of pre-Kinsey sex research in the United
States includes summaries of the work of such researchers as
Katharine Bement Davis, Gilbert Van Tassel Hamilton, and Robert
Latou Dickinson. Krich places special emphasis on describing research methodology and its impact on the studies' results. He
justly points out that Kinsey's research was not the first of its
kind and that it exhibited many methodological deficiencies, as had
its predecessors. Krich argues, however, that used in tandem with
Kinsey's reports, the earlier studies provide an essential corrective to Kinsey's statistical fragmentation. An excellent introduction to the interpretation of sex research data, the ideas in this
article can also be applied to other survey interpretations as well.

61   LOWRY, THOMAS P., ed. The Classic Clitoris: Historic
     Contributions to Scientific Sexuality. Chicago: Nelson-Hall,
     1978. 120 pp.
     This is a collection of three essays presented in English
translation for the first time: Marcel Cohen, "The Mysterious
Origins of the Word 'Clitoris'" (1937); George Ludwig Kobelt, "The
Female Sex Organs in Humans and Some Mammals" (1844); and Ulrich
Gerhardt, "Female Cloaca and Copulatory Organs: Comparative
Anatomy" (1933). Each translation is preceded by an introduction
by Lowry, a former associate of Masters and Johnson. There is
also a comcluding section by Kermit E. Krantz, which summarizes
contemporary knowledge of the anatomy and physiology of the clitoris.

62   MAGLIN, NAN BAUER. "Vida to Florence: 'Comrade and Companion.'"
     Frontiers 4, no. 3 (Fall 1979):13-20.
     Maglin describes the quasi-lesbian relationships in the fiction
of Florence Converse and Vida Scudder and their connection to
Converse and Scudder's own lives. As close friends and constant
companions for over forty years, Converse and Scudder participated
in a number of woman-oriented institutions and networks. Maglin
finds their writings to be both a literary expression of their
own experience and a depiction of the kinds of female homosocial
relationships being built in late nineteenth- and early twentieth-
century America.

63   MELLEN, JOAN. <u>Women and Their Sexuality in the New Film.</u>
      New York: Horizon Press, 1973. 255 pp.
          In this study of the portrayal of women and their sexuality
      in contemporary cinema, Joan Mellen paints an uncomfortable picture
      of a medium depicting women as "sick, anxious, and unsure," re-
      flecting little impact of feminist political perspectives. Par-
      ticular emphasis is placed on the role of the director in creating
      the overall image of woman in the film, and Mellen selects films
      and directors (many of them European) which display this strong
      interrelationship.
          The initial chapter, "Bourgeois Woman: A Disturbance in
      Mirrors," provides an overview of the remaining essays in the book.
      One, on Mae West, is the most "historical" chapter, and Mellen pro-
      vides a fresh insight into that actress's characterizations:
      "West . . . transforms sexual allure on the part of women into an
      item of pride, power and autonomy. She transcends the cultural
      meaning of sexual availability in women because she separates it
      from servility and servitude."
          This is a useful survey of media imagery, focusing on films
      produced in the late 1960s and early 1970s. It would have been
      helpful if Mellen had included a list, with standard production
      data, of the various films discussed, especially since there is
      no index.

64   MORGAN, EDMUND S. "The Puritans and Sex." <u>New England Quarterly</u>
      15, no. 4 (December 1942):591-607.
          "The Puritans and Sex" was a pioneering piece of historical
      analysis which made extensive use of court records to show that
      all was not prudery in Puritan Massachusetts. It is still one of
      the few works that deals specifically with pre-nineteenth-century
      sexual behavior in the United States. While Morgan can give only
      a brief overview, his numerous references to women suggest addi-
      tional areas of research. The article is completely heterosexual
      in focus.

65   MUNCY, RAYMOND LEE. <u>Sex and Marriage in Utopian Communities:</u>
      <u>19th-century America.</u> Bloomington: Indiana University Press,
      1973. 275 pp.
          Nineteenth-century utopian communities in America which had
      unique approaches to questions of sex and marriage are examined
      in this work. Monogamous marriage, Muncy argues, was the primary
      institution of traditional society that caused concern among
      communitarians, chiefly because it placed family welfare above
      the good of the community as a whole. A wide range of alternatives,
      including celibacy, polygyny, and free love, were implemented by
      various groups, who often saw the active restructuring of women's
      economic and social position as one of their goals. Muncy's sources
      are chiefly published materials, and he sometimes fails to perceive
      how their innate biases have influenced his own arguments. Use
      this work with caution, although it is a fruitful source of ideas
      for further research. There are footnotes and an index, but no
      bibliography.

66 NISSENBAUM, STEPHEN. Sex, Diet, and Debility in Jacksonian
    America: Sylvester Graham and Health Reform. Westport, Conn.:
    Greenwood Press, 1980. 198 pp.
        Although there is not much specifically on women in its
    pages, Sex, Diet, and Debility sets the tone of the time in which
    many nineteenth-century theorists were writing. It also includes
    an excellent bibliography of sexual hygiene literature in America,
    1830-80, which extends beyond sexuality to nutrition, water cures,
    and other popular health material. Chapter nine is an especially
    good demonstration of the interlocking of reforms and reformers in
    mid-nineteenth-century America.

67 PIERSON, RUTH ROACH. "The Double Bind of the Double Standard:
    VD Control and the CWAC in World War II." Canadian Historical
    Review 52 (March 1981):31-58.
        Based largely on materials in Record Group 24 in the Public
    Archives of Canada, this article describes official attitudes to-
    ward and control of venereal disease in the Canadian Women's Army
    Corps and, to a lesser degree, the Canadian armed forces in general
    during World War II. Beginning in 1942, a policy of equal medical
    treatment for men and women was in effect, and women were no longer
    discharged from the service if they had contracted a venereal dis-
    ease. Despite this policy, however, discrimination in treatment
    and attitudes remained, because of society's double standard of
    sexual morality. For example, servicemen were routinely issued
    condoms and prophylactic kits and were accorded special VD preven-
    tive treatment centers. Women were not. This is a useful analysis
    of how social attitudes can have a significant impact on perceptions
    and treatment of a purely medical problem when the origin of that
    problem lies in sexual behavior.

68 POMEROY, WARDELL B. Dr. Kinsey and the Institute for Sex
    Research. New York: Harper and Row, 1972. 479 pp.
        This biography, written by one of Kinsey's research associ-
    ates, is best in its description of the climate in which sex re-
    searchers tried to do their work and of the opposition to and
    criticism of the female volume after its publication. Material
    on methodology is largely anecdotal. There are no footnotes or
    bibliography.

69 REED, JAMES. From Private Vice to Public Virtue: The Birth
    Control Movement and American Society Since 1930. New York:
    Basic Books, 1978. 456 pp.
        Meticulously researched, Reed's study of the birth control
    movement focuses on the work of three key figures: Robert Latou
    Dickinson, Clarence Gamble, and Margaret Sanger. Although Reed
    may be too sanguine in his evaluation of contemporary birth con-
    trol practice as a "public virtue" (there is still a pattern of
    linking contraception among the unmarried with immorality), there
    is no doubt that a revolution in social and political attitudes
    toward the practice has occurred during the twentieth century.

Coincident with providing information on birth control per
se, From Private Vice to Public Virtue also furnishes its readers
with substantial material on sexual attitudes and behavior, as
well as the scientific study of sex in the United States. The
notes and bibliography are especially detailed and useful.

70   ROBINSON, PAUL A. The Modernization of Sex: Havelock Ellis,
     Alfred Kinsey, William Masters and Virginia Johnson. New York:
     Harper and Row, 1976. 200 pp.
         In this critique of the major writings of four of the leading
     sexologists of the twentieth century, Robinson, who is a member of
     the history department at Stanford, places special emphasis on
     evaluating the empirical bases for his subjects' conclusions and
     is especially perceptive of cultural influences on their thought.
     He compares the various studies to the others, as well as to Freud,
     but does not draw comparisons between their work and those of
     other contemporary sex researchers. Female sexuality is given
     equal time, although Robinson is quick to point out certain ambi-
     guities in Ellis's thought on this subject, as well as Kinsey's
     occasional sexism and Masters and Johnson's feminist bias. There
     is an index but no bibliography, and footnote citations are pri-
     marily to the works being discussed.

71   ROSENBERG, CHARLES E. "Sexuality, Class and Role in 19th-
     century America." American Quarterly 25, no. 2 (May 1973):
     131-53.
         This is an important theoretical article tracing the main
     currents of nineteenth-century sexual attitudes as reflected in
     prescriptive literature. Rosenberg, one of the leading medical
     historians of the United States, summarizes common themes--
     repression, inconsistency and ambivalence, the persistence of a
     "male-oriented antirepressive behavioral ethos," and standardiza-
     tion of language and imagery--all tied to a pervasive gender and
     class role ideology. Although woman's sexuality was consistently
     linked to her maternal function and masturbation was consistently
     decried, nevertheless, nineteenth-century America accorded a
     variety of sexual behavior options. Extensive footnote references
     are included.

72   ROWBOTHAM, SHEILA, and JEFFREY WEEKS. Socialism and the New
     Life: The Personal and Sexual Politics of Edward Carpenter and
     Havelock Ellis. London: Pluto, 1977. 198 pp.
         Actually this book consists of two separate essays. The
     first, on Edward Carpenter, is by Sheila Rowbotham, while the
     second, shorter piece on Havelock Ellis is by Jeffrey Weeks.
     Originally delivered as a series of talks to the Gay Culture Society
     at the London School of Economics in 1974, they are unified not only
     by the two subjects' common bond of sexual reform, but also by their
     attempt to relate sexual ideology to a broader philosophy of social-
     ism. The essays, though suggestive, are somewhat uneven and cannot
     substitute for full-scale intellectual biographies of both of these

figures. A bibliography is included, which provides a useful guide
for additional research.

73   RULE, JANE. Lesbian Images. Garden City, N.Y.: Doubleday,
      1975. 246 pp.
      When Jane Rule wrote Lesbian Images in the early 1970s, the
tide of lesbian writing that was to emerge from the contemporary
women's movement was just beginning. Seen in retrospect, therefore,
Rule's book appears as one of the first of many works exploring
images of lesbians and the role of lesbian authors of fiction,
biography, and autobiography.
      Bringing her own experience as a writer to bear on the sub-
ject, Rule begins with an autobiographical introduction and two
chapters tracing the cultural origins of twentieth-century attitudes toward lesbians, the religious and psychiatric context in
which all the writers discussed have lived and worked. Rule then
discusses the life and work of individual authors, both well known
--Gertrude Stein, May Sarton--and obscure figures, such as Dorothy
Baker.
      Rule adopts a liberal definition of lesbians as simply women
who love other women, with or without specific sexual contact, and
therefore is able to include a wide range of authors and titles
that might be excluded by a less catholic definition. Her concluding chapters on "recent" nonfiction and individual works demonstrate
how far lesbian authors and literature have come in the past decade.

74   SAHLI, NANCY. "Sexuality in 19th and 20th Century America:
      The Sources and Their Problems." Radical History Review 20
      (Spring-Summer 1979):89-96.
      Because researchers often find materials relating to sexual-
ity difficult to locate and interpret, this article, which offers
suggestions for possible sources, is a welcome addition to the how-
to research literature. Sahli also discusses some of the methodological problems involved in using particular kinds of items, such
as surveys, as well as problems of access to, bias in, and preservation of sources for sexuality research.

75   _____. "Smashing: Women's Relationships before the Fall."
      Chrysalis, no. 8 (1979), pp. 17-27.
      Building on the work begun by Carroll Smith-Rosenberg in "The
Female World of Love and Ritual," Nancy Sahli shows how loving relationships between women became increasingly suspect in the late
nineteenth and early twentieth centuries. This was due largely to
the pejorative definition of such relationships as lesbian by sexologists, psychiatrists, and other scientific/medical researchers
and writers of that time. Of special interest is Sahli's discussion of smashing, a nineteenth-century term used for female-female
crushes, particularly among schoolgirls and college students. A
wide variety of source materials, from fiction to college records,
is used.

76 SCHLOSSMAN, STEPHEN, and STEPHANIE WALLACH. "The Crime of
    Precocious Sexuality: Female Juvenile Delinquency in the
    Progressive Era." Harvard Educational Review 48, no. 1
    (February 1978):65-94.
        Using a 1,200-case sample from Milwaukee Children's Court
    (1901-20), Schlossman and Wallach describe how girls were persist-
    ently discriminated against under the law. They were charged with
    offenses, primarily "immorality," which connoted some form of
    sexual misbehavior, but would not have been prosecuted under the
    adult criminal code, while boys were charged with adult crimes.
    Moreover, the girls' treatment in court often resulted in exposés
    of their sexual behavior whose primary purpose seems to have been
    the titillation of the court itself. A conventional "Victorian"
    code of morality circumscribed the justice process and condemned
    girls whose sexual behavior did not conform to those boundaries.
        Sexual regulation and gender-role stereotyping continued in
    the reformatories themselves. "In an era becoming increasingly
    fascinated with all things sexual, reformatories offered a warning
    that society would still not tolerate girls who showed the same
    interest in sex as boys and reinforced the traditional belief that
    'normal' girls were sexually impassive." The authors conclude that
    the discriminatory treatment of girl delinquents resulted from eth-
    nic prejudice, new theories of adolescence, and Progressive-era
    goals of purifying society. In addition to their use of case ma-
    terial, Schlossman and Wallach have marshaled a wide array of other
    sources to substantiate their arguments. Researchers will find
    many ideas for further study in their narrative and documentation.

77 SEARS, HAL D. The Sex Radicals: Free Love in High Victorian
    America. Lawrence: Regents Press of Kansas, 1977. 342 pp.
        Sears discusses the work of the post-Woodhull generation of
    free love advocates and sex reformers, with particular emphasis on
    Moses Harman, Lillian Harman, Edwin C. Walker, Ezra and Angela
    Heywood, D.M. Bennett, Edward Bliss Foote, Edward Bond Foote, Elmina
    Slenker, and Lois Waisbrooker. Based on his reading of such sources
    as Harman's paper Lucifer and a wide range of other materials, Sears
    traces the connections between the feminist free love ideology,
    which stressed woman's right to control her own body and be mistress
    of her own person, and other threads of the movement: anarchism,
    libertarianism, secularism, and spiritualism. His discussion of
    the impact of the Comstock laws and their use as a form of deliber-
    ate social reform repression is particularly relevant in the con-
    text of contemporary discussions on pornography and obscenity.
    This is a work rich in sources and detail and is suggestive of
    many additional lines of research into the history of female sexu-
    ality and feminist reform.

78 SEATON, ESTA. "Sex and the Nubile Girl in Edward Bok's Ladies
    Home Journal (1890-1919)." University of Michigan Papers in
    Women's Studies 2, no. 4 (1978):31-54.
        After Edward Bok assumed the editorship of the Ladies Home

Journal in 1890, its place as the premier women's magazine in the
United States (in terms of circulation) was even more assured.
Bok was conservative to the point of prudery in his sexual attitudes, and Seaton shows how these attitudes were reflected in the
fiction and nonfiction appearing in the Journal between 1890 and
1919. Above all, the Journal tried to promote a position of strict
propriety, wherein unmarried women would be sweet, loving, innocent,
and totally passive. Typical advice in one of the Journal's columns
might read as follows: "A lady is not supposed to recognize a gen-
tleman when he is one of a group standing in front of a hotel, since
a modest girl would not permit her eyes to rest upon such an assem-
blage." Although, in the interests of promoting self-control and
social purity, Bok launched a sex education campaign in 1906, it
was not until after 1912 that strict propriety began to be loosened,
and more liberal behavior accepted as a norm.

79   SHADE, WILLIAM G. "'A Mental Passion': Female Sexuality in
      Victorian America." International Journal of Women's Studies 1,
      no. 1 (January–February 1978):13–29.
         Although William Shade claims that his article acts as a tool
to clarify Carl Degler's arguments in "What Ought to Be and What
Was," the result is an unsatisfying assembly of materials taken
largely out of context. Shade seems to have missed Degler's main
point--that prescriptive literature and real behavior can be radi-
cally different--and his continued use of such literature in an
attempt to show why a decline in childbirth rates occurred from
1800 to 1900 does little to shed light on the question. At one
point he asserts that the declining birth rate was due to a decline
in frequency of heterosexual activity, but offers nothing to substantiate this claim other than some statistics from Katharine
Bement Davis's 1929 study. He also summarizes the views of several
nineteenth-century feminists on the sexual nature of men and women,
but fails to indicate why these women should be considered to be
representative of the wide range of opinion--even among feminists,
let alone all women writers--at that time.

80   SIMMONS, CHRISTINA. "Companionate Marriage and the Lesbian
      Threat." Frontiers 4, no. 3 (Fall 1979):54–59.
         Why was fear of lesbianism such a significant problem in the
heterosexual ideology of the 1920s and 1930s? At this time, a new
marriage ideology emphasizing woman's role as a psychological companion to her husband, an equal in the relationship, was developing.
Part of this ideology was a denigration of lesbians as "failed"
heterosexuals, whose behavior was the result of social rather than
hereditary sources. Simmons argues that these writers used lesbianism as a metaphor for women's autonomy in various forms and
that their underlying goal was to perpetuate a single role for
women, one focused on marriage and the service of men.

81   SMITH, DANIEL SCOTT, and MICHAEL S. HINDUS. "Premarital
      Pregnancy in America 1640-1971: An Overview and Interpretation."

Journal of Interdisciplinary History 5, no. 4 (Spring 1975): 537-70.

The authors trace variations in premarital pregnancy rates throughout American history. They find that low rates typify times when relationships between generations were well defined, when family moral authority was augmented by outside controls, and when there was little deviance from a central core of values. Higher rates of premarital sexual activity characterized eras in which parent-child relationships were somewhat ambiguous, when social controls on morality were uncertain, and when there was diversity in value identification among the population. The authors' conclusions are supported by statistics, charts, and references.

82 SMITH-ROSENBERG, CARROLL. "The Female World of Love and Ritual: Relations between Women in Nineteenth-century America." Signs 1, no. 1 (Autumn 1975):1-29.

In this now classic article, Carroll Smith-Rosenberg paints a rich picture of loving relationships between women in the nineteenth century. While not denying that these relationships may have had a sexual or homoerotic component, Smith-Rosenberg argues that twentieth-century tendencies to dichotomize such behavior into heterosexual/homosexual categories obscure the complexity of the sexual and emotional spectrum in which these women functioned. Utilizing letters and diaries from thirty-five families, "The Female World of Love and Ritual" demonstrates the possibilities for studying actual sexual/emotional behavior in the absence of surveys, case studies, and other commonly used sources.

83 _____. "Puberty to Menopause: The Cycle of Femininity in Nineteenth-century America." In Clio's Consciousness Raised: New Perspectives on the History of Women, edited by Mary S. Hartman and Lois Banner, 23-37. New York: Harper and Row, 1974.

This article summarizes attitudes of the medical profession in Victorian America toward puberty and menopause in women. In their view, women were governed by their reproductive organs, specifically their ovaries, which began their reign at puberty, relinquishing it only with menopause. Smith-Rosenberg indicates that while physicians regarded menopause as pathological, or at least debilitating, many women viewed it positively, as a release from the trials of childbirth. This is an insightful examination of nineteenth-century medical etiology of the female condition.

84 SNITOW, ANN BARR. "Mass Market Romance: Pornography for Women Is Different." Radical History Review 20 (Spring-Summer 1979): 141-61.

Snitow analyzes the sexual messages conveyed to millions of women readers by the Harlequin romance series. "Virginity is a given here; sex means marriage and marriage, promised at the end, means, finally, there can be sex." Snitow finds that the novels glorify the distance between men and women and reinforce the cultural code that pleasure for women is men, in fact, sexualizing every contact between women and men.

85   STILES, HENRY REED. <u>Bundling, Its Origin, Progress, and Decline in America</u>. Albany, N.Y.: J. Munsell, 1869. 139 pp.
      Bundling was the New England custom, apparently originating in the British Isles, of two members of opposite sexes sleeping together with all their clothes on. It was not necessarily confined to courtship, sometimes occurring by necessity when strangers required a sleeping place for the night. Stiles, a Connecticut antiquarian, was convinced that there was nothing immoral in the practice, arguing that it led to much less sexual activity than contemporary (1869) customs of courtship. Nevertheless, it was primarily a lower-class pattern, and ended at the end of the eighteenth century, largely because of clerical and popular criticism. Stiles reproduces excerpts from many sources describing the custom, including eighteenth-century poetry and travelers' accounts and other nineteenth-century antiquarian works. Because of the comparative scarcity of sources on sexuality during the colonial period, this is still a useful work for students of that era.

86   STIMPSON, CATHARINE R. "The Mind, the Body, and Gertrude Stein." <u>Critical Inquiry</u> 3, no. 3 (Spring 1977):489-506.
      Between the years 1900 and 1910, Gertrude Stein's lesbian sexuality affected both her writing and social relationships. Through an examination of Stein's fiction of this era, works such as <u>Q.E.D.</u>, <u>Three Lives</u>, and <u>Fernhurst</u>, Catharine Stimpson traces Stein's strategies for dealing with this mind/body dilemma. First, Stein apparently interacted differently with her friends, depending on the degree of their knowledge about her sexuality. Second, she often used heterosexual terms and gender definitions when describing her life. And third, her fiction uses an encoding or disguise pattern when dealing with lesbian and quasi-lesbian images. Stimpson's conclusion is a provocative one: "One must wonder if future scholars will not ask about us, 'Why were they so interested in sexuality? What did the fascination with sexuality itself encode, disguise, and hide? For what was sexuality their metaphor?'"

87   WALTERS, RONALD G., ed. <u>Primers for Prudery: Sexual Advice to Victorian America</u>. Englewood Cliffs, N.J.: Prentice-Hall, 1974. 175 pp.
      <u>Primers for Prudery</u> is a collection of brief excerpts from nineteenth-century American sexual advice literature. Although there is a topical arrangement to the material, including one chapter exclusively on women, Walters, a history professor at Johns Hopkins, does not display much awareness of the underlying social, political, and psychological bases that influenced opinions on "appropriate" sexual behavior for women. Nor does he attempt to trace changes in theory during the period, although he does cite materials from diverse modes of thought. Some of the excerpts have been taken out of context, and it is difficult for the reader

to determine how representative his selections are of the whole of sexual advice literature being written and read by both profession-al physicians and lay people. As Walters notes, the relationship between this literature and real behavior is a matter of conjec-ture and inference.

88   WALTERS, RONALD G. "Sexual Matters as Historical Problems: A Framework of Analysis." Societas 6 (Summer 1976):157-75.
        Walters suggests various methodological approaches to the study of the history of human sexuality. The thinking is, at times, rather muddy.

89   YOUNG, KIMBALL. Isn't One Wife Enough? New York: Henry Holt, 1954. 476 pp.
        One of the most controversial aspects of Mormonism in the nineteenth and early twentieth centuries was its system of polygamy. In this history of the practice, Young examines a variety of view-points, including the experience of families who were part of the plural marriage system. Young emphasizes religious, social, and economic aspects of polygamy rather than sexual behavior (he notes that it is difficult to obtain data on this subject). He observes, however, that critics of polygamy often saw in it only the exercise of unrestrained male lust, rather than the complex of doctrine and behavior it really was. Unfortunately, there is no documentation of Young's sources other than what may be gleaned from the text.

90   BEALL, OTHO T., Jr. "Aristotle's Master Piece in America: A Landmark in the Folklore of Medicine." William and Mary Quarterly 20, no. 2 (April 1963):207-22.

91   BRADLEY, MARION ZIMMER. "Feminine Equivalents of Greek Love in Modern Fiction." International Journal of Greek Love 1, no. 1 (January 1965):48-58. ISR, LC.

92   BRECHER, EDWARD M. "Krafft-Ebing Vs. Havelock Ellis: Contrast-ing Attitudes in Two Pioneering Students of Sexual Behavior." Medical Aspects of Human Sexuality 7, no. 7 (July 1973):147-57.

93   BULLOUGH, VERN L. "An Early American Sex Manual, or Aristotle Who?" Early American Literature 7, no. 3 (Winter 1973):236-46.

94   _____. "Sex in History: A Virgin Field." Journal of Sex Research 8, no. 2 (May 1972):101-16.

95   BULLOUGH, VERN L., and MARTHA VOIGHT. "Homosexuality and Its Confusion with the 'Secret Sin' in Pre-Freudian America." Journal of the History of Medicine and Allied Sciences 28, no. 2 (April 1973):143-55.

96   CANBY, HENRY SEIDEL. "Sex and Marriage in the Nineties." Harper's Magazine 169 (June-November 1934):429-36.

97   CANNON, CHARLES A. "The Awesome Power of Sex: The Polemical
     Campaign against Mormon Polygamy." Pacific Historical Review
     43, no. 1 (February 1974):61-82.

98   CHURCHILL, FREDERICK B. "Sex and the Single Organism: Bio-
     logical Theories of Sexuality in Mid-Nineteenth Century."
     Studies in the History of Biology 3 (1979):139-77.

99   COMINOS, PETER T. "Late-Victorian Sexual Respectability and
     the Social System." International Review of Social History 8,
     pt. 1 (1963):18-48, 216-50.

100 COOK, BLANCHE WIESEN. "Female Support Networks and Political
     Activism." Chrysalis, no. 3 (1977), pp. 43-61.

101 CURTIS, B. "Victorians Abed: William Graham Sumner on the
     Family, Women and Sex." American Studies 18 (1977):101-22.

102 DUBERMAN, MARTIN BAUML. "'I Am Not Contented': Female
     Masochism and Lesbianism in Early Twentieth Century New England."
     Signs 5, no. 4 (Summer 1980):825-41.

103 FADERMAN, LILLIAN. "Lesbian Magazine Fiction in the Early
     Twentieth Century." Journal of Popular Culture 11, no. 4
     (Spring 1978):800-817.

104 _____. "The Morbidification of Love between Women by Nineteenth-
     century Sexologists." Journal of Homosexuality 4, no. 1 (Fall
     1978):73-90.

105 FELLMAN, ANITA CLAIR, and MICHAEL FELLMAN. "The Rule of
     Moderation in Late Nineteenth-century American Sexual Ideology."
     Journal of Sex Research 17, no. 3 (August 1981):238-55.

106 GILBERT, ARTHUR N. "Doctor, Patient, and Onanist Diseases in
     the Nineteenth Century." Journal of the History of Medicine
     and Allied Sciences 30, no. 3 (July 1975):217-34.

107 GORDON, MICHAEL. "Sex Manuals: Past and Present." Medical
     Aspects of Human Sexuality 5, no. 9 (September 1971):21-37.

108 HALLER, JOHN S., Jr. "From Maidenhood to Menopause: Sex
     Education for Women in Victorian America." Journal of Popular
     Culture 6, no. 1 (Summer 1972):49-69.

109 HALLER, WILLIAM, and MALLEVILLE HALLER. "The Puritan Art of
     Love." Huntington Library Quarterly 5, no. 2 (January 1942):
     235-72.

110 HOLLENDER, MARC H. "The Medical Profession and Sex in 1900."
     American Journal of Obstetrics and Gynecology 108, no. 1
     (1 September 1970):39-48.

111 KERN, LOUIS J. "Ideology and Reality: Sexuality and Women's Status in the Oneida Community." Radical History Review 20 (Spring-Summer 1979):180-204.

112 McGOVERN, JAMES R. "The American Woman's Pre-World War I Freedom in Manners and Morals." Journal of American History 55, no. 2 (September 1968):315-33.

113 MAW, WALLACE H. Fifty Years of Sex Education in the Public Schools of the United States (1900-1950): A History of Ideas. Ed.D. dissertation, University of Cincinnati, 1953. 556 pp. ISR.

114 MONEY, JOHN. "The Way Sex Was--75 Years Ago." Sexology 41, no. 11 (June 1975):27-30.

115 PERRY, LEWIS. "'Progress, Not Pleasure, Is Our Aim': The Sexual Advice of an Antebellum Radical." Journal of Social History 12, no. 3 (Spring 1979):354-66.

116 ROLLESTON, J.D. "Penis Captivus: A Historical Note." Janus 39 (November-December 1935):196-202.

117 ROSENBAUM, BETTY B. "The Sociological Basis of the Laws Relating to Women Sex Offenders in Massachusetts (1620-1860). Journal of Criminal Law and Criminology 28, no. 6 (March-April 1938):815-46.

118 RUGEN, HELEN M. "Women on the Borderland of Pathology: Dominant Conceptions of Female Sexuality 1900-1920." Society for the Social History of Medicine Bulletin, no. 18 (June 1976), pp. 11-12.

119 SHOCKLEY, ANN ALLEN. "The Black Lesbian in American Literature: An Overview." Conditions 5 (1979):133-42.

120 SMITH, DANIEL SCOTT. "The Dating of the American Sexual Revolution: Evidence and Interpretation." In The American Family in Social-Historical Perspective. Edited by Michael Gordon, 321-35. New York: St. Martin's Press, 1973.

121 _____. "Family Limitation, Sexual Control and Domestic Feminism in Victorian America." Feminist Studies 1, nos. 3-4 (Winter-Spring 1973):40-57.

122 SMITH-ROSENBERG, CARROLL. "Beauty, the Beast and the Militant Woman: A Case Study in Sex Roles and Social Stress in Jacksonian America." American Quarterly 23, no. 4 (October 1971):562-84.

123 _____. "The Hysterical Woman: Sex Roles and Role Conflict in 19th-century America." Social Research 39, no. 4 (Winter 1972): 652-78.

124   SMITH-ROSENBERG, CARROLL, and CHARLES E. ROSENBERG. "The
       Female Animal: Medical and Biological Views of Woman and Her
       Role in Nineteenth-century America." Journal of American History
       60, no. 2 (September 1973):332-56.

125   SNITOW, ANN BARR. "The Front Line: Notes on Sex in Novels by
       Women, 1969-1979." Signs 5, no. 4 (Summer 1980):702-18.

126   STAGE, SARAH J. "Out of the Attic: Studies of Victorian
       Sexuality." American Quarterly 27, no. 4 (October 1975):480-85.

127   THOMAS, KEITH. "The Double Standard." Journal of the History
       of Ideas 20, no. 2 (April 1959):195-216.

128   VEITH, ILZE. Hysteria: The History of a Disease. Chicago:
       University of Chicago Press, 1965. 301 pp.

Social and Political Analysis and Theory

How does woman's nature as a sexual being influence her position in society? How, in turn, has a traditionally male-dominated power structure determined woman's role? How do women perceive their own sexuality, and to what extent do they agree or disagree with an ideology that would define their economic, social, and political roles in terms of their sexuality and destiny as wives and mothers?

In attempting to relate questions of woman's sexuality to broader problems of society and politics, authors have frequently chosen to focus on specific institutions that bridge the gap. Marriage was perhaps the most susceptible of these in the late nineteenth and early twentieth centuries. Free love advocates such as Victoria Woodhull argued for an end to what they called sexual slavery, while Judge Ben Lindsey and his fellow supporters of companionate marriage sought radical reform of the traditional marriage relationship. More contemporary analyses, such as Susan Brownmiller's Against Our Will: Men, Women and Rape (entry 136) and Phyllis Chesler's Women and Madness (entry 142) examine areas in which ideas about women's sexuality have been used by men and male-dominated institutions as the means for denying women the integrity of their minds and bodies.

Although many works by feminist theorists are to be found in this section, this is by no means the only point of view represented. Floyd Dell (entry 145), for example, while claiming to call for a revolt against the patriarchy, displayed not only a perverse homophobia, but also a general insensitivity to women's concerns. Nineteenth-century Italian theorist Paolo Mantegazza (entry 185), whose works were still being reprinted in translation in the United States in the 1930s, saw women as objects to be "given" to men, yet advocated sex education and opposed clitoridectomy. Perhaps in the theoretical arena more than in any other do subjective opinions masquerade as facts. Any yet these words are those that lead ultimately to social reform and political change.

31

129   The Annals of the American Academy of Political and Social
      Science 376 (March 1968). Special issue on sex and the contempo-
      rary American scene.
         Edited by Edward Sagarin, this was the first issue of the
      Annals to be devoted completely to the subject of sexuality. There
      are seventeen essays, covering a wide range of subjects, some, such
      as abortion, prostitution, sex and aging, and the double standard,
      relating directly to women. Authors represented included Mary
      Steichen Calderone, Isadore Rubin, Albert Ellis, and John Gagnon.
      Sagarin's introductory essay, "Taking Stock of Studies of Sex,"
      contains some useful guidelines for evaluating sex research.

130   BARDWICK, JUDITH M. Psychology of Women: A Study of Bio-
      cultural Conflicts. New York: Harper and Row, 1971. 242 pp.
         Biological determinism, the idea that psychological sex dif-
      ferences may be caused by the presence of different reproductive
      systems in men and women and by genetic sex differences, is a
      dominant theme in Bardwick's work. Although she acknowledges the
      role of culturally transmitted sex-linked values, these play a
      secondary role. As she notes in her introduction, many of her
      ideas are opinions rather than iron-clad empirical proofs; some-
      times research with small-group populations is extrapolated to pro-
      vide the basis for generalizations about a presumed larger whole.
      For example, Bardwick asserts, "The mature woman is her body--it
      is the way in which she attracts men, manipulates them, loves them,
      secures love, and gratifies both of their sexual and reproductive
      needs." This definition is not only filled with heterosexist bias,
      but assumes that female maturity is actively sexual to the core in
      a way that male maturity is not. The very concept of "maturity,"
      of course, is culturally determined.

131   BAUER, BERNHARD ADAM. Woman and Love. 2 vols. Vol. 1 trans-
      lated by Eden and Cedar Paul; vol. 2 translated by E.S. Jerdan
      and Norman Haire. New York: Boni and Liveright, 1927. 353,
      396 pp.
         Like many Germanic writers on women and sexuality in the late
      nineteenth and early twentieth centuries--Bachhofen, Krafft-Ebing,
      Hirschfeld--Bauer, a Viennese gynecologist, seemed to be intent
      on producing a mammoth encyclopedia of information. Woman and Love
      suffers not only from diffuse organization but from repetition and
      broad generalizations--"A woman is naturally polygamous, just like
      a man," or "Woman in the prime of life is the absolute slave of
      her sexuality"--as well. Bauer's sources are not well documented,
      and although he refers to many authors by name, his reliance on
      conjecture and hearsay in many cases make his arguments suspect.
      Volume 1 focuses on what might be called concepts of women's love
      and sexuality--pain, pleasure, crime, and so on--while the second
      volume presents more straightforward details regarding anatomy,
      physiology, sexual behavior, and prostitution.

132   BEACH, FRANK A., ed. Human Sexuality in Four Perspectives.

Baltimore: Johns Hopkins University Press, 1977. 330 pp.
This is a collection of original essays by ten male authors
on such topics as hermaphroditism, sex differences, and the impact
of hormones on behavior. The four perspectives, which serve to
unify the book or at least give it a structure as outlined by
Beach in his introduction, are those of developmental psychology
and biology, sociology, physiology, and evolution. Several of the
essays seem to be hurriedly and even subjectively researched. The
one on homosexuality by Martin Hoffman, for example, adopts a male
emphasis, claiming that sources do not exist for lesbians. Yet an
examination of sources used as well as Hoffman's "suggested readings" simply reveals that the author does not know what is available.
Other essays, such as that on hormonal changes in women and their
psychological impact, do display an awareness of "male" problems
in diagnosing women's ills: "Physicians, mostly men, often dis-
count a woman's premenstrual or menstrual complaints as being all
'in her head' and therefore not worthy of medical attention. This
is an error, which stems partly from difficulties that a male physician has in empathising with a woman and partly from Western
cultural factors of the masculine self-image which derogates emotional displays as evidence of weakness."

133   _____. Sex and Behavior. New York: John Wiley & Sons, 1965.
       592 pp.
This collection of papers is the tangible product of two
conferences held in 1961 and 1962 at the University of California,
Berkeley. In addition to providing a forum for the presentation
of new research on human and animal sexuality, these conferences
were of no slight historical interest, being the terminal under-
taking of the Committee for Research in Problems of Sex of the
National Academy of Sciences. Of note in this volume are a preliminary report by Masters and Johnson on their work and Paul H.
Gebhard's "Situational Factors Affecting Human Sexual Behavior."
Essays are accompanied by an edited transcript of the conference
discussion following each presentation, as well as a resource list.
There is also a concluding summary chapter by Frank A. Beach.

134   BERNARD, JESSIE. The Sex Game. Englewood Cliffs, N.J.:
       Prentice-Hall, 1968. 372 pp.
Although The Sex Game is primarily a discussion of the factors involved in and sociological implications of sex roles and
gender roles, Bernard includes significant material on sexuality
and sexual behavior, especially in chapter 2, "No Figments."
Throughout the book she highlights real differences in male and
female sexuality: "Perhaps because it is so irrelevant to reproduction, female sexuality, as expressed in orgasm, appears to be
surprisingly amenable to cultural constraints. . . . If cultural
proscription of male orgasm were possible, the population would
suffer severe attrition." She also maintains that twentieth-
century sexologists and authors of marriage manuals, by emphasizing the importance of female orgasm and the "correctness" of

vaginal orgasm, have placed new pressures for performance on men and women, which in some cases, as that of the vaginal orgasm, are contrary to physiological possibility. As with Bernard's other writings, a wide range of sources and imaginative analogies form the basis of her arguments.

135   BROWNE, FRANCES WORSLEY STELLA. Sexual Variety and Variability among Women, and Their Bearing upon Social Reconstruction. British Society for the Study of Sex Psychology Publication, no. 3. London: Beaumont, 1915. 14 pp. Reprinted in Sheila Rowbotham, A New World for Women: Stella Browne--Socialist Feminist (London: Pluto, 1977), pp. 87-105.
    During the 1920s, Stella Browne was one of the first social-ists to perceive the connection between economics and woman's re-productive role. This essay, originally presented at a meeting of the British Society for the Study of Sex Psychology, begins with a discussion of conventional views of woman's sexuality, her apathy and supposedly instinctive monogamy. Browne argues that these views are in error and that women's sexuality is really more dif-fuse and variable than men's and cannot be satisfied either by traditional patriarchal marriage or by prostitution. She was not, however, in favor of all the sexual variations and indeed felt that some of them were due only to patriarchal lingerings: "Our maintenance of outworn traditions is manufacturing habitual auto-erotists and perverts, out of women who would instinctively prefer the love of a man." She also called for legalization and promotion of abortion and contraception.

136   BROWNMILLER, SUSAN. Against Our Will: Men, Women and Rape. New York: Simon and Schuster, 1975. 472 pp.
    Rape, most feminists would agree, is a crime of violence de-ploying the penis as weapon (Susan Brownmiller's words), and such a view is stunningly articulated in this book. Yet, as Brownmiller shows in the chapter, "Victims: The Setting," women, while not responsible for the crime, are trained and sexually socialized to be rape victims. Popular culture conditions women to be passive, to want to be raped, and Brownmiller traces the origin of this conditioning to Freud, Deutsch, Horney, and other psychoanalytic and psychological theorists who have emphasized the "superiority" of the male. "Because men control the definitions of sex, women are allotted a poor assortment of options." Other models for sexu-al passivity are furnished by the Roman Catholic church as well as images of popular culture in films, books, and the media. Brownmiller sees rape as a key issue of the women's movement and urges women to fight back.

137   CALVERTON, V.F., and SAMUEL D. SCHMALHAUSEN, eds. Sex in Civilization. New York: Macaulay, 1929. 719 pp.
    "The intellectuals are in revolt against an entire civiliza-tion. The revolt against the old sex attitudes, with their si-lences and stupidities, is a vital part of this entire revolt

against a decaying culture." Placing sexuality in the context of social evolution and group relations was the primary motive of Calverton and Schmalhausen in editing this collection of essays. Psychoanalytic theory is given its due, although the editors feel that such an individually oriented theory is not the complete explanation for human behavior. Some of the essays on women, such as those by authors Phyllis Blanchard and G.V. Hamilton, reflect ideas found in more detail in their monographs, while Charlotte Perkins Gilman's "Sex and Race Progress" calls for the promotion of eugenics as well as women's involvement in "lifting the quality of the human race." Other well-known contributors include Robert Briffault, Harry Elmer Barnes, Mary Ware Dennett, and Margaret Sanger.

138   CARPENTER, EDWARD. Love's Coming-of-Age. New York: Mitchell Kennerly, 1911. 199 pp.
　　Sex reform was only one of many causes undertaken by Edward Carpenter, an English socialist whose works were widely read in the United States and in Europe. Love's Coming-of-Age, originally published privately in 1896, is a radical plea for changes in the legal rigidity of conventional marriage, as well as a freer, more open approach to sexuality. Carpenter, who was a homosexual, included a chapter on homosexuality, and although his descriptions of both lesbians and gay men may seem to be dominated by traditional stereotypes, his voice was an important early force in calling for a humanitarian, nonpejorative attitude toward this sexual minority. Carpenter was also a firm supporter of women's rights, maintaining that the future of woman depended on her ability to control her sexuality, recognizing that the male treatment of woman as a serf (or in Havelock Ellis's words, quoted by Carpenter, as "a cross between an angel and an idiot") had determined her condition so far. Although Carpenter believed in the depth of mother feeling in women and was as critical of masturbation as most of his contemporaries, his clear sense of the effect of patriarchal tradition and the relationship between economic power and sexuality show him as much in advance of his time. Although some of his notions, such as his advocacy of nudity and his preoccupation with star and sex worship, may strike readers as simply eccentric, other ideas, such as his advocacy of open marriage and individually agreed upon marriage contracts, are still being advocated today.

139   _____. Sex-Love and Its Place in a Free Society. Manchester: Labour Press Society, 1894. 25 pp.
　　In 1894 Edward Carpenter, the British socialist and sexual reformer, published three related pamphlets on the themes of woman, marriage, and sex. This one on "sex-love" deals most directly with sexuality, which Carpenter saw as an underlying universal experience indispensable for personality development. Indeed, he maintained that the enforced celibacy of single women in his culture was very wrong. He advocated sex education from an early age, retaining, however, his time's belief in the danger of masturbation

35

and the need for self-control. Self-control, however, was only to prevent libertinism and should not be enforced if true love and passion were present. Carpenter's Love's Coming-of-Age (entry 138) provides a fuller exposition of many of these ideas.

140   CHAPMAN, JANE ROBERTS, and MARGARET GATES, eds. The Victimiza-
       tion of Women. Beverly Hills, Calif.: Sage Publications, 1978.
       320 pp.
       A collection of essays on various aspects of women's victim-
ization in a male-dominated culture, this book is part of a series
of Sage yearbooks in women's policy studies. Of particular relevance to female sexuality are the introductory conceptual essay by
Margaret Gates and those by Kee MacFarlane and Del Martin on the
sexual abuse of children and battered women, respectively. A
feminist perspective is maintained throughout.

141   CHAPMAN, R.D. Freelove a Law of Nature. New York: published
       by the author, 1881. 36 pp.
       Linking free love to other libertarian causes, such as free
trade and free speech, Chapman saw monogamy as an impediment to
social and sexual happiness. Underlying this argument was a belief in the electromagnetic attraction between the sexes, an attraction that died in conventional marriage because of "prolonged
application of the same stimulus." Chapman quoted extensively from
the works of Foote, the elder, and Hollick, and also argued in favor of contraception. This rare pamphlet has been reprinted in the
RPI "History of Women" microfilm series.

142   CHESLER, PHYLLIS. Women and Madness. Garden City, N.Y.:
       Doubleday, 1972. 359 pp.
       Because sexuality and sexual behavior have been used so
frequently to define women's mental health or illness, psychologist
Phyllis Chesler's Women and Madness is essential for a full understanding of how society uses and misuses its knowledge of these
fields. Chapters on sex between patients and therapists and on
lesbians provide concise introductions to these topics; the lesbian
chapter is especially useful in its differentiation between lesbians
and male homosexuals. Chesler is, of course, writing for a popular
audience, and some readers may wish for more detailed documentation
of her sources. Her feminist viewpoint is clearly expressed and
her indictment of past psychiatric theory and practice as being
harmful to and repressive of women is strongly and convincingly
set forth.

143   CROLY, DAVID GOODMAN. The Truth about Love: A Proposed Sexual
       Morality Based upon the Doctrine of Evolution, and Recent
       Discoveries in Medical Science. New York: David Wesley, 1872.
       259 pp.
       The free love movement, which came to the fore in the early
1870s, sparked much moralistic criticism, but also led to some
thoughtful analysis of sexual relationships. David Croly, managing

editor of the New York <u>World</u> and husband of Jennie June Croly, one
of the best-known journalists and women's club leaders of her day,
was no advocate of free love, but he also had little use for conventional monogamy either. The public was no stranger to Croly's
views on sex; his <u>Miscegenation</u> (1864) had shocked readers by advocating the amalgamation of the races to improve civilization.
Now, as Croly saw it, free love was too purely hedonistic, taking
too little account of the needs of society. What was needed was
legislative and societal reform in order to legitimize all forms
of sexual relationships from polyandry to sodomy and to encourage
such desiderata as scientific propagation of children and voluntary male sterilization. Croly was especially favorable toward
John Humphrey Noyes's Oneida model for male continence, since
Croly himself believed that sex was for much more than the begetting of children. "It is the brutal and inferior morality which
simply allows the sexes to come together for purposes of propagation; and the higher, the human civilized morality which allows
intercourse without reference to propagation."

Although Croly had no clear strategy for achieving his many
goals, it is interesting to reflect on how many of them fore-
shadowed behavior patterns and political positions commonly associated with the Progressive era, from the legitimization of social
dancing as a quasi-sexual form of expression to the movement to
legally regulate prostitution. It is perhaps no accident that his
son Herbert, first editor of the <u>New Republic</u>, was one of that
era's most representative spokesmen. Note that some sources attribute authorship to Jane Cunningham (Jennie June) Croly, although
the <u>National Union Catalog</u> lists David Goodman Croly as the author.

144   de BEAUVOIR, SIMONE. <u>The Second Sex</u>. Translated and edited by
       H.M. Parshley. New York: Knopf, 1953. 732 pp.
       Material on women's sexuality is scattered throughout <u>The</u>
<u>Second Sex</u>, although most of it is found in the sections where de
Beauvoir discusses the female life cycle. Her initial chapters,
however, include a critique of Freud and psychoanalysis. De
Beauvoir remarks on psychoanalytic utilization of masculine patterns when defining women, theoretical definitions of man as a
human being and woman as an alienated other, and the dead-end
quality of this approach: "All psychoanalysts systematically re-
ject the idea of <u>choice</u> and the correlated concept of value, and
therein lies the intrinsic weakness of the system."

Chapter 14, "Sexual Initiation," analyzes the complexity of
woman's eroticism. De Beauvoir compares clitoral and vaginal sexual response, calling them systems "one of which perpetuates juvenile independence while the other consigns woman to man and childbearing. The normal sexual act in effect puts woman into a state
of dependency upon the male and the species." Asserting that
penetration is a violation, she calls for an authentic female
eroticism which will demand that woman overcome her passivity and
establish a relationship of reciprocity with her partner.

A chapter on lesbians is less satisfactory in its perpetuation of visual stereotypes. "The lesbian often likes to drink hard liquor, smoke strong tobacco, use rough language, take violent exercise" conveys a somewhat negative image. Subsequent material on marriage argues that it is intended to suppress woman's erotic life and also that sexual love inevitably dies in marriage.

De Beauvoir's sources merit some comment. Although The Second Sex was written prior to publication of Kinsey's female volume, she does make use of Sexual Behavior in the Human Male. Another much-used authority is Wilhelm Stekel's book on frigidity in women. De Beauvoir does not seem to have used any studies by Katharine Bement Davis, Margaret Mead, or similar American scholars. We do, however, find references to such various Anglo-American literary works as Little Women and Lady Chatterley's Lover. Clearly De Beauvoir's thought and imagery reflect a broad but somewhat eclectic selection of sources, perhaps dependent on their availability in French translation.

145 DELL, FLOYD. Love in the Machine Age: A Psychological Study of the Transition from Patriarchal Society. New York: Farrar and Rinehart, 1930. 428 pp.

Novelist Floyd Dell thought he had produced the epitome of iconoclasm with Love in the Machine Age. Old-fashioned views must go, he declared. Tradition is leading to neurosis, as people struggle to conform to an outmoded patriarchal social system.

Dell, unfortunately, is his own worst enemy, for what he seems to be proposing is the substitution of one rigid system for another. Particularly striking is his obsession with homosexuality, a vague term that he appropriates whenever convenient. Claiming it to be part of the patriarchal social system, he asserts, for example, that open marriages (in our contemporary sense) "are symptoms of pre-adult sexuality. They are attaining an inner and usually unconscious satisfaction of their homosexual wishes by their mutual infidelities." Women's colleges have a homosexual and quasi-homosexual atmosphere. "A certain proportion have graduated either into life-long homosexuality or into permanent lay nunship."

With his constant emphasis on "normal" heterosexuality and his lack of sensitivity to women's concerns, Dell becomes merely an inverted parrot of the old patriarchal system which he pretends to oppose.

146 De MARTINO, MANFRED F., ed. Sexual Behavior and Personality Characteristics. New York: Citadel Press, 1963. 412 pp.

This is a collection of essays, mostly reprints of previously published articles, in some cases abridged from the original. Exceptions are De Martino's "Dominance-Feeling, Security-Insecurity, and Sexuality in Women," and "Some Reactions to First Remembered Sexual Climax" by Glen A. and Yvonne Brackbill. Some of the material dates from the 1940s and seems out of date even for 1963. Although subject coverage is balanced between men and women, De Martino's selection criteria seem to be rather eclectic; several items originally appeared in the International Journal of Sexology, an Indian publication. There is also little attempt to relate essays to one another through introductory narrative or explanations of context and significance.

147   ELLIS, ALBERT, and ALBERT ABARBANEL, eds. The Encyclopedia of Sexual Behavior. 2 vols. New York: Hawthorn Books, 1961.
      The Encyclopedia of Sexual Behavior is really a collection of essays prepared by individual authors on a wide range of topics. Some of those relating specifically to women include "Femininity," by Clara Thompson, "Frigidity," by Albert Ellis, and "Anatomy of the Female Orgasm," by William H. Masters and Virginia E. Johnson. Each essay reflects the point of view of the individual author(s) and is usually accompanied by a reference list of sources cited in the text.

148   ELLIS, HAVELOCK. "The Evolution of Modesty." In Studies in the Psychology of Sex. Vol. 1, pt. 1, 1-84. New York: Random House, 1936.
      "The Evolution of Modesty," along with Ellis's essays on sexual periodicity and autoerotism, were published together in 1899, two years after "Sexual Inversion," the first of the Studies. Like much of Ellis's work, it was extensively rewritten in subsequent years, and the Random House edition reflects these changes.
      Ellis saw modesty as an especially feminine trait, "so that it may almost be regarded as the chief secondary sexual character of women on the psychical side." Basing his conclusions largely on anthropological observation and travelers' accounts, he believed that sexual modesty in women was rooted in periodicity "and is an involuntary expression of the organic fact that the time for love is not now." Blushing is seen as a physiological sanction of modesty, while the conception of women as property adds a new dimension to an old emotion.

149   _____. Sex and Marriage: Eros in Contemporary Life. Edited, with a note, by John Gawsworth. London: Williams and Norgate, 1951. 211 pp.
      Reprinted as recently as 1977 by Greenwood Press, this is a collection of essays by Ellis, part of a larger series of his works edited posthumously by John Gawsworth. "The Sexual Life of Woman" critiques studies done in the United States by G.V. Hamilton, Katharine Bement Davis, and Robert Latou Dickinson. Another essay of interest, "The Supposed Frigidity of Women," argues that frigidity is a condition of male definition rather than a reflection of a constitutional incapacity in women. He supports this view by references to women's wider range of sexual response. Other items worthy of note include "Eros in Contemporary Life," "The Future of Marriage," and "Parents as Sexual Advisers."

150   _____. "Sex in Relation to Society." In Studies in the Psychology of Sex, vol. 4, 1-750. New York: Random House, 1936.

Originally published in 1910, "Sex in Relation to Society" was seen by Ellis as the logical conclusion to his earlier Studies. Here, rather than describing the relationship of the individual to particular choices of object or of sexually related behavior, he integrated his earlier findings into a study of social and cultural attitudes and institutions: motherhood, sex education, prostitution, morality, marriage.

Ellis believed that although medical, legal, and moral demands had to be considered, the needs of the individual should be given first consideration: "The main task before us must be to ascertain what best expresses, and what best satisfies the totality of the impulses and ideas of civilized men and women." Although he was an advocate of conventional motherhood, recommending rest during the last three months of pregnancy, he also believed in woman's sexual autonomy and moral responsibility: "In controlling her own sexual life, and in realizing that her responsibility for such control can no longer be shifted on to the shoulders of the other sex, women will also indirectly affect the sexual lives of men, much as men already affect the sexual lives of women." Yet Ellis's "sacred motherhood" with its corollary of marriage centering in the child, raises more questions about sexual economy than it resolves. It is with these dilemmas that we are still struggling today.

151 FINOT, JEAN. Problems of the Sexes. Translated by Mary J. Stafford. New York and London: G.P. Putnam's Sons, 1913. 408 pp.

Primarily concerned with tracing the need for women's emancipation, as well as the future prospects of the "new woman," Finot believed that inequality of the sexes had resulted in mutual distrust, hatred, and scorn. Women were defined only in terms of their sexual nature: "Confined to sexual life, she can be only a mother or a courtesan." Even women of genius, like Sappho, whose lesbianism Finot discusses at some length, are judged not by their achievements (as men would be) but by the vagaries of their private or sexual lives. Although Finot held some traditional views ("Sexual emotions are less strong in woman than in man"), he overwhelmingly supported woman's emancipation as a means for improving her economic and social position, as well as conventional institutions such as marriage. The purity of women would be extended to men, resulting in a higher standard of chastity and less divorce.

152 FOERSTER, FRIEDRICH WILHELM. Marriage and the Sex-Problem. Translated by Meyrick Booth. New York: Frederick A. Stokes, 1912. 228 pp.

Although his writing has a sophistication that earlier theorists' lacked, Foerster's arguments calling for an ascetic Christian sexual ethic based on self-control hearken back to the ideas of the mid-nineteenth century. In this translation of Sexual ethick und Sexualpädagogik, Meyrick Booth provides an introduction outlining Foerster's life and thought. Professor of education at the University of Vienna, Foerster was skeptical of Freud's ideas about the interrelationship between sexuality and neuroses. This comment foreshadows similar ones to be made in the future by other critics of Freud's research methods: "A nerve-doctor, who sees, for the most part, only the darker side of sexual life, is from the very beginning extremely liable to construct his views upon his abnormal experience alone, and thus unconsciously to pervert the truth." Reacting against intellectualism and materialism, Foerster called for a return to fundamental Christian ethics, including a monogamic ideal based on love and loyalty. Birth control, divorce, and the pursuit of sexual pleasure undermined this ideal. Foerster was also opposed to sex education in the schools, at least of the biological variety, and felt that character development should be stressed, too much exposure to sexual enlightenment posing a potential for sexual tyranny of the will.

153   FOOTE, EDWARD BLISS. Dr. Foote's Replies to the Alphites, Giving Some Cogent Reasons for Believing that Sexual Continence Is Not Conducive to Health. New York: Murray Hill, 1883. 126 pp. ISR.

One of the classics of nineteenth-century free love literature, Dr. Foote's Replies had its roots in the controversy over whether sexual intercourse should be limited only to reproduction or whether pleasure was also a legitimate aim. Foote took a eugenic position, maintaining that birth control would serve to improve the race and at any rate was more feasible than the Alphites' doctrine of self-control and self-denial. In this collection of letters, replies, articles, and reviews, dating from May 1881 to March 1883, Foote takes on several so-called Alphites (named for the journal Alpha, which expressed their views), including Caroline B. Winslow and Parker Pillsbury. Much of the material consists of letters from both sides, reprinted from Foote's Health Monthly.

154   FORBAT, SANDOR, ed. Love and Marriage. New York: Liveright, 1938. 432 pp.

This collection of essays by such authors as Havelock Ellis, Julian Huxley, and Wilhelm Stekel includes a variety of points of view on such subjects as love, monogamy, and morality. There is a certain amount of misinformation, as in this comment by P. Orlovski: "The muscular contraction which, according to some investigators, is said to be identical with the feminine orgasm, has in actual fact nothing to do with it, as the orgasm can occur without it." On the other hand, Ellis's remarks anticipate the 1960s and 1970s controversy over vaginal versus clitoral orgasm: "The clitoris is a normal focus of sexual sensation and tends so to continue frequently as the chief if not the only focus. That with the initiation of adult intercourse the vagina should also become a focus of pleasurable sensation is natural, but it is incorrect to speak of any 'transfer.'" Love and Marriage was also published in England under the title, Love, Marriage, Jealousy, with minor alteration in its content.

155   FOREL, AUGUSTE HENRI. The Sexual Question: A Scientific, Psychological, Hygienic, and Sociological Study for the Cultured Classes. Translated by C.F. Marshall. New York: Rebman, 1908. 536 pp.

This all-encompassing compendium on the subject of sex by Swiss psychiatrist Forel was a popular work in its day, being reprinted many times in both its German- and English-language editions. Individual subjects discussed include the history of sexual life and marriage, sexual jurisprudence, and pathology, Forel's object being to demonstrate the integral relationship between sex and society. Although Forel claimed to be making a clean sweep of prejudices, traditions, and prudery, he nevertheless perpetuated many of the conventional stereotypes of female sexuality and gender behavior: "The instinct of procreation is much stronger in woman than in man, and is combined with the desire to give herself passively, to play the part of one who devotes herself, who is conquered, mastered and subjugated. These negative aspirations form part of the normal sexual appetite of woman." Yet Forel also took a comparatively liberal view of homosexuality and of abortion: "The right of the embryo to life should depend on the wish of the bearers of each of the two germs by which it is formed, at the moment of conception." Perhaps such inconsistency only serves to demonstrate the culture-bound yet totally subjective quality of much writing on human sexuality.

156   FORSTER, DORA. Sex Radicalism as Seen by an Emancipated Woman of the New Time. Chicago: M. Harman, 1905. 57 pp. ISR.

This is a comparatively late free love tract in the free thought tradition of Moses Harman and Lucifer, and the pamphlet closes with an advertisement for that journal. Forster calls for abolition of the power of the church and its control of sexual relations. "Society should not interfere with the sex-life of an individual, except when his actions are injurious to others. Its issue of licenses to depart from chastity, called marriage, is an impertinence." Like other free love advocates, Forster believed that the position of woman would be improved by giving her equal control of the sexual relationship. She notes that under the current "Puritan" system masturbation is often continued in adult life due to a lack of permissible outlets, but that women often find other substitutes for sex, such as religious enthusiasm or same-sex friendships. An appendix reprints selections by Edward Carpenter, R.B. Kerr (on Moses Harman), and others.

157   FRIEDAN, BETTY. The Feminine Mystique. New York: W.W. Norton, 1963. 380 pp.

Friedan devotes only one chapter, somewhat sensationally titled "The Sex-Seekers," to a direct discussion of women's sexuality, although the topic is dealt with indirectly throughout much of the book. The book's reputation rests on its role as a catalyst in the contemporary women's movement, and while its overall impact and importance cannot be denied, one sometimes wishes that Friedan's arguments were based more on solid historical or social science analysis than on inference from sources taken somewhat out of context. For example, Friedan rejects Freud's ideas about women as being culturally biased and determined, yet fails to apply the same criteria to his and other theorists' ideas on the causes and characteristics of homosexuality.

158   GAGNON, JOHN H., and WILLIAM SIMON. Sexual Conduct: The Social
       Sources of Human Sexuality. Chicago: Aldine, 1973. 316 pp.
            Much of the material in Sexual Conduct is a recasting of pre-
       viously published articles, giving a slightly disjointed cast to
       the book. Gagnon and Simon's thesis is that sexual behavior is
       the outcome of a complex psychosocial development process, which
       orders, rather than is ordered by, biological circumstance. So-
       called natural sexual behavior is therefore a myth. "The social
       meaning given to the physical acts releases biological events."
       Thus, sexual behavior is a unified mind-body process. In addition
       to the theoretical material, several of the other essays, such as
       those on childhood and adolescence and on sex education, relate
       equally to males and females, while others, on lesbians and prosti-
       tutes, deal exclusively with women.

159   GEBHARD, PAUL H.; JAN RABOCH, and HANS GIESE. The Sexuality of
       Women. Library of Sexual Behavior, vol. 1. Translated by Colin
       Bearne. New York: Stein and Day, 1970. 144 pp.
            Originally published in Germany, The Sexuality of Women con-
       sists of three sections prepared separately by Gebhard, Raboch,
       and Giese. Gebhard's contribution summarizes previously published
       material on women's sexuality prepared by the Institute for Sex
       Research and is based on a series of lectures given in 1966 at the
       University of Hamburg. Raboch's essay presents information on dis-
       turbances of sexual responsiveness in women based on research con-
       ducted at the Sexological Institute of Charles University in Prague,
       the first scientific sex institute to be established (1922) in a
       university. Giese, a specialist in psychiatry and neurology who
       in 1950 became director of the Institute for Sex Research in
       Frankfurt am Main, offers more impressionistic evidence, based on
       his case experience and some cursory statistical studies.

160   GEDDES, PATRICK, and ARTHUR J. THOMPSON. Sex. New York:
       Henry Holt, 1914. 256 pp.
            Geddes and Thompson were, respectively, professor of botany
       at the University of St. Andrews and professor of natural history
       at the University of Aberdeen. Although much of this work reflects
       their background, their overall intent, to dispel human ignorance,
       was clearly evinced: "For lack of a little instruction many are
       made miserable when they should be happy, many even ruined, in
       soul and in body." Advocates of self-control, they nevertheless
       warn that women's emancipation may lead them to demand greater re-
       straint from men than they are willing to give. They counter this,
       however, by giving greater weight to the control over their own

bodies which women will thereby achieve. One interesting observation: "Woman's greater control over her passions--for organic, ethical, and social reasons, and for fear of consequences--may lead man to conclude quite erroneously that these passions are much less strong than his."

161   GOLDSMID, JOSEPH ALBERT. Companionate Marriage from the Medical and Social Aspects. London: William Heinemann, 1934. 63 pp.
      Incorporating the ideas of Judge Ben Lindsey, Goldsmid presents arguments favoring the adoption of companionate marriage as a viable legal and social institution. He analyzes the four characteristics of the system set forth by Lindsey: freely available birth control, divorce by mutual consent, equitable alimony and support arrangements, and sex and marriage education for youth. Goldsmid believes that goals of continence and celibacy before marriage are not realistic and that companionate marriage would cut down people's involvement in extramarital relations, masturbation, and homosexuality. A corollary, which he discusses, is that the new system would lead to women's equality in the marriage relationship.

162   GROSS, LEONARD, ed. Sexual Behavior: Current Issues, An Interdisciplinary Approach. Flushing, N.Y.: Spectrum, 1974. 291 pp.
      This anthology reprints articles from Sexual Behavior, a now defunct periodical published in the early 1970s, which has limited availability because of its short publication span. Among the essays relating to women are Robert R. Bell, "Female Sexual Satisfaction as Related to Levels of Education"; Robert Staples, "The Sexuality of Black Women"; and Robert Seidenberg, "Older Women and Younger Men." Many articles are accompanied by comments from such authorities as Cynthia Fuchs Epstein and Jessie Bernard. There is no material on lesbianism or childhood and adolescent sexuality.

163   HAIRE, NORMAN. Hymen or the Future of Marriage. London: Kegan Paul, Trench, Trubner, 1927. 96 pp.
      In this book of social commentary and prophecy, Haire pleads for increased individual freedom and an improved sexual morality. Marriage, he says, is in trouble because of sexual unhappiness, and this unhappiness is in turn due to lack of proper sex education and faulty standards of sexual conduct. Sex codes, he felt, needed to adapt to changing social conditions and advances in scientific knowledge. Because he felt that thwarting of sexual impulses was dangerous to the health, Haire believed in the desirability of either early marriage or premarital sex. He also advocated sterilization of hereditarily disabled people before they were permitted to marry. His other predictions included an increase in polygamy, divorce reform, and strict eugenic laws governing reproduction.

164   HAMMER, SIGNE, ed. Women: Body and Culture: Essays on the

Sexuality of Women in a Changing Society. New York: Perennial
Library, 1975. 342 pp.
   With the exception of one selection from an unpublished Ph.D.
dissertation, all the material in this reader originally appeared
in some other publication. There are four sections to the book
dealing in turn with sexual identity; masturbation, sexual intercourse, and orgasm; menstruation and menopause; and pregnancy,
birth, and child care. Authors represented include Masters and
Johnson, Karen Horney, and Margaret Mead. An original essay by
Hammer introduces each topic section. Some essays are extensively
documented, and there is a short bibliography.

165   HARTLEY, CATHERINE GASQUOINE. The Truth about Woman. New York:
      Dodd, Mead, 1913. 404 pp.
      Hartley, an Englishwoman whose works up until this time had
focused exclusively on Spain and Spanish culture, saw this book as
a personal statement of her faith in woman as the predominant and
responsible partner in the relations of the sexes. Although much
of the book deals with sexual biology in birds, nonhuman mammals,
and other species, as well as with the history of relations between the sexes, Hartley does include significant material on sexuality. She was an advocate of female superiority based on the
maternal role and saw a difference between the force of "male
sexual hunger" and woman's own desire, which was motivated by the
purpose of "continuing the race." Women should have the right
of selection of sexual partners and should fix sexual standards,
"the True Female Franchise." She also called attention to the relationship between religious salvation and sexuality in women:
"In both cases the surrender, the renunciation of personal will,
is an experience fraught with passionate pleasure."

166   HENSLIN, JAMES M., ed. Studies in the Sociology of Sex. New
      York: Appleton-Century-Crofts, 1971. 410 pp.
      A collection of sixteen original essays, Studies emphasizes
the impact and influence of group membership on sexual behavior.
In addition to several general essays, topics dealt with include
orgasm, sex among swingers, abortion, rape, the involvement of
sex in certain occupations, and male homosexuality. Of particular
interest are Michael Gordon, "From an Unfortunate Necessity to a
Cult of Mutual Orgasm: Sex in American Marital Education Literature, 1830-1940"; Carolyn Symonds, "Sexual Mate-Swapping: Violation of Norms and Reconciliation of Guilt"; and James M. Henslin
and Mae A. Biggs, "Dramaturgical Desexualization: The Sociology
of the Vaginal Examination." Notes and bibliographic citations
accompany each essay.

167   HEYWOOD, EZRA H. Cupid's Yokes; Or, the Binding Forces of
      Conjugal Life. Princeton, Mass.: Co-operative Publishing Co.,
      1876. 23 pp.
      One of the many free love tracts published during the 1870s,
Cupid's Yokes had a wide distribution, estimated at anywhere

between 50,000 and 200,000 copies. Reform of the institution of marriage was Heywood's primary goal, but an underlying theme in the work is that such rational reform would give women equal power in controlling relationships. Heywood's vision of a rationally controlled sex would lead, he felt, to the elimination of such sexual abuses as prostitution, masturbation, and celibate abstinence, and he advocated nonclimactic intercourse on the pattern of the Oneida community. Cupid's Yokes also linked economic reform to sexual reform; Heywood claimed that the accumulation of property without work by capitalists, that is, the profit system, would be eliminated by sexual reform, and vice versa. Unfortunately, Heywood was arrested under the Comstock law for sending such "obscene" material through the mail, and was convicted and sentenced to a fine and two years in prison. Hal Sears's The Sex Radicals contains a detailed discussion of the tract and Heywood's subsequent legal difficulties.

168   HITZ, GERTRUDE. The Importance of Knowledge Concerning the
       Sexual Nature. A Suggestive Essay. Washington, D.C.:
       Washington Society for Moral Education, 1884. 32 pp.
          Arguing in favor of a single standard of sexual morality,
Gertrude Hitz maintained that sexual relations should be undertaken
for reproductive purposes only: "Strict continence, except for
procreation, is the highest law of sexual life." Hitz advocated
sex education and repression as means of achieving this goal, ad-
vising young women to avoid all activities and appearances that
might excite passionate feelings in men. She also commented on
masturbation, "a poisonous habit," and prostitution, which she regarded as economic in origin.

169   HOCH, PAUL H., and JOSEPH ZUBIN, eds. Psychosexual Development
       in Health and Disease. New York: Grune and Stratton, 1949.
       283 pp.
          Much of the material in this collection of papers read at
the 38th annual meeting of the American Psychopathological Association focuses on the work of Alfred C. Kinsey, whose Sexual Behavior
in the Human Male had just been published. This does not, however,
negate its relevance for the study of female sexuality. Especially
useful is the essay by Kinsey et al., "Concepts of Normality and
Abnormality in Sexual Behavior," which concludes that "current concepts of normality and abnormality in human sexual behavior represent what are primarily moral evaluations. They have little if
any biologic justification." David Levy's rejoinder to such Kinsey
critics as Gustav Bychowski puts such opposition in a rational,
scientific perspective, and evaluates Kinsey's findings vis à vis
psychoanalytic theory. Other essays by such authors as Margaret
Mead examine sexuality from a variety of anthropological, sociological, and cross-cultural, cross-species perspectives.

170   HUTT, CORINNE. Males and Females. Middlesex, England:
       Penguin Books, 1972. 158 pp.

Part of the Penguin "Science of Behaviour" series, Males and Females discusses sexual and sex-based (gender-determined) differences in both sexual and nonsexual behavior. Particular emphasis is placed on biologically determined differences, and Hutt bases much of her argument on studies of sex-related behavior in other mammalian species. The author displays a decided lack of sensitivity to the nuances of cultural conditioning, including her own: "A woman's primary role is that of motherhood and most women have some or other of the attributes which fit them for this role." As with all biological determinists, one must ask whether biological and sex differences are the cause of or merely the accompaniment to and "justification" for various forms of gender distinction and discrimination.

171   JAMES, C.L. The Future Relations of the Sexes. St. Louis: published by the author, 1872. 27 pp.
      This short free love tract presents the common argument that marriage is a state of virtual slavery for women. James is more concerned about other aspects of the women's rights question than some other writers and also offers a synopsis of communal models for alternatives to monogamous marriage and a critique of consanguinous marriage. Free love, as might be expected, is destined to triumph, although not without difficulty: "Free love implies a conception of chastity so high, that the cut-throat defenders of the bloody law of marriage consider it impracticable." Future Relations is available on microfilm as part of Research Publications, Inc.'s "History of Women" series.

172   JANEWAY, ELIZABETH. "Who Is Sylvia? On the Loss of Sexual Paradigms." Signs 5, no. 4 (Summer 1980):573-89.
      Utilizing Thomas Kuhn's definition of paradigm, Janeway describes how men's visions of female sexuality in Western culture have dichotomized into a good/bad, Mary/Eve image that has been used to manipulate women and deny them their full human potential. The "Mary" conception and its corollary economic motivators, which have worked to maintain a paradigm of female sexual purity, are breaking down in contemporary society. The male mythology of Eve, however, has not broken down, and Janeway sees its perpetuation as damaging to women. Janeway calls for a cautious creation of new paradigms of women's sexuality, indeed, new woman-generated definitions of self.

173   Journal of Sex & Marital Therapy 1, no. 2 (Winter 1974).
      Special issue on female sexuality.
      This special issue includes seven essays, as well as an introductory editorial by Helen Singer Kaplan. One theme governing the material is that while there are significant biopsychological differences between men and women, this in no way justifies the idea that one sex is superior or inferior to the other. Some of the essays raise more questions than they answer, and all point the way to additional research. Kaplan's article, "The

Classification of the Female Sexual Dysfunctions," is an especially good summary of the psychology and physiology of female orgasm. Ariel Compton's "Who's Hysterical" compares character traits of the so-called hysterical personality with those of "normal" women and finds that those traits "are not only the very ones that are often seen as belonging naturally to women but are often claimed by both men and women as being 'feminine.'"

174   KISCH, ENOCH HEINRICH. The Sexual Life of Woman in Its
       Physiological, Pathological and Hygienic Aspects. Translated
       by M. Eden Paul. New York: Rebman, 1910. 686 pp.
            Originally published in Berlin in 1904, The Sexual Life of
       Woman appeared in several English-language editions. Kisch's
       previous work had included monographs on such subjects as the meno-
       pause and sterility in women, and this work places decided emphasis
       on biological and medical aspects of the subject, although Kisch
       does not refrain from making comments on social questions.
            Dividing woman's sexual life cycle into three segments--
       menarche, menacme, and menopause--the author examines the anatomi-
       cal characteristics, pathology, and other conditions typifying
       these segments of woman's life. In the social and political sphere,
       Kisch felt that the movement for the emancipation of women had gone
       too far and regarded free love as "a barbaric retrogression toward
       the rude sexual habits of savage people." He did, however, advocate
       sex education prior to marriage for young women and the importance
       of hygiene in sexual relations. There are frequent citations by
       author's name in the text to Kisch's sources, but the absence of
       title citations makes these difficult for the researcher to trace.

175   KOEDT, ANN. "The Myth of the Vaginal Orgasm." In Notes from
       the Second Year, edited by Shulamith Firestone and Ann Koedt,
       37-41. n.p.: 1970.
            One of the most influential essays on sexuality to come out
       of the early stages of the contemporary women's movement, "The
       Myth of the Vaginal Orgasm" focuses on the primary role of the
       clitoris in producing orgasm in women. Kinsey's and Masters and
       Johnson's research are cited as evidence of the physiological fal-
       libility of Freud's view of the superiority of the vaginal orgasm.
       Koedt sees the Freudian definition having arisen as part of an
       overall tendency to define women sexually in terms of what pleases
       men, even though it is anatomically "correct," because men see the
       clitoris as a threat to their masculinity. The establishment of
       clitoral orgasm as fact and norm would threaten the institution
       of heterosexuality. Notes and the essay have been microfilmed as
       part of the Bell and Howell "Herstory" series.

176   KOGAN, BENJAMIN A. Human Sexual Expression. New York:
       Harcourt Brace Jovanovich, 1973. 385 pp.
            The central concept of Kogan's book is that human sexuality
       is an expression of the total personality. He reviews much of the
       recent research in such areas as sexual and reproductive physiology,

genetics, sexual dysfunction, and related topics such as pregnancy and birth control. Kogan is careful to avoid value judgments when reporting on variant sexual behaviors and attitudes and accords equal coverage to men and women. Much effort is made to debunk old myths: "As Judd Marmor has pointed out, Sigmund Freud's patriarchal notions about women are invalid. . . . 'penis envy' (like 'womb envy') is now understood to depend largely on environmental cues." There is extensive footnote documentation and a glossary of sex-related terms.

177   KRICH, ARON M., ed. Women: The Variety and Meaning of Their Sexual Experience. New York: Dell, 1953. 317 pp.
     An original introduction by Margaret Mead highlights this mass-market paperback, which reprints selections from several well-known works on various aspects of female sexuality. Authors represented include Laura Hutton, Helene Deutsch, and Havelock Ellis. Some of the material, such as Robert Latou Dickinson's critique of the Kinsey male volume, relates only indirectly to women, while other essays, such as that by Frederick W. Goodrich, Jr., on natural childbirth, imply a broad interpretation of the phrase "sexual experience."

178   KRONHAUSEN, PHYLLIS, and EBERHARD KRONHAUSEN. The Sexually Responsive Woman. New York: Grove Press, 1964. 255 pp.
     Masters and Johnson's research on sexual physiology comprises one full chapter of this book, but, oddly, the Kronhausens never refer to them by name. The authors' objective of dispelling some of the mythology of female sexuality, such as certain psychoanalytic viewpoints and the concept of the vaginal orgasm, is laudable, as is their vision of women as physiologically and psychologically autonomous, but their methodology, such as the unattributed material mentioned above, as well as their use of four "interviews" with women as the bulk of their empirical evidence, is rather unconvincing. Among the topics covered in this strange mixture of impressionistic recollections and factual evidence are the anatomy of orgasm, premarital sex, and sexual technique.

179   LAMARE, NOEL. Love and Fulfillment in Woman. Translated by Adrienne and Ralph Case. New York: Macmillan, 1957. 179 pp.
     Published in France in 1952 as Connaissance sensuelle de la femme, this work reflects the traditional theory that woman's behavior is at the mercy of her reproductive system. "Her life . . . is an unceasing and anxious search for balance, which she can find in love alone." Focusing on the negative aspects of female sexuality, Lamare devotes fully half of the book to a discussion of such sexual problems as frigidity, congenital malformations, and "accidents of defloration." Lamare recognizes that woman's sexuality is more complex than man's, especially in its psychological and emotional aspects, but some of his ideas, such as the following one on vaginal sensitivity, are questionable: "It is solely upon the male partner that the awakening of this sensitiveness depends

--upon his culture, his delicacy, and his skill." There is no documentation and little text citation of authorities.

180   LAWS, JUDITH LONG. "Toward a Model of Female Sexual Identity." Midway 11, no. 1 (Summer 1970):39-75.
        Laws begins by reviewing and discussing literature from Freud to date, which may contribute to a perception or understanding of female sexuality and sexual identity. Her review is by no means uncritical, nor, it should be noted, is it at all comprehensive (the subject is rather broad for an article of this length). She concludes by proposing a model for an "integrative approach to the study of sexual identity" and a research agenda for the field.

181   LAWS, JUDITH LONG, and PEPPER SCHWARTZ. Sexual Scripts: The Social Construction of Female Sexuality. Hinsdale, Ill.: Dryden Press, 1977. 243 pp.
        Sexual behavior, rather than being innate or instinctual, is patterned by scripts or traditional learned modes. For women, most of these scripts have been fashioned by men, just as a masculine bias is found in much sex research. With the rise of laboratory-based sex research, joined with feminist consciousness, women are beginning to change the old scripts and to develop new ones that reflect both the new empirical research base as well as their own subjective realities.
        Feminist in perspective, Sexual Scripts examines five key areas: sexual identity, biological processes, sexual interaction, life-styles, and women as sexual victims. Laws and Schwartz seek to answer the following questions in regard to each of these topics: "What are the available social scripts? How are they enforced? What competing constructions exist? What research does not exist and why?" The book is well documented and summarizes a broad range of recent research and writing on sexuality, psychology, sociology, and feminism.

182   LIPMAN-BLUMEN, JEAN, and ANN R. TICKAMYER. "Sex Roles in Transition: A Ten-Year Perspective." Annual Review of Sociology 1 (1975):297-337.
        A useful complement to Astin, Parelman, and Fisher, this review essay includes a 350-item bibliography. The authors discuss the literature topically, with particular focus on the impact of sex-role research on women, as well as on feminist critiques of sexual inequality. Materials discussed are primarily from the 1960s and 1970s, although some earlier citations are also included, as are historical studies.

183   LOEWENSTEIN, SOPHIE. "An Overview of Some Aspects of Female Sexuality." Social Casework 59, no. 2 (February 1978):106-15.
        This review article provides a concise summary of current opinion of the vaginal-clitoral orgasm controversy, sexual diversity, marriage, masturbation, and "normal" sexuality.

184   McCOWAN, DON CABOT. <u>Love and Life: Sex Urge and Its</u>
<u>Consequences</u>. Chicago: Pascal Covici, 1928. 205 pp.
       Including chapters on such subjects as sex education, sex
and crime, and sex psychology, McCowan presents a combination of
myth, hearsay, and scientific fact. His social outlook is in many
cases enlightened, as when he defines woman's status in many modern
marriages as that of a mere slave or prostitute, love itself being
founded on romantic fiction. In other areas, however, such as his
recommendation of state intervention in the breeding and raising of
children, he strikes modern readers as reactionary. Characteristic
of his "mythological" approach is this passage, in which coitus
during menstruation "would be bad for the female, as it would increase congestion, and aside from common decency and cleanliness,
the flow from the female is very irritating and is liable to set
up urethritism in the male." He also claims that at least 50 percent of all women are frigid and recommends Krafft-Ebing as <u>the</u>
text for the study of "perversions." Other topics discussed include sexual physiology, menstruation, and birth control.

185   MANTEGAZZA, PAOLO. <u>The Sexual Relations of Mankind</u>. Translated
by Samuel Putnam. New York: Eugenics Publishing Co., 1935.
335 pp.
       Mantegazza (1831-1910) was a versatile Italian physician
turned anthropologist who, among other achievements, first publi-
cized the coca plant in Europe. A forerunner of such later soci-
ologists as Havelock Ellis, he first published <u>The Sexual Relations</u>
<u>of Mankind</u> in 1885. Part of his <u>Trilogy of Love</u>, it was frequently
reprinted and translated into many languages. More of an anthropological and literary account than a scientific study based on
empirical evidence, it ranges over many subjects, often moralizing
in the process and contributing its share to the folklore of misinformation that characterizes so much of nineteenth- and twentieth-
century writing on sex. "Negroes have a highly developed sexual
apparatus and the energy that goes with it. Their pubic precocity
finds a correspondence in lust, polygamy and debauchery." Or,
"Until such time as this convulsed and scrofulous civilization of
ours shall learn to give to every man born of woman a loaf of bread
and a woman, the nauseous stench of solitary vice will continue
to contaminate every vein of our body social, transforming love's
joyous grape-cluster into a handful of musty corn devoured by cryp-
togamia." And yet he also condemned clitoridectomy and advocated
sex education!

186   MARTIN, VICTORIA CLAFLIN WOODHULL. <u>Tried as by Fire; Or, the</u>
<u>True and the False, Socially</u>. New York: Woodhull & Claflin,
1874. 44 pp.
       Victoria Woodhull claimed to have delivered this address to
a quarter of a million people. In it, she freely expresses her
radical ideas on free love and the need for revolution in marriage:
"Marriage is an assumption by the community that it can regulate
the sexual instincts of individuals better than they can themselves;

and they have been so well regulated that there is scarcely such
a thing known as a natural sexual instinct in the race; indeed,
the regulations have been so at war with nature that this instinct
has become a morbid disease, running rampant or riotous in one sex,
and feeding its insatiable maw upon the vitality of the other,
finally resulting in disgust or impotency in both." Often dramatic
("Nine women in ten are so diseased sexually, as to make them unfit to become mothers"), Woodhull painted a picture of insatiable
male lust, arguing that free love and stirpiculture were the only
salvation for women and society.

187 _____. The Victoria Woodhull Reader. Edited by Madeleine B.
 Stern. Weston, Mass.: M & S Press, 1974. 640 pp. in various
 pagings.
 Stern has collected and reprinted in facsimile form twenty-
four of Victoria Woodhull's choicest pamphlets, orations, and
articles. This is a welcome addition to the literature, since
many of Woodhull's original publications are hard to locate. One
section of the book includes five pieces on sexuality: "A Speech
on the Principles of Social Freedom" (1871); "Victoria C. Woodhull's
Complete and Detailed Version of the Beecher-Tilton Affair (1872);
"The Naked Truth; Or, the Situation Reviewed!" (1873); "To Women
Who Have an Interest in Humanity, Present and Future" (1874); and
"Tried as by Fire; Or, The True and the False, Socially" (1874).
In addition to these free love tracts, there are two essays on
eugenics, the remainder of the volume dealing with political and
economic issues. Stern provides brief introductory notes, as well
as a short bibliography.

188 MEAD, MARGARET. Male and Female: A Study of the Sexes in a
 Changing World. New York: Morrow, 1949. 477 pp.
 Sex differences, concepts of maleness and femaleness, and
gender roles as culturally determined, learned behavior are Margaret
Mead's focal points in this classic study. Drawing on evidence from
her studies of Pacific societies as well as post-World War II
American culture, Mead argues against strictly defined gender roles
and definitions of masculine and feminine. "Normal" sexual behavior, like other behavior, is relative, varying from culture to
culture. She especially emphasizes the role of learning in determining male and female roles: "Men have to learn as children to
want to beget and cherish children. . . . Women on the other hand,
have to learn to want children only under socially prescribed conditions." Mead examines the contradictory nature of much American
sexual behavior. Women, for example, get one message before marriage and a totally different one after, leading to potential difficulty: "The complete total relaxation of feminine surrender, as
distinguished from specific orgasmic behaviour, is hardly available to women who have had to live through years of bridling their
every impulse to yield and surrender." The major significance of
this work, however, is in its call for equity between men and wo-
en: "If we once accept the premise that we can build a better

world by using the different gifts of each sex, we shall have two
kinds of freedom, freedom to use untapped gifts of each sex, and
freedom to admit freely and cultivate in each sex their special
superiorities."

189   MEISEL-HESS, GRETE.   The Sexual Crisis: A Critique of Our Sex
      Life. Translated by Eden and Cedar Paul. New York: Critic
      and Guide, 1917. 345 pp.
        Originally published in Jena in 1909, The Sexual Crisis
      called for sexual reform in the shape of eugenics, sexual freedom
      of choice for women, socialist education and social services, and
      recognition of motherhood. Such a reform of women's economic and
      social relationship to men, Meisel-Hess believed, would bring an
      end to forcible monogamy. Man and woman "must be free to procreate
      when at the climax of their reproductive energies, in unions con-
      tracted from pure inclination and uninfluenced by calculations of
      social advantage."

190   MILLER, PATRICIA Y., and MARTHA R. FOWLKES. "Social and
      Behavioral Constructions of Female Sexuality." Signs 5, no. 4
      (Summer 1980):783-800.
        In this general review of twentieth-century studies of female
      sexuality, Miller and Fowlkes pay particular attention to ways in
      which culturally determined biases of researchers impact their
      otherwise scientifically based research. Specifically, definitions
      of "normal" behavior tend to be derived not from any scrutiny of
      actual normative behaviors but from the researchers' own social
      norms.

191   MILLETT, KATE. Sexual Politics. Garden City, N.Y.: Doubleday,
      1970. 393 pp.
        In this stunning attack on the male cultural tradition, Kate
      Millet presents a contemporary American intellectual counterpart
      to Simone de Beauvoir's The Second Sex (entry 144). Millett's use
      of hyperbole and wit is superb, but the seriousness of her intent
      is never compromised.
        Much of Millett's analysis is devoted to literature and the
      depiction of female sexuality by such authors as D.H. Lawrence,
      Henry Miller, and Norman Mailer. Freud is seen as a key male re-
      actionary force, both because of his emphasis on so-called bio-
      logical destiny and because of his positing an irreducible, sexu-
      ally determined human nature. Millett is skeptical, as well, about
      Freud's lucidity: "Until the awesome lapsarian moment when the fe-
      male discovers her inferiority, her castration, we are asked to be-
      lieve that she had assumed her clitoris a penis. One wonders why."
      Or, "One cannot separate Freud's account of how a child reasons
      from how Freud himself reasons, and his own language, invariably
      pejorative, tends to confuse the issue irremediably." Freud's
      followers and successors, Marie Bonaparte, Helene Deutsch, and
      Erik Erikson, are treated no less severely.
        Millett's criticism set the standard for much of the feminist

analysis that grew out of the newly emerged women's movement of
the 1970s. It also engendered criticism of its own, as in Juliet
Mitchell's Psychoanalysis and Feminism: "With Millett, . . . em-
piricism run riot denies more than the unconscious; it denies any
attribute of the mind other than rationality. As a result it must
also end up denying the importance of childhood experiences" (see
entry 343). One suspects that the last word has yet to be said.

192   PALMER, RACHEL LYNN, and SARAH K. GREENBERG. Facts and Frauds
      in Woman's Hygiene: A Medical Guide against Misleading Claims
      and Dangerous Products. New York: Vanguard Press, 1936. 311
      pp.
        An early, consumer-oriented publication on female sexual
hygiene, Facts and Frauds includes evaluations of products ranging
from sanitary napkins to abortifacients. Physiological and medical
information is also presented. Well written, carefully researched,
and prowoman in perspective, it includes a 149-item bibliography.

193   [PARKHURST, HENRY M.] Diana: A Psychofyziological Essay on
      Sexual Relations for Married Men and Women. 2d ed., rev. and
      enlarged. New York: Burnz & Company, 1882. 48 pp.
        Dividing sexual desire into affectional and generative com-
ponents, Diana called for satisfaction of affectional desire without genital or amorous activity. Dianists, as they came to be
called, were expected to achieve satisfaction from such actions as
a conversation or hand clasp. Nudity was encouraged as a means of
expressing affectionate feelings. Since orgasm was seen to be injurious, abstinence from conventional sexual relationships was a
virtue, except when the "high and holy purpose" of procreation was
to occur. One of the pamphlet's supporters was Leo Tolstoy, who
published an essay in the Russian journal Nedelya, which is reproduced in translation in Hal Sears's The Sex Radicals (entry 77),
which also includes a full discussion of Diana's message and impact,
especially as promoted by Elmina Slenker. Note the would-be pho-
netic spelling.

194   PIERSON, ELAINE C., and WILLIAM V. D'ANTONIO. Female and Male:
      Dimensions of Human Sexuality. Philadelphia: J.B. Lippincott,
      1974. 349 pp.
        Written for late adolescents, Female and Male is based in
part on the authors' experience in teaching and counseling at the
University of Pennsylvania and the University of Connecticut.
Pierson and D'Antonio display a humanistic, nonsexist perspective
which emphasizes emotional and social aspects of sexuality: "We
both believe that there is an emotional and physical 'magic' involved in human sexual interaction. . . . orgasmic ability does
not necessarily make a sexually whole human being, nor does it
account for an intense attraction to another human being of either
sex." Nevertheless, the authors provide extensive coverage of reproductive and sexual biology and physiology, as well as social
conditions (marriage, nonmarital sex) and problems (rape, venereal

disease). Many of their ideas merit further consideration: "Sexual expression in marriage has focused more on the reduction of male tension and childbearing than on love." There is a glossary and bibliography, but the book would have also benefited from additional illustrations.

195   A Portfolio of Illustrations Which Comprise a Picture Story of Woman's Sexual Life. New York: Eugenics Publishing Co., [1934]. 32 pp.
      This pamphlet contains a series of line drawings depicting various aspects of woman's reproductive anatomy and physiology, such as the position of the ovum during pregnancy, the hymen, and the uterus. There are no illustrations of sex technique or activity.

196   RAMUS, CARL. Marriage and Efficiency. New York and London: G.P. Putnam's Sons, 1922. 239 pp.
      Marriage and Efficiency consists of eighteen discrete essays, including "Psychoanalysis" and "Roosevelt on Marriage," none of which reflects the theme of the title. Ramus is, however, concerned with the state of marriage as an institution, one which he finds suffering from a variety of problems ranging from snoring to sexual incompatibility: "The sexual indifference and resulting unhappiness that so often occur in marriage are largely due to the continuous intimacy that is forced upon husband and wife by conventional views on marriage and economic necessity." He recommends adoption of knowledge of the female sexual cycle, as articulated by Marie C. Stopes, as a method for improving marital happiness and advocates birth control and personal hygiene, including use of a bidet and separate beds.

197   ROBINSON, VICTOR, ed. The Encyclopaedia Sexualis: A Comprehensive Encyclopaedia-Dictionary of the Sexual Sciences. New York: Dingwall-Rock, 1936. 819 pp.
      Contributors as varied as Margaret Mead and Wilhelm Stekel can be found in this anthology of topical articles and short, dictionary-like definitions. Some of the material, such as the selection on the World League for Sexual Reform, is contemporary in focus, while elsewhere, as in the section "Girdle of Chastity," historical perspectives predominate. Illustrated with photographs, diagrams, and reproductions, The Encyclopaedia Sexualis is a treasure trove of trivia as well as of obscure historical, literary, and medical references. Logical balance is not always achieved; there is a ten-page entry for "Sex Problems in Icelandic Literature," but none whatsoever for orgasm.

198   SANGER, MARGARET. Woman and the New Race. New York: Brentano's, 1920. 234 pp.
      In Woman and the New Race, Margaret Sanger articulated her belief that birth control, and hence diminished population growth, was the key to an improved quality of life in the American nation.

Her primary concern, as always, was for the health of women, endangered by indiscriminate childbearing, but she was equally concerned about the economic and social conditions confronting the urban masses, especially new immigrant groups. Birth control and voluntary motherhood would enable women to choose and to control their own lives. "No woman can call herself free who does not own and control her own body. No woman can call herself free until she can choose consciously whether she will or will not be a mother." Of particular interest are Sanger's comments regarding the relationship of birth control to infant mortality and her discussion of legal strictures on birth control in the United States.

199   SEAMAN, BARBARA. Free and Female: The Sex Life of the
       Contemporary Woman. New York: Coward, McCann & Geoghegan,
       1972. 288 pp.
       Seaman, a feminist journalist specializing in scientific and medical subjects, reviews contemporary research on female sexuality, including the work of Mary Jane Sherfey. Seaman feels that women must discover and express their own sexuality and must play an active role in teaching men appropriate sex techniques. One chapter, "How to Liberate Yourself from Your Gynecologist," contains some trenchant criticism of the medical profession and asks hard questions about health care for women. Other topics covered in the book include marriage, venereal disease, and contraception.

200   SEVERANCE, JULIET H. Marriage. Chicago: M. Harman, 1901.
       41 pp.
       Originally delivered at the International Congress of Freethinkers in Chicago in 1893, Marriage called that sacred institution a fetish of liberals, which placed woman "in an enslaved and inferior position." Love alone, according to Severance, was necessary for unions between men and women. She also criticized divorce laws for not allowing divorce on the simple grounds of mutual assent, maintaining that they forced the continuation of marriages damaging to women and children alike. This pamphlet also reprints Severance's article, "The Medical Monopoly," which had originally appeared in Truth Seeker. Marriage is included in the RPI "History of Women" microfilm series.

201   SEWARD, GEORGENE H. Sex and the Social Order. New York and
       London: McGraw-Hill, 1946. 301 pp.
       A psychologist on the faculty of Simmons College, Seward is concerned here with the social aspects of sexual behavior. About half of the book deals with nonhuman sexual behavior as well as so-called primitive societies, including material on gender role. The remainder reviews scientific literature of psychosexual development and behavior, sex differences, patterns of relationship, and such related topics as "sexual decline," using sources reflecting contemporary American culture. Seward generally refrains from interjecting her own views and analysis except for the final chapter, "Sex in Postwar Society," where her ideas will strike 1980s readers

as naively optimistic: "Victory for the democratic way of living
means a democratic reformulation of sex roles. Although fighting
prowess may be defensible in a militaristic ideology, it has no
place around the peace table. The masculine drive to power can be
sublimated in constructive achievement." There is a 701-item bibliography.

202   SHULMAN, ALIX KATES. "Organs and Orgasms." In Woman in Sexist
       Society, edited by Vivian Gornick and Barbara K. Moran, 292-303.
       New York: New American Library, 1971.
           Shulman calls for a recognition of the role of the clitoris
       in producing female sexual pleasure. Like Ann Koedt, in "The Myth
       of the Vaginal Orgasm," she sees male emphasis on the vagina and
       vaginal orgasm as being motivated by male desire for male pleasure;
       she is unstinting in her criticism of Freud and his followers.
       Shulman calls for the re-education of men and women and the educa-
       tion of male children regarding the role of the clitoris, quoting
       extensively from Masters and Johnson to demonstrate woman's present
       disadvantaged sexual role. She concludes that women's sexual plea-
       sure is as much a political question as it is an anatomical one.

203   _____. "Sex and Power: Sexual Bases of Radical Feminism."
       Signs 5, no. 4 (Summer 1980):590-604.
           "Sex and Power" discusses radical feminist ideas about female
       sexuality as an aspect of the power relations between men and women.
       Shulman feels that the insights into the political nature of sexu-
       ality gained during the early stages of the contemporary women's
       movement are in danger of being eroded by the forces of complacency
       and antifeminism. She urges feminists to increase their awareness
       of the politics of sexuality in order to aid in building a strong
       feminist movement.

204   SMART, CAROL, and BARRY SMART, eds. Women, Sexuality and Social
       Control. Boston: Routledge & Kegan Paul, 1978. 121 pp.
           For this collection of feminist-oriented essays by American,
       English, and Norwegian authors, the Smarts have assembled material
       that demonstrates the role of sexuality and sex-related problems,
       such as rape, in contributing to social divisions between men and
       women and to social control of women by men. Mary McIntosh's arti-
       cle, "Who Needs Prostitutes? The Ideology of Male Sexual Needs,"
       critiques various interpretations of male and female sexual differ-
       ences, while Deirdre Wilson's "Sexual Codes and Conduct: A Study
       of Teenage Girls," examines ideas and behavior in two groups of
       thirteen-to-fifteen-year-old English girls. The book's bibliogra-
       phy includes some English and European citations which may not be
       familiar to American readers and therefore is of special interest.

205   SMITH, BLANCHE MARIE [M.B.]. The Single Woman of Today: Her
       Problems and Adjustment. London: Watts, 1951. 130 pp.
           Reprinted in New York by the Philosophical Library in 1952
       and again by Greenwood Press in 1973, The Single Woman of Today

merits comparison with Laura Hutton's work (entry 1334) on the
same subject. Smith takes a decidedly negative view of her topic,
beginning by calling singleness "an unnatural state" and "a disastrous denial of woman's natural rights to biological and psychological completion." She claims that single women suffer from a
variety of health problems, such as diseases of the reproductive
system, prompted by their status, and that many crack under the
strain. She also finds that they are often narcissistic, frigid,
or lesbian. Her solution is to call for elevation of women's status so that their value will not be predicated solely on their
marital condition. Until that time, single women will remain "forever incomplete."

206   SWATOS, WILLIAM H., Jr., and CYNTHIA H. HARRIS. "To Be a
       Woman: 'Nonfiction' on Female Sexuality." International
       Journal of Women's Studies 2, no. 5 (September–October 1979):
       489–500.
           Swatos and Harris analyze and compare ten popular "femaleness-
       womanhood" books, which appeared between 1959 and 1976, in terms of
       their views on role playing in sexual relations, sexual dysfunction,
       orgasm, noncoital sex, and learning and liberation. They find that
       there are distinctions in the books, based primarily on whether
       they portray woman's sexual role as that of a servant or of an in-
       dependent self. There is a marked tendency to place blame for sexu-
       al dysfunction on the female partner. On the whole, the books are
       seen as offering disparate and sometimes contradictory information
       to their readers.

207   TALMEY, BERNARD SIMON. Woman: A Treatise on the Normal and
       Pathological Emotions of Feminine Love. 7th ed. New York:
       Practitioners' Publishing Co., 1912. 262 pp.
           The seventh edition of Woman is the final and most complete
       version of this work, which first appeared in 1904. Ostensibly
       written for the medical profession, much of the book deals with
       so-called pathology--frigidity, masturbation, lesbianism, bestial-
       ity--and makes free use of case citations from Krafft-Ebing, Moll,
       and similar authors. Because of his indiscriminate reliance on
       other authorities, Talmey is often contradictory (for example,
       denying woman's multiorgasmic potential in one place and affirming
       it in another) and is not reluctant to set forth as truth the wild-
       est theories without any empirical proof: "Bananas are often used
       for onanistic purposes. Country girls use cucumbers in masturba-
       tion." In addition to this melange of folklore and medical-
       pathological narrative, Talmey also includes information on repro-
       ductive anatomy and biology, coital positions and frequency, sexual
       hygiene, and the psychology of love. Since many of his cases are
       of European origin and appeared in translation here for the first
       time, Talmey's Woman is of more than incidental interest for schol-
       ars wishing to study the transmission of ideas from the European
       to the American scene. It is a vivid example of how total non-
       sense, hearsay, myth, and fantasy were accepted as truth by the

medical world (and no one knows how many lay readers) not so many years ago.

208   TENENBAUM, JOSEPH. The Riddle of Women: A Study of the Social Psychology of Sex. New York: Lee Furman, 1936. 477 pp.
       In this study of the impact of woman's sexual identity on her social role, Tenenbaum fully subscribes to the "biology is destiny" point of view. "She is the mother of the race, and her physiology and biology are primarily and principally concerned with the business of propagation." Although Tenenbaum mentions much recent research in his text, his is still a highly subjective account. Some of his ideas, such as the role played by images of idealized motherhood in muddling ideas on women's sexuality, still ring true, while others have a touch of fantasy: "Owing to the superior imagination and diffused sexuality of the female, dreams replenish and color the conscious mind long after the shadows have vanished with the dusk of sleep." Focusing on the cultural deriva- tion of ideas regarding woman's sexuality, he includes material on sexual relations, marriage, adultery, divorce, widowhood, and sin- gle women, or as he calls them, spinsters. The latter fare none too well, and his comments clearly show Tenenbaum's feelings on woman's "appropriate" sphere--matrimony and motherhood: "Denied motherhood, they are driven by an insatiable desire to be near children, to mother them, to teach or to spoil them. . . . The younger spinster may be able to compensate her sexual disappoint- ments and pose as a madonna, but the older spinster is commonly a nagger and hypochondriac."

209   TOBIAS, ROSCOE BURDETTE, and MARY E. MARCY. Women as Sex Vendors or Why Women Are Conservative (Being a View of the Economic Status of Woman). Chicago: Charles H. Kerr, 1918. 59 pp.
       Tobias and Marcy argue that women are politically and eco- nomically conservative because they are the "owners" and vendors of sexual pleasure to men. "The private possession of a commodity necessary to man, the lower cost of living for women, are the natu- ral causes of lower wages for women than for men, and explains why women are actually able to live on lower wages, as a sex, than men." The authors say that because of this women do not try to advance themselves as individuals, but figure up ways to barter for men's favors. Tobias and Marcy prophesy a change in this con- dition as a result of post-World War I economic developments.

210   WAGNER, NATHANIEL N., ed. Perspectives on Human Sexuality: Psychological, Social and Cultural Research Findings. New York: Behavioral Publications, 1974. 517 pp.
       Wagner has grouped this collection of previously published material into four sections: sex difference and the development of sexuality, psychological factors in sexual behavior, sexual behavior in cross-cultural perspective, and studies of special populations. Several of the articles relate specifically to women,

such as Joseph LoPiccolo's "Mothers and Daughters: Perceived and Real Differences in Sexual Values" and Philip Goldberg's "Are Women Prejudiced Against Women?" Most of the material originally appeared between 1960 and 1973.

211   WALKER, EDWIN COX. What the Young Need to Know: A Primer of Sexual Rationalism. Chicago: M. Harman, n.d. 42 pp.
      Another Harmanesque free thought/free love tract (Walker was Moses Harman's close associate), this essay is not written for children, but its question-and-answer format is intended to suggest the types of information they should receive. Active, free sexuality on the part of women is seen as necessary to health and happiness. "Sexual attraction will be manifested differently by different individuals, by the same individuals at different times, and in both monogamic and varietist relations, even by the same individuals, in different periods of life." The Christian religion is freely criticized: "The ascetic doctrine has been an unmitigated curse to mankind, a veritable 'Asiatic mildew.'" Also discussed are clothing, nudity, literature, and the utility of legal sanctions to protect women from undesired sexual relations.

212   WEIDEGER, PAULA. Menstruation and Menopause. New York: Alfred A. Knopf, 1976. 257 pp.
      Weideger includes a discussion of the relationship between the menstrual taboo and woman's perception of her own sexuality, as well as the impact of the menstrual or reproductive cycle on sexuality. She also incorporates the results of a questionnaire answered by 558 women. Unfortunately, her opinions are frequently antilesbian and politically myopic.

213   WEININGER, OTTO. Sex and Character. London: William Heinemann; New York: G.P. Putnam's Sons, 1906. 356 pp.
      Weininger, who was less than thirty when he penned this treatise, is really concerned here with outlining what he perceives to be the chief differences between men and women and how these relate to "character" or personality. Highly subjective, he seems unable to distinguish between inherent and culturally determined characteristics. Much of his thought reflects prevalent stereotypes: "The condition of sexual excitement is the supreme moment of a woman's life. The woman is devoted wholly to sexual matters, that is to say, to the spheres of begetting and of reproduction." Other theories, such as homosexuality being a "higher form" than heterosexuality, are more creative. Intellectual women, according to Weininger, are a sexually intermediate form. Weininger sees sexual abstinence on the part of men as the key to changing their view of woman as only a sexual object. Likewise, only when women give up their sexual selves will they be truly emancipated.

214   WESTERMARCK, EDWARD A. The Future of Marriage in Western Civilisation. London: Macmillan, 1936. 281 pp.
      Written as a sequel to Westermarck's earlier volume, The

History of Human Marriage, this work is more contemporary in orientation, although it contains abundant historical material, and in
many cases replicates material found in the earlier book. Topics
discussed include sexual maladjustment, divorce, free love, and
sexual morality. Westermarck's sources, which include such varied
items as Katharine Bement Davis's Factors in the Sex Life of Twenty-
two Hundred Women (entry 951) and Thomas Hobbes's Leviathan, are
especially well documented. He concludes, not surprisingly, by
predicting the survival of marriage and the family. He also anticipated the decline in criminal penalties for sexual acts involving
consenting adults, a trend that can be witnessed at the present
time.

215   WILE, IRA S. The Sex Life of the Unmarried Adult: An Inquiry
      into and an Interpretation of Current Sex Practices. New York:
      Vanguard Press, 1934. 320 pp.
           A lecturer at Columbia University, physician Ira S. Wile pre-
      pared this work in part as a protest against the propensity of
      writing on sex to be directed to and about the married alone.
      Wile not only recognized that sexual behavior is largely cultural-
      ly determined, but that the 1920s and 1930s were seeing freer sex
      behavior and more open sexual relationships between men and women.
           This collection of eleven essays looks at various aspects of
      the sexual behavior of unmarried individuals. Mary Beard, for ex-
      ample, in "The Economic Background of the Sex Life of the Unmarried
      Adult," examines the impact of economic conditions on sexual behav-
      ior from a worldwide, historical perspective. Robert Latou
      Dickinson's "Medical Reflections upon Some Life Histories" analyzes
      the possibilities when "the sex act becomes immune to ancient haz-
      ards, protected from sequels of venereal suffering and long obliga-
      tion."

216   WILLARD, ELIZABETH OSGOOD GOODRICH. Sexology as the Philosophy
      of Life: Implying Social Organization and Government. Chicago:
      J.R. Walsh, 1867. 483 pp.
           In many ways a direct antecedent of Antoinette Brown
      Blackwell's The Sexes Throughout Nature (1875) (entry 221),
      Willard's Sexology attempts to demonstrate the necessity for in-
      corporating so-called natural laws governing sexual differentia-
      tion in the adoption of political and social systems. Influenced
      by Herbert Spencer, Willard includes extensive discussions of re-
      productive biology and female sexuality, although many of her bio-
      logical theories were sadly unscientific. She argued in favor of
      woman's right to control over man in sexual relations, although,
      like many of her crypto-feminist contemporaries, she maintained a
      belief in separate male and female spheres. She advocated coitus
      at one-month intervals and maintained that all "normal" sexual de-
      sire in women was only a means to the end of maternity. Willard
      offers additional commentary on a variety of sexual topics, includ-
      ing abortion and prostitution.

217 YARROS, RACHELLE S. <u>Modern Woman and Sex: A Feminist Physician</u>
     <u>Speaks</u>. New York: Vanguard Press, 1933. 218 pp.
        <u>Modern Woman and Sex</u> is a forum for Yarros's views on a vari-
     ety of sex-related subjects. Generally, she feels that there is
     too much emphasis on sex technique rather than on emotional and
     social aspects of sexual behavior. What has resulted is a situa-
     tion wherein woman's situation is sometimes less than equitable.
     "The modern sophisticated young girl or woman . . . demands equal-
     ity and full control of her own body. She does not care to be a
     mere instrument of pleasure to her husband or lover."
        Yarros advocates a middle ground between the old and new and
     proposes reform of marriage and divorce laws as the first step to-
     ward rational change. Nevertheless, she supports monogamic mar-
     riage as an institution. A foe of abortion, she advocates birth
     control and sex education. Other topics discussed by Yarros in-
     clude prostitution, venereal disease, and the marriage night.

218 ZUBIN, JOSEPH, and JOHN MONEY, eds. <u>Contemporary Sexual</u>
     <u>Behavior: Critical Issues in the 1970's</u>. Baltimore: Johns
     Hopkins University Press, 1973. 468 pp.
        Based on the proceedings of the 61st annual meeting of the
     American Psychopathological Association, this collection of papers
     follows in the tradition of such earlier symposia as 1949's "Psy-
     chosexual Development in Health and Disease." One group of five
     essays focuses on maternity and women's sexuality and includes the
     following essays: "Interrelationships between Sexual Responsive-
     ness, Birth, and Breast Feeding" by Niles Newton, "Maternalism in
     Fetal Hormonal and Related Syndromes" by Anke A. Ehrhardt, "Women's
     Sexual Arousal" by Gunter Schmidt and Volkmar Sigusch, "Maternalism,
     Sexuality and the New Feminism" by Alice S. Rossi, and "The New
     Black Feminism: A Minority Report" by Julia Mayo. Other chapters
     relating to women include those on pornography, comarital sex, and
     public attitudes on sexual issues.

219 ATKINSON, TI-GRACE. "The Institution of Sexual Intercourse."
     In <u>Notes from the Second Year</u>, edited by Shulamith Firestone
     and Ann Koedt, 42-47. n.p.: 1970.

220 BERKELEY-HILL, OWEN. "The Erotic Rights of Women." <u>Marriage</u>
     <u>Hygiene</u> 4, no. 1 (August 1937):30-33.

221 BLACKWELL, ANTOINETTE BROWN. <u>The Sexes Throughout Nature</u>. New
     York: G.P. Putnam's Sons, 1875. 240 pp.

222 DELL 'OLIO, ANSELMA. "The Sexual Revolution Wasn't Our War."
     In <u>The First MS. Reader</u>, edited by Francine Klagsbrun, 124-32.
     New York: Warner, 1972.

223 DENSMORE, DANA. "On Celibacy." In <u>Voices from Women's Libera-</u>
     <u>tion</u>, edited by Leslie Tanner, 264-68. New York: New American
     Library, 1970.

224   ELLIS, HAVELOCK. The Love Rights of Women. New York: Birth
      Control Review, 1918. 15 pp. Also known as The Erotic Rights
      of Women.

225   FAUNCE, PATRICIA SPENCER, and SUSAN PHIPPS-YONAS. "Women's
      Liberation and Human Sexual Response." International Journal
      of Women's Studies 1, no. 1 (January-February 1978):83-95.

226   FIRESTONE, SHULAMITH. The Dialectic of Sex: The Case for
      Feminist Revolution. New York: William Morrow, 1970.   274 pp.

227   GREER, GERMAINE. The Female Eunuch. New York: McGraw-Hill,
      1971. 349 pp.

228   HARDING, MARY ESTHER. The Way of All Women: A Psychological
      Interpretation. New York: Longmans, Green, 1933. 335 pp.

229   HERSCHBERGER, RUTH. Adam's Rib. New York: Pellegrini &
      Cudahy, 1948. 221 pp.

230   HOWELL, MARY C. "Brief Guide to Office Counseling: The
      'Sexual Revolution' and the Feminist Movement." Medical Aspects
      of Human Sexuality 9, no. 2 (February 1975):175-76.

231   HUBBARD, SUSAN DICKES. "An Overview of Female Sexuality."
      Humanist 36, no. 6 (November-December 1976):9-19.

232   _____. "Social Pressures on Feminine Sexuality." Frontiers 1
      no. 3 (Winter 1976):31-33.

233   JONES, GEORGE L., and HENRY WATSON. "Some Sex Problems En-
      countered by Social Workers." Proceedings of the National
      Conference of Charities and Corrections 39 (1912):300-303.

234   KELLEY, FLORENCE. "The Sex Problems in Industrial Hygiene."
      American Journal of Public Hygiene 20, no. 2 (May 1910):252-57.

235   KEY, ELLEN. Love and Marriage. Translated by Arthur G. Chater.
      New York: G.P. Putnam's Sons, 1911. 399 pp.

236   KIERNAN, JAMES G. "The Significance of Sex in Modern Literature."
      Urologic and Cutaneous Review 27, no. 5 (May 1923):285-95.

237   LYDON, SUSAN. "The Politics of Orgasm." In Sisterhood Is
      Powerful: An Anthology of Writings from the Women's Liberation
      Movement, edited by Robin Morgan, 219-28. New York: Vintage
      Books, 1970.

238   MITCHELL, JULIET. "The Second Marie Stopes Memorial Lecture:
      Female Sexuality." Journal of Biosocial Science 5, no. 1
      (January 1973):123-36.

239   PARSONS, ELSIE CLEWS. The Old-Fashioned Woman: Primitive
      Fancies about the Sex. New York and London: G.P. Putnam's
      Sons, 1913. 373 pp.

240   PRUETTE, LORINE. "Sex and Marriage in a Modern Age." Birth
      Control Review 14, no. 3 (March 1930):69-71.

241   ROHLEDER, HERMANN. "Incest in Modern Civilization." American
      Journal of Urology and Sexology 13, no. 9 (September 1917):
      406-11.

242   ROYDEN, AGNES MAUDE. "Modern Love." In The Making of Women:
      Oxford Essays in Feminism, edited by Victor Gollancz, 36-63.
      London: George Allen & Unwin; New York: Macmillan, 1917.

243   SHUFELDT, R.W. "Havelock Ellis on the Psychology of Sex."
      Pacific Medical Journal 44, no. 2 (February 1901):84-92.

244   SMITH, JAMES R., and LYNN G. SMITH. "Co-marital Sex and the
      Sexual Freedom Movement." Journal of Sex Research 6, no. 2
      (May 1970):131-42.

245   SONENSCHEIN, DAVID, and MARK J.M. ROSS. "Sex Information in
      the 'Romance' and 'Confession' Magazines." Medical Aspects of
      Human Sexuality 5, no. 8 (August 1971):136-59.

246   "Viewpoints: Has Women's Liberation Become a Cause of Marital
      and Sexual Strife?" Medical Aspects of Human Sexuality 5, no.
      9 (September 1971):12-19.

247   "Viewpoints: What Is the Effect on Women of Today's Sexual
      Climate?" Medical Aspects of Human Sexuality 12, no. 4 (April
      1978):58+.

248   WALSH, ROBERT H., and WILBERT M. LEONARD. "Usage of Terms for
      Sexual Intercourse by Men and Women." Archives of Sexual
      Behavior 3, no. 4 (July 1974):373-76.

249   WILLIAMS, EDWARD HUNTINGTON. "The Sexual Significance of
      Recent Fashions." Medical Record 86, no. 21 (21 November 1914):
      874-77.

250   "A Women's Petition for Sexual Sanity." MS. 3, no. 8 (February
      1975):80-81.

Legal and Ethical Perspectives

Many of Western civilization's fundamental beliefs regarding woman's sexuality and sex-related institutions, such as marriage, stem from Judeo-Christian traditions. Beginning with scripture itself, theologians have interpreted what they believe to be absolute truths into a far more complex ideology which has been used not only to constrain woman's sexual behavior, but her social, economic, and political roles as well. Drawing on this tradition, legislators have codified many of these customs and beliefs into an elaborate system of laws aimed at setting limits to sexual behavior and sex-related practices.

As many of the authors represented in this section show, however, theological interpretations and legal restrictions frequently reflect outmoded or biased points of view, failing to mirror the mores and behavior of the people whose interests and attitudes they are supposed to reflect. While religious belief is a matter of personal choice and conscience, the law's impact is more pervasive. The problem is particularly acute in the United States, where there is still much inconsistency in the law and patterns of its enforcement from state to state and region to region. Although women have traditionally been responsible for the commission of only a small minority, if even that, of many sex-related crimes (rape, incest, child molestation, exhibitionism, and the like), their more common role as victims has heightened their awareness of the need for the equitable administration of justice in these areas.

Underlying many questions of sexual ethics and the law is the issue of the double standard. While most theorists have agreed that it must be eliminated in order to achieve true equality between men and women, there has been less agreement as to what should take its place. Late nineteenth-century social purity advocates maintained that a single standard of chastity and adherence to the existing "female" model of self-control should govern male-female relationships. Another trend, however, seen particularly since World War II, has been toward women having the same freedom to engage in nonmarital sexual relations as men. Some feminists and other critics argue that such adherence to the traditional male model is ethically questionable and does little to lead women toward true liberation from male domination.

Other religious, ethical, and legal issues discussed here include the question of virginity, the role of love in sexual relations, the institution of marriage, and ethical issues involved in sex research and sex therapy.

251   BAILEY, DERRICK SHERWIN. The Mystery of Love and Marriage: A
      Study of the Theology of Sexual Relation. New York: Harper
      and Brothers, 1952. 145 pp.
         Bailey, an Anglican clergyman, examines the theological un-
      derpinnings and interpretations of the "one flesh" concept, and
      the broader significance of sex and sexuality in the Christian re-
      ligion. "Early Christianity left to succeeding ages an unbalanced
      conception of sex and sexual intercourse, and an entirely mistaken
      view of sexual pleasure. . . . This failure to understand sex con-
      tributed to the exaltation of celibacy, which in its turn deprived
      most of the Western clergy and theologians of the experience which
      would have given them, as married men, a more sympathetic approach
      to the subject." Scholarly in tone and approach, this book, which
      was reprinted by Greenwood in 1977, will be of use to scholars in-
      vestigating the relationship, already empirically demonstrated by
      Kinsey and others, between religion and sexual behavior in our
      culture, as well as the religious background for much of the nine-
      teenth century's sexual ideology.

252   BARNETT, WALTER. Sexual Freedom and the Constitution: An
      Inquiry into the Constitutionality of Repressive Sex Laws.
      Albuquerque: University of New Mexico Press, 1973. 333 pp.
         In this study, Barnett's topic is one not usually dealt with
      by writers on female sexuality. Although most of his references
      relate to male homosexuality, the material on "sodomy" and other
      "deviations" is applicable to women.

253   "Editorial: Review of European Legislation for Control of
      Prostitution." New Orleans Medical and Surgical Journal 11
      (March 1855):667-705.
         This detailed review is an early precursor of similar arti-
      cles which appeared regularly later in the century, largely as a
      result of the advent of the social purity movement. It is also
      of interest because of its detailed discussion of female masturba-
      tion.

254   GINDER, RICHARD. Binding with Briars: Sex and Sin in the
      Catholic Church. Englewood Cliffs, N.J.: Prentice-Hall, 1975.
      251 pp.
         Ordained in 1940, Richard Ginder served for several years as
      official censor of books for the Roman Catholic diocese of
      Pittsburgh, writing extensively on a wide range of church-related
      topics. Over the years, as he came to acknowledge the validity of
      his own sexuality, he gathered the material for this book. "As I
      pondered the different aspects of the subject . . . the classical

morality on sex became increasingly implausible." Ginder analyzes
the Roman Catholic church's attitudes toward sexuality and finds,
simply, that they are unrealistic for the contemporary world. He
is not at all reluctant to take a stand on controversial issues,
and although he does not favor abortion, he does support birth
control and gay rights. Although many of Ginder's arguments draw
upon male behavior for examples and precedents, nevertheless this
is a useful work for providing background in understanding Judeo-
Christian cultural attitudes toward human sexuality as a whole.

255 GRAY, ARTHUR HERBERT. Men, Women, and God: A Discussion of
     Sex Questions from the Christian Point of View. Rev. ed. New
     York and London: Harper & Brothers, 1938. 149 pp.
         Originally published in 1922 and frequently reprinted there-
     after in both Britain and the United States, Men, Women, and God
     was the work of the English clergyman and popular religious writer
     Arthur Herbert Gray. Intended as a guide to sexual morality inside
     and outside marriage, it incorporates New Testament principles of
     love and faith into much of its argument. Generally conservative,
     Gray believes that relations between men and women are essential
     to render the two sexes "complete," and he doubts the validity of
     the arguments of some women who claim they can exist independently
     of men. He criticizes masturbation as being unnatural, evil, and
     productive of bad psychic consequences and warns against grandes
     passions between women: "It is not a relationship which can per-
     manently satisfy. It cannot give a woman children. It leaves
     part of her hungry." Because he did see women as sexual beings,
     however, Gray advises those not married to sublimate their sexual
     feelings into the path of Christian religion. He also criticizes
     couples who refuse to have children as "unChristian," although he
     does approve of birth control for those with enough.

256 GUYON, RENÉ. The Ethics of Sexual Acts. Translated by J.C.
     and Ingeborg Flugel. New York: A.A. Knopf, 1934. 383 pp.
         This translation of La Legitimité des actes sexuels was also
     published in England under the title Sex Life and Sex Ethics.
     Guyon saw archaic principles dominating contemporary attitudes
     toward sexuality. In an effort to bring about rational change,
     he offers observations on sexual attitudes and behavior drawn from
     historical, anthropological, and medicopsychological authorities as
     well as his own wide experience. Anticipating the ideas of Thomas
     Szasz, Guyon criticizes psychiatric definitions of normality and
     pathology: "Influenced by a thousand obscure and unavowed motives,
     psychiatry has sided with the social conventions, and has therefore
     inevitably changed the natural roles, reversed the usual terminol-
     ogy of medicine, and looked upon those who do not conform to the
     conventional rules as being abnormal and therefore pathological."
     To Guyon, sexual variations, such as homosexuality, were not aber-
     rations, but normal manifestations of a multidimensional universe
     of possible sexual behavior. Guyon concludes by calling for a
     system of sexual liberty allowing for the true natural variety of
     human sexual bevaior.

257 HARTLEY, CATHERINE GASQUOINE. Women's Wild Oats: Essays on
     the Re-fixing of Moral Standards. London: T. Werner Laurie,
     1919. 256 pp.
          Of particular interest here is the essay "Foreseeing Evil,"
     which deals with sexual relationships outside of marriage and which
     also appeared, in an earlier version, in a work entitled Women and
     Morality. Hartley saw morally hypocritical modern civilization
     making healthy sexual expression difficult. What women needed
     was not more sex education but a new morality, "some open recogni-
     tion of honourable, partnerships outside of marriage . . . in the
     form of a registered contract before the relationship was entered
     upon." Such responsibility would replace secret sexual relation-
     ships "in the new order."

258 Information on Transexualism [sic] for Law Enforcement Officers.
     Baton Rouge, La.: Erickson Educational Foundation, 1973. 30
     pp. ISR.
          Prior to its dissolution in 1977, the Erickson Educational
     Foundation financially supported the work of such students of sexu-
     ality as Vern Bullough and Thomas P. Lowry. It also engaged in
     educational publishing, focusing on homosexuality, transvestism,
     and transsexualism. This pamphlet, in question-and-answer format,
     provides information on transsexuals to the law enforcement com-
     munity. It includes material on both male-to-female and female-
     to-male transsexuals, with emphasis on the former. Erickson esti-
     mated at the time that more than 1,800 Americans had undergone sex
     reassignment surgery.

259 KIMMEL, VIOLA MIZELL. The Double Standard of Conduct for Men
     and Women To-day: Its Origin and Results. New York: n.p.,
     1916. 57 pp.
          Kimmel, who billed herself as a "specialist in the training
     of parents and children," believed in a holistic approach to the
     relationship between sexuality and bodily health, in which sexual
     functions were no more sacred or special than any other physical
     function. This holistic approach, however, also led her to embrace
     the nineteenth-century idea of the body as a closed system. Orgasm,
     which resulted in the loss of "vital fluids" from this system,
     should therefore be avoided, except for procreation. Indeed,
     Kimmel saw the sex act as harmful to women's health and orgasm as
     a selfish act, the antithesis of love. At the root of all sexual
     problems lay the double standard, whose abolition Kimmel proposed.
          The last eleven pages of this tract, which has been micro-
     filmed as part of RPI's "History of Women" series, advertise
     Kimmel's correspondence courses, including "The Truth about Sex"
     and "Competent Motherhood." Also included are ads for individual
     works, such as Kimmel's Right Eating a Science and a Fine Art and
     a volume with the intriguing title, Horses, Their Food and Their
     Feet.

260 KING, MORGAN D. The Cohabitation Handbook: Living Together

and the Law. Berkeley, Calif.: Ten Speed Press, 1975. 182 pp.

Attorney Morgan D. King is concerned primarily with the legal ramifications of heterosexual unmarried couples living together, and deals with such questions as community property, insurance, and travel abroad. Two chapters, on sex practices and babies (including abortion and contraception), relate directly to sexuality. King notes that although many states have laws prohibiting fornication and "unnatural" sex practices, people are seldom arrested for them in their own homes. His examples and legal references relate to California and New York, although a final chapter compares the various state laws relating to cohabitation. King is often very funny and is quick to point out the ambiguity, inconsistency, and fustiness of many of the United States's state laws relating to sex.

261   KIRCHWEY, FREDA, ed. Our Changing Morality: A Symposium. New
       York: Albert & Charles Boni, 1924. 249 pp.

Reflecting the new morality of the 1920s, this collection of articles which appeared in the Nation focuses on the connection between changing standards of sexual behavior and the increasing freedom of women. The list of contributors is stellar. Bertrand Russell argues for sexual intercourse "sprung from the free impulse of both parties, based upon mutual inclination and nothing else." Charlotte Perkins Gilman, among other arguments, attacks Freudianism as a "physical theory disguised in the technical verbiage of 'psychology,'" while noted Jungian Beatrice Hinkle asserts that the single standard is, unfortunately, interpreted as the male, not female, standard. Other contributors range from Floyd Dell to Elsie Clews Parsons.

262   KLING, SAMUEL G. Sexual Behavior and the Law. New York:
       Bernard Geis, 1965. 300 pp.

This is one of several books by Kling in the areas of sex, marriage, and the law. His primary concerns here are the disparity between what social custom permits and what is allowable under the law and, as a logical result, the necessity for reform to bring the law into conformity with actual social practice. A question-and-answer format covering such topics as criminal penalties, evidence, characteristics of offenders, and historical and cultural background, is followed in each chapter. Chapters are organized by subject and include sixteen areas of conduct, such as incest, sterilization, impotence and frigidity, and sex rights in marriage and divorce. Although Kling relies on inaccurate or questionable authorities in some areas, the book succeeds in portraying the archaic, almost folkloristic quality of much of the sex-related legislation of the time (1965), and makes a concerted appeal for total reform of the statutes in most states. Because of the insensitivity of the legislation to women's rights and needs, this area should be of especial interest to activists intent on reform.

263   LAY, WILFRID. A Plea for Monogamy. New York: Boni and

Liveright, 1923. 305 pp.

That Lay was a firm believer in monogamy should be evident from the title of this work, which enshrines his belief that all conscious and unconscious "love cravings" should be satisfied in marriage. Such satisfaction, however, was primarily the responsibility of the husband, "the leading factor in the erotic sphere." Women and men had different roles to play: "It is masculine to give and to create and to change external reality. It is feminine to receive, and to respond to the activity of the male." Lay advocated Karezza, also known as male continence, as the method to achieve his goal of a perfect, monogamous marriage.

264   LOLLINI, CLELIA. "A New Sexual Morality." In Proceedings of the International Conference of Women Physicians, vol. 4, Moral Codes and Personality, 30-36. New York: Woman's Press, 1919.
Lollini calls for the elimination of the double standard, liberalization of divorce laws, and women's rights.

265   MASTERS, WILLIAM H., et al., eds. Ethical Issues in Sex Therapy and Research. 2 vols. Boston: Little, Brown, 1977 and 1980. 227; 436 pp.
Because of controversy generated around the ethical propriety of both sex therapy and sex research, the Reproductive Biology Research Foundation (now the Masters and Johnson Institute) decided in 1974 to sponsor a series of forums to discuss ethical problems in the sex therapy and sex research fields, with an ultimate goal of drafting ethics guidelines for these areas. The first volume of this set prints the transcribed proceedings of the first conference, held in January 1976, while the second includes background papers and discussion from a second conference held in January 1978. Issues covered include consent, privacy, confidentiality, and values. The second volume also includes copies of the draft and revised ethics guidelines.

266   MAY, GEOFFREY. Social Control of Sex Expression. New York: W. Morrow, 1931. 307 pp.
Geoffrey May's distinguished legal career included work as counsel for the Russell Sage Foundation as well as service with the United States government. Equally knowledgeable in British and American law (he was a member of the Inner Temple), he drew upon anthropological, historical, legal, and religious sources for this study of the basis of Anglo-American law over voluntary sex expression. Most of the book, however, focuses on Great Britain, with only two chapters relating to the United States. Like other works on this theme dealing with the United States, it emphasizes the obsolescence and lack of uniformity from state to state of many American statutes.

267   NORTHCOTE, HUGH. Christianity and Sex Problems. 2d ed., rev. and enlarged. Philadelphia: F.A. Davis, 1916. 478 pp.
Originally published in 1906, Christianity and Sex Problems

nearly doubled in length at its reissue ten years later. Northcote incorporates much new material, such as Ellis's Studies in the Psychology of Sex, which had appeared in the interim, and he attempts to reconcile those ideas with the traditions of Christian religion and sexual ethics. Although his stated emphasis is on aspects of male sexuality, such as chastity, Northcote includes much material relating to women or to both sexes. He devotes several chapters to a discussion of prostitution, but has no realistic solutions to the problem (he advocates missionary-type rescue work as an effective approach and also supports sterilization of "sexual degenerates"). Influenced by Freud, Northcote counseled sublimation of sexual desire as a means of self-control and had this comment on sublimation in women: "Christ's personality, by winning the affections and dominating the will of women, subjugates the perfect female organism, and attracts to itself the whole range of feminine emotion. One of the chief elements in this mental condition in the woman is an unconscious sublimated sexuality."

268   REISS, IRA L. Premarital Sexual Standards in America: A
       Sociological Investigation of the Relative Social and Cultural
       Integration of American Sexual Standards. Glencoe, Ill.: Free
       Press, 1960. 286 pp.
       Standards for behavior, not behavior itself, are the focus
of this semipopular examination of attitudes in American society.
Reiss gets off to a rather unfortunate beginning in his survey of
past standards and the origins of present day ones, for at times
his statements are distorted and inaccurate: "By the turn of the
century, the feminists were winning their battles on all fronts.
Women were now wearing lipstick and rouge and were beginning to
smoke."
       Still working in an impressionistic vein, Reiss looks at the
contemporary scene, where he distinguishes four possible standards:
abstinence, permissiveness with affection, permissiveness without
affection, and the double standard. He compares the four, including the positive and negative consequences they offer, and their
relation to American culture. Reiss also discusses the "abstinence
standard," which encompasses sexual behaviors other than actual
genital intercourse. Not surprisingly, he finds an overall liberalizing trend as young people fashion standards for themselves
rather than merely accept those handed down by authority figures.

269   ROYDEN, AGNES MAUDE. Sex and Common-Sense. New York and
       London: G.P. Putnam's Sons, 1922. 211 pp.
       Maude Royden was a leading British feminist who had been
educated at Oxford. A large part of this book consists of edited
lectures given in 1921 at Kensington Hall in London. Royden's
overriding theme is the need for honest Christian morality to
govern relations between men and women. Nevertheless, she was no
prude, maintaining that women who deny their sexuality pay a heavy
price, criticizing the "ancient but un-Christlike belief that women miss their object in life if they are not wives and mothers."

And while she thought that homosexual behavior was unnatural and immoral, she did not think society should condemn homosexuals as people. Her chief plea was for sexuality to be seen as a union of spirit and body.

270   Sex Problems Court Digest, 1970–.
      This periodical provides a monthly summary of the reported and published state and federal court opinions concerning issues related to sex problems involved in criminal and civil court procedures. Topics discussed include sex crimes, obscenity, obscene literature, entertainment, transsexualism, homosexuality, transvestism, sexual dysfunction, loitering, morals, and similar problems. The Digest has been edited by Emanuel Bund since its founding.

271   SLOVENKO, RALPH, ed.   Sexual Behavior and the Law.   Springfield, Ill.:   Charles C. Thomas, 1965.   886 pp.
      This collection of thirty-eight essays covers a wide range of topics, many of them relating directly to women––"Polygamous Women," "The Unmarried Mother," "Female Homosexuality"––and others containing incidental information. The majority of the authors are psychiatrists or psychoanalysts, although Slovenko was a law professor at Tulane. Other disciplines, such as sociology, are also represented. The essays display their authors' beliefs about the subject at hand, are often undocumented by any empirical evidence, and generally do not refer to any existing legislation or instances of its enforcement. There are some exceptions, such as Walter O. Weyrauch's essay, "Informal Marriage and Common Law Marriage," but on the whole the quality of the material is largely subjective, impressionistic, and subject to sharp analysis and evaluation by those with a mind toward factual, rational enquiry.

272   SOROKIN, PITIRIM ALEKSANDROVICH.   The American Sex Revolution.   Boston: Porter Sargent, 1956.   186 pp.
      Founder of the sociology department at Harvard University, Pitirim Sorokin was alarmed by the sex revolution he perceived to be occurring in the United States. An increase in illicit sex, a rising divorce rate, a decline of parental instinct, and a general sexualization of American culture could only lead, he felt, to a rise in sexual anarchy and the destruction of society. He felt that psychiatry, psychoanalysis, and counseling were of no help (he vigorously opposed Freud's views of sexuality) and that the only solution was rigorous control of sexual expression. Not surprisingly, he favored keeping all sexual influences away from young people and condemned such anarchistic tendencies as premarital sex.

273   THOINOT, LEON HENRI.   Medicolegal Aspects of Moral Offenses.   Translated by Arthur W. Weysse.   Philadelphia: F.A. Davis, 1911.   487 pp.
      Originally published in France in 1898, this work on medical jurisprudence was being reprinted by Davis as late as 1930. Moral

offenses, of course, are so-called sexual offenses, and Thoinot considers rape, child molestation, bestiality ("Cases of bestiality chargeable to women are very rare, and the animal concerned is always the dog"), lesbianism, and nymphomania, among the conditions involving women. Although Thoinot's examples are drawn largely from the Continent, Weysse has appended additional material illustrative of American law. Krafft-Ebing is relied on heavily, and there is a sensational cast to much of the material.

274 WITTHAUS, R.A., and TRACY C. BECKER. Medical Jurisprudence: Forensic Medicine and Toxicology. Vol. 2. New York: William Wood & Co., 1894. 751 pp.

There are several essays in this second volume of original material assembled by Witthaus and Becker relating to women's sexuality and medical jurisprudence. Among these are chapters on such topics as abortion, pregnancy, rape, sexual incapacity, and so-called unnatural crimes, such as oral sex and lesbianism. The information presented varies widely from author to author and ranges from the purely physiological to unsubstantiated folklore and moralistic pronouncements. Particularly disappointing is the failure of some authors to refer to any actual laws or court cases in the United States or, if they do so, to omit specific citations which would facilitate further research. Nevertheless, Medical Jurisprudence does indicate predominant currents of thought in the medicolegal community, and is of interest in that regard.

275 BENSING, R.C. "A Comparative Study of American Sex Statutes." Journal of Criminal Law, Criminology and Police Science 42, no. 1 (May-June 1951):57-72.

276 BERGER, DAVID G., and MORTON G. WENGER. "The Ideology of Virginity." Journal of Marriage and the Family 35, no. 4 (November 1973):666-76.

277 BERNARD, JESSIE. "Infidelity: Some Moral and Social Issues." In The Dynamics of Work and Marriage; Scientific Proceedings, edited by Jules H. Masserman, 99-126. Science and Psychoanalysis, no. 16. New York: Grune & Stratton, 1970.

278 BERTINE, ELEANOR. "Health and Morality in the Light of the New Psychology." In Proceedings of the International Conference of Women Physicians, vol. 4, Moral Codes and Personality, 5-14. New York: Woman's Press, 1919.

279 BIGELOW, HORATIO R. "The Moral Significance of Sterility." Obstetric Gazette 6, no. 1 (January 1883):1-24.

280 BLACKWELL, ELIZABETH. Counsel to Parents on the Moral Education of Their Children. New York: Brentano's Literary Emporium, 1879. 160 pp.

281   BOAS, CONRAD VAN EMDE. "Some Reflections on Sexual Relations between Physicians and Patients." Journal of Sex Research 2, no. 3 (November 1966):215-18.

282   BOGART, G. HENRI. "One Bane of Prudery." Texas Medical Journal 27, no. 5 (November 1911):165-75.

283   BYRNE, THOMAS R., Jr., and FRANCIS M. MULLIGAN. "'Psychopathic Personality' and 'Sexual Deviation': Medical Terms or Legal Catch-alls--Analysis of the Status of the Homosexual Alien." Temple Law Quarterly 40, nos. 3-4 (Spring-Summer 1967):328-47.

284   CHADDOCK, CHARLES GILBERT. "Sexual Crimes." In A System of Legal Medicine, edited by Allan McLane Hamilton and Lawrence Godkin, 525-72. New York: E.B. Treat, 1894.

285   CONWAY, ALLAN, and CAROL BOGDAN. "Sexual Delinquency--the Persistence of a Double Standard." Crime and Delinquency 23, no. 2 (April 1977):131-35.

286   DAHLBERG, CHARLES CLAY. "Sexual Contact between Patient and Therapist." Medical Aspects of Human Sexuality 5, no. 7 (July 1971):34+.

287   DRENNAN, JENNIE G. "Sexual Intemperance: Some Explanation of What Is Meant by the Term." New York Medical Journal 74 (13 July 1901):70.

288   DRUMMOND, ISABEL. The Sex Paradox: An Analytic Survey of Sex and the Law in the United States Today. New York: G.P. Putnam's Sons, 1953. 369 pp.

289   EIGEN, MICHAEL. "Female Sexual Responsiveness and the Therapist's Feelings." Psychoanalytic Review 66, no. 1 (Spring 1979):3-8.

290   EXNER, MAX J. "Sex Education in Colleges." Proceedings of the International Conference of Women Physicians, vol. 5, Adaptation of the Individual to Life, 159-206. New York: Woman's Press, 1919.

291   FARNSWORTH, DANA L. "Sexual Morality and the Dilemma of the Colleges." Medical Aspects of Human Sexuality 4, no. 10 (October 1970):64+.

292   GARTMAN, LEO. "The Female Sex Instinct in Its Relation to Our Morality." American Journal of Urology and Sexology 11, no. 11 (November 1915):439-51.

293   GLAISTER, JOHN. "The Medico-legal Aspects of Impotency in the Sexes." Practitioner 95 (July 1915):23-30.

294   HALL, RUFUS B. "The Education of the Laity upon Sexual Matters; When Shall They Be Taught and to What Extent?" American Journal of Obstetrics and Diseases of Women and Children 42, no. 5 (November 1900):577-84.

295   HAMILTON, ALLAN McLANE. "The Civil Responsibility of Sexual Perverts." American Journal of Insanity 52 (April 1896):503-11.

296   HUGHES, CHARLES H. "Erotism (Normal and Morbid) and the Un-written Law in Our Courts." Alienist and Neurologist 28, no. 2 (May 1907):205-23.

297   JACKSON, A. REEVES. "The Ethics of Female Sterility." Physician's Magazine 1, no. 2 (December 1885):178-87.

298   KENNARD, K. SELLERS. "A Medical View of the Triennial Cohabita-tion Doctrine, as Applied in the Case of Tompkins v. Tompkins, III Atl. Rep. 599." Medico-Legal Journal 38 (1921):52-59.

299   LEE, RICHARD V. "The Importance of Virginity in 1972." Yale Journal of Biology and Medicine 45, no. 5 (October 1972):iii-v.

300   MORGAN, ELAINE. "In Defense of Virgins." Medical Aspects of Human Sexuality 12, no. 6 (June 1978):85-102.

301   MORTON, JAMES F., Jr. "Sex Morality--Past, Present, and Future or Monogamy Versus Variety." Medico-Pharmaceutical Critic and Guide 14, no. 10 (October 1911):365-68.

302   PERKINS, NELLIE L. "Mental and Moral Problems of the Woman Probationer." Hospital Social Service 9 (1924):1-15.

303   SCHROEDER, THEODORE. "Censorship of Sex Literature." Medical Council 14, no. 3 (March 1909):91-98.

304   _____. "Legal Obscenity and Sexual Psychology." Alienist and Neurologist 29, no. 3 (August 1908):354-88.

305   _____. "One Religio-sexual Maniac." Psychoanalytic Review 23, no. 1 (January 1936):26-45.

306   SHAINESS, NATALIE. "The Danger of Orgasm Worship." Medical Aspects of Human Sexuality 4, no. 5 (May 1970):73-79.

307   SHUFELDT, R.W. "On the Medico-Legal Aspect of Impotency in Women." Medico-Legal Journal 14, no. 3 (1896):289-96.

308   _____. "The Medico-Legal Consideration of Perverts and Inverts." Pacific Medical Journal 48, no. 7 (July 1905):385-93.

309   SLOVENKO, RALPH, and CYRIL PHILLIPS. "Psychosexuality and the Criminal Law." Vanderbilt Law Review 15, no. 2 (June 1962): 797–828.

310   SMITH, EDITH LIVINGSTON, and HUGH CABOT. "A Study in Sexual Morality." Social Hygiene 2, no. 4 (October 1916):527+.

311   STEKEL, WILHELM. "The Sexual Root of Kleptomania." Journal of the American Institute of Criminal Law and Criminology 2, no. 2 (July 1911):239–46.

312   SWAN, ARTHUR. "Sex on the Stage, with Especial Reference to Its Influence on the Adolescent Mind." American Journal of Urology and Sexology 12, no. 7 (July 1916):300–309.

313   TALMEY, BERNARD SIMON. "Female Chastity; Its Psychology and Eugenics." American Medicine, n.s. 12, no. 7 (July 1917): 497–510.

314   WALKER, EDWIN COX. "Sex Morality--Past, Present and Future, or Monogamy Versus Variety." Medico-Pharmaceutical Critic and Guide 14, no. 11 (November 1911):401–8.

315   WHATHAM, ARTHUR E. "Modesty and the Modern Woman." American Journal of Urology and Sexology 15, no. 7 (July 1919):289–93.

Contributions of Psychoanalysis

Psychoanalysis in the tradition of Sigmund Freud has been by no means the only school of psychological theory to have gained acceptance and influence in the twentieth century. Yet, in its emphasis on the sexual origins of the neuroses, as well as the pervading influence of psychosexual development on psychological functioning, it has, at least in the United States, played a major role in defining how women have been seen as sexual beings in our society.

As Juliet Mitchell emphasizes in Psychoanalysis and Feminism (entry 343), Freud's followers and popularizers sometimes distorted his original theories. Yet this observation fails to confront other key problems in the psychoanalytic approach, such as its reliance on specific, often atypical, case analyses as the proof for much more widely reaching theories, or its fundamental assumption of the existence of the unconscious. There has also been a tendency to regard Freudian theory as truth writ in stone, and in former times revisionists such as Karen Horney were ostracized by their more orthodox colleagues.

The laboratory research of Masters and Johnson played a critical role in initiating the questioning of some classical psychoanalytic tenets, such as the transfer of sexual sensitivity from the clitoris to the vagina. This new scientific data, coupled with an awareness of the role that Freud's own cultural milieu and traditions played in determining his thinking, has led to a re-evaluation in recent years of much psychoanalytic and psychiatric theory and writing. Mary Jane Sherfey's The Nature and Evolution of Female Sexuality (entry 349), Jean Strouse's Women and Analysis (entry 351), and Ethel Spector Person's Signs article, "Sexuality as the Mainstay of Identity" (entry 345), all reflect this new direction, as do many of the pieces by feminist theorists found in other sections of this book.

316   BENEDEK, THERESE. Studies in Psychosomatic Medicine: Psycho-
      sexual Function in Women. New York: Ronald Press, 1952. 435
      pp.
          The first eleven chapters of this collection of Benedek's
      studies on female psychosexuality reprint Benedek and Boris

Rubenstein's 1942 work on the sexual cycle in women (see entry 317). Three of the other four essays draw upon this earlier work: "The Psychosomatic Implications of the Primary Unit: Mother-Child," "Climacterium: A Developmental Phase," and "Some Psycho-physiological Problems of Motherhood." The remaining essay is a brief review of sexual and reproductive functions ranging from homosexuality to dysmenorrhea. Benedek was convinced that motherhood was a biological and psychological "need" for women, and warned against women who denied their passive role and ignored their maternal function: "It may lead to regression of the need and in this way it may cause frigidity. In time it may influence the ovarian function itself, causing functional sterility."

317   BENEDEK, THERESE, and BORIS B. RUBENSTEIN. The Sexual Cycle in Women: The Relation between Ovarian Function and Psychodynamic Processes. Psychosomatic Medicine Monographs, vol. 3, nos. 1 and 2. Washington, D.C.: National Research Council, 1942. 307 pp.
      Drawing upon a previous research base of hormone studies as well as psychoanalytic theory, Benedek and Rubenstein aimed at finding out "whether the psychoanalytic material reflects an ebb and flow of recurring emotions which, independent of environmental influences, are fundamentally related to hormonal function." Using vaginal smear and basal body temperature techniques, Benedek and Rubenstein studied 152 full menstrual cycles of fifteen women in psychoanalysis. Comparing their physiological findings with the psychoanalytic record of these cases, they found that parallel to and correlated with the hormonal cycle there was an identifiable emotional cycle, both of which constituted what they described as "the sexual cycle in women." Benedek and Rubenstein were fully aware of the possibility for criticism of their findings and techniques, and therefore not only described their methods in detail, but also discussed perceived shortcomings. Regardless of its problems, the study represented a significant advance in its interdisciplinary approach in attempting to find a physiological basis for human behavior and is a marked departure from psychoanalytic generalization based on case observation alone.

318   BLUM, HAROLD P., ed. Female Psychology: Contemporary Psychoanalytic Views. New York: International Universities Press, 1977. 454 pp.
      Many of the pieces in this collection of essays were included in a supplement on female psychology that appeared in 1976 as part of volume 24 of the Journal of the American Psychoanalytic Association and in a 1968 issue of that same journal devoted to female sexuality. Beginning with an analysis of Freud's views on early female sexuality, the articles proceed through the female psychosexual life cycle, offering revisionist views of classic psychoanalytic theory. Roy Schafer's "Problems in Freud's Psychology of Women" discusses the impact of "traditional patriarchal and evolutionary values" on psychoanalytic principles, while Peter Barglow

and Margret Schaefer's "A New Female Psychology?" critiques several revisionist interpretations. References are included for all essays, although a few rely heavily on what might be atypical case reports to make their point.

319   BONAPARTE, MARIE. Female Sexuality. New York: International Universities Press, 1953. 225 pp.

Marie Bonaparte's Female Sexuality is perhaps the ultimate theoretical expression of the myth of the vaginal orgasm. Certainly later popularizers, such as Marie N. Robinson, depend heavily on Bonaparte's thinking. Bonaparte's argument is by now a familiar one. The clitoris is "essentially male and inappropriate to the feminine function." It is an "atrophied" penis, and women who experience clitoral rather than vaginal orgasms have been arrested in development. "It is in the vagina itself and, more or less distant from the entrance according to the individual that, for the functionally adapted, evolved and adult woman, true erotic sensitivity dwells; it is from this point that, in coitus, the terminal orgasm starts." In an accusing tone she observes, "We know, besides, that women who show too great an aversion to men's brutal games may be suspected of masculine protest and excessive bisexuality. Such women may very well be clitoridal."

Bonaparte believes that masochism and passivity are "proper" female attributes. The basis for her theories and generalizations, such as that all healthy children masturbate, is often unclear. She admits, on page 104, that she has never analyzed a little girl, and a list of works referred to in the text is noticeably devoid of any but other psychoanalytic works, aside from a few references to such questionable "documentation" as Michelet's 1858 L'Amour. Bonaparte even goes so far as to infer that the missionary position is the only position for "normal" coitus.

320   CHAPMAN, JOSEPH DUDLEY. The Feminine Mind and Body: The Psychosexual and Psychosomatic Reactions of Women. New York: Vision, 1967. 325 pp.

Chapman, an osteopathic obstetrician, is concerned in this book with the application of psychoanalytic theory and psychosomatic concepts of illness to woman's sexual development and sexual problems. Treating the stages of woman's sexual life from infancy to menopause, he embraces such ideas as penis envy and innate female passivity. "A woman is passive sexually. This anatomic and physiologic fact is re-created in her psychologic makeup. The female is pursued, wooed, and finally submits to the sexual act."

According to Chapman, women sublimate and spiritualize their erotic needs, and the majority of them fail to experience any pleasure from sexual activities. Motherhood is woman's chief goal. Most of Chapman's conclusions seem to be based on his reading of Freud and other psychoanalytic theorists. He offers some case material, chiefly to bolster his arguments about the psychosomatic origin of sexual disturbance.

321   CHASSEGUET-SMIRGEL, JANINE.   Female Sexuality: New Psycho-
      analytic Views.   Ann Arbor: University of Michigan Press, 1970.
      220 pp.
          Another contribution to the continuing reappraisal of psycho-
      analytic theory is this collection of essays by French analysts,
      originally published there in 1964 as Recherches psychanalytiques
      nouvelles sur la sexualité feminine.   Although the authors general-
      ly subscribe to such ideas as the importance of the mother for
      personality development and sexual adjustment, especially as ar-
      ticulated by Melanie Klein and Ernest Jones, they also agree that
      it is misleading to examine female sexuality from the point of
      view of theories about male sexuality.   Chasseguet-Smirgel in her
      introduction further articulates this revision-without-rejection
      philosophy: "The vitality of any doctrine depends on the possi-
      bility of rethinking certain aspects without disrupting the whole
      structure."   In addition to the six essays, which cover such topics
      as narcissism, penis envy, and homosexuality in women, Chasseguet-
      Smirgel's introduction features brief historical summaries of the
      key elements of Freud's theory of female sexuality, the theories
      of other analysts supporting Freud, and the ideas of psychoanalysts
      who differ from Freud in their theories on this subject.

322   DEUTSCH, HELENE.   The Psychology of Women: A Psychoanalytic
      Interpretation.   2 vols.   New York: Grune & Stratton, 1944 and
      1945.   399; 498 pp.
          The popularity of Helene Deutsch's The Psychology of Women
      may be judged by its having been reprinted eighteen times between
      1944 and 1971, finally being issued as a mass-market Bantam paper-
      back in 1973.   Building on the tenets of classical Freudian theory,
      Deutsch divides the work into two volumes, the first providing a
      general introduction to female psychology and the second focusing
      on motherhood, or as Deutsch calls it, woman's "role as servant of
      the species."
          Deutsch hoped in this work to restate, reassert, and, where
      necessary, revise the views expressed in her Psychoanalysis of the
      Sexual Functions of Women (1925).   She included extensive case
      documents and also turned to literature for evidence: "Instructive
      data for this book have been found in creative literature, which is
      less objective than clinical observation but all the more true be-
      cause more inspired."   This equation of truth with inspiration, a
      subjective quality at best, makes one doubt Deutsch's claim to em-
      pirical validity.
          According to Deutsch, three essential traits--narcissism,
      passivity, and masochism--characterize normal femininity.   Biology
      is brought in to support these theories: "The anatomy of the sex
      organs leaves no doubt as to the character of their aims: the
      masculine organ is made for active penetration, the feminine for
      passive reception."   From there it is but a short step to biologi-
      cally determined "normal" behavior patterns.   For example, those
      who advocate an active female sexual role are warned that "such
      behavior goes against biologic and psychologic laws."   This in

turn may lead to the "masculinity complex" in which "fear" of femininity marshals the forces of "masculine tendencies," such as intellectuality.

Deutsch's remarks about orgasm and women's sexual behavior are a bit more tentative. She disagreed with Freud regarding the "resignation" of the clitoris in favor of the vagina in adult life, noting that neither biology nor psychology had as yet given totally adequate information about the sexual function. Unlike many psychoanalytic theorists, Deutsch merely glosses over the question of frigidity. Not so menopause, which she sees as a time characterized by almost universal depression and other symptoms: "The suggestibility of women in this life period increases markedly, their judgement fails, and they readily fall victim to evil counselors." One wonders if this had ever happened to Deutsch who, after all, was sixty when The Psychology of Women was published.

323   EICHLER, LOIS S. "Feminine Narcissism": An Empirical Investigation. Ph.D. dissertation, Boston University, 1972. 90 pp. ISR, LC.
      This is an empirical study of the psychoanalytic concept of narcissism--the positive evaluation of the self and one's body (body cathexis) and the perception of oneself as distinctly feminine. Using certain standard psychological testing procedures, Eichler tested a sample of senior college women at Boston University and Brandeis University in order to chart different patterns between those aspiring to careers and those aspiring to be homemakers. In the area of sexuality, it was found that "body cathexis was positively related to the early experience of sexual intercourse, to greater enjoyment of intercourse and negatively related to menstrual discomfort." Particularly useful is Eichler's chapter reviewing literature on feminine narcissism and related concepts.

324   FREUD, SIGMUND. "'Civilized' Sexual Morality and Modern Nervous Illness." In The Standard Edition of the Complete Psychological Works of Sigmund Freud, translated and edited by James Strachey, vol. 9, 177-204. London: Hogarth Press and the Institute of Psycho-Analysis, 1959.
      Freud questions whether "civilized" sexual morality, requiring abstinence before marriage and monogamy during marriage, doesn't lead to more harm than good. He believes that such ethics repress the instinctual life and often cause neuroses. In women, abstinence leads to frigidity in marriage, and as a result sexual relations in marriage are good only for three, four, or five years. Suppression of sexuality in women also leads to suppression of other functions, such as intellect. Freud generalizes freely about the so-called sexual failure of most marriages, yet offers no empirical proof to support his claims. This essay was printed several times in the United States (it was written in 1908), and its ideas may have led to the conclusion (hardly avoidable) that Freud advocated unrestricted sexual activity.

325 ____. "Female Sexuality." In The Standard Edition of the
Complete Psychological Works of Sigmund Freud, translated and
edited by James Strachey, vol. 21, 221-43. London: Hogarth
Press and the Institute of Psycho-Analysis, 1961.

"Female Sexuality" is to a large degree a restatement of the
ideas in the 1925 essay, "Some Psychical Consequences of the Anatomical Distinction between the Sexes" (entry 331). Published in
1931, it focuses on the significance of the girl's pre-Oedipal attachment to her mother in determining her later psychosexual behavior. Freud is convinced that this attachment assumes a sexual
form, but statements like the following make one pause in accepting his claims: "It is difficult to give a detailed account of
those [the sexual activities] because they are often obscure instinctual impulses which it was impossible for the child to grasp
psychically at the time of their occurrence, which were therefore
only interpreted by her later, and which then appear in the analysis in forms of expression that were certainly not the original
ones."
He also assumes certain "facts," such as clitoral masturbation being the "culmination" of sexual activity in the pre-Oedipal
phase. Such assumptions, of course, are based on patient recall
in analysis, not on actual observations of young children.
In a departure from his usual practice, Freud concludes this
essay with a critique of other papers on the same subject. Editor
Strachey notes that these had largely been written in reaction to
"Psychical Consequences," but Freud fails to mention this fact,
even omitting any reference to the essay itself.

326 ____. "Femininity (New Introductory Lecture on Psycho-
Analysis No. 33)." In The Standard Edition of the Complete
Psychological Works of Sigmund Freud, translated and edited by
James Strachey, vol. 22, 112-35. London: Hogarth Press and
the Institute of Psycho-Analysis, 1964.

To a large degree, "Femininity" duplicates material presented
by Freud in two earlier papers, "Some Psychical Consequences of
the Anatomical Distinction between the Sexes" (1925) (entry 331)
and "Female Sexuality" (1931) (entry 325). As in his earlier work,
Freud emphasizes the role played by the pre-Oedipal and Oedipal
phases in determining adult psychosexual behavior, in other words,
the mechanisms involved in the girl's transferring her love from
mother to father along with her sexual object choice.
Readers accustomed to feminist criticism of Freud, as well
as to the necessity of empirical evidence in proving theories,
will have a field day pointing out the misconceptions in Freud's
arguments. Most evident is Freud's biological determinism: "The
anatomical distinction between the sexes must express itself in
psychical consequences." His pro-male bias is evident in his references to certain female sexual organs as being male organs "in
an atrophied state" and in his use of the phrase "boy's far superior equipment." Superior for what? Apparent also is his inability
to see how cultural conditioning influences behavior and psychological development. Thus, in maintaining that the so-called wish

for a penis is transformed into a wish for a baby from the father, as in the following statement, he fails to perceive how much of the female reaction is conditioned by the values of the society in which she lives: "Her happiness is great if later on this wish for a baby finds fulfillment in reality, and quite especially so if the baby is a little boy who brings the longed for penis with him." As usual, the conclusions are drawn from observations in analysis. Freud's advice at the essay's conclusion hardly affirms our confidence in what has preceded it: "If you want to know more about femininity, enquire from your own experiences of life, or turn to the poets, or wait until science can give you deeper and more coherent information."

327   _____. "Fragment of an Analysis of a Case of Hysteria." In *The Standard Edition of the Complete Psychological Works of Sigmund Freud*, translated and edited by James Strachey, vol. 7, 1-122. London: Hogarth Press and the Institute of Psycho-Analysis, 1953.

Written in 1901, but not published until 1905, this long essay describes the famous case of "Dora," whom Freud analyzed between October and December 1900. It forms a link between the ideas expressed in *The Interpretation of Dreams* and *Three Essays on the Theory of Sexuality* (entry 333). Certainly Freud's statement that "sexuality . . . provides the motive power for every single symptom, and for every single manifestation of a symptom" underlies his theories of psychosexual development.

"Dora" has been a favorite target of feminist critics, who perceive in Freud's interpretation evidence of his own patriarchal, sexist biases. Indeed, one can only wonder at the following analysis of Dora's disgust at being passionately kissed by Herr K., a friend of her father's (and husband of his mistress), at the age of only fourteen: "In this scene . . . the behaviour of this child of fourteen was already entirely and completely hysterical. I should without question consider a person hysterical in whom an occasion for sexual excitement elicited feelings that were preponderantly or exclusively unpleasurable." Freud's ultimate analysis, focusing on two dreams, showed that Dora had been in love, not only with Herr K., but with his wife and her own father. Masturbation during childhood lurked in the background, as did the venereal disease which Dora's father apparently transmitted to his wife and, possibly, through her to Dora herself.

This case also gives us insight into Freud's methods. The narrative was written, not from notes compiled at the conclusion of each session, but from Freud's memory after the patient had broken off treatment. Freud admitted to "filling up the gaps" in his interpretation with insights gained from other cases. One cannot help wondering, in the light of this, whether the two dreams Freud chose to analyze were the only two the patient had or whether they were the only two that could obviously be interpreted in light of his symbolic theories. "Dora" is evidence of Freud's imaginative and creative approach to interpretation of the workings of the human mind, but it raises more questions about method and interpretation than it answers.

328 _____. "Observations on Transference-Love (Further Recommendations on the Technique of Psycho-Analysis III)." In The Standard
Edition of the Complete Psychological Works of Sigmund Freud,
translated and edited by James Strachey, vol. 12, 157-71.
London: Hogarth Press and the Institute of Psycho-Analysis,
1958.
   First published in 1915 as part of a group of essays on
psychoanalytic technique, "Observations on Transference-Love" describes the phenomenon, induced by the analytic situation, of women
patients falling in love with their analysts. Although these women
declare their "readiness for sexual surrender," Freud feels that it
is simply a manifestation of resistance to analytic treatment.
Analysts are advised to be totally neutral (i.e., to neither return the woman's feelings nor stifle them) and to preserve the
erotic transference for the purpose of advancing the analytic work.
Freud does not comment on how women analysts should react to similar behavior in male patients. He dismissed the love emotions of
these women patients simply as acting out of previously developed
patterns of love relationships.

329 _____. "On the Universal Tendency to Debasement in the Sphere
of Love (Contributions to the Psychology of Love II)." In The
Standard Edition of the Complete Psychological Works of Sigmund
Freud, translated and edited by James Strachey, vol. 11, 177-90.
London: Hogarth Press and the Institute of Psycho-Analysis,
1957.
   Written in 1912, this essay is one of three brought together
by Freud as "Contributions to the Psychology of Love." Primarily
a study of psychical impotence in men, this piece contains some
material on frigidity in women, which Freud believed was comparable
to the need on the part of men to debase their sexual object.
   Freud maintained that women's sexual repression prior to
marriage often caused them to be frigid when sexual activity was
at last sanctioned through matrimony. This was because they still
carried the old prohibitions along in their minds. He also discussed the theme of tension between civilization and instinctual
behavior, which had been developed in more detail in the 1908 essay, "'Civilized' Sexual Morality and Modern Nervous Illness"
(entry 324).

330 _____. "The Psychogenesis of a Case of Homosexuality in a
Woman." In The Standard Edition of the Complete Psychological
Works of Sigmund Freud, translated and edited by James Strachey,
vol. 18, 146-74. London: Hogarth Press and the Institute of
Psycho-Analysis, 1961.
   The woman in this case was an eighteen-year-old girl who had
developed a genitally unconsummated relationship with an apparently
bisexual woman about ten years her senior. Freud concluded that

the older woman was in fact a substitute for the girl's own mother.
Many interesting points are raised in this paper, such as Freud's
belief that the girl's dreams were deliberately intended to mis-
lead him and his tacit admission that penis envy might be only a
metaphor. After saying that the girl had pronounced penis envy of
her brother, he adds, "She was in fact a feminist; she felt it un-
just that girls should not enjoy the same freedom as boys, and
rebelled against the lot of woman in general." It is also significant that the young woman was defined by Freud as being homosexual
even though genital sexual relations had never occurred with this
or any other partner.

331 _____. "Some Psychical Consequences of the Anatomical Distinc-
tion between the Sexes." In The Standard Edition of the Complete
Psychological Works of Sigmund Freud, translated and edited by
James Strachey, vol. 19, 241-58. London: Hogarth Press and the
Institute of Psycho-Analysis, 1961.

Sigmund Freud's ideas on the topic of female sexuality were
by no means static. For many years, Freud maintained that psychosexual development in boys and girls ran on parallel tracks, merely
substituting one gender for the other (what boys felt towards mothers, girls felt toward fathers). By the time this paper was completed in 1925, however, Freud had abandoned his assumption of a
developmental analogy and was seeking more precise theories, based
on fresh clinical observations.

In this essay, Freud synthesized various ideas originally
stated in his other work. He introduced the concept of the importance of the mother in the pre-Oedipal phase of the female
child. Penis envy is given its full due: "They notice the penis
of a brother or playmate, strikingly visible and of large propor-
tions, at once recognize it as the superior counterpart of their
own small and inconspicuous organ, and from that time forward fall
a victim to envy for the penis." This envy leads to feelings of
inferiority in the girl, feelings shared by "the contempt felt by
men for a sex which is the lesser in so important a respect." Accepting this, the girl gives up her wish for a penis and substitutes for it a wish for a child, taking her father as a love object.
Freud concludes that there is a difference in the relationship between the castration complex and the Oedipus complex in boys and
girls. In boys the castration complex destroys the Oedipus complex, whereas in girls the castration complex makes the Oedipus
complex possible.

Freud, acknowledging the contributions of Abraham, Horney,
and Deutsch, admits that his findings are based on "a handful of
cases" and, in an aside, admonishes his readers not to be deflected
from his views by the arguments of feminists favoring equality "in
position and worth" between the two sexes.

332 _____. "The Taboo of Virginity (Contributions to the Psychology
of Love III)." In The Standard Edition of the Complete Psychological Works of Sigmund Freud, translated and edited by James

Strachey, vol. 11, 191-208. London: Hogarth Press and the
Institute of Psycho-Analysis, 1957.

Expanding on the theme of frigidity discussed in "On the
Universal Tendency to Debasement in the Sphere of Love," Freud
links frigidity to the universal taboo of virginity. Drawing on
some anthropological observations, he observes that the taboo of
virginity has been established because men perceive sexual intercourse with a virgin as representing danger. This is because of
the blood shed and, more importantly, because the husband perceives
hostility on the part of the wife. Freud argues that this hostility is due to the wife's predisposition to grant her lasting love
to the first man to satisfy her "virgin's desire for love," usually
the father. The ideas in this essay are almost totally culturally
determined, something not recognized by its author. Moreover, in
our contemporary culture, where the taboo of virginity is broken
far more than it is respected (is it, indeed, a taboo any more?),
can one accept psychological theories based on its existence as a
given?

333   _____. Three Essays on the Theory of Sexuality. Translated
and newly edited by James Strachey. New York: Basic Books,
1962. 130 pp.

The text of this edition is identical to that found in volume
7 of The Standard Edition of the Complete Psychological Works of
Sigmund Freud, but includes some additional editorial footnotes,
as well as a bibliography and index. Three Essays forms the core
of Freud's writing on sexuality and consists of three parts: "The
Sexual Aberrations," "Infantile Sexuality," and "The Transformations
of Puberty." Although the essays were originally published in 1905,
they were continually revised by Freud for subsequent editions.
This text is based on the sixth German edition of 1925, the last
published in Freud's lifetime.

"The Sexual Aberrations" is based on the work of such writers
as Krafft-Ebing, Ellis, Bloch, and Hirschfeld, and deals with such
topics as homosexuality, oral sex, and fetishism. There is scant
material specifically on women, and in several places Freud notes
the "impenetrable obscurity" surrounding knowledge of female sexuality. In this essay, Freud articulates his philosophy of the
sexual nature of neurotic and hysterical behavior and his idea
that the potential for all the sexual variations is present in
each individual.

"Infantile Sexuality" posits the existence of active sexual
instinct in prepubescent children. No memory of this early sexual
behavior, however, is retained in adult life, hence the value of
psychoanalysis in making "what has been forgotten conscious." This
essay also summarizes such familiar concepts as penis envy and the
castration complex.

The final essay, "The Transformations of Puberty," discusses
changes in sexuality from childhood to puberty and contains a description of the transfer of "erotogenic susceptibility to stimulation" in women from the clitoris to the vagina.

Freud based his conclusions in Three Essays on his analytical
case experience. In at least one instance (as in the "Touching and
Looking" section of "The Sexual Aberrations"), a single case served
as the basis for a generalization (Freud was so conscious of this
problem that he altered his original text from "a single analysis"
to "several analyses," a fact revealed in Strachey's notes to this
edition). The reader is, of course, given no indication of how
many analyses served to confirm Freud's conclusions, and there is
always a nagging suspicion about the role of the analyst in "suggesting" certain interpretations. Three Essays deserves to be
read, however, if for no other reason than its importance in determining so much of what was to follow.

334   FREUD, SIGMUND, and JOSEF BREUER. Studies on Hysteria. In
      The Standard Edition of the Complete Psychological Works of
      Sigmund Freud, translated and edited by James Strachey, vol. 2.
      London: Hogarth Press and the Institute of Psycho-Analysis,
      1955. 335 pp.
            Studies on Hysteria is generally acknowledged as the starting
      point of psychoanalysis. Publication of the initial "Preliminary
      Communication," which lays the groundwork for the case material
      and conclusions that follow, occurred in 1893, but the entire work
      did not appear until 1895.
            Freud's belief in the sexual origin of hysteria can be in-
      ferred, but he does not assert, as he did later (cf. the "Dora"
      case) that sexual causes were always present. Indeed, at this
      time, Breuer would seem to have held much stronger views regarding
      the role of sexuality in causing neuroses than did his younger col-
      league. It was, after all, Breuer who said, "The great majority
      of severe neuroses in women have their origin in the marriage bed."
      It is clear, however, that one firm belief was in the ability of
      different sexual factors to produce different neurotic disorders.
            The five cases used as supporting evidence for Freud and
      Breuer's theories are all women, mostly members of the educated
      middle class. One subject, however, was English, while another
      was a country girl Freud met while vacationing and whose dialect
      he reproduced in the original German version. Unfortunately, this
      case did not advance beyond a brief conversation between Freud and
      the girl. In a revealing footnote added in 1924, he indicates that
      he falsified the original case report, indicating that an attempted
      seduction by an uncle had really been the work of the girl's own
      father. A similar distortion also occurred in the case of Elisabeth
      von R. In later years, Freud was to claim that these incestuous
      episodes were no more than fantasies in the minds of his subjects.

335   GARRISON, DEE. "Karen Horney and Feminism." Signs 6, no. 4
      (Summer 1981):672-91.
            This article summarizes Karen Horney's views on the psycholo-
      gy of women, their reception by the psychoanalytic profession, and
      their relationship to psychoanalytic theory in the 1920s and 1930s.
      Garrison emphasizes the personal and social context in which

Horney's ideas developed and discusses factors behind the Freudian psychoanalytic establishment's antagonism to Horney's theories and its general lack of interest in a revisionist psychology of women.

336   GOLDMAN, GEORGE D., and DONALD S. MILMAN, comps. and eds. <u>Modern Woman: Her Psychology and Sexuality</u>. Springfield, Ill.: Charles C. Thomas, 1969. 275 pp.
      This is a collection of papers prepared for a conference sponsored by Adelphi University's Program in Psychotherapy. In addition to the paper texts, the discussion/commentary is also included. The presenters were primarily psychoanalysts, both psychologists and psychiatrists. Topics discussed include female body image, female sexual functioning, and frigidity. Some of the material is not well documented, and despite the editors' intention to present new material accurately reflecting woman's true sexual nature, some stereotypes still remain. For example, Leon Hammer, in his discussion of Leah Cahan Schaefer's paper on frigidity, comments: "The one thing which defines a woman's awareness of her femininity is her awareness of her desire for men. Her freedom to desire, her actual desire, is her femininity." Or, examine these comments by Ruth-Jean Eisenbud on lesbians: "We find the mothers of homosexual women dominant and narcissistic, adored queens, or dead or distant, and the child abandoned. . . . We find the fathers brutal, or aloof and exalted, or traumatized and inconsistent, or close and absorbing."

337   HIGDON, JOHN F. <u>Power and Sexual Dynamics in Female Paranoids and Nonparanoids Assessed by Interpersonal Check List, Sex Attitudes Questionnaire, and Thematic Stimuli</u>. Ph.D. dissertation, Southern Illinois University, 1972. 96 pp.
      Studying the history of research into the relationship between power and sexuality in paranoids, Higdon concludes that theories have traditionally focused on homosexuality as a decisive factor and, to a lesser extent, power anxieties. Since most empirical studies aimed at substantiating these theories of Freud and others deal only with male subjects, Higdon was interested in testing women to see if the results would hold. Working with patients at Anna State Hospital, he found that his results substantiated neither the power nor the homosexuality theories, although he suggests that further refinement of existing theories and standardized testing procedures might produce the expected results in women as well as men.

338   HORNEY, KAREN. <u>Feminine Psychology</u>. Edited and with an introduction by Harold Kelman. New York: W.W. Norton, 1967. 269 pp.
      One of the best known of Freud's followers, in part because of her rediscovery by the contemporary feminist movement, Karen Horney made her primary contribution to psychoanalytic revisionism with her emphasis on the role of cultural as well as biological factors in determining human behavior. Classical penis envy, for

example, was transformed by Horney into the masculinity complex, a symbolic metaphor representing women's envy of men's power and dominance in society.

Feminine Psychology is one of a series of anthologies of Horney's works edited by Harold Kelman and published by Norton. It includes such well-known essays as "The Flight from Womanhood" and "The Denial of the Vagina" and is basic reading for people seeking an understanding of revisionist psychoanalytic theory. Karen Horney, who died in 1952, was expelled from the New York Psychoanalytic Society because of the "heresy" of her views, going on to help found the Association for the Advancement of Psychoanalysis and the American Institute for Psychoanalysis.

339 Journal of the American Psychoanalytic Association 16, no. 3 (July 1968). Special issue on female sexuality.

Discussions of Mary Jane Sherfey's theories of female sexuality highlight this special issue. Other significant contributions include Judith S. Kestenberg's "Outside-Inside, Male-Female," in which the author proposes that the universal repudiation of femininity is based on the anxiety-provoking nature of inner genital sensations; a review article on orgasm by Jules Glenn and Eugene H. Kaplan; and observations by Marjorie C. Bennett on sex differences.

340 KARASU, TOKSOZ B., and CHARLES W. SOCARIDES, eds. On Sexuality: Psychoanalytic Observations. New York: International Universities Press, 1979. 412 pp.

On Sexuality is a collection of original essays reflecting psychoanalytic perspectives and trying to integrate these with new research findings in human sexuality. The editors' primary commitment to their discipline is, however, apparent: "It is our conviction that sexual behavior is primarily a motivated field, and motivational analysis supplied by psychoanalysis is the only method by which science can reach the whole individual on the behavior level."

Although most articles deal with both sexes, some relate to women only, including "Modern Woman and Motherhood" by Edith Buxbaum and "Feminism and the New Psychology of Women" by Virginia L. Clower. There is an extensive list of references. The editors offer only brief introductory remarks and do not really attempt to relate the essays to one another.

341 LONG, CONSTANCE. "A Psycho-analytic Study of the Basis of Character." In Proceedings of the International Conference of Women Physicians, vol. 4, Moral Codes and Personality, 67-90. New York: Woman's Press, 1919.

Among the many papers presented at the International Conference that touch on questions of sexuality, that of Constance Long, an English gynecologist and translator of Jung's Analytical Psychology, is of interest to contemporary readers because of its foreshadowing of issues still being debated. Specifically, Long and the discussants of her paper raise many salient points regarding the definition of sexuality and whether it should be regarded as a physical or emotional phenomenon, or both. Long leans heavily toward an emotional definition: "Homosexuality then is love for members of the same sex." Questions regarding homosexuality dominate the discussion, and comments of a Dr. Jackson of Pasadena regarding lesbian relationships are of special interest. The proceedings as a whole demonstrate the degree to which Freudian psychology, as well as Jungian and other theories, had already found a receptive audience in the United States. Citations to other conference papers may be found under their authors' names.

342   MILLER, JEAN BAKER, ed. Psychoanalysis and Women. Baltimore: Penguin Books, 1973. 415 pp.

Although it was published in 1973, Psychoanalysis and Women does not consist of the new feminist critiques of Freud inspired by the women's movement (Juliet Mitchell's Psychoanalysis and Feminism (entry 343) is perhaps the best-known example). Rather, it is a collection of essays by psychoanalysts, all of whom have taken exception to some aspect of Freud's theories of female psychology and sexuality.

Many of the pieces, such as those by Karen Horney and Mary Jane Sherfey, are frequently reprinted; others are less familiar. Especially useful are those that critique Freud's conceptual and methodological validity in the light of more recent empirical research. A bibliography of the most frequently cited sources and other works consists largely of references to psychoanalytic literature.

343   MITCHELL, JULIET. Psychoanalysis and Feminism. New York: Pantheon Books, 1974. 456 pp.

In this intellectually challenging work, Juliet Mitchell maintains that feminist theorists and other critics of Sigmund Freud have erred in their appraisal of psychoanalysis. This is usually due to their misreading of Freud's own work, their mistaken equation of his followers' theories with "true" psychoanalytic theory, or as in the case of Simone de Beauvoir, their summary rejection of basic tenets of his theory, such as the existence of the unconscious. She also notes that "if you study Freud's writings on femininity outside the context of the main concepts of psychoanalysis they are doomed to sound absurd and/or reactionary."

Beginning with a synopsis of basic psychoanalytic theory and Freud's ideas on femininity, Mitchell then analyzes the ideas of Wilhelm Reich, R.D. Laing, and feminist critics Simone de Beauvoir, Betty Friedan, Eva Figes, Germaine Greer, Shulamith Firestone, and Kate Millett. She concludes by turning to the anthropological theory of Claude Levi-Strauss in an attempt to demonstrate the inevitability of the Freudian schema for patriarchal culture.

Although Mitchell persistently attacks the so-called misinterpretations and inconsistencies of others, her own work is not free from internal contradictions. In her chapter on Betty

Friedan, for example, she asserts, "Psychoanalysis must be one of the very few scientific professions that, from its inception, exercised no discrimination against women." And yet, she later discusses a vote taken in 1910 by the Viennese psychoanalytic group on whether to admit women to their discussions. The very fact of the vote plus the negative position of three members (Freud was not among them) do not strike one as evidence of no discrimination.

More significant than such minor inconsistencies, however, is her neglect of the role of scientific method and language in the evolution and establishment of psychoanalysis as a science. How accurate, for example, is language as an expressive tool for unconscious "events" which may, in the individual, have predated the development of language skills? How constrained or circumscribed is psychoanalytic theory by its own choice of language? Mitchell, for example, comments that Freud's use and meaning of certain terms changed during his lifetime. Indeed, the evolution of Freud's own theories and his frequent admission of the need for further exploration and confirmation/revision would seem to indicate that psychoanalytic theory is not writ in stone. Relating to the question of language is that of how psychoanalytic theory can be "proven" when, with language as its medium and the individual as its laboratory subject, it is simply impossible to replicate test situations in the same way one might in studying the laws of physics or cell growth in an amoeba.

Indeed, Mitchell is really dealing with two problems. The first, to demonstrate errors in the appraisal and criticism of psychoanalysis, she handles extremely well. The second, to demonstrate that Freudian psychoanalytic theory is an exact science with a "proof" lying in the roots of patriarchal culture, she handles less convincingly. Her final argument--"When the potentialities of the complexities of capitalism--both economic and ideological-- are released by its overthrow, new structures will gradually come to be represented in the unconscious"--must be taken on faith alone, the same faith that remains the underlying ethos of psychoanalysis itself.

344   NELSON, MARIE COLEMAN, and JEAN IKENBERRY, eds. Psychosexual
       Imperatives: Their Role in Identity Formation. New York:
       Human Sciences Press, 1979. 397 pp.
       This collection of twelve original essays uses a psycho-
analytically oriented approach to contemporary issues of psychosexual development, gender identity, and self-image. Much of the
material reflects on the changing role of women in contemporary
society and our culture's increasing diversity of sexual behavior.
Cultural and historical antecedents of the present situation are
also discussed. There is, however, wide variation in the individual author's points of view, ranging from traditional Freudians to
feminist revisionists. An extensive bibliography complements the
essays.

345   PERSON, ETHEL SPECTOR. "Sexuality as the Mainstay of Identity:

Psychoanalytic Perspectives." Signs 5, no. 4 (Summer 1980): 605-30.

Person reviews and critiques psychoanalytic, psychiatric, and other theories of sexuality. Gender, not sex per se, orders sexuality for both men and women, but genital sexual activity is much more significant for male personality organization than it is for women. The sex print of "sexual preference" is another key factor. Person criticizes the all too common use of the male model of sexuality as the norm by which female sexuality is judged. She particularly cautions against viewing sexual liberation as synonymous with female liberation and autonomy.

346   ROTHGEB, CARRIE LEE, ed. Abstracts of "The Standard Edition of the Complete Psychological Works of Sigmund Freud". New York: International Universities Press, 1973. 761 pp.

This extremely useful reference work contains abstracts of each paper as well as its accompanying editorial notes from James Strachey's twenty-three-volume Standard Edition of the Complete Psychological Works of Sigmund Freud. Prepared by the National Clearinghouse for Mental Health Information, a unit of the National Institute of Mental Health, with the cooperation of the American Psychoanalytic Association, the book is arranged chronologically, in the same order as the Standard Edition, enabling the reader to trace the development of Freud's ideas over time.

There is also a KWOC subject index to titles, which, unfortunately, is not an adequate tool for subject access to the abstracts themselves. Readers will still have to skim the abstracts for relevant references to women, but this, at least, is easier than searching through the twenty-three volumes of the Standard Edition.

347   RUITENBEEK, HENDRIK M., ed. Psychoanalysis and Female Sexuality. New Haven: College & University Press, 1966. 251 pp.

This anthology reprints fifteen essays by psychoanalysts, many of which were first published in the International Journal of Psycho-analysis. Freud's 1931 essay on female sexuality appears, as does Clara Thompson's classic work on penis envy. Other authors represented include Karen Horney, Judd Marmor, and Marie Bonaparte.

348   Sexuality of Women: Scientific Proceedings of the Tenth Annual Spring Meeting of the American Academy of Psychoanalysis. Edited by Jules H. Masserman. Science and Psychoanalysis, no. 10. New York: Grune & Stratton, 1966. 168 pp.

Only four of the essays in this collection of papers presented at the spring 1966 meeting of the American Academy of Psychoanalysis relate directly to female sexuality. These include "Feminine Psychology and Infantile Sexuality" by Paul Chodoff, "Erotic and Affectional Components of Female Sexuality" by Marvin G. Drellich and Sheldon E. Waxenberg, "A Re-assessment of Feminine Sexuality and Erotic Experience" by Natalie Shainess, and Ruth Moulton's "Multiple Factors in Frigidity." The remaining essays,

eight in all, cover such diverse topics as women in classical
Greece, dependency patterns in pregnancy, and the future of the
academy and psychiatry, and include a panel discussion on educated
women in modern society, featuring such speakers as Mary Bunting
and Esther Raushenbush.

349   SHERFEY, MARY JANE. The Nature and Evolution of Female Sexuality.
      New York: Random House, 1972. 188 pp.
          Originally published in the Journal of the American Psycho-
      analytic Association in 1966, The Nature and Evolution of Female
      Sexuality was planned to be the first part of a two-part study,
      the second part envisioned as a tracing of female sexual develop-
      ment "through the primate line of descent." This latter work, how-
      ever, was never published, perhaps because of the controversy en-
      gendered by Nature and Evolution. Thus, many of Sherfey's ideas,
      such as that on "the relationships . . . between the reduction in
      clitoral size, the evolution of the vagina, the menstrual cycle,
      and the escape from estrus cyclicity along with the evolving modes
      of human sexual behavior" are articulated, but never substantiated
      with empirical proof. Other ideas, such as women being originally
      responsible for the initiation of male circumcision, following
      observation of animal coitus, are simply fanciful.
          Sherfey's training as a psychiatrist has led her to re-
      evaluate fundamental psychoanalytic theories in the light of con-
      temporary research in sexual physiology and biology. Here she is
      on stronger ground than in the sociohistorical portions of the
      book. Relying heavily on the work of Masters and Johnson, she
      shows how two fundamental tenets of classical psychoanalytic theory
      --inherent human embryonic bisexuality and the so-called vaginal
      orgasm--are biologically and physiologically false. Indeed, one
      of the most important implications of her work is the need for an
      overall re-evaluation of psychological, psychoanalytic, and social
      evolutionary theory from the perspective of biological and physio-
      logical structure and evolution.
          Her conclusion, that "forceful suppression of women's in-
      ordinate sexual demands was a prerequisite to the dawn of every
      modern civilization and almost every living culture," has been
      heavily criticized. Indeed, it relies on a particular sort of
      biological determinism which equates capacity with performance.
      Moreover, orgasmic capacity and "sexual demands" are not the same.
      One can only draw an analogy with the human mind, which is capable
      of highly advanced, creative thought, but which, unfortunately,
      usually settles for far, far less.

350   STOLLER, ROBERT J. Sexual Excitement: Dynamics of Erotic Life.
      New York: Pantheon Books, 1979. 281 pp.
          In this book Stoller describes the psychoanalysis of a woman
      whose dominant sexual fantasy scenario was "being raped by a horse
      while a group of silent men watched, the performance controlled by
      a sadistic Director." The subject developed this daydream until
      it became the fantasy form necessary for her adult sexual life.

From this case, as well as other material, Stoller concludes
that hostility, or the urge to harm the sexual object, is the central dynamic in sexual excitement. "The hostility of erotism is
an attempt, repeated over and over, to undo childhood traumas and
frustrations that threatened the development of one's masculinity
or femininity." To support this assertion, Stoller discusses his
ideas on what he calls "primary femininity" and articulates his
belief in the necessity of firm male/female gender identity and
identification for psychic health. Stoller, however, offers no
mass data or statistics in support of his theories and, more significantly, glosses over differences in erotic behavior in men and
women.

351   STROUSE, JEAN, ed. Women and Analysis: Dialogues on Psycho-
      analytic Views of Femininity. New York: Grossman, 1974. 375
      pp.
      One of the constant threads running through contemporary
feminism has been the re-examination of psychoanalytic theory,
especially its assumptions about female sexuality and gender role.
In some cases, such analysis has resulted in a total rejection of
the ideas of Freud and his followers, whereas other writers, such
as Juliet Mitchell, have produced positive reappraisals. A novel
approach has been taken by Jean Strouse in this collection. Ten
essays written by psychoanalysts about women, all of them previously published, have been reprinted. Their authors include Freud,
Abraham, Deutsch, Horney, Bonaparte, Thompson, Erikson, and Emma
Jung. Each essay is accompanied by a new critique prepared specially for this volume by scholars representing a variety of subject fields, among them Ethel Spector Person, Juliet Mitchell, and
Margaret Mead. This approach enables the authors to focus their
criticism and, by reproducing the original documents, enables
readers to evaluate each critique against its source.

352   TRIDON, ANDRÉ. Psychoanalysis and Love. New York: Brentano's,
      1922. 333 pp.
      André Tridon was a prolific popularizer of psychoanalytic
theory. His technique for doing so, however, was to snatch at
likely quotations from Freud, Stekel, and others, and to interweave
these with his own broad generalizations and stray facts. Most of
the chapters are short and do not necessarily relate to one another.
"Glandular Personalities" is followed by "Love and Mother Love,"
which in turn is followed by "Should Winter Mate With Spring?"
      Tridon, for all his weaknesses as an author, could be for-
ward looking in his philosophy. His chapter on "The New Woman and
Love" lauds woman's financial independence, for it "can remove from
her love all taint of even mild commercialism, returning favors
in kind, or accepting presents, no longer as a bribe, but as a
token of affection on the part of a man she loves." At the same
time, he could reflect prevailing stereotypes: "Normal man is
physiologically aggressive in love, normal woman is submissive."

353   ABRAHAM, HILDA C. "A Contribution to the Problems of Female
       Sexuality." International Journal of Psycho-analysis 37, nos.
       4-5 (July-October 1956):351-53.

354   ABRAHAM, KARL. "Manifestations of the Female Castration Com-
       plex." International Journal of Psycho-analysis 3, pt. 1
       (March 1922):1-29.

355   BOUSFIELD, PAUL. "The Castration Complex in Women." Psycho-
       analytical Review 11, no. 2 (April 1924):121-43.

356   BRIERLEY, MARJORIE. "Some Problems of Integration in Women."
       International Journal of Psycho-analysis 13, pt. 4 (October
       1932):433-48.

357   _____. "Specific Determinants in Feminine Development."
       International Journal of Psycho-analysis 17, pt. 2 (April 1936):
       163-80.

358   EISSLER, KURT. "On Certain Problems of Female Sexual Develop-
       ment." Psychoanalytic Quarterly 8 (1939):191-210.

359   FLIEGEL, ZENIA ODES. "Feminine Psychosexual Development in
       Freudian Theory, a Historical Reconstruction." Psychoanalytic
       Quarterly 42, no. 3 (July 1973):385-409.

360   FOULKES, S.H. "The Idea of Change of Sex in Women."
       International Journal of Psycho-analysis 24, pts. 1 and 2
       (1943):53-56.

361   GALEN, AMY F. "Rethinking Freud on Female Sexuality: A Look
       at the New Orthodox Defense." Psychoanalytic Review 66, no. 2
       (Summer 1979):173-86.

362   HARRIS, HELENA. "Some Linguistic Considerations Related to the
       Issue of Female Orgasm." Psychoanalytic Review 66, no. 2
       (Summer 1979):187-200.

363   HEIMAN, MARCEL. "Sexual Response in Women: A Correlation of
       Physiological Findings With Psychoanalytic Concepts." Journal
       of the American Psychoanalytic Association 11, no. 2 (April
       1963):360-85.

364   HINKLE, BEATRICE. "On the Arbitrary Use of the Terms 'Masculine'
       and 'Feminine.'" Psychoanalytic Review 7, no. 1 (January 1920):
       15-30.

365   JONES, ERNEST. "The Early Development of Female Sexuality."
       International Journal of Psycho-analysis 8, pt. 4 (October 1927):
       459-72.

366   _____. "Early Female Sexuality." International Journal of Psycho-analysis 16, pt. 3 (July 1935):263-73.

367   LESTER, EVA P. "On the Psychosexual Development of the Female Child." Journal of the American Academy of Psychoanalysis 4, no. 4 (October 1976):515-28.

368   LISTER, MILTON. "The Analysis of an Unconscious Beating Fantasy in a Woman." International Journal of Psycho-analysis 38, no. 1 (January-February 1957):22-31.

369   LORAND, SANDOR. "Contribution to the Problem of Vaginal Orgasm." International Journal of Psycho-analysis 20, pts. 3 and 4 (July and October 1939):432-38.

370   MENNINGER, KARL A. "Impotence and Frigidity from the Standpoint of Psychoanalysis." Journal of Urology 34 (1935):166-83.

371   MEYERS, THOMAS J. "The Clitorid Woman." Psychiatric Quarterly 40, no. 2 (April 1966):248-57.

372   MÜLLER, JOSINE. "A Contribution to the Problem of Libidinal Development of the Genital Phase in Girls." International Journal of Psycho-analysis 13, no. 3 (July 1932):362-68.

373   NAGERA, HUMBERTO. Female Sexuality and the Oedipus Complex. New York: Jason Aronson, 1975. 143 pp.

374   OPHUIJSEN, J.H.W. VAN. "Contributions to Masculinity Complex in Women." International Journal of Psycho-analysis 5, pt. 1 (January 1924):39-49.

375   PUTNAM, JAMES JACKSON. "Comments on Sex Issues from the Freudian Standpoint." New York Medical Journal 45, no. 24 (15 June 1912):1249-54; no. 25 (22 June 1912):1306-9.

376   _____. "Personal Impressions of Sigmund Freud and His Work, with Special References to His Recent Lectures at Clark University." Journal of Abnormal Psychology 4 (December-January 1909-10):293-310; (February-March 1910):372-79.

377   RADO, SANDOR. "Fear of Castration in Women." Psychoanalytic Quarterly 2 (July-August 1933):425-75.

378   ROSS, NATHANIEL. "The Primacy of Genitality in the Light of Ego Psychology; Introductory Remarks." Journal of the American Psychoanalytic Association 18, no. 2 (April 1970):267-84.

379   SARLIN, CHARLES. "Feminine Identity." Journal of the American Psychoanalytic Association 11, no. 4 (October 1963):790-816.

380   SCHAFER, ROY. "Problems in Freud's Psychology of Women."
       Journal of the American Psychoanalytic Association 22, no. 3
       (1974):459-85.

381   THOMPSON, CLARA. "Penis Envy in Women." Psychiatry 6, no. 1
       (February 1943):123-25.

382   WEISSMAN, PHILIP. "Psychosexual Development in a Case of
       Neurotic Virginity and Old Maidenhood." International Journal
       of Psycho-analysis 45, no. 1 (1964):110-20.

383   WITTELS, FRITZ. "Mona Lisa and Feminine Beauty: A Study in
       Bisexuality." International Journal of Psycho-analysis 15, pt.
       1 (January 1934):25-40.

384   _____. "Motherhood and Bisexuality." Psychoanalytic Review 21,
       no. 2 (April 1934):180-93.

385   _____. "A Type of Woman with a Three-Fold Love Life."
       International Journal of Psycho-analysis 16, pt. 4 (October
       1935):462-73.

Medical and Scientific Writing
before 1920

Clitoridectomy, venereal disease, hysteria, and coital frequency
were but a few of the topics relating to women's sexuality covered by
physicians and other scientific professionals writing before 1920.
Laboratory-based sex research was still, for the most part, in the future, and these writers set forth a wide range of theories, in some
cases based on actual observation, but in others derived from mere
folklore or traditional concepts of "truth." Writing primarily for an
audience of colleagues, rather than for the general public, their ideas,
in many cases, were obviously intended to have an impact far beyond
what we now consider to be the medical realm.

The nineteenth century was a time of great advances in gynecological surgery and the treatment of other disorders of the sexual system
in women. Yet, as G.J. Barker-Benfield has observed, such innovations
in treatment were not always motivated by the highest ideals. Isaac
Baker Brown (entry 389), who espoused clitoridectomy as a cure for insanity and other conditions affecting women, had his opponents, but he
also had followers in both his native Britain and in the United States.
Physicians commonly took moral stands on issues such as birth control
and abortion, and masturbation was seen not only as a disease but as
the cause of a wide range of problems ranging from nymphomania to
tuberculosis.

Many works by European writers, such as Richard von Krafft-Ebing,
were published in the United States, and Havelock Ellis's Studies in
the Psychology of Sex (entries 393-397), which began to appear in the
1890s, were widely read and reprinted. There was also an active
American medical press, and one of the more interesting characteristics
of writing on women's sexuality at this time was the extent to which
articles on the subject were published in state and local medical periodicals. Firms in Boston, Philadelphia, and New York continued to
dominate book publishing. There was regional activity here as well,
but never to the extent that it existed for mass audience prescriptive
literature.

Although William Acton's ideas on the asexuality of women (entry
386) found many supporters, the range of medical opinion on women's

sexuality was far more diverse than some historians might have us believe. Elizabeth Blackwell, for example, argued in The Human Element
in Sex (entry 388) that women's sexuality was different from that of
men and should not be evaluated in terms of a male model. C.W. Malchow's
The Sexual Life (entry 407), published in Minneapolis in 1904, called
for a recognition of the periodicity of women's sexual desire, as well
as for recognition of three erogenous zones: the clitoris, vagina, and
breasts.

Looked at from a feminist perspective, there is much that is ob-
jectionable in the medicoscientific writing of the nineteenth and early
twentieth centuries. We should not forget, however, that whatever
their underlying motivations and beliefs, these individuals were exploring new topics and areas of investigation never before subjected
to scientific inquiry. Their failings and biases should not blind us
to that fact, nor to the role of such investigation as a catalyst for
social change.

386   ACTON, WILLIAM. The Functions and Disorders of the Reproductive
      Organs in Youth, in Adult Age, and in Advanced Life. Considered
      in their Physiological, Social, and Psychological Relations.
      London: John Churchill, 1857. 106 pp.
         William Acton's views on female sexuality have been cited
      frequently by historians seeking to demonstrate that women were
      regarded as asexual creatures in Victorian England and America.
      Interestingly, the first few editions of Functions and Disorders
      contained virtually nothing about women, and even by the sixth
      edition (1875), male sexuality was still the overwhelming focus.
      This edition, however, does contain some of the statements that
      have formed many people's impressions of women's sexuality at this
      time: "I should say that the majority of women (happily for so-
      ciety) are not very much troubled with sexual feeling of any kind.
      . . . I am fully convinced that in many women there is no special
      sexual sensation in the clitoris. . . . As a general rule, a mod-
      est woman seldom desires any sexual gratification for herself."
      But these ideas form such a minor part of the whole (7 pages out
      of 266 in the sixth edition) that it seems curious that they should
      have grown into the stereotype they became, especially since many
      of Acton's contemporaries, at least in the United States, did not
      share his views. Acton's method was hardly scientific and his pro-
      nouncements on women seem to have sprung fully grown from his own
      imagination. For the historian, the later editions of Acton are
      essential reading, not because they necessarily reflect the current
      of Victorian thought, but because of the influence they subsequent-
      ly seem to have had.

387   BERGERET, L.F.E. The Preventive Obstacle, or Conjugal Onanism.
      Translated by P. De Marmon. New York: Turner & Mignard, 1870.
      182 pp.
         This translation of Bergeret was apparently the only edition

of the work issued in the United States, although it was frequently reprinted in France. Bergeret, chief physician of the Arbois Hospital in the Jura, was an absolute foe of any sort of deviance from so-called natural sexual intercourse, coition solely for the sake of procreation. He opposed birth control practices, as well as such sexual variations as fellatio, cunnilingus, and mutual masturbation, claiming that they caused a variety of mental and physical diseases in men and women. Unfortunately, Bergeret, despite the bolstering of his argument by 128 cases, confused cause with coincidence and was more intent on pushing his argument than providing incontrovertible empirical proof of its legitimacy. In addition to condemning "artificial" forms of sexual expression, Bergeret also censured sexual excess (which he never clearly defined) and claimed that a chief danger of "fraudulent" relations and birth control was their tendency to encourage extramarital sexual activity on the part of women. His case studies are of interest, not because of their relation to his thesis, but because of the evidence they present on French women's sexual behavior in the nineteenth century.

388   BLACKWELL, ELIZABETH. The Human Element in Sex: A Medical
      Enquiry into the Relation of Sexual Physiology to Christian
      Morality. London: J. & A. Churchill, 1884. 120 pp.
         Typical of Blackwell's writings on sexuality and sexual morality, The Human Element in Sex emphasizes the importance of chastity as a means of sexual and social self-control. Sexual physiology is also treated in detail. Unlike her contemporaries, such as William Acton, Blackwell argued for the existence of strong sexual passion in women, noting that women tended to sublimate physical passion through the mind into the emotion of love. This different character of women's sexuality had led to the development of a common fallacy which argued that sexual passion was an almost exclusive attribute of men. Blackwell was far ahead of her time in recognizing that a common attribute, sexuality, could evince different "normal" characteristics in men and women, and that women's nonconformity to a male-defined norm did not necessarily mean the absence of the quality itself.

389   BROWN, ISAAC BAKER. On the Curability of Certain Forms of
      Insanity, Epilepsy, Catalepsy, and Hysteria in Females. London:
      Robert Hardwicke, 1866. 85 pp.
         Readers of The Horrors of the Half-known Life (entry 36) will find much familiar material in this short work by English physician Isaac Baker Brown. Its pages contain case after case involving Brown's use of clitoridectomy as a cure-all for a wide range of women's health problems, ranging from menstrual irregularities to epileptic fits. Brown was heavily censured by the medical profession following the revelation of his practices, which had apparently been going on since 1859, involving, in some cases, girls as young as seventeen years. Yet even in the face of this opposition and in the face of failures of his operation to effect a cure,

Brown insisted on the righteousness of his theory: "It is no fault
of the operation if it fail in such cases." From the tone of this
work it is obvious that Brown was singlemindedly bent on selling
his operation to the profession and to his patients, some of whom
raised no small objections when he revealed his plans (they seem
always to have acquiesced in the end).

As Barker-Benfield noted in The Horrors, the study of genital
mutilative surgery in the nineteenth century must be seen in the
context of an ethos of psychological as well as physical control
over women. Isaac Baker Brown was merely an extreme example of
a common type of dominant male bent on asserting his power over
woman regardless of its ultimate impact on her.

390   CALHOUN, GEORGE R. Report of the Consulting Surgeon on
      Spermatorrhea, or Seminal Weakness, Impotence, the Vice of
      Onanism, Masturbation, or Self-abuse, and Other Diseases of the
      Sexual Organs. Philadelphia: Howard Association, 1858.   23 pp.
         In this extreme antimasturbation tract predicting dire con-
      sequences for the vice's practitioners, Calhoun maintains that
      masturbation was practiced equally by men and women, the latter
      exhibiting such symptoms of the habit as nervous prostration, di-
      gestive disorders, decayed teeth, and vaginal discharges. A com-
      mon accompaniment was nymphomania, and more women than men were
      rendered insane by the "vile habit." Calhoun was consulting sur-
      geon to the Howard Association of Philadelphia, a philanthropic
      organization with similarly named counterparts in London and sev-
      eral American cities dedicated to the relief of "virulent and epi-
      demic diseases." Apparently masturbation was considered to be one
      of these by the Philadelphia group.

391   COLOMBAT, MARC. A Treatise on the Diseases and Special Hygiene
      of Females. Translated by Charles D. Meigs. Philadelphia:
      Lea and Blanchard, 1845.   719 pp.
         Although this is primarily a medical work on the pathology
      and treatment of physical diseases of the female reproductive sys-
      tem, Colombat devotes one section to what he calls "functional
      lesions and the neuroses peculiar to females." Included are dis-
      cussions of such conditions as nymphomania and hysteria, as well
      as of general hygienic and preventive techniques. Because Colombat
      includes references to other printed works on these subjects and
      cites opinions of specific authorities, this book is a useful start-
      ing point for tracing the development of ideas relating to women's
      sexual and gynecological condition. Originally published in France
      in 1838, Colombat's treatise was given extensive supplementary an-
      notation by its American translator, Charles D. Meigs, in order to
      bring its contents up to date.

392   DICKINSON, ROBERT LATOU. "Bicycling for Women from the Stand-
      point of the Gynecologist." American Journal of Obstetrics and
      Diseases of Women and Children 31, no. 1 (January 1895):24-37.
         Dickinson advocates bicycling as a form of recreation and

exercise for women, noting that certain critics argue that it encourages masturbation. While agreeing that such a use of the bicycle saddle would be possible, Dickinson denies that this is common, citing his failure to find any case literature on the topic.
Dickinson, at this time an obstetrician in Brooklyn, is perhaps
best known for his sex research studies published in the 1930s,
as well as his involvement in the birth control movement.

393   ELLIS, HAVELOCK. "Eonism." In Studies in the Psychology of
      Sex, vol. 3, pt. 2, 1-110. New York: Random House, 1936.
         "Eonism" is part of a group of essays in the Studies that
Ellis arranged under the heading "Eonism and Other Supplementary
Studies." In this essay, he is concerned with the question of
transvestism, taking his term for this variation from the Chevalier
d'Eon, an eighteenth-century French nobleman who dressed as a woman, although he appears to have had no sexual relations with either
sex.
         Ellis offers numerous historical examples of cross dressing
by women as well as a summary of current opinions on the practice
and its relation to fetishism, homosexuality, and other variations.
Some of Ellis's cases would probably be recognized today as exhibiting the characteristics of transsexualism rather than simple
transvestism, such as "A.T.," who felt that "the sexual experiences
of a woman were needed for the complete gratification of his state
of feeling."

394   _____. "The History of Florrie and the Mechanism of Sexual
      Deviation." In Studies in the Psychology of Sex, vol. 3, pt.
      2, 121-212. New York: Random House, 1936.
         One of the more unusual essays in Ellis's Studies is this
case analysis included in the section "Eonism and Other Supplementary Studies." Some time after the publication of the initial
volumes in the series, a woman wrote to Ellis enclosing a lengthy
narrative describing her sexual history, which focused on an obsession with whipping and autoflagellation. During the next three
years, via written communications and personal interviews, she
revealed further information, which is arranged and presented here,
including material from fantasies and dreams. Through this form
of self-analysis, aided by Ellis's sympathetic comprehension, she
gradually modified her variant interests. In addition to the fas-
cinating case material, this essay is also of interest because of
its discussion of Freud's psychoanalytic technique and its relation
to the methods used in this case.

395   _____. "The Mechanism of Detumescence." In Studies in the
      Psychology of Sex, vol. 3, pt. 1, 115-200. New York: Random
      House, 1936.
         In this rather cryptically titled essay (cryptic, at least,
for those unfamiliar with Ellis's deployment of sexual terminology), the physical features of sexual intercourse are described,
including the anatomical structures involved. The clitoris is

defined as a "rudimentary analogue of the masculine penis," its function being to "receive and transmit the stimulatory voluptuous sensations imparted to it by friction with the masculine genital apparatus." Freud's views are referred to in passing, as is some of Robert Latou Dickinson's early work.

Ellis's comments reflect the general lack of knowledge then common regarding the nature of women's orgasm. Such statements as the following are not uncommon: "The association of the aptitude for detumescence with a tendency to a deep, rather than to a high voice, both in men and women, has frequently been noted and has seldom been denied." No substitute for Masters and Johnson, this essay is chiefly of interest as an indicator of the state of knowledge on this subject at the time.

396 _____. "The Phenomena of Sexual Periodicity." In Studies in the Psychology of Sex, vol. 1, pt. 1, 85-160. New York: Random House, 1936.

Along with his essays on modesty and autoerotism, Havelock Ellis considered this study to be an essential introduction to the psychology of sex. Examining the natural world as a whole, Ellis marshals evidence from anthropological as well as medical sources to discuss periodicity in both men and women. Ellis was among the first researchers to draw attention to the relationship between sexual desire and the menstrual cycle: "Heightening [of sexual emotion] occurs usually a few days before, and especially during, the latter part of the flow, and immediately after it ceases." Stepping outside the usual boundaries of sexuality, he also discusses such evidence of periodicity as seasonal fluctuations in scarlet fever rates and bread consumption in prison.

397 _____. "The Sexual Impulse in Women." In Studies in the Psychology of Sex, vol. 1, pt. 2, 189-256. New York: Random House, 1936.

Ellis's special study of women's sexuality forms part of a trilogy, which includes material on the sexual impulse in general, as well as sadism and masochism. Particularly, he feels that the elusive nature of the sexual impulse in women (a characteristic also noted by Sigmund Freud) and divergent opinions of so-called experts necessitate a special approach to the female sex.

Historically, Ellis traces two threads of thought on women's sexuality. The first created the dichotomy of woman as devil and angel. The second, a nineteenth-century creation, found women to be naturally frigid and devoid of sexual feeling. Demonstrating the contradictory and inconclusive quality of contemporary views, Ellis concludes that the sexuality of women is unduly minimized.

He also argues that women's sexuality is qualitatively different from men's, especially in its greater complexity. Inherent frigidity is a false concept: "The fact that it is almost normally the function of the male to arouse the female, and that the greater complexity of the sexual mechanism in women leads to more frequent disturbance of that mechanism, produces a simulation of organic

sexual coldness which has deceived many." He concludes: "Fairly
uniform, on the whole, in men generally and in the same man throughout mature life, sexual impulse varies widely between woman and
woman, and even in the same woman at different periods."

398   GOODELL, WILLIAM. "Clinical Lecture on Conjugal Onanism and
      Kindred Sins." Philadelphia Medical Times 2 (1 February 1872):
      161-63.
          In this anti-birth control article, Goodell argues that wives
      must experience orgasm if organic problems are not to result. Un-
      fortunately, Goodell is very foggy on the nature of female orgasm,
      confusing it with the resolution of male climax. There is also no
      acknowledgement of the role of the clitoris in female sexual plea-
      sure.

399   _____. Lessons in Gynecology. Philadelpha: D.G. Brinton,
      1879. 380 pp.
          Several chapters of Lessons in Gynecology relate directly to
      sexuality, for Goodell did not see his subject as a purely medical
      one. A colleague of S. Weir Mitchell, to whom he dedicated this
      book, Goodell shared many of Mitchell's views on women's sexual
      nature, including the relationship of nervous disorders to dis-
      turbances of the reproductive system, and employed Mitchell's rest
      cure in the treatment of his own patients. In the chapter "The
      Sexual Relations as Causes of Uterine Disorders," Goodell criti-
      cized long, prudish courtships for wearing down women's nerves,
      but expressed equal apprehension at the idea of licentious behavior
      before marriage. He advised separate beds and separate rooms to
      protect women from honeymoon excesses, and attacked contraception
      as being sinful and tending to degrade the woman into the status
      of a mistress, in addition to causing damage to her reproductive
      system. Goodell, who was opposed to continence as well, believed
      that women's reproductive organs needed to be bathed by semen in
      order to be healthy. While ostensibly advocating a traditional
      role for women and believing that women were governed by the sexu-
      al sphere, Goodell did not place them on a pedestal. Indeed, his
      advice on female attendants is a clue to an underlying fear of and
      ambivalence toward the gentler sex: "It is an excellent plan to
      have a female attendant in one's office. . . . her presence tends
      to protect [the physician] from evil-speaking or from designing
      women."

400   HAMMOND, WILLIAM ALEXANDER. Sexual Impotence in the Male and
      Female. Detroit: Davis, 1887. 305 pp.
          This is an expansion of an 1883 work by Hammond entitled
      Sexual Impotence in the Male. Although impotence has been a term
      traditionally used only in reference to men, Hammond used it in
      reference to women as well, outlining three causes for the condi-
      tion: absence of sexual desire, physical malformation or disease
      of the vagina and external genitalia, and absence of the ability
      to experience orgasm. Although Hammond believed that lack of

development of the clitoris was the primary cause of absence of sexual desire, he also believed that an "original absence" could exist, a retarded development of sexual feelings. He discusses vaginism, the pain and spasm caused during coitus or by the introduction of foreign objects into the vagina, maintaining that it was due chiefly to spinal nerve irritation; his treatments for the condition were barbaric and quackish. Hammond's solution to orgasmic inability was somewhat more pleasant--the woman was to take marijuana (in a medicinal dosage) three times a day!

401 HOWE, JOSEPH W. Excessive Venery, Masturbation, and Continence: The Etiology, Pathology and Treatment of the Diseases Resulting from Venereal Excesses, Masturbation and Continence. New York: Bermingham, 1883. 291 pp.

Perhaps the epitome of nineteenth-century antimasturbation literature, this work was based on lectures given by Howe at New York University. Women, while discussed, do not engage Howe's attention to the same degree as do men. Howe does, however, see masturbation as a cause of insanity among both sexes and charges that mothers who masturbate can cause hereditary consumption in their offspring. Nymphomania is another result, the only cure for which is marriage or clitoridectomy. Excessive Venery was frequently reprinted well into the twentieth century, including a 1974 Arno Press reprint of the 1887 edition.

402 HUHNER, MAX. A Practical Treatise on Disorders of the Sexual Function in the Male and Female. Philadelphia: F.A. Davis, 1916. 318 pp.

Huhner, a genitourinary specialist at Mount Sinai Hospital in New York, wrote this book largely because of his concern that neurologists with little empirical or practical knowledge of the sexual organs were dominating the field of diagnosis and treatment of neuroses and other conditions relating to the sexual functions. Huhner's own use, however, of a wide range of both reliable and suspect sources (from Joseph W. Howe's Excessive Venery, Masturbation and Continence [entry 401] to Howard A. Kelly's Medical Gynecology [entry 478]) makes his conclusions somewhat uneven.

Masturbation is seen as a disease, although Huhner is quick to point out that its use among married women is due frequently to the sexual incompetence of their husbands. Nymphomania is characterized as a hereditary psychopathology, and the author includes not a small amount of imaginative description: "'Now! Now!' exclaimed the patient when the entire speculum was within the vagina. A convulsive movement seized her entire body, a thrill went through her, and she made all the movements of a passionate coition."

Other chapters relating to women cover such topics as frigidity, vaginismus, dyspareunia, and absence of orgasm. Huhner was not averse to recommending that women should fake orgasms in order to prevent marital discord, although he also recognized the importance of clitoral stimulation in the achievement of the orgasm.

403 JACKSON, JAMES C. <u>The Sexual Organism, and Its Healthful
Management</u>. Boston: B. Leverett Emerson, 1861. 279 pp.
A belief in the universal efficacy of the water cure and
vehement condemnation of drugs characterized James C. Jackson's
medical philosophy. His conviction that too many quacks were
treating and prescribing for sexual problems apparently led him
to write this book. An abolitionist by background, Jackson advocated John Humphrey Noyes's technique of male continence as a means
of birth control and of gratification of sexual desire; full coition should be engaged in only for propagation. He was equally
opposed to masturbation and detailed a wide variety of pathological,
behavioral, and visual characteristics by which its practitioners
could be identified (girls and women, for example, developed a
peculiar wiggle in their walk). Another of his beliefs was that
women who engaged in excessive intercourse, such as prostitutes,
would be rendered sterile, while preadolescent girl masturbators
would never attain normal menstruation. Although he appended an
"M.D." to his name, Jackson's only medical credentials seem to have
been the proprietorship of several water cures and his willingness
to expound a wide range of moralistic theories aimed ultimately at
achieving his own particular brand of human perfection.

404 KING, A.A. "Hysteria." <u>American Journal of Obstetrics and
Diseases of Women and Children</u> 24, no. 5 (May 1891):513-32.
After reviewing literature on and definitions of hysteria,
King, who was a Washington, D.C., obstetrician, asserts that most
hysteria attacks in women are sexual in origin and are a manipula-
tive tool used unconsciously by the reproductive system to invite
sexual contact with men. The more sexual desire is frustrated,
the more hysteria is likely to occur. King prescribes marriage,
intellectual and physical exercise, and other forms of treatment.
No empirical evidence is used in this subtle, often convoluted
argument on behalf of positive assertion of women's sexuality.

405 KRAFFT-EBING, RICHARD von. <u>Psychopathia Sexualis</u>. Translated
by Harry E. Wedeck. New York: G.P. Putnam's Sons, 1965. 640
pp.
This classic taxonomy of sexual variations was originally
published in 1886. This edition is the first with the text completely in English; other translations retained key passages in
their original Latin. Drawing on case histories gathered in his
own practice, communications of colleagues, published reports, and
even court records, Krafft-Ebing utilized primarily European
sources, although more American material is present than one might
imagine. Although the author cited the sources for his material
in the text, these are often in abbreviated form and the absence
of any reference list makes it somewhat difficult for the reader
to trace them further.
<u>Psychopathia Sexualis</u>, especially its case histories, served
as the source of data for much subsequent writing, including that
of Sigmund Freud. Krafft-Ebing's inclusion of certain categories

of behavior, such as masturbation and oral-genital sex, in his classification of "perversions" strikes contemporary readers as being as antiquated as his moral pronouncements. His influence, both on professional and lay audiences (many lay people learned of their "perverted" natures for the first time after reading Krafft-Ebing), should not be underestimated.

Although the majority of the case histories describe men, a substantial number relate to women. Not to be overlooked, either, are the ways in which women figure in the behavior of the male cases.

406   LEWIS, WILLIAM HERBERT DENSLOW. The Gynecological Consideration of the Sexual Act. Edited, with supplementary material, by Marc H. Hollender. Weston, Mass.: M & S Press, 1970. 49+ pp.

Originally read at the American Medical Association meeting of 1899 and published in 1900, The Gynecological Consideration of the Sexual Act demonstrates Lewis's commitment to the cause of public health and his concern with ignorance and injustice. Hollender's introduction includes information on the Lewis paper's publication history--it was rejected by the AMA Journal on the grounds of obscenity--and on Lewis's life and other writings. Lewis's description of the physiological characteristics of hetero-sexual intercourse is as frank as was possible for the time, and he is fully aware of woman's multiorgasmic potential. Despite pay-ing lip service to women's rights in the relationship, Lewis's at-titude toward nonconventional sexual behavior was rigid, insensi-tive, and moralistic, and he was not averse to recommending the application of heroic methods in the treatment of, for example, extreme cases of frigidity. In addition to the text of the talk, the original published version, reproduced here, included a summary of the discussion at the AMA session where the paper was read, as well as Lewis's account of his struggle to have it published. Also reprinted is Lewis's 1906 Pacific Medical Journal article, "The Advocacy of Publicity Regarding Venereal Prophylaxis: A Personal Experience," which offers further details regarding the medical profession's reactions to the talk.

407   MALCHOW, C.W. The Sexual Life: A Scientific Treatise Designed for Advanced Students and the Professions, Embracing the Natural Sexual Impulse, Normal Sexual Habits and Propagation, Together with Sexual Physiology and Hygiene. Minneapolis: Burton, 1904. 308 pp.

Influenced by Havelock Ellis, Krafft-Ebing, and other European writers on sex, Malchow, a prominent Minneapolis physi-cian, departed markedly from nineteenth-century practice by openly discussing sexual technique. This modern cast is typical. For example, Malchow noted that women have three erogenous zones: the clitoris, vagina, and breasts. "A woman lays more stress upon the preliminary caresses to the sexual act proper than does the man be-cause of the greater diffusion of the sexual zones." He also ob-served that sexual desire in women was heightened around the time

of their menstrual periods, although he also retained the old folkloristic belief in the ability of train riding, bicycle saddles,
and sewing machine treadles to cause orgasm. An extremely popular
work, The Sexual Life ran to at least twenty-seven printings and
was still being issued as late as 1931.

408   MEIGS, CHARLES D. Woman: Her Diseases and Remedies. A Series
        of Letters to His Class. 2d ed., rev. and enlarged. Philadelphia:
        Lea and Blanchard, 1851. 690 pp.
        Originally published in 1848 as Females and Their Diseases,
Woman: Her Diseases and Remedies was the work of Charles D. Meigs,
one of his time's best-known gynecologists. In this book Meigs
did not confine himself simply to pathological and medical matters,
but offered frequent comments on sexuality as well. In his chapter
on the clitoris, for example, Meigs discussed nymphomania ("nothing
can be found more revolting"), which he equated with masturbation,
citing the case of a child only nine years old. Menopause was
seen as a pathological condition: "Henceforth, what has she to
expect save gray hairs, wrinkles, the gradual decay of those physical or personal attractions which heretofore have commanded the
flattering homage of society." Hysteria is linked to a diseased
condition of the sexual organs, and opium suggested to relieve its
symptoms.

409   PARKE, J. RICHARDSON. Human Sexuality: A Medico-Literary
        Treatise on the Laws, Anomalies, and Relations of Sex With
        Especial Reference to Contrary Sexual Desire. 2d ed.
        Philadelphia: Professional Publishing Co., 1908. 476 pp.
        In his introduction, Parke, a former U.S. Army physician,
notes that he prepared this volume in order to summarize and present in orderly arrangement the ideas of such sex writers as
Krafft-Ebing, Ellis, Ulrichs, Moll, and others. Parke does not
attempt any sort of evaluation of the validity of these authors'
views, accepting their assertions at face value, even those that
are clearly only imaginary folklore. In relation to women, he believes that the feminist movement is leading to an indifference
of women to heterosexual relations. Women, however, are also seen
in the tradition of Acton as having less sexual need than men.
Topics covered by Parke include sexual desire, marriage, contraception, and so-called artificial eroticism, with much emphasis
on "abnormal" and unconventional practices.

410   SCHRENK von NOTZING, ALBERT PHILIBERT FRANZ, FREIHERR von.
        Therapeutic Suggestion in Psychopathia Sexualis (Pathological
        Manifestations of the Sexual Sense), with Especial Reference to
        Contrary Sexual Instinct. Translated by Charles Gilbert
        Chaddock. Philadelphia: F.A. Davis, 1895. 320 pp.
        Primarily concerned with hypnotic "treatment" of male homo-
sexuals, Schrenk von Notzing noted the paucity of materials relating to women: "The phenomena of sexual anaesthesia and uranism
in the female sex could be given but brief consideration--first,

because in medical practice and social life they have attained
nothing like the importance of male homo-sexuality; and, secondly,
because, owing to the infrequency of these anomalies, I have had
no opportunity for personal observation of them." Nevertheless,
women are discussed in this German "nerve-doctor's" book, in sections on masturbation and nymphomania, as well as occasional references in those on homosexuality. Schrenk von Notzing, like most
of his contemporaries, had a narrow definition of normality and
saw his role as that of a curer of disease: "To convince the patient that he or she has become the victim of an abnormal, dominating impulse, whether an onanist or a nymphomaniac,--that is, self-
knowledge,--constitutes an important step toward improvement."

   Schrenk von Notzing's case studies document the frequency of
prescription of heterosexual intercourse (presumably with prostitutes, since many patients were unmarried), a "therapy" that in-
curred the enmity of social purity advocates in Europe and the
United States and raises some interesting questions about these
practitioners' views of women as sexual objects. In addition, the
book documents the harm that works such as Krafft-Ebing's Psychopathia Sexualis (and presumably this one as well) worked on people,
convincing them that their natural, genuine behavior was abnormal
and in need of treatment. "If we have been successful in demonstrating that this therapeutic result, so important for the life
of such unfortunates, may be obtained by suggestive treatment;
that useful members of society can be made of such perverted individuals,--then the object of this work has been attained."

411   STORER, HORATIO ROBINSON. The Causation, Course and Treatment
      of Reflex Insanity in Women. Boston: Lee and Shephard, 1871.
      236 pp.
         Nineteenth-century beliefs in the pervasive influence of her
      reproductive system on woman's behavior are no better seen than
      in this work by Boston physician Horatio R. Storer, best known for
      his opposition to abortion. Storer's thesis was that functional
      or organic disturbance of the reproductive system was the major
      cause of mental illness among women. Such disturbance did not have
      to be direct; for example, a case of insanity appearing to be
      caused by alcoholism could really be traced to the patient's con-
      sumption of liquor in order to relieve the pain caused by uterine
      disease. Underlying Storer's argument was another purpose: the
      closer amalgamation of the American Medical Association and the
      Association of Medical Superintendents of American Institutions
      for the Insane. Thus, Storer's plea for the establishment of pro-
      fessional medical staffs at asylums in order to assure the proper
      tracing and treatment of insanity originating in the reproductive
      system can also be seen as a political maneuver to assert the power
      of the AMA over the administration of mental institutions.
      Storer's arguments were met with skepticism by many of his pro-
      fessional peers, who thought he overstated his case, and, indeed,
      it is impossible to find in his text any empirical proof of a di-
      rect link between reproductive pathology and mental illness. Yet

Storer's impact should not be discounted, especially on those physicians who were to advocate gynecological surgery as a treatment for women's mental ills. The treatise was originally published in 1865 in somewhat different form in the Transactions of the American Medical Association.

412 _____. Female Hygiene: A Lecture Delivered at Sacramento and San Francisco, by Request of the State Board of Health of California. Boston: James Campbell, 1872. 20 pp.

In this wide-ranging discussion of so-called sexual dissipation among California women, Storer warns against sewing machines as instruments of masturbation, advocacy of birth control by the Protestant clergy, and masculine "third sex" women. He also rails against higher education for women, arguing that women's value is as wives, not voters, although they were not created as objects of passion alone.

413 TALMEY, BERNARD SIMON. Love: A Treatise on the Science of Sex-Attraction. For the Use of Physicians and Students of Medical Jurisprudence. New York: Practitioner's Publishing Co., 1915. 438 pp.

There is little material here that cannot be found in Talmey's other works, such as Woman (entry 207) and Neurasthenia Sexualis (entry 1590). Talmey is concerned less here with love than with plain old sex, and he discusses such topics as reproductive physiology, sexual pathology, and sexual hygiene. Readers are given a certain amount of misinformation (loss of the ovaries in woman prevents her from experiencing orgasm) and subjective opinion masquerading as fact: "Men and women with blunt intellects also have blunt feelings and are incapable of experiencing true love."

414 THORNTON, AUGUSTUS W. Hysterical Women; Their Trials, Tears, Tricks and Tantrums. Chicago: Donohue & Henneberry, 1893. 195 pp.

Thornton, a Whatcom County, Washington, physician, admittedly prepared this book as "a commercial literary enterprise." Commercial it certainly was, being peddled mail order from his home by the good doctor, but its literary merits are most questionable. It is a sensational, semihysterical account of symptoms and cases of the malady gleaned from a wide range of sources. Thornton himself blamed nineteenth-century civilization for the condition's rise at that time: "abortion . . . and the vile, abominable, disgusting and damnable practices, of the French, to prevent the blessings of motherhood, became well known, and exercised, as well by lecherous husbands, as sensuous wives; no wonder under such advances in the march of civilization . . . the nervous system of our men, and women, become deranged and result in an excess of hysterical and nervous affections." Also to blame was woman's "morbid desire for the excitement of the sexual organs, caused by the frequent and unnecessary insertion of the speculum." Thornton was obviously a man with a message.

415   ABBOTT, A.W. "Artificial Vagina Utilizing a Single Portion of
       Ileum." Surgery, Gynecology and Obstetrics 27, no. 2 (August
       1918), 227-29.

416   "Aberrations of the Sexual Instinct." Medical Times and Gazette
       1 (9 February 1867):141-46.

417   ALLEN, NATHAN. "The Normal Standard of Woman for Propagation."
       American Journal of Obstetrics and Diseases of Women and Children
       9, no. 1 (April 1876):1-39.

418   ARKWRIGHT, J. "Excision of the Clitoris and Nymphae." British
       Medical Journal 1 (28 January 1871):88.

419   BALDWIN, J.F., and A.W. ABBOTT. "The Baldwin Operation for
       Artificial Vagina." Surgery, Gynecology and Obstetrics 27, no.
       6 (December 1918):631.

420   BAYLES, GEORGE. "The Residence and Agencies of the Passions."
       Virginia Medical Monthly 1, no. 8 (November 1874):476-89; no. 9
       (December 1874):533-43; no. 10 (January 1875):581-94.

421   BEEBE, H.E. "The Clitoris." Journal of Orificial Surgery 6,
       no. 1 (July 1897):8-12.

422   BELL, SANFORD. "A Preliminary Study of the Emotion of Love
       between the Sexes." American Journal of Psychology 13, no. 3
       (July 1902):325-54.

423   BONNEY, VICTOR. "Formation of an Artificial Vagina by Trans-
       plantation of a Portion of the Ileum (Baldwin's Operation);
       with Remarks on the Ethical Aspect of the Procedure." Lancet
       2 (11 October 1913):1059-61.

424   BRADFIELD, T. NAYLOR. "Vaginismus vs. Insanity." Medical
       Record 8 (4 May 1878):356.

425   BROWN, CHARLES W. "Is the Presence of the Hymen a Proof of
       Virginity?" Philadelphia Medical Times 4 (8 November 1873):
       83-84.

426   BROWN, ISAAC BAKER. "Clitoridectomy." British Medical Journal
       1 (5 January 1867):18.

427   BURNETT, J.A. "The Clitoris." Regular Medical Visitor 4, no.
       9 (15 September 1903):201-3.

428   CLARK, A. CAMPBELL. "Relations of the Sexual and Reproductive
       Functions to Insanity." American Journal of Insanity 45, no. 2
       (October 1888):292-97.

429   CONNOR, J.J.   "What a Country Doctor Knows about Marital
       Excesses."   St. Louis Courier of Medicine and Collateral
       Sciences 10, no. 4 (October–November 1883):471–73.

430   CONRAD, J.S.   "Moral Insanity."   Transactions of the Medical
       Society of Virginia (1887):197–211.

431   COOTE, HOLMES.   "Clitoridectomy."   British Medical Journal 2
       (22 December 1866):705.

432   CORNING, J. LEONARD.   "Erotomania; Considerations on Its
       Manifestations and Pathogenesis."   American Medicine 9, no. 3
       (21 January 1905):109–12.

433   CRANDALL, F.H.   "Active Hemorrhage Produced by Coitus."
       Medical and Surgical Reporter 35, no. 18 (28 October 1876):
       352–53.

434   DANA, C.L.   "On Certain Sexual Neuroses."   Medical and Surgical
       Reporter 65, no. 7 (15 August 1891):241–45.

435   De ARMAND, J.A.   "Women as Sexual Nondescripts."   St. Louis
       Medical Era 12, no. 5 (January 1903):152–57.

436   De SÉRÉ, G. LOUIS.   "Sexual Activity and the Critical Period
       in Man and Woman."   Wood's Medical and Surgical Monographs 3
       (1889):797–834.

437   DOANE, L.G.   "Excessive Coitus as a Cause of Uterine Disease."
       Arkansaw Doctor 1, no. 3 (1881):4.

438   "Does Male Copulation without Emission Injure Female Health?"
       Medical News 45, no. 9 (30 August 1884):240.

439   DOUGLASS, THOMAS.   "Erotomania."   Journal of the Arkansas
       Medical Society 13, no. 4 (September 1916):67–77.

440   DÜCK, JOHANNES.   "Sexual Abstinence in Men and Women."
       American Journal of Urology and Sexology 12, no. 5 (May 1916):
       204–9.

441   DUGGAN, MALONE.   "The Instruction of Woman on the Questions of
       Sex, Venereal Diseases and the Early Detection of Cancer."
       Texas State Journal of Medicine 3, no. 11 (March 1908):286–87.

442   "Editorial: Clitoridectomy."   Southern Journal of the Medical
       Sciences 1 (February 1867):794.

443   ELLIS, HAVELOCK.   "Kleptolagnia."   In Studies in the Psychology
       of Sex, vol. 3, pt. 2, 477–91. New York: Random House, 1936.

444   _____. "The Menstrual Curve of Sexual Impulse." In Studies in the Psychology of Sex, vol. 3, pt. 2, 213-36. New York: Random House, 1936.

445   ENGELMANN, GEORGE J. "Clitoridectomy." American Practitioner 25 (January 1882):1-12.

446   _____. "The Increasing Sterility of American Women." Journal of the American Medical Association 37, no. 14 (5 October 1901): 890-97.

447   ENGSTAD, J.E. "Artificial Vagina." Journal-Lancet 37, no. 10 (15 May 1917):329-37.

448   ERICH, Dr. "Paroxysms in the Female Resembling Nocturnal Emmissions in the Male." Maryland Medical Journal 9, no. 15 (December 1882):348.

449   ESKRIDGE, BELLE C. "Why Not Circumcise the Girl as Well as the Boy?" Texas State Journal of Medicine 14, no. 1 (May 1918): 17-19.

450   EULENBURG, ALBERT. "Sexual Abstinence and Its Influence on Health." American Journal of Urology and Sexology 14, no. 6 (June 1918):252-72.

451   EVANS, T.H. "The Problem of Sexual Variants." St. Louis Medical Review 54, no. 10 (8 September 1906):213-15.

452   FORT, C.H. "Some Corroborative Facts in Regard to the Anatomical Difference between the Negro and White Races." American Journal of Obstetrics and Diseases of Women and Children 10, no. 2 (April 1877):258.

453   FOSTER, BURNSIDE. "A Brief History of the Origin and Practice of Mutilating Operations on the Sexual Organs." Northwestern Lancet 17 (1 December 1897):464-68.

454   GOFFE, J. RIDDLE. "The After-Effects of Hysterectomy on the Nervous System, the General Health and the Sexual Functions." American Medicine 8, no. 21 (19 November 1904):885-86.

455   GOLDSMITH, W.B. "A Case of Moral Insanity (with Removal of Ovaries and Recovery)." American Journal of Insanity 40 (October 1883):162-77.

456   GORDON, ALFRED. "Nervous and Mental Disturbances Following Castration in Women." Journal of the American Medical Association 63, no. 16 (17 October 1914):1345-48.

457   GORTON, D.A. "Moral Insanity." American Medical Monthly 16, no. 2 (May 1898):56-64; no. 3 (June 1898):81-92; no. 5 (August 1898):201-8.

458   GRANDIN, EGBERT H. "The Role of the Clitoris in the Production of Neuroses." Pediatrics 3, no. 4 (15 February 1897):145-48.

459   GREEN, CHARLES M. "Lacerations of the Vagina by Coitus." Boston Medical and Surgical Journal 128, no. 15 (13 April 1893): 364.

460   GREENHALGH, ROBERT. "Clitoridectomy." British Medical Journal 2 (29 December 1866):729.

461   GRISWOLD, RUFUS W. "Some Observations on the Physiology of Coitus from the Female Side of the Matter." Clinical News 1 (11 September 1880):445-49.

462   HAGENMANN, J.A. "The Correlation between Olfactory and Genital Functions in the Human Female." Medical Press and Circular 152, no. 9 (1 March 1916):195.

463   HARLING, ROBERT D. "Clitoridectomy." British Medical Journal 1 (12 January 1867):40.

464   HERSMAN, C.C. "The Medico-Legal Aspect of Erotochoreic Insanities." Alienist and Neurologist 18, no. 3 (July 1897):414-18.

465   HILL, CHARLES G. "Sexual Excesses in the Nervous and Insane." Maryland Medical Journal 29, no. 6 (3 June 1893):111-13; 116-18.

466   "The History and Present Position of the Doctrine of Moral Insanity." Medico-Legal Journal 9 (1891-92):249-64; 356-83.

467   HOWARD, WILLIAM LEE. "The Desire for Detumescence and Contrectation Equally Balanced in the Sexually Normal Man and Woman." Pacific Medical Journal 50, no. 1 (January 1907):22-24.

468   HUGHES, CHARLES H. "The Erratic Erotic Princess Chimay; a Psychological Analysis." Alienist and Neurologist 25, no. 3 (August 1904):359-66.

469   _____. "The Erotopath in Society." Alienist and Neurologist 24, no. 1 (February 1903):72-78.

470   _____. Erotopathia; Morbid Eroticism." Alienist and Neurologist 14, no. 4 (October 1893):531-78.

471   HUHNER, MAX. "Continence." Urologic and Cutaneous Review 20 no. 4 (April 1916):184-93.

472 ISHAM, MARY KEYT. "Report of a Case of Degeneracy with Con-
     clusions." Woman's Medical Journal 23, no. 5 (May 1913):100-102.

473 JACOBI, LEO. "Sexual Intercourse; a Physiological Interpreta-
     tion." American Journal of Urology 6, no. 2 (February 1910):
     73-76.

474 JENKINS, J.O. "Sex; Its Relation to Woman's Life." Kentucky
     Medical Journal 13, no. 9 (1 August 1915):360-64.

475 JONES, H. MACNAUGHTON. "The Sexual Element in the Neurasthenia
     of Women." Practitioner 86 (January 1911):61-75.

476 JONES, HERBERT C. "An Abnormal Sexual Condition." Medical
     Fortnightly 16, no. 3 (1 August 1899):457-58.

477 KARPAS, MORRIS J. "Paraphrenia Erotica, a Contribution to the
     Study of Synthetic Psychiatry." American Journal of Insanity
     72, no. 2 (October 1915):291-96.

478 KELLY, HOWARD A. Medical Gynecology. New York: D. Appleton,
     1908. 662 pp.

479 _____. "The Preservation of the Hymen." American Journal of
     Obstetrics and Diseases of Women and Children 37, no. 1
     (January 1898):7-14; 641-43.

480 KENNER, ROBERT C. "Some Clinical and Historical Notes on
     Erotomania." Alienist and Neurologist 39, no. 1 (January 1918):
     49-51.

481 KIERNAN, JAMES G. "Kleptomania and Pyromania." Alienist and
     Neurologist 37, no. 3 (August 1916):252-58.

482 _____. "Sex Transformation and Psychic Impotence." American
     Journal of Dermatology and Genito-Urinary Diseases 9, no. 2
     (March 1905):67-74.

483 KOSSAK, MARGARETHE. "The Sexual Life of the Hysteric."
     American Journal of Urology and Sexology 11, no. 12 (December
     1915):505-8.

484 LANDRUM, LINTON D. "Epilepsy Resulting from Sexual Excesses."
     Charlotte Medical Journal 31, no. 6 (December 1907):299-301.

485 LESZYNSKY, WILLIAM M. "Sexual Disorders Associated with
     Disease of the Nervous System and Remarks on Present-day Sexual
     Problems." Medical Record 83, no. 15 (12 April 1913):661-64.

486 LEWIS, WILLIAM HERBERT DENSLOW. "The Control of the Sexual
     Instinct." Medical Examiner and Practitioner 18, no. 295 (April
     1908):105-9.

487   LOCKWOOD, T.F. "Sexual Orgasm a Physiological Function Requisite
to Maintain Healthy Sexual Capacity." Kansas City Medical Record
21, no. 5 (May 1904):145–47.

488   LOEWENFELD, L. "Virginity and Sexuality." American Journal of
Urology and Sexology 12, no. 10 (October 1916):463–71.

489   LYDSTON, GEORGE FRANK. "Sexual Hygiene." Southern Practitioner
9, no. 6 (June 1887):235–41.

490   McCOLGAN, T.J. "The Revelations of a Woman Doctor Reviewed."
Southern Practitioner 9, no. 7 (July 1887):291–94.

491   McKEE, E.S. "Consanguinity in Marriage." Transactions of the
Ohio State Medical Society 41 (1886):93–108.

492   _____. "The Hymen; Anatomically, Medico-Legally and Historically
Considered." Lancet-Clinic 99, no. 10 (7 March 1908):240–46.

493   McLAUREY, WILLIAM M. "Remarks on the Relation of Menstruation
to the Sexual Function." American Journal of Obstetrics and
Diseases of Women and Children 20, no. 2 (February 1887):158–64.

494   McMURTRIE, DOUGLAS C. "Sexual Psychology." American Journal
of Urology, Venereal and Sexual Diseases 9, no. 11 (November
1913):531–38; no. 12 (December 1913):582–85; 10, no. 2 (February
1914):91–94; no. 4 (April 1914):195–200; no. 9 (September 1914):
432–35.

495   MALCHOW, C.W. "Unequalized Sexual Sense and Development the
Great Cause of Domestic Infelicity and Nervousness in Women."
Northwestern Lancet 23, no. 4 (15 February 1903):64–68.

496   MESROPIAN, M. "Physical and Sexual Frailty of the Average
American Woman." Western Medical Review 12, no. 10 (15 October
1907):350–56.

497   MILLARD, F.R. "Sexual Appetite and Sexual Instinct." New
Albany Medical Herald 21, no. 245 (May 1901):479–80.

498   MILLIGAN, FRANCIS H. "On So-Called 'Enlightened Sexology.'"
Medical and Surgical Reporter 33, no. 16 (16 October 1875):305.

499   MOEBIUS, P.J. "Gall's Special Organology; the Sexual Instinct;
Statement and Criticism." Alienist and Neurologist 23, no. 2
(April 1902):138–62.

500   MONTGOMERY, E.E. "Results of Removal of Uterine Appendages."
Annals of Gynecology and Pediatry 8, no. 9 (June 1895):661–63.

501   MORRIS, J. "Alarming Hemorrhage Following Coitus." Transactions

of the Medical and Chirurgical Faculty of Maryland 79 (1877): 91–93.

502 _____. "Nocturnal Emissions in Women." Transactions of the Medical and Chirurgical Faculty of Maryland 79 (1877):93–96.

503 MORRIS, ROBERT T. "Is Evolution Trying to Do Away with the Clitoris?" Transactions of the American Association of Obstetricians and Gynecologists, 1892 5 (1893):288–302.

504 MORTON, THOMAS G. "Removal of the Ovaries as a Cure for Insanity." American Journal of Insanity 49 (January 1893):397–401.

505 MOYER, HAROLD. "Is Sexual Perversion Insanity?" Alienist and Neurologist 28, no. 2 (May 1907):193–204.

506 MUNDÉ, PAUL F. "The Physical and Moral Effects of Absence of the Internal Female Sexual Organs; with Remarks on Congenital Sexual Malformations in the Female." American Journal of Obstetrics and Diseases of Women and Children 39, no. 3 (March 1899):289–304.

507 NORTHRUP, H.L. "Moral Degeneracy and Its Surgical Treatment." Hahnemannian Monthly 54 (April 1919):193–212.

508 NOVAK. EMIL. "Congenital Absence of the Uterus and Vagina." Surgery, Gynecology, and Obstetrics 25, no. 5 (November 1917): 532–37.

509 OBERNDORF, C.P. "Intermediary Stages in Sexual Development." Journal of Nervous and Mental Disease 50, no. 5 (November 1919): 453–55.

510 "The Obstetrical Society. Meeting to Consider the Proposition of the Council for the Removal of I.B. Brown." British Medical Journal 1 (6 April 1867):395–410.

511 PARSONS, R.L. "Erotomania." Journal of Psychological Medicine 5, no. 3 (July 1871):456–68.

512 PARVIN, THEOPHILUS. "Coition in Pregnancy." American Practitioner 24 (July 1881):12–16.

513 PERRY, RALPH St. J. "Sexual Hunger as a Factor in the Diseases of Women." American Journal of Dermatology and Genito-Urinary Disease 3, no. 1 (January 1899):5–8.

514 PETERKIN, G. SHEARMAN. "Cultivation and Control as against Suppression of Sex Instinct." Urologic and Cutaneous Review 23, no. 4 (April 1919):201–4.

515   PETTRES [PETTUS], COWLEY S. "Moral Effect of Professional
       Instruction on Proper Sexual Union." Southwest Journal of
       Medicine and Surgery 23, no. 12 (December 1915):361-68.

516   PETTUS [PETTRES], COWLEY S. "The Importance of Legitimate
       Scientific Sexual Union in Development of Character and Produc-
       tion of Contentment and Happiness." Journal of the Arkansas
       Medical Society 12, no. 3 (August 1915):61-65.

517   PIGG, W.B. "The Effects of Incomplete Coition." Tri-State
       Medical Journal and Practitioner 5, no. 9 (September 1898):
       418-21.

518   POPE, CURRAN. "Mental Disturbances Caused by Sexual Excesses."
       American Journal of Dermatology and Genito-Urinary Disease 11,
       no. 10 (October 1907):439-41.

519   PRESTON, ROBERT J. "Sexual Vices--Their Relation to Insanity
       --Causative or Consequent." Virginia Medical Monthly 19, no. 3
       (June 1892):193-201.

520   PRINCE, MORTON. "Sexual Perversion or Vice? A Pathological
       and Therapeutic Inquiry." Journal of Nervous and Mental Disease
       25 (1898):237-56.

521   RAY, ISAAC. "The Insanity of Women Produced by Desertion or
       Seduction." American Journal of Insanity 23, no. 2 (October
       1866):263-74.

522   "Remarkable Case of Sexual Abstinence." American Journal of
       Urology and Sexology 15, no. 1 (January 1919):31-33.

523   REMONDINO, P.C. "Some Observations on Continence as a Factor
       in Health and Disease." American Journal of Dermatology and
       Genito-Urinary Diseases 4, no. 1 (January 1900):1-12; no. 2
       (March 1900):59-72.

524   RICHARDSON, A.B. "Perversions of the Moral Sense in Insanity."
       American Journal of Insanity 46 (January 1890):363-69.

525   RIVERS, W.C. "A New Theory of Kissing, Cunnilingus, and
       Fellatio." Alienist and Neurologist 36, no. 3 (August 1915):
       253-68.

526   ROBINSON, BYRON. "The Clitoris." Interstate Medical Journal
       7, no. 1 (January 1900):18-23.

527   _____. "The Sexual Phases and Crises of Woman." American
       Medical Compendium 16, no. 12 (December 1900):724-28.

528   ROSSE, IRVING C. "Sexual Hypochondriasis and Perversion of the

Genesic Instinct." <u>Journal of Nervous and Mental Disease</u> 19, no. 11 (November 1892):795-811.

529 "Sexual Abstinence in Woman." <u>American Journal of Urology and Sexology</u> 13, no. 4 (April 1917):168-70.

530 "Sexual Hygiene." <u>Alkaloidal Clinic</u> 6, no. 10 (October 1899): 645-50.

531 SHUFELDT, R.W. "Beauty and Sexual Education in Women." <u>American Journal of Dermatology and Genito-Urinary Disease</u> 14, no. 10 (October 1910):468-71.

532 _____. "Continence in the Two Sexes." <u>Medico-Pharmaceutical Critic and Guide</u> 14, no. 8 (August 1911):304-7.

533 _____. "Popular and Medical Opinions in Regard to the Hymen." <u>Pacific Medical Journal</u> 49, no. 1 (January 1906):1-9.

534 _____. "Psychopathia Sexualis and Divorce." <u>Pacific Medical Journal</u> 43, no. 10 (October 1900):734-43.

535 SMITH, A. LAPTHORN. "The Effect of Removal of the Ovaries upon the Sexual Appetite." <u>Medical Record</u> 48, no. 8 (24 August 1895): 273.

536 SMYTHE, A.G. "The Position of the Hymen in the Negro Race." <u>American Journal of Obstetrics and Diseases of Women and Children</u> 10, no. 4 (October 1877):638.

537 SOULE, J. <u>Science of Reproduction and Reproductive Control. The Necessity of Some Abstaining from Having Children--The Duty of All to Limit Their Families according to Their Circumstances Demonstrated. Effects of Continence--Effects of Self-Pollution --Abusive Practices, Seminal Secretion--Its Connection with Life. How to Preserve Youthful Vigor, and How to Attain to the Acme of Physical, Moral, and Intellectual Perfection. Laws and Philosophy of Impregnation, with an Explanation of the Seminal Animalculae, and Female System. With All the Different Modes of Preventing Conception, and the Philosophy of Each.</u> New York: n.p., 1856. 70 pp.

538 SPRATLING, W.P. "Moral Insanity." <u>Medico-Legal Journal</u> 8 (1890-91):220-26.

539 STEKEL, WILHELM. "Sexual Abstinence and Health." <u>American Journal of Urology and Sexology</u> 14, no. 5 (May 1918):193-225.

540 STERNBERG, WILHELM. "Differences between Man's and Woman's Love Life." <u>American Journal of Urology and Sexology</u> 12, no. 10 (October 1916):455-62.

541   STEVENS, JOHN W.   "Insane Lovers."   Medical Record 70, no. 7
      (18 August 1906):244-51.

542   STORER, HORATIO ROBINSON.   "Haemorrhage from Rupture of the
      Hymen."   Boston Medical and Surgical Journal, n.s. 7, no. 2
      (12 January 1871):24.

543   _____.   "Obstinate Erotomania."   American Journal of Obstetrics
      and Diseases of Women and Children 1, no. 4 (February 1869):
      423-26.

544   SWAYZE, GEORGE B.H.   "Daughters of Eve."   Medical Times 37
      (October 1909):298-303.

545   TALMEY, BERNARD SIMON.   "Transvestism, a Contribution to the
      Study of the Psychology of Sex."   New York Medical Journal 99,
      no. 8 (21 February 1914):362-68.

546   TANNENBAUM, SAMUEL A.   "Sexual Abstinence and Nervous Disorders."
      Medico-Pharmaceutical Critic and Guide 16, no. 8 (August 1913):
      271-93.

547   TANNER, T. HAWKES.   "On Excision of the Clitoris as a Cure for
      Hysteria, etc."   Transactions of the Obstetrical Society of
      London 8 (1866):360-84.

548   TAYLOR, CHARLES FAYETTE.   "Effect on Women of Imperfect Hygiene
      of the Sexual Function."   American Journal of Obstetrics and
      Diseases of Women and Children 15, no. 1 (January 1882):161-77.

549   "Tests of Virginity."   Urologic and Cutaneous Review 19, no. 9
      (September 1915):529.

550   THOMPSON, HANNAH M.   "The Preservation of the Hymen."
      Philadelphia Medical Journal 2, no. 23 (December 1898):1192-94.

551   THOROUGHBRED, A [pseud.].   "Chacun à Son Goût; Mauriceau or
      Dionis; Which?"   [Coitus during pregnancy].   Southern Practitioner
      3, no. 9 (September 1881):272-79.

552   VAN de WARKER, ELY.   "Effects of Railroad Travel upon the Health
      of Women."   Georgia Medical Companion 2 (1872):192-206.

553   _____.   "The Fetich of the Ovary."   American Journal of
      Obstetrics and Diseases of Women and Children 54, no. 3
      (September 1906):366-73.

554   _____.   "A Gynecological Study of the Oneida Community."
      American Journal of Obstetrics and Diseases of Women and Children
      17, no. 8 (August 1884):785-810.

555 VANDERVEER, A. "'She Thought It Was Her Change of Life.'" Journal of the American Medical Association 15, no. 1 (5 July 1890):4-6.

556 VINEBERG, HIRAM N. "The Effect of Hysterectomy on the Sexual Function." Medical News 85, no. 27 (December 1904):1249.

557 "Violent Spasmodic or Gradual Aspiratory Movements of the Uterus during the Female Orgasm, Which?" Peoria Medical Monthly 5, no. 5 (September 1884):283-87.

558 WALLIAN, SAMUEL S. "The Physiological, Pathological and Psychological Bearings of Sex." Transactions of the Medical Society of New York (1890):247-59.

559 WAUGH, WILLIAM FRANCIS. "Are Women Polygamists?" Alienist and Neurologist 34, no. 3 (August 1913):319-26.

560 WEBB, De WITT. "The Influence of Immaturity and Degeneration in Some Forms of Thinking, Especially Sexual Thinking." Virginia Medical Monthly 20, no. 2 (May 1893):153-60.

561 WEST, CHARLES. "Clitoridectomy." British Medical Journal 2 (24 November 1866):585.

562 WHATHAM, ARTHUR E. "Has Woman Stronger Sexual Desire than Man?" American Journal of Urology and Sexology 14, no. 7 (July 1918): 307-18.

563 WHOLEY, C.C. "Cases of Insanity Arising from Inherent Moral Defectiveness." Journal of the American Medical Association 62, no. 12 (21 March 1914):926-28.

564 WINDELL, J.T. "Casualties of Copulation." Kentucky Medical Journal 7, no. 8 (15 May 1909):408-11.

565 WYLIE, W. GILL. "Amputation of the Clitoris." American Journal of Obstetrics and Diseases of Women and Children 43, no. 5 (May 1901):720-23.

566 YEOMANS, T.G. "Some Concepts of Human Sexuality." Medical Sentinel 27, no. 10 (October 1919):1096-1111.

Medical and Scientific Writing, 1920 and After

The development of scientific research methodology and laboratory techniques has been a consistent emphasis in the medical and scientific investigation of women's sexuality in the twentieth century. The zenith of this trend was reached perhaps in 1966 with the publication of William H. Masters and Virginia E. Johnson's Human Sexual Response (entry 580), a work that has had far-reaching effects on both professional and lay audiences. Subsequent symposia and research on such topics as the vagina, women's orgasm, and periodicity have further expanded our knowledge of the female sexual system.

Although much of the material in such fields as prenatal development, sexual physiology, and endocrinology is technically beyond the scope of this bibliography, findings in these areas have been incorporated not only into standard texts on human sexuality but into works intended for popular audiences as well. Yet, as Diana Scully and Pauline Bart pointed out in their survey of gynecology textbooks (entry 584), there has also been a continuing tendency by some writers to perpetuate traditional, inaccurate, and stereotyped views of women's sexuality. Periodicals such as Medical Aspects of Human Sexuality attempt to overcome the problem of communicating this new research to the general medical audience.

Another difference between much recent research and the writing generated by the medical profession in the nineteenth and early twentieth centuries is its separation of the sexual and reproductive functions. This can be seen in a greater emphasis on female sexual response for its own sake, rather than as a subordinate part of the reproductive function. A further distinction can be made between those who would view and study sexual response as primarily a physiological phenomenon and those who feel that equal emphasis should be placed on its psychological and emotional components. Victorian moralizing may have fallen by the wayside, but the medicoscientific debate over the nature of women's sexuality continues.

567   AMERICAN MEDICAL ASSOCIATION, COMMITTEE ON HUMAN SEXUALITY. Human Sexuality. Chicago: American Medical Association, 1972. 246 pp.

Recognizing that physicians are often called upon to give advice regarding sexual matters and yet often know little beyond reproductive anatomy and physiology, the American Medical Association prepared this book as a guide for practitioners in sexual counseling. Necessarily concise, it incorporates much of the research of the 1960s in its examination of such subjects as sexual response, sexual development, and sex and society. Appendices include a sample sexual performance evaluation form to be used in taking case histories of patients with sexual problems, a bibliography of sex education literature, and a special section on sex and the law, reprinted from the Journal of the American Medical Association.

568   BRECHER, RUTH, and EDWARD M. BRECHER, eds. An Analysis of Human
       Sexual Response. Boston: Little, Brown, 1966. 318 pp.
       In the first part of this book, popular health and medical
writers Edward and Ruth Brecher present in lay language a summary
of the material in Masters and Johnson's Human Sexual Response
(entry 580), material from earlier Masters-Johnson research, and
additional information prompted by questions arising from their
research and conclusions, such as biographical material. The second section of the book prints several essays on various aspects
of sex research, including practical applications, by such authors
as Wardell Pomeroy, tracing connections between Kinsey and Masters-
Johnson, Daniel G. Brown on female orgasm, and Mary Steichen
Calderone on sex education. Several bibliographies complement the
narrative. In some ways, this is a more useful work than Human
Sexual Response, simply because of the diversity of material it
presents. For example, the Brown essay is a summary of the clitoral-vaginal orgasm controversy, predating later feminist discussions on the same theme by such writers as Ann Koedt.

569   De MERRE, LEON J. The Female Sex Hormones. New York: Vantage,
       1954. 219 pp.
       De Merre attempted to achieve a balance between the scientific and sensational in this account of the various female sex
hormones. His recommendations regarding their therapeutic application are cautious, given the cancer-producing linkages already observed in laboratory experiments. A final chapter, on sex determination and homosexuality, shows that De Merre subscribed to conventional, repressive views: "The psychologically maladjusted
types of women who wear masculine clothes and try to affect a male
attitude . . . should be treated for disorders of the mind and not
for probable physiological troubles. . . . It goes without saying
that these individuals should make a serious effort to achieve
normality, instead of exhibiting publicly an abnormal condition.
. . . Homosexuals require real medication because their hormone
equilibrium has been disrupted; they are not to be indiscriminately
included among those who feign the condition for various ulterior
motives."

570   DOISY, EDWARD A., et al. Female Sex Hormones. Philadelphia:

University of Pennsylvania Press, 1941. 58 pp.
This is a collection of four essays: "The Ovarian Follicular
Hormone," "Gonadotropic Hormones," "Diagnostic Procedures in Female
Sex Endocrine Problems," and "Uses and Limitations of Female Sex
Endocrine Therapy." The first two essays provide a historical summary of research and a state of the art report for their respective
topics. The essay on diagnostic procedures is primarily a summary
of research done between 1925 and 1941 in the Endocrine Laboratory
of Mount Sinai Hospital in New York City. The fourth essay provides historical background for analyzing the use (and misuse) of
hormone therapy to treat a variety of conditions in women. Doisy,
incidentally, was one of the discoverers of estrogen.

571   DOUGHERTY, CARY M., and ROWENA SPENCER. Female Sex Anomalies.
      Hagerstown, Md.: Harper & Row, 1972. 273 pp.
      A collection of clinical essays on physical malformation and
unusual conditions of the female genitals and reproductive system,
this book is based largely on case records and other clinical evidence from files of Charity Hospital at New Orleans and records
collected by the authors. Dougherty and Spencer feel that erroneous information and ill-founded beliefs about such anatomical and
physiological conditions often lead to an expectation by both medical and nonmedical persons of peculiar sexual or social behavior
on the part of the affected individual. In order to combat such
misinformation, the authors categorize the various conditions by
major organ affected and also differentiate among anomalies occurring in various age categories: the intrauterine period, the neo-
natal period, and at sexual maturity.

572   FILLER, JULIET PARKER. The Female Hormones. New York:
      Booktab, 1947. 184 pp.
      Popular books on hormone therapy such as this one document
the faddish quality often assumed by that form of treatment, as
well as some of the mystique surrounding the discovery of these
substances and reception of this knowledge by the medical profession and general public. Filler describes the evolution of endocrinology and cases where female hormones have been administered
therapeutically, but she cautions readers that despite their
"miracle quality, hormones should only be used for treatment based
on sound scientific analysis." Nevertheless, statements such as
"we can say without exaggeration that woman's emancipation, in a
new and exciting meaning of the word, is being achieved through
hormone research in many fields" tend to sensationalize what is
chemically and physiologically a most complex problem. Students
of women's culture and attitudes toward women should note especially the chapters on hormones and sex desire, beauty, and hormone
cosmetics.

573   FISHER, SEYMOUR. The Female Orgasm: Psychology, Physiology,
      Fantasy. New York: Basic Books, 1973. 533 pp.
      The title of this book is somewhat misleading, for Fisher's

study goes far beyond a mere investigation of women's sexual orgasm. Dealing with the influence of psychological as well as body functions on female sexual response, he begins with a review of previous research and writing in this field. He then examines the evidence presented by psychological tests, laboratory observation, and interviews with a sample population in Syracuse, New York.

Fisher concludes that many accepted ideas about female sexuality are erroneous. For example, "Contrary to psychoanalytic theory, it cannot be said that a woman's sexual responsiveness is an index of her emotional maturity or stability." Fisher's research is extremely well documented by source references and descriptions of testing and measurement techniques.

574 GREEN, RICHARD, ed. Human Sexuality: A Health Practitioner's Text. Baltimore: Williams & Wilkins, 1975. 251 pp.
This is an anthology of eighteen essays with accompanying material by Green, written to be used as a text in human sexuality courses taught in medical schools. Much of the book seems to be male oriented, and there are only two women authors in the group of twenty contributors. There are, however, a few pieces that focus on women alone: "Pelvic Examination of Women" by Diane S. Fordney Settlage, "Sexuality during Pregnancy and Postpartum" by Julius C. Butler, Jr., and Nathaniel N. Wagner, and "Treating Sexual Dysfunction: The Solo Female Physician," also by Settlage.

575 HAFEZ, E.S.E., and T.N. EVANS, eds. The Human Vagina. Human Reproductive Medicine, vol. 2. Amsterdam and New York: North-Holland, 1978. 515 pp.
This collection of papers represents the proceedings of the seventh Symposium in Reproductive Medicine held at the C.S. Mott Center for Human Growth and Development, Wayne State University, in 1976. The authors present state of the art and research reports on a variety of topics relating to this sexual organ, including anatomy, viral infections, plastic surgery, and morphology. Of particular interest are J.P. Semmens and F.J. Semmens, "Role of the Vagina in Female Sexuality" and L.I. Lipshultz and J.N. Corriere, Jr., "Construction of a Neovagina in Male Transsexuals." Surgical procedures and pathological examples are illustrated with photographs, and extensive documentation accompanies all thirty-four chapters.

576 KAPLAN, HAROLD I., ALFRED M. FREEDMAN, and BENJAMIN J. SADOCK, eds. Comprehensive Textbook of Psychiatry. Vol. 2. 3d ed. Baltimore: Williams & Wilkins, 1980. 1164 pp.
Readers may wish to compare the more than 250 pages on sexuality in this standard text with earlier editions of the same work, especially since the editors have selected material reflective of the rapid development and change in the psychiatric field, and particularly since this is one of the primary reference texts in that field. There are several subsections in the sexuality portion, including discussions of sexual physiology and technique, gender

disorders, sex and the life cycle, homosexuality, psychosexual dysfunctions, and related topics such as abortion and contraception. Robert Stoller's discussion of transsexualism reveals a "blame mother" philosophy of diagnosis and treatment evolved by many institutions dealing with this problem, a philosophy that speaks to many levels of sexism. Ira Pauly's essay on sex and the life cycle, however, displays sensitivity to women's concerns as well as a broad historical perspective on the literature--one example of this (frequently absent from medical literature) is his use of both male and female gender designations when referring to physicians. Richard Green's essay on homosexuality dispels many myths about this subject and outspokenly questions many psychiatric assumptions and presumptions: "Much confusion has been rendered by reports in the psychiatric literature of impressions of psychopathology [in gay people] derived from clinical samples. The fallacy here is patent. If one were to inspect files of heterosexual psychiatric patients and generalize the psychopathology found there to non-patient heterosexuals, heterosexuality would 'obviously' be a mental illness." Other sections of the entire three-volume set may be of collateral interest to students of female sexuality.

577 KATCHADOURIAN, HERANT A., and DONALD T. LUNDE. Fundamentals of Human Sexuality. 2d ed. New York: Holt, Rinehart and Winston, 1975. 595 pp.
     This second edition of an undergraduate text originally published in 1972 shows considerable revision when compared to the first edition, a task made easier by the authors' thorough discussion of those changes. Comparable in format and approach to biology and social science texts, Fundamentals of Human Sexuality is the work of two psychiatrists who, in addition to including the usual material on anatomy, physiology, and sexual behavior, also feature a section on cultural aspects of sexuality with chapters on literature, film, art, and the law. Illustrations range from scientific drawings to photos of erotic art objects. Although the text itself is not heavily documented, there is a bibliography. Fundamentals, because of the breadth of its coverage, is a good starting point for the study of human sexuality in all its aspects.

578 LOWRY, THOMAS P., and THEA SNYDER LOWRY. The Clitoris. St. Louis: Warren H. Green, 1976. 255 pp.
     Twelve authors in addition to the Lowrys have contributed to this unique collection of essays, which presents summary information on the clitoris from the perspectives of anatomy, pathology, anthropology, linguistics, and other fields. Although the Lowrys' perspective is clearly feminist, the essays present a diverse range of viewpoints. Of particular interest to historians and social scientists are essays by Ben R. Huelsman on the anthropology and history of female genital mutilation and by Thomas P. Lowry on the etymology of the word clitoris. The text is supplemented by illustrations, charts, bibliographies, and twenty-eight stereoscopic color photos (for use with a Sawyer's Viewmaster) of normal clitorides.

579   MADDOCK, JAMES W., and DEBORAH L. DICKMAN, eds. Human Sexuality:
       A Resource Book. 3 vols. Minneapolis: University of Minnesota
       Medical School, 1972. Unpaged. ISR.
           As part of a general curriculum revision in the early 1970s,
       the University of Minnesota Medical School introduced an inter-
       disciplinary program in human sexuality. These volumes comprise
       a guide to the course's structure and include all the required
       readings. Reprints and some original documents were photorepro-
       duced verbatim. The overall focus of the material is humanist,
       and the compilers include such feminist items as Alix Kates
       Shulman's "Organs and Orgasms" and Del Martin and Phyllis Lyon's
       "The New Sexuality and the Homosexual." A section on the history
       of the development of the course is of special interest to those
       wishing to develop similar courses or other innovative teaching
       approaches to interdisciplinary questions.

580   MASTERS, WILLIAM H., and VIRGINIA E. JOHNSON. Human Sexual
       Response. Boston: Little, Brown, 1966. 366 pp.
           Human Sexual Response, the first book-length study of human
       sexual physiology, was the culmination of twelve years of research
       conducted by Masters and Johnson at the Reproductive Biology
       Research Foundation. As the authors note in their introductory
       remarks, despite the existence of such massive efforts as Alfred
       C. Kinsey's compendiums on male and female sexual behavior, there
       had been no adequate medical research into what precisely happens
       to the human body during the sexual response cycle. Clearly,
       Masters and Johnson perceived a mission: "Without adequate support
       from basic sexual physiology, much of psychologic theory will re-
       main theory and much of sociologic concept will remain concept."
           Two basic questions underlay the investigation: "What physi-
       cal reactions develop as the human male and female respond to ef-
       fective sexual stimulation? Why do men and women behave as they
       do when responding to effective sexual stimulation?" Partly because
       of the study's failure to deal with psychological factors, the sec-
       ond of these questions was not adequately answered by the research,
       but physical reactions were amply documented. Laboratory study of
       382 women and 312 men, drawn mostly from the upper socioeconomic
       and intellectual strata of the St. Louis academic community, re-
       vealed the behavior of the uterus, vagina, clitoris, and other body
       parts during the phases of sexual response.
           Masters and Johnson are outspoken in much of their criticism
       of what had formerly passed as "scientific" knowledge. "Conceptu-
       alization of the role of the clitoris in female sexual response
       has created a literature that is a potpourri of behavioral concept
       unsupported by biologic fact." Women welcomed, for example, their
       evidence on orgasm. "Are clitoral and vaginal orgasms truly sepa-
       rate anatomic entities? From a biologic point of view, the answer
       to this question is an unequivocal No." They also demonstrate the
       multiorgasmic potential of many women and devote special chapters
       to pregnancy and sexual response and sexual response in aging women.
       Of particular interest is their documentation of earlier opinions,

128

based on what they term "phallic fantasy," countered by their presentation of demonstrable empirical fact. Although the scientific
documentary style of the book makes it rather heavy going, its impact on everything from the foundations of psychoanalytic theory
to the women's rights movement makes Human Sexual Response essential reading.

581   NEWTON, NILES. Maternal Emotions: A Study of Women's Feelings
       toward Menstruation, Pregnancy, Childbirth, Breast Feeding,
       Infant Care, and Other Aspects of Their Femininity. New York:
       Paul B. Hoeber, 1955. 140 pp.
            Newton set out to answer the question "Are women's feelings
       toward sexual intercourse, menstruation, pregnancy, childbirth,
       breast feeding, and infant care related to each other?" Using
       literature in these fields and interviews with mothers in a
       Philadelphia maternity ward, she concludes that all these areas
       are interrelated aspects of women's sexuality: "Women's experiences
       in sexual intercourse are related to their feeling and experiences
       in the realm of menstruation, pregnancy, childbirth, breast feeding,
       and motherhood." Other conclusions were reached about sex and gen-
       der roles: "The most culturally feminine women almost always showed
       deep feelings of inferiority by saying they wished to be men; the
       least culturally feminine women very seldom felt so inferior that
       they said they wished to be men." Newton's work is significant
       because it attempts to define a distinctive psychology of woman.
       One wonders, however, whether a different group of respondents--a
       nonmother female population--might have yielded significantly dif-
       ferent conclusions.

582   O'NEILL, MARION VERONICA. Hysterical Personality: An Empirical
       Investigation of a Sexual Approach-Avoidance Conflict. Ph.D.
       dissertation, Emory University, 1967. 79+ pp.
            O'Neill's thesis is that the observed behavior characteristics
       of hysterical women (as personality types) are the result of a con-
       flict concerning sexual motives and feminine identity. According
       to this thesis, hysterical women engage in sexually provocative
       behavior, but then avoid the sexual act itself. O'Neill selected
       her test subjects from a pool of 150 undergraduate female students.
       She concludes: "Under sexually seductive conditions the hysteric
       avoids sexual stimuli and denies their relevance to herself. Under
       relatively neutral conditions she is attentive to sexual stimuli
       and maximizes the sexual implications of her surroundings."
       O'Neill's study, though not without flaws, suggests a possible
       approach to the study of hysteria in the nineteenth century.

583   The Personnel and Guidance Journal 54, no. 7 (March 1976).
       Special issue on the counselor and human sexuality.
            Only one article in this special issue--"Group Process for
       Women with Orgasmic Difficulties" by Lonnie Garfield Barbach and
       Toni Ayres--relates specifically to women. The other articles,
       however, do generally provide a nonsexist approach to their themes

(such topics as literature and resources and human sexuality and the handicapped) and are useful for assessing the attitudes of the personnel and guidance field in this area. One disappointment, however, is "The Homosexual and Counseling," which, although well intentioned, is noticeably lacking in relevant references to problems and resources relating specifically to lesbians.

584   SCULLY, DIANA, and PAULINE BART. "A Funny Thing Happened on the Way to the Orifice: Women in Gynecology Textbooks." American Journal of Sociology 78, no. 4 (January 1973):1045-50.
      Scully and Bart analyze twenty-seven general gynecology texts published in the United States since 1943, with particular emphasis on their presentation of female sexuality. The authors conclude that throughout the period texts actively perpetuated traditional, inaccurate views of female sexuality and generally failed to incorporate new findings of such sex researchers as Kinsey and Masters and Johnson.

585   SEX INFORMATION AND EDUCATION COUNCIL OF THE UNITED STATES, ed. Sexuality and Man. New York: Charles Scribner's Sons, 1970. 239 pp.
      Originally published as a series of individual SIECUS study guides, Sexuality and Man was reviewed and approved by the entire SIECUS Board of Directors. Its eleven chapters cover such topics as premarital sexual standards, sexual relations during pregnancy and the postdelivery period, and sex education and moral values. Several chapters were prepared by Isadore Rubin; other authors include Wardell Pomeroy and John Gagnon. In addition to the essays, there are a list of film resources for sex education, reference notes, and a bibliography.

586   VINCENT, CLARK E., ed. Human Sexuality in Medical Education and Practice. Springfield, Ill.: Charles C. Thomas, 1968. 595 pp.
      Designed to be used as a text in human sexuality courses in medical schools, Human Sexuality in Medical Education and Practice is an outgrowth of three training institutes held at Bowman Gray School of Medicine, Wake Forest University, in 1966 and 1967. Most of the chapters, each of which was prepared by a different author, integrate material on both men and women, although there are only two women authors, each writing jointly with a male. Some of the material is reprinted from other sources, including several SIECUS Discussion Guides.

587   WEISSKOPF, SUSAN CONTRATTO. "Maternal Sexuality and Asexual Motherhood." Signs 5, no. 4 (Summer 1980):766-82.
      Weisskopf reviews recent literature on maternal sexuality-- "a woman's sexual feelings or behaviors while she is involved in tasks normally associated with motherhood"--and asexual motherhood, the cultural belief (and consequent prescription for behavior and feelings) that "mothers are not, and should not be sexual persons."

Materials surveyed include professional as well as popular medical, psychological, and sociological works.

588   ADAMS, DAVID B., ALICE ROSS GOLD, and ANNE D. BURT. "Rise in Female-initiated Sexual Activity at Ovulation and Its Suppression by Oral Contraceptives." New England Journal of Medicine 299, no. 21 (23 November 1978):1145-50.

589   ADDIEGO, FRANK, et al. "Female Ejaculation: A Case Study." Journal of Sex Research 17, no. 1 (February 1981):13-21.

590   AVERY, WANDA, CAROLYN GARDNER, and SUZANNE PALMER. "Vulvectomy." American Journal of Nursing 74, no. 3 (March 1974):453-55.

591   BARON, RBOERT A. "Heightened Sexual Arousal and Physical Aggression: An Extension to Females." Journal of Research in Personality 13, no. 1 (March 1979):91-102.

592   BELL, ROBERT R. "Sex as a Weapon and Changing Social Roles." Medical Aspects of Human Sexuality 4, no. 6 (June 1970):99-111.

593   BELZER, EDWIN G., Jr. "Orgasmic Expulsions of Women: A Review and Heuristic Inquiry." Journal of Sex Research 17, no. 1 (February 1981):1-12.

594   BENTLER, P.M., and WILLIAM H. PEELER. "Models of Female Orgasm." Archives of Sexual Behavior 8, no. 5 (September 1979):405-24.

595   BERNARD, JESSIE. "Sex in Remarriage." Medical Aspects of Human Sexuality 2, no. 10 (October 1968):54-61.

596   BERNSTEIN, ISIDOR. "The Female Orgasm--A Panel Discussion." Journal of the Hillside Hospital 17, no. 1 (January 1968):44-49.

597   BILLER, HENRY B. "Fathering and Female Sexual Development." Medical Aspects of Human Sexuality 5, no. 11 (November 1971): 126-38.

598   BLUM, LUCILLE HOLLANDER. "Darkness in an Enlightened Era: Women's Drawings of Their Sexual Organs." Psychological Reports 42, no. 3, pt. 1 (June 1978):867-73.

599   BLUMSTEIN, PHILIP, and PEPPER SCHWARTZ. "Bisexuality in Women." Archives of Sexual Behavior 5, no. 2 (March 1976):171-81.

600   BYRD, BENJAMIN. "Brief Guide to Office Counseling: Sex after Mastectomy." Medical Aspects of Human Sexuality 9, no. 4 (April 1975):53-54.

601   CARNS, DONALD E. "Talking about Sex: Notes on First Coitus

and the Double Sexual Standard." Journal of Marriage and the Family 35, no. 4 (November 1973):677–88.

602   CAVANAUGH, JOHN. "Rhythm of Sexual Desire in Women." Medical Aspects of Human Sexuality 3, no. 2 (February 1969):29–39.

603   CHEZ, RONALD A. "Obtaining the Sexual History in the Female Patient." GP (Kansas City, Missouri) 30, no. 4 (October 1964): 120–24.

604   CHILMAN, CATHERINE S. "Some Psychosocial Aspects of Female Sexuality." Family Coordinator 23, no. 2 (April 1974):123–31.

605   "Circumcision of Women." Sexology 1, no. 2 (October 1933):82–84.

606   CLARK, Le MON. "Is There a Difference between a Clitoral and a Vaginal Orgasm?" Journal of Sex Research 6, no. 1 (February 1970):25–28.

607   CLAVAN, SYLVIA. "Changing Female Sexual Behavior and Future Family Structure." Pacific Sociological Review 15, no. 3 (July 1972):295–308.

608   COLEMAN, JAMES. "Female Status and Premarital Sexual Codes." American Journal of Sociology 72, no. 2 (September 1966):217.

609   COLMEIRO–La FORET, CARLOS. "Pregnancy in Virgins." International Journal of Sexology 5, no. 1 (August 1951):7–9.

610   CONSTANTINE, LARRY L., and JOAN M. CONSTANTINE. "Sexual Aspects of Multilateral Relations." Journal of Sex Research 7, no. 3 (August 1971):204–25.

611   DALY, MICHAEL JOSEPH. "The Clitoris as Related to Human Sexuality." Medical Aspects of Human Sexuality 5, no. 2 (February 1971):80–97.

612   DEARBORN, GEORGE VAN NESS. "The Two-love Question; an Example of Unconscious Erotic Symbolism." Journal of Abnormal Psychology 22, no. 1 (April–June 1927):62–88.

613   DENBER, HERMAN C.B. "The Use of Sexuality to Externalize Inner Conflict." Medical Aspects of Human Sexuality 7, no. 9 (September 1973):44–60.

614   DEVEREUX, GEORGE. "The Female Castration Complex and Its Repercussions in Modesty, Appearance and Courtship Etiquette." American Imago 17, no. 1 (Spring 1960):3–19.

615   DICKINSON, ROBERT LATOU. "Premarital Examination as Routine Preventive Gynecology." Transactions of the American Gynecological Society 53 (1928):51–66.

616   DMOWSKI, W. PAUL, MANUEL LUNA, and ANTONIO SCOMMEGNA.   "Hormonal
      Aspects of Female Sexual Response." Medical Aspects of Human
      Sexuality 8, no. 6 (June 1974):92-113.

617   DRELLICH, MARVIN G. "Sex after Hysterectomy." Medical Aspects
      of Human Sexuality 1, no. 3 (November 1967):62-64.

618   DRELLICH, MARVIN G., and IRVING BIEBER. "The Psychological
      Importance of the Uterus and Its Functions." Journal of Nervous
      and Mental Disease 126, no. 4 (April 1958):322-36.

619   DUENHOETTER, JOHANN H. "Quiz: Sex and Pregnancy." Medical
      Aspects of Human Sexuality 12, no. 5 (May 1978):45-50.

620   EASTMAN, WILLIAM F., et al. "Sexual Problems and Personality
      Adjustment of College Women." Journal of the American College
      Health Association 18, no. 2 (18 December 1969):144-47.

621   ELKAN, EDWARD. "Evolution of Female Orgastic Ability--A
      Biological Survey." International Journal of Sexology 2, no. 1
      (August 1948):1-13; no. 2 (November 1948):84-93.

622   ELLIS, ALBERT. "Female Sexual Response and Marital Relations."
      Social Problems 1, no. 4 (April 1954):152-55.

623   EVERETT, HENRY COFFIN. "Competition in Bed." Medical Aspects
      of Human Sexuality 5, no. 4 (April 1971):10-22.

624   FALICOV, CELIA J. "Sexual Adjustment during First Pregnancy
      and Post Partum." American Journal of Obstetrics and Gynecology
      117, no. 7 (1 December 1973):991-1000.

625   FELLER, WILLIAM, and WARNER C. HALL. "Castration in the Female."
      Medical Aspects of Human Sexuality 3, no. 3 (March 1969):31-42.

626   "Female Orgasm: An Interview with Seymour Fisher, Ph.D."
      Medical Aspects of Human Sexuality 7, no. 4 (April 1973):76-91.

627   FILLER, WILLIAM, and NATHAN DREZNER. "The Results of Surgical
      Castration in Women under Forty." American Journal of Obstetrics
      and Gynecology 47, no. 1 (January 1944):122-24.

628   FISHER, SEYMOUR, and HOWARD J. OSOFSKY. "Sexual Responsiveness
      in Women; Psychological Correlates." Archives of General
      Psychiatry 17, no. 2 (August 1967):214-26.

629   FISHER, WILLIAM A., and DONN BYRNE. "Sex Differences in
      Response to Erotica? Love Versus Lust." Journal of Personality
      and Social Psychology 36, no. 2 (February 1978):117-25.

630   FREEMAN, HARROP A., and RUTH S. FREEMAN. "Senior College Women:

Their Sexual Standards and Activity, Part 1, To Whom Does the College Woman Turn for Sex Counseling?" Journal of the National Association of Women Deans and Counselors 29, no. 2 (Winter 1966): 59-64.

631   FRY, WILLIAM. "Psycho-dynamics of Sexual Humor: Women's View of Sex." Medical Aspects of Human Sexuality 6, no. 4 (April 1972):124-39.

632   GARTMAN, LEO. "Divorce and Sexuality." American Journal of Urology and Sexology 16, no. 4 (October 1920):163-85.

633   GEBHARD, PAUL H. "Factors in Marital Orgasm." Journal of Social Issues 22, no. 2 (April 1966):88-95.

634   GILLESPIE, W.H. "Concepts of Vaginal Orgasm." International Journal of Psycho-analysis 50, no. 4 (October 1969):495-97.

635   GINSBERG, GEORGE L. "Effects on Men of Increased Sexual Freedom for Women." Medical Aspects of Human Sexuality 7, no. 2 (February 1973):66-89.

636   GOLDEN, JOSHUA S. "Sexual Problems of Beautiful Women." Sexual Behavior 1, no. 1 (April 1971):73-78.

637   GOODLIN, ROBERT C., DAVID W. KELLER, and MARGARET RAFFIN. "Orgasm during Late Pregnancy: Possible Deleterious Effects." Obstetrics and Gynecology 38, no. 6 (December 1971):916-20.

638   GRABER, BENJAMIN, and GEORGIA KLINE-GRABER. "Clitoral Foreskin Adhesions and Female Sexual Function." Journal of Sex Research 15, no. 3 (August 1979):205-12.

639   GRAFENBERG, ERNEST. "The Role of the Urethra in Female Orgasm." International Journal of Sexology 3, no. 3 (February 1950):145-48.

640   GRANT, IGOR. "Anxiety about Orgasm." Medical Aspects of Human Sexuality 6, no. 3 (March 1972):14-46.

641   GREENBLATT, ROBERT B., FRANK MORTARA, and RICHARD TORPIN. "Sexual Libido in the Female." American Journal of Obstetrics and Gynecology 44, no. 4 (October 1942):658-63.

642   GREENWALD, HAROLD. "Fashion Models and Sex." Medical Aspects of Human Sexuality 4, no. 6 (June 1970):83-95.

643   HAFT, JAY STUART, H.B. BENJAMIN, and WALTER ZEIT. "Foreign Bodies in the Female Genitourinary Tract: Some Psychosexual Aspects." Medical Aspects of Human Sexuality 8, no. 10 (October 1974):54-78.

644 HAMBLIN, ROBERT L., and ROBERT O. BLOOD. "Pre-marital Experience and the Wife's Sexual Adjustment." Social Problems 4, no. 2 (October 1956):122-30.

645 HARDENBERGH, E.W. "The Psychology of Feminine Sex Experience." International Journal of Sexology 2, no. 4 (May 1949):224-28.

646 HATHAWAY, BRUCE. "Female Orgasm Research Challenges Traditional Views." Psychiatric News 17, no. 12 (18 June 1982):34+.

647 _____. "Female Orgasm Studies Challenge Older Views." Psychiatric News 17, no. 10 (4 June 1982):22+.

648 HAYWARD, EMELINE P. "Types of Female Castration Reaction." Psychoanalytic Quarterly 12, no. 1 (1943):45-66.

649 HEIMAN, JULIA R. "Women's Sexual Arousal." Psychology Today 8, no. 11 (April 1975):91-94.

650 HOLLENDER, MARC H. "Hysterectomy and Feelings of Femininity." Medical Aspects of Human Sexuality 3, no. 7 (July 1969):6-18.

651 _____. "Women's Wish to Be Held: Sexual and Nonsexual Aspects." Medical Aspects of Human Sexuality 5, no. 10 (October 1971):12-26.

652 HOLLENDER, MARC H., LESTER LUBORSKY, and ROBERTA B. HARVEY. "Correlates of the Desire to Be Held in Women." Journal of Psychosomatic Research 14, no. 4 (Decmeber 1970):387-90.

653 HOON, EMILY FRANCK, and PETER W. HOON. "Styles of Sexual Expression in Women: Clinical Implications of Multivariate Analyses." Archives of Sexual Behavior 7, no. 2 (March 1978):105-16.

654 HUFFMAN, JOHN W. "Sex after Hysterectomy." Sexual Behavior 3, no. 2 (February 1973):42-43.

655 HYAMS, LEONARD L. "The Vagina: Abnormalities, Functional Aspects, and Size." Medical Aspects of Human Sexuality 7, no. 1 (January 1973):116-33.

656 IAMS, FRANK J. "Female Circumcision." Medical Record and Annals 31, no. 4 (April 1937):171-73.

657 "An Interview with Masters and Johnson on Human Sexual Inadequacy." Medical Aspects of Human Sexuality 4, no. 7 (July 1970):21-45.

658 JAYNE, CYNTHIA. "A Two Dimensional Model of Female Sexual Response." Journal of Sex and Marital Therapy 7, no. 1 (Spring 1981):3-30.

659   JONES, J. DAVID, and ILA H. GEHMAN. "The Taboo of Virginity: Resistances of Male Therapists and Early Adolescent Girl Patients in Treatment." Journal of the American Academy of Child Psychiatry 10, no. 2 (April 1971):351-57.

660   KANE, FRANCIS J., MORRIS A. LIPTON, and JOHN A. EWING. "Hormonal Influences in Female Sexual Response." Archives of General Psychiatry 20, no. 2 (February 1969):202-9.

661   KANIN, EUGENE J., KAREN R. DAVIDSON, and SONIA R. SCHECK. "A Research Note on Male-Female Differentials in the Experience of Heterosexual Love." Journal of Sex Research 6, no. 1 (February 1970):64-72.

662   KAPLAN, L. "Parent-eroticism." Journal of Sexology and Psychanalysis 2, no. 6 (November-December 1924):577-84.

663   KARPF, MAURICE J. "Counseling with the Unmarried Woman--the Singleton, the Widow and the Divorcee." International Journal of Sexology 8, no. 4 (May 1955):209-13.

664   KEGEL, ARNOLD H. "Sexual Functions of the Pubococcygeus Muscle." Western Journal of Surgery, Obstetrics and Gynecology 60, no. 10 (October 1952):521-24.

665   KENNY, JAMES A. "Sexuality of Pregnant and Breast-feeding Women." Archives of Sexual Behavior 2, no. 3 (June 1973): 215-29.

666   KIERNAN, JAMES G. "Human Bisexuality." Urologic and Cutaneous Review 27, no. 2 (February 1923):75-82.

667   KOLIN, IRVING S., JAMES L. BAKER, Jr., and EDMUND S. BARTLETT. "Psychosexual Aspects of Mammary Augmentation." Medical Aspects of Human Sexuality 8, no. 12 (December 1974):88-100.

668   KOLODNY, ROBERT C. "Observations on the New Masters and Johnson Report." Medical Aspects of Human Sexuality 4, no. 7 (July 1970):47-60.

669   KRAFT, THOMAS. "Sexual Factors in the Development of the Housebound Housewife Syndrome." Journal of Sex Research 6, no. 1 (February 1970):59-63.

670   KRAUSE, CHARLOTTE. "The Femininity Complex and Women Therapists." Journal of Marriage and the Family 33, no. 3 (August 1971):476-82.

671   KUTNER, NANCY G., and DONNA BROGAN. "An Investigation of Sex-related Slang Vocabulary and Sex-role Orientation among Male and Female University Students." Journal of Marriage and the Family 36, no. 3 (August 1974):474-84.

672   LANE, MARY E. "Brief Guide to Office Counseling: Sex during Menstruation." Medical Aspects of Human Sexuality 8, no. 10 (October 1974):143-44.

673   LANGMYHR, GEORGE. "Brief Guide to Office Counseling: Clitoral Stimulation: Do's and Don'ts." Medical Aspects of Human Sexuality 9, no. 8 (August 1975):51-52.

674   LLEWELLYN, CHARLES E., Jr. "Sex Demands Which Cause Marital Conflict." Medical Aspects of Human Sexuality 7, no. 8 (August 1973):125-47.

675   LUSCHEN, MARY E., and DAVID M. PIERCE. "Effect of the Menstrual Cycle on Mood and Sexual Arousability." Journal of Sex Research 8, no. 1 (February 1972):41-47.

676   McCAHEY, JAMES F., and ANDREW J. RAMSAY. "Virilism and Female Pseudohermaphroditism with Relation to the Bisexual Nature of the Ovary." American Journal of Obstetrics and Gynecology 36, no. 1 (July 1938):108-15.

677   McCAULEY, ELIZABETH A., and ANKE A. EHRHARDT. "Female Sexual Response." In Psychosomatic Obstetrics and Gynecology, edited by David D. Youngs and Anke A. Ehrhardt, 39-66. New York: Appleton-Century-Crofts, 1980.

678   MACOMBER, DONALD. "The Emotional Life of Woman in Relation to the Practice of Gynecology." American Journal of Obstetrics and Gynecology 13, no. 6 (June 1927):732-41; 804-6.

679   MALLESON, JOAN. "Sex Problems in Marriage." Practitioner 172, no. 1030 (April 1954):389-96.

680   MALOY, BERNARD. "Insanity and the Shortness of Human Life Attributed to Ancient and Modern Sensuality." Illinois Medical Journal 49, no. 1 (January 1926):45-61.

681   MARBACK, A. HERBERT. "Sexual Problems and Gynecologic Illness." Medical Aspects of Human Sexuality 4, no. 12 (December 1970): 48-57.

682   MARCOTTE, DAVID B. "Quiz: Prevalent Misinformation about Male and Female Sexuality." Medical Aspects of Human Sexuality 12, no. 5 (May 1978):44-52.

683   MARMOR, JUDD. "Some Considerations Concerning Orgasm in the Female." Psychosomatic Medicine 16, no. 3 (May-June 1954): 240-45.

684   MARSHALL, SUMNER. "Cystitis and Urethritis in Women Related to Sexual Activity." Medical Aspects of Human Sexuality 8, no. 5 (May 1974):165-76.

685   MARTIN, CHARLES B., Jr., and EUGENE M. LONG, Jr. "Sex
      during the Menstrual Period." Medical Aspects of Human Sexuality
      3, no. 6 (June 1969):37-49.

686   MASLOW, ABRAHAM H. "Self-Esteem (Dominance-Feeling) and Sexu-
      ality in Women." Journal of Social Psychology 16, pt. 2
      (November 1942):259-94.

687   MATHIS, JAMES L. "The Sexual Tease." Medical Aspects of Human
      Sexuality 4, no. 12 (December 1970):21-25.

688   MEAD, BEVERLEY T. "Women's Complaints with Sexual Connotation."
      Medical Aspects of Human Sexuality 6, no. 4 (April 1972):12-27.

689   MELODY, GEORGE F. "Gynecologic Illness and Sexual Behavior."
      Medical Aspects of Human Sexuality 2, no. 10 (October 1968):
      6-11.

690   MENNINGER, KARL A. "Somatic Correlations with the Unconscious
      Repudiation of Femininity in Women." Journal of Nervous and
      Mental Disease 89, no. 4 (April 1939):514-27.

691   MEYERS, THOMAS J. "The Psychological Effects of Gynecic
      Surgery." Pacific Medicine and Surgery 73, no. 6 (November-
      December 1965):429-32.

692   MOLL, THEOPHILUS J. "Sexual Abnormalities as Factors in
      Divorce Cases." Medico-Legal Journal 40, no. 5 (September-
      October 1923):128-49; no. 6 (November-December 1923):151-70.

693   MORGENTHAU, JOAN E., and NATALIE J. SOKOLOFF. "The Sexual
      Revolution: Myth or Fact?" Pediatric Clinics of North America
      19, no. 3 (August 1972):779-89.

694   MOSHER, DONALD L., and IRENE GREENBERG. "Females' Affective
      Responses to Reading Erotic Literature." Journal of Consulting
      and Clinical Psychology 33, no. 4 (August 1969):472-77.

695   MOULTON, RUTH. "A Survey and Re-evaluation of the Concept of
      Penis-Envy." Contemporary Psychoanalysis 7, no. 1 (Fall 1970):
      84-104.

696   MUNJACK, DENNIS. "Reciprocity in Sexual Relations." Medical
      Aspects of Human Sexuality 8, no. 1 (January 1974):156-88.

697   NEWTON, NILES. "Trebly Sensuous Woman." Psychology Today 5,
      no. 2 (July 1971):68-71; 98-99.

698   OCHSNER, ALTON. "Influence of Smoking on Sexuality and Preg-
      nancy." Medical Aspects of Human Sexuality 5, no. 11 (November
      1971):78-92.

699   "Opinion: Is There Any Difference between 'Vaginal' and 'Clitoral' Orgasm?" Sexual Behavior 2, no. 3 (March 1972): 41-45.

700   "Opinion: Should Women Ever Pretend to Climax?" Sexual Behavior 1, no. 1 (April 1971):11-13.

701   OVESEY, LIONEL. "Masculine Aspirations in Women." Psychiatry 19, no. 4 (November 1956):341-51.

702   PARSHLEY, H.M. "Sexual Abstinence as a Biological Question; Is Sexual Intercourse a Physiological Necessity?" Sexology 1, no. 1 (Summer 1933):31-36.

703   PERRY, JOHN DELBERT, and BEVERLY WHIPPLE. "Pelvic Muscle Strength of Female Ejaculators: Evidence in Support of a New Theory of Orgasm." Journal of Sex Research 17, no. 1 (February 1981):22-39.

704   PHILIPP, ELLIOT. "Hairy Women, Manly Women and the Stein-Leventhal Problem." British Journal of Sexual Medicine 1, no. 8 (November-December 1974):12-17.

705   PINES, M. "Human Sexual Response--A Discussion of the Work of Masters and Johnson." Journal of Psychosomatic Research 12, no. 1 (June 1968):39-49.

706   PODOLSKY, EDWARD. "The Influence of Olfactory Perceptions on Sexual Activity." Journal of Sexology and Psychanalysis 1, no. 3 (May 1923):303-4.

707   RABOCH, JAN, VLAD BARTAK, and KAREL NEDOMA. "Types of Sexual Reactivity in Gynecological Patients." Journal of Sex Research 4, no. 4 (November 1968):282-87.

708   RASKIN, DAVID E., and KATHLEEN A. SULLIVAN. "Erotomania." American Journal of Psychiatry 131, no. 9 (September 1974): 1033-35.

709   RAY, ROSE E., and WILLIAM D. THOMPSON. "Autonomic Correlates of Female Guilt Responses to Erotic Visual Stimuli." Psychological Reports 34, no. 3, pt. 2 (June 1974):1299-1306.

710   REICH, WILHELM. "The Function of the Orgasm (Psychopathology and Sociology of Sex Life)." Archives of Psychoanalysis 1, pt. 4 (July 1927):1141-1218.

711   ROBERTIELLO, RICHARD C. "Masochism and the Female Sexual Role." Journal of Sex Research 6, no. 1 (February 1970):56-58.

712   ROBERTIELLO, RICHARD C., and RENA M. SHADMI. "An Important Set

of Dynamics in Female Sexual Problems." Journal of Contemporary Psychotherapy 1, no. 1 (Fall 1968):19-25.

713 ROSANOFF, AARON J. "Human Sexuality, Normal and Abnormal, from a Psychiatric Standpoint." Urologic and Cutaneous Review 33, no. 8 (August 1929):523-30.

714 ROSENBAUM, SALO. "Pretended Orgasm." Medical Aspects of Human Sexuality 4, no. 4 (April 1970):84-96.

715 ROTHMAN, DAVID. "Habitual Abortion and Sexual Conflict." Medical Aspects of Human Sexuality 7, no. 7 (July 1973):56-69.

716 "Roundtable: Female Orgasm." Medical Aspects of Human Sexuality 2, no. 4 (April 1968):37-47.

717 "Roundtable: Foreplay." Medical Aspects of Human Sexuality 2, no. 6 (June 1968):6-13.

718 "Roundtable: Foreplay." Medical Aspects of Human Sexuality 5, no. 7 (July 1971):60-81.

719 "Roundtable: Is There a Relationship between a Woman's Physical Appearance and Her Sexual Behavior?" Medical Aspects of Human Sexuality 4, no. 10 (October 1970):8-23.

720 RUBIN, ZICK. "Measurement of Romantic Love." Journal of Personality and Social Psychology 16, no. 2 (October 1970): 265-73.

721 RUTGERS, JOHANNES. "Sexual Continence with Special Reference to Sexual Continence in Women." Journal of Sexology and Psychanalysis 1, no. 3 (May 1923):266-73.

722 SALZMAN, LEON. "Family Infidelity." Medical Aspects of Human Sexuality 6, no. 2 (February 1972):118-36.

723 _____. "Psychiatric and Clinical Aspects of Infidelity." In The Dynamics of Work and Marriage; Scientific Proceedings, edited by Jules H. Masserman, 127-39. Science and Psychoanalysis, no. 16. New York: Grune & Stratton, 1970.

724 SCHON, MARTHA. "The Meaning of Death and Sex to Cancer Patients." Journal of Sex Research 4, no. 4 (November 1968):288-302.

725 SCHUCKIT, MARC A. "Sexual Disturbance in the Woman Alcoholic." Medical Aspects of Human Sexuality 6, no. 9 (September 1972): 44-65.

726 SEDGWICK, RAE. "Myths in Human Sexuality: A Social-Psychological Perspective." Nursing Clinics of North America 10, no. 3 (September 1975):539-50.

727   SEIDENBERG, ROBERT. "Psychosexual Adjustment of the Unattractive Woman." Medical Aspects of Human Sexuality 7, no. 5 (May 1973): 60-81.

728   SEVELY, J. LOWNDES, and J.W. BENNETT. "Concerning Female Ejaculation and the Female Prostate." Journal of Sex Research 14, no. 1 (February 1978):1-20.

729   SHADER, RICHARD I., and JANE I. OHLY. "Premenstrual Tension, Femininity, and Sexual Drive." Medical Aspects of Human Sexuality 4, no. 4 (April 1970):42-49.

730   SHAINESS, NATALIE. "The Problem of Sex Today." American Journal of Psychiatry 124, no. 8 (February 1968):1076-84.

731   _____. "Sexual Problems of Women." Journal of Sex and Marital Therapy 1, no. 2 (Winter 1974):110-23.

732   _____. "Vulnerability to Violence: Masochism as Process." American Journal of Psychotherapy 33, no. 2 (April 1979):174-89.

733   SHERMAN, JULIA A. "What Men Do Not Know about Women's Sexuality." Medical Aspects of Human Sexuality 6, no. 11 (November 1972):138-53.

734   SINGER, JOSEPHINE, and IRVING SINGER. "Types of Female Orgasm." Journal of Sex Research 8, no. 4 (November 1972):255-67.

735   STANLEY, ELIZABETH. "Perspectives on the Need for Continuity of Physical Stimulation in Female Sexual Arousal." Medical Aspects of Human Sexuality 8, no. 2 (February 1974):98-133.

736   STERN, ADOLPH. "Clinical Manifestations of Female Sexual Deviations." Archives of Neurology and Psychiatry 32, no. 4 (October 1934):879.

737   STOPES, MARIE CHARLOTTE CARMICHAEL. "Coital Interlocking; a Physiologic Discovery." Clinical Medicine and Surgery 38, no. 3 (March 1931):179-80.

738   TANNENBAUM, SAMUEL A. "Orgasm in the Female." Journal of Sexology and Psychanalysis 2, no. 1 (January 1924):31-36.

739   _____. "Psychanalytic Sketches, No. 4." Journal of Sexology and Psychanalysis 2, no. 3 (May 1924):286-90.

740   TUNNADINE, PRUDENCE. "Psychological Aspects of the Vaginal Examination." Medical Aspects of Human Sexuality 7, no. 4 (April 1973):116-38.

741   TWOMBLY, GRAY H. "Sex after Radical Gynecological Surgery." Journal of Sex Research 4, no. 4 (November 1968):275-81.

742   VALENTINE, JOHN, and JOHN PAUL BRADY. "Interview: Female
       Sexual Responsiveness." Medical Aspects of Human Sexuality 8,
       no. 9 (September 1974):117-25.

743   VERKAUF, BARRY STEPHEN. "Acquired Clitoral Enlargement."
       Medical Aspects of Human Sexuality 9, no. 4 (April 1975):134-45;
       151.

744   "Viewpoints: Can One Tell if a Woman Has an Orgasm?" Medical
       Aspects of Human Sexuality 4, no. 8 (August 1970):91-101.

745   "Viewpoints: Can Women Enjoy Sex without Orgasm?" Medical
       Aspects of Human Sexuality 7, no. 1 (January 1973):102-14.

746   "Viewpoints: How Do You Advise the Man Who Is Overly Concerned
       about the Female Orgasm?" Medical Aspects of Human Sexuality 7,
       no. 3 (March 1973):12-20.

747   "Viewpoints: Should a Woman Pretend to Reach Orgasm to Please
       Her Husband?" Medical Aspects of Human Sexuality 8, no. 2
       (February 1974):7-26.

748   "Viewpoints: What Are the Effects of Premarital Sex on the
       Marital Relationship?" Medical Aspects of Human Sexuality 7,
       no. 4 (April 1973):143-67.

749   "Viewpoints: What Is the Basis for the Distinction Many
       Patients Make between Vaginal and Clitoral Orgasms?" Medical
       Aspects of Human Sexuality 7, no. 11 (November 1973):84-103.

750   WAGNER, NATHANIEL N., and DON A. SOLBERG. "Pregnancy and
       Sexuality." Medical Aspects of Human Sexuality 8, no. 3 (March
       1974):44-79.

751   WALL, JAMES H. "Significant Factors in the Readjustment of
       Women Patients with Masculine Tendencies." Psychiatric Quarterly
       14, no. 3 (July 1940):504-12.

752   WALLIN, PAUL. "A Study of Orgasm as a Condition of Women's
       Enjoyment of Intercourse." Journal of Social Psychology 51
       (February 1960):191-98.

753   WEINER, MYRON F. "Wives Who Refuse Their Husbands."
       Psychosomatics 14, no. 5 (September-October 1973):277-82.

754   WELLS, W. FRANK. "A Plastic Operation for Congenital Absence
       of Vagina." American Journal of Surgery 29, no. 2 (August
       1935):253-55.

755   WHATHAM, ARTHUR E. "Eroticism in Women." Medical Life 28, no.
       4 (April 1921):179-87.

756   WILE, IRA S. "The Psychology of the Hymen." Journal of Nervous and Mental Disease 85, no. 2 (February 1937):143-56.

757   WILSON, FITZPATRICK, and DONALD P. SWARTZ. "Coital Injuries of the Vagina." Obstetrics and Gynecology 39, no. 2 (February 1972):182-84.

758   WINCZE, JOHN P., PETER HOON, and EMILY FRANCK HOON. "Sexual Arousal in Women: A Comparison of Cognitive and Physiological Responses by Continuous Measurement." Archives of Sexual Behavior 6, no. 2 (March 1977):121-34.

759   WINOKUR, GEORGE, SAMUEL B. GUZE, and ERIC PFEIFFER. "Nocturnal Orgasm in Women." American Medical Association Archives of General Psychiatry 1, no. 2 (August 1959):180-84.

760   WOLLMAN, LEO. "Female Circumcision." Journal of the American Society of Psychosomatic Dentistry and Medicine 20, no. 4 (1973):130-31.

761   _____. "Hooded Clitoris: Preliminary Report." Journal of the American Society of Psychosomatic Dentistry and Medicine 20, no. 1 (1973):3-4.

762   WOODWARD, CHARLES. "The Degeneration of the Human Race from the Excessive Practice of the Social Evil and Other Causes, and Its Control by a Verified Method." North American Journal of Homeopathy 70, no. 5 (May 1922):403-6.

763   WRIGHT, THEW. "Congenital Absence of Vagina, Accompanied by Marked Nervous Symptoms; Baldwin's Operation and Removal of Ovarian Tissue." American Journal of Surgery 36, no. 5 (May 1922):114-15.

764   ZAVITZIANOS, GEORGE. "Fetishism and Exhibitionism in the Female and Their Relationship to Psychopathy and Kleptomania." International Journal of Psycho-analysis 52, pt. 3 (1971): 297-305.

765   ZUSSMAN, SHIRLEY, and LEON ZUSSMAN. "Brief Guide to Office Counseling: Keys to Understanding Female Sexuality." Medical Aspects of Human Sexuality 8, no. 8 (August 1974):125-26.

Prescriptive Literature before 1920

Written for popular audiences, prescriptive literature can tell
its readers much about attitudes toward women's sexuality during a
given period. What it cannot indicate, of course, when examined outside of its total historical context, is whether its authors were reflecting primarily their own individual points of view or whether their
opinions and conclusions reflected dominant social mores and behavior
of the time. More importantly, what effect, if any, did they have on
the behavior of their readers? How many women, for example, even tried
to follow Eliza B. Duffey's recommendation of once monthly coital frequency (entry 780) or Martin L. Holbrook's call for sexual abstinence
during pregnancy and lactation (entry 797, 798)?

Beginning with such early works as Aristotle's <u>Masterpiece</u> (entry
767) and proceeding up to such twentieth-century products as William
Josephus Robinson's <u>Woman: Her Sex and Love Life</u> (entry 832), prescriptive literature is characterized by a variety of viewpoints, as well
as a frequent lack of attention to scientific fact. George W. Savory,
for example, recommended "the sexual gymnastics of the Egyptian dancing
girls" as a means to health, while Alice Stockham advocated reading
works by Browning and Emerson prior to coitus. Plagiarism was not uncommon, and some authors, clearly motivated by commercial gain, issued
the same work at different times under different titles. Authors or
firms they controlled often published their own works, selling them
through the mails and using them to advertise products and services
ranging from sexual counseling to patent medicine and, of course, other
advice books. Many books provided general advice on such topics as
maternal health and infant care, whereas others focused more specifically on such sex-related questions as chastity, gynecological disorders,
or venereal disease.

Prescriptive literature could also serve broader purposes of social
reform. Some writers, such as Henry C. Wright (entry 852), used their
work to call for woman's control of sexual relations; others, such as
the Fowler brothers (entries 786-789), connected sexual behavior to
broader philosophical questions, in their case, the "science" of
phrenology. John Humphrey Noyes (entry 822) claimed that male continence not only heightened women's sexual pleasure, but led its

145

practitioners along the road to spiritual perfection.

Throughout the nineteenth century, women began, in increasing numbers, to prescribe for their own sex. Yet most of the literature directed toward women continued to be written by men, often reflecting their own goals of domination and control of women's sexual expression. Such a pattern, one must observe, has persisted to the present day.

766   ALCOTT, WILLIAM A. The Physiology of Marriage. Boston: J.P.
      Jewett, 1856. 259 pp.
          Although The Physiology of Marriage was addressed primarily
      to a male audience, Alcott included frequent references to women's
      sexuality. "Woman, I say, is naturally and constitutionally pure,"
      but Alcott feared that she could be easily perverted or seduced
      by those who would teach her to masturbate or who would procure
      her for a life of prostitution. Alcott especially feared masturba-
      tion, arguing that in women it was more dangerous than bearing and
      raising children and would cut years off a woman's life. Other
      taboos included intercourse at night, a frequency of more than once
      a month, and sexual relations after childbirth until the child had
      acquired its first teeth. Because women were not supposed to feel
      sexual desire, such controls imposed a greater need for self-
      control on men than on women. Sex education and diet reform (pic-
      kled and preserved meats were especially suspect) were Alcott's
      primary means for achieving his own particular brand of sexual re-
      form.

767   ARISTOTLE [pseud.]. The Works of Aristotle, the Famous
      Philosopher. New England [sic]: Printed for the Proprietor,
      1813. 264 pp.
          According to Charles Rosenberg and Carroll Smith-Rosenberg,
      editors of the Arno Press reprint series "Sex, Marriage and Society"
      [1974], which includes this particular edition, Aristotle's
      Masterpiece was the most widely read popular medical book in
      America prior to the mid-nineteenth century. Originally written
      in the late seventeenth century, it went through many editions,
      variations, and reprintings, each a mixture of folklore and would-
      be scientific thought. A typical passage describes the clitoris:
      "The next thing is the clitoris, which is a sinewy and hard part
      of the womb, replete with spongy and black matter within, in the
      same manner as the side ligaments of the yard suffers erection
      and falling in the same manner, and both stirs up lust and gives
      delight in copulation, for without this, the fair sex neither de-
      sire nuptial embraces nor have pleasure in them, nor conceive by
      them; and according to the greatness or smallness of this part,
      they are more or less fond of men's embraces; so that it may
      properly be styled the seat of lust."
          In addition to the Masterpiece, which deals most directly
      with questions of sexuality, other sections of the Works relate
      to midwifery, sterility, and various questions and answers about

life and the natural world: "How comes women's bodies to be
looser, softer, and their veins lesser than men's: And why do
they want hair? By reason of their menses: for with them their
superfluities, which would produce hair, go away; and where the
flesh is filled, consequently their veins are more hid than men's."

768   AUSTIN, GEORGE LOWELL. Perils of American Women or a Doctor's
       Talk with Maiden, Wife and Mother. Boston: Lee and Shepard,
       1883. 240 pp.
            Reprinted in 1907 as A Doctor's Talk with Maiden, Wife, and
       Mother, this work is a basic sex and marriage manual which dis-
       cusses all aspects of woman's reproductive life. Austin was not
       especially original in his ideas on female sexuality, most of which
       are included in the chapter entitled "The Hygiene of the Marriage
       Bed." His opposition to birth control, abortion, and sexual excess
       was unequivocal, and he informed his readers that the latter would
       lead to "leucorrhea, hemorrhages, ulceration of the neck of the
       uterus, polypi, or uterine cancer, nymphomania, frequent miscar-
       riages, and barrenness." He did not, however, deny an active
       sexuality for women, noting that the clitoris was "usually regarded
       as the seat of voluptuous sensations" and affirming that post-
       menopausal women could still experience sexual pleasure. Some of
       his other ideas--that semen fecundates a woman's body as well as
       the ovum and that 50 percent of all miscarriages are caused by
       intercourse during pregnancy--are somewhat less believable.

769   BEECHER, CATHARINE E. Letters to the People on Health and
       Happiness. New York: Harper & Brothers, 1855. 192 pp.
            Catharine Beecher's chief aim in presenting this series of
       letters was to suggest methods for improving what she saw to be the
       dangerously deteriorating health of the American people, especially
       women. Letter 22 deals with the danger of masturbation, which is
       the only sexual theme on which Beecher touches, apparently because
       of her extreme modesty and prudishness in regard to matters sexual.
       She hints at the possibility of "the power which a teacher, even
       of the same sex, may exert on the affections and susceptibilities
       of pupils, so that in some cases they may become morbid and ex-
       cessive," but never develops this theme into a full discussion of
       same-sex relationships. Material written by Mrs. R.B. Gleason of
       the Elmira, New York, Water Cure and appended to the end of
       Beecher's letters, sets forth much the same view: "Death and the
       mad-house are the last resort of these most miserable victims [of
       masturbation]."

770   BIGELOW, MAURICE A. Sex-education: A Series of Lectures
       Concerning Knowledge of Sex in Its Relation to Human Life.
       New York: Macmillan, 1916. 251 pp.
            The origins of the sex education movement in the social
       purity movement can be clearly seen in this guide for parents and
       sex educators in the schools. Originally given by Bigelow as lec-
       tures at Teachers College, Columbia University, the book grew out

of the activities of the American Federation for Sex Hygiene. In outlining his curriculum and dealing with questions such as who should give sex instruction to the young, Bigelow reveals himself as a conservative traditionalist. Advocating separate instruction for boys and girls, perferably by members of their own sex, he maintains, for example, that adolescent girls should not be given detailed descriptions of their external genitalia because this "might arouse curiosity that leads to exploration and irritation." Bigelow encouraged formal instruction of girls in "scientific facts regarding mothercraft or the care of small children," but warned against sexual freedom for women, which he felt derived from the interest many young women found in "more or less superficial studies of radical socialism." A bibliography of sex education materials in the final chapter will be of interest to researchers.

771 CONGER, HORACE O., and CAROLINE P. CRANE. Obstetrics and Womanly Beauty: A Treatise on the Physical Life of Woman, Embracing Full Information on All Important Matters for Both Mothers and Maidens. Chicago: American Publishing House, 1900. 541 pp.

The emphasis on beauty in the title of this book was probably a promotional gimmick, since most of the work was concerned with such mundane matters as care of the sick, pregnancy, and woman's physiology (there are a few beauty aids, such as recipes for once-a-week tooth powder and a freckle remover). The material on sexuality is a mixture of the old and new. Therefore, while masturbation is still seen as leading to paralysis and insanity, sexual intercourse during pregnancy is given the go-ahead, except during those days during which the woman would otherwise have been having her menstrual period. Moderation and restraint in sexual relations --but not abstinence--is advised, as is limitation of salt intake: "It is such a goad toward carnalism that the ancient fable depicted Venus as born of the salt sea-wave."

772 [COOKE, NICHOLAS FRANCIS.] Satan in Society. By a Physician. Cincinnati: Vent, 1871. 412 pp.

A dramatic style, mixed with a high measure of moralizing, characterizes Cooke's presentation. Seeing the sexual behavior of the time as a danger to the future of the nation, Cooke enumerated various "vices" that he believed were prime targets for moral reform: divorce, free love, flirting, women's rights, commingling of the sexes, abortion, and even reading newspapers (by children). Convinced that most marriages were unhappy because of sexual excesses immediately following the wedding, Cooke painted an especially distressing picture of the bride on her marriage night: "Through the long hours of that dreary night, she listens to the heavy respirations of her gross companion, whose lightest movement causes her to shrink with terror." A strong believer in a traditional role for woman, Cooke devotes several chapters to a discussion of her past, present, and future. Satan in Society was heavily plagiarized by William H. Walling for his Sexology (entry 846).

773   CRADDOCK, IDA C. <u>Letter to a Prospective Bride</u>. Philadelphia: published by the author, 1897. 18 pp. LC.
      There is some duplication in both content and language be-tween this tract and <u>Right Marital Living</u> (entry 774). Craddock encourages brides to teach their husbands the self-control needed to engage in intercourse without emission. Above all, women are to control the sexual relationship. The pamphlet also advertises Craddock's lecture and consultative services, given at her offices, Room 6, 1230 Arch Street, Philadelphia.

774   _____. <u>Right Marital Living</u>. Chicago: published by the author, 1899. 54 pp. LC.
      Ida Craddock billed herself on the cover of this tract as a "lecturer and correspondent on social purity." Her boldness, how-ever, in describing sexual techniques is unlike anything found in conventional purity literature. Her guiding philosophy was that women should control sexual relations, and she clearly separated the "love function" and reproductive functions. Although her idea that mental self-control could successfully inhibit orgasm seems fanciful, her emphasis on the importance of foreplay and woman's active role in sexual intercourse is not. Surprisingly, she was also a believer in vaginal orgasm: "The clitoris should play a very secondary part indeed, and the orgasm should be induced within the vagina." Craddock also used this pamphlet to advertise her lecture course, "The Psychology of Sex," offered at her offices, Suite 38-40, 80 Dearborn Street, Chicago.

775   CUTTER, CALVIN. <u>The Female Guide: Containing Facts and Information upon the Effects of Masturbation, and the Causes, Prevention, Treatment, and Cure of Hernia or Rupture, Cositive-ness, Liver Complaints, Piles, Deformities, and Painful Diseases of the Spine, Suppression and Irregular Painful Monthly Periods, Prolapsus Uteri, or Falling of the Womb, Attended with Weakness of the Bowels, Pain in the Sides and Back, Difficulty of Passing Urine, etc., etc.</u> West Brookfield, Mass.: Charles A. Mirick, 1844. 72 pp.
      There is little unique information in the sections of Cutter's pamphlet dealing with masturbation, since the author lifted passages verbatim from works of Gove, Woodward, and Tissot. The primary putpose of the work was to call the reader's attention to a variety of women's ailments which could be treated by purchas-ing and wearing Cutter's patent abdominal supporter, the "Spino."

776   DIRIX, M.E. <u>Woman's Complete Guide to Health</u>. New York: W.A. Townsend & Adams, 1869. 342 pp.
      Dirix's chapter on hysteria includes two case histories which suggest that hysterical symptoms were an accompaniment to fear of or aversion to heterosexual intercourse originating in physical discomfort or concern about the danger of pregnancy. The book, which was apparently written to help promote Dirix's medical prac-tice in Brooklyn, is primarily a discussion of medicopathological conditions of the reproductive system.

149

777   DRAKE, EMMA FRANCES ANGELL. What a Young Wife Ought to Know.
      New rev. ed. Philadelphia: Vir Publishing Co., 1908. 293 pp.
          Sex education manuals published by Vir geared to different
      sexes and age groups were widely acclaimed by religious and social
      reform leaders alike. A companion volume, What a Young Husband
      Ought to Know, was written by Sylvanus Stall; Mary Wood-Allen was
      also a contributor to the series.

778   DRESSLER, FLORENCE. Feminology: A Guide for Womankind, Giving
      in Detail Instructions as to Motherhood, Maidenhood, and the
      Nursery. Chicago: C.L. Dressler, 1902. 702 pp.
          A general health guide, Feminology is notable for its full-
      color lithographs of such pathological delights as crusted ringworm
      and "Ear in Confluent Small-pox/Mature Stage." Other less vivid
      illustrations depict woman's nature, physical culture exercises,
      and the reproductive system. While the emphasis is on physiology
      and disease, sexuality is not neglected. Calling those who oppose
      birth control "Pharisees," Dressler advocates intercourse only
      when it is agreeable to both parties, giving the woman additional
      control over questions of maternity. Although she believed in ab-
      stinence by the unmarried (masturbation and sexual excess were
      equally culpable), Dressler did not advocate such an extreme as a
      birth control technique. Probably from fear of prosecution under
      the Comstock laws, she also did not specifically discuss any al-
      ternative birth control techniques, limiting her argument to a
      general plea.

779   DUBOIS, JEAN. The Secret Habits of the Female Sex: Letters
      Addressed to a Mother on the Evils of Solitude, and Its Seductive
      Temptations to Young Girls, the Premature Victims of a Pernicious
      Passion, with All Its Frightful Consequences: Deformity of Mind
      and Body, Destruction of Beauty, and Entailing Disease and Death;
      but from Which, by Attention to the Timely Warnings Here Given,
      the Devotee May Be Saved, and Become an Ornament to Society, a
      Virtuous Wife, and a Refulgent Mother!. New York: n.p., 1848.
      185 pp. ISR.
          Largely derived from the works of such writers as Alibert and
      Tissot, The Secret Habits of the Female Sex is a typical antimastur-
      bation tract of the nineteenth century. Written in the form of let-
      ters "to a young invalid, who had brought on her illness by addic-
      tion to this very life-destroying habit," it predicted the typical
      dire consequences of the practice: consumption, insanity, and even
      death. It includes "melancholy confessions of the victims them-
      selves" and urges decency and chastity as the highest virtues for
      women. The final section of the book consists of "cures," includ-
      ing this one: "Simple application to calm irritation of the stom-
      ach, resulting from Onanism; also vomitings from the same cause.--
      A hare skin dressed with the hair on placed on the epigastrum next
      the skin." Also recommended was drinking marshmallow water with a
      syrup of violets.

780   DUFFEY, ELIZA BISBEE. <u>The Relations of the Sexes</u>. New York:
      Wood & Holbrook, 1876. 320 pp.
      Eliza B. Duffey's <u>The Relations of the Sexes</u> demonstrates the
growing feminist consciousness that typified so many of the women
writing on sexuality in the post-Civil War era. An outspoken advocate of birth control who took the necessary post-Comstock precau-
tions against actually describing birth control practices, Duffey
firmly believed that a woman's body was her own. Her attitude toward sexuality was somewhat ambivalent; while she never denied that
women had sexual feelings, she did feel that they were largely un-
developed until marriage and even then took second place to maternal
instincts. Seeking to downplay the importance of purely sexual
relationships in marriage, Duffey recommended once-a-month coital
frequency and continence and chastity whenever possible. She opposed free love, polygamy, prostitution, and abortion, and extolled
the American legal institution of marriage as being more perfect
and equal than any other on earth. Duffey was certainly no physician, nor did she clearly espouse any but the most generally feminist position of social reform, but her belief in her own arguments
and her appeal to common sense in the face of sexist prejudice give
her work a credibility often lacking in the writing of her more
histrionic male counterparts.

781   _____. What Women Should Know: A Woman's Book about Women.
      Philadelphia: J.M. Stoddart, 1873. 320 pp.
      Her belief that women's advice books written by men often
told only partial truths was a primary factor leading Eliza Duffey
to write <u>What Women Should Know</u>. Equally important, however, was
her conviction that overall improvement in women's health was a
sine qua non to their political and economic advancement. Duffey's
zeal to demonstrate women's potential sometimes led her to make
unrealistic claims (she contended, for example, that healthy women
would be totally free from menstrual pain), and she was as fanati-
cal as her male counterparts in her opposition to masturbation.
Her recommendations for courtship behavior included no kissing or
touching unless the couple was engaged; control of the situation
lay with the woman since "the passions of men are much stronger
and more easily inflamed than their own." Such control extended
into marriage, and Duffey outlined the situations in which woman's
right to refuse was justified. A large part of the book is devoted
to pregnancy and maternal and infant health. However, there is no
discussion of menopause. Despite her intention of presenting the
"truth" to women, Duffey to a large degree presented only her own
views about their behavior.

782   ENGLISH, VIRGIL PRIMROSE. <u>The Doctor's Plain Talk to Young
      Women: Anatomy, Physiology, and Hygiene of the Sexual System
      and the Relation of This System to Health, Beauty, and Popularity</u>.
      Cleveland: Ohio State Publishing Co., 1902. 220 pp.
      English, a Cleveland physician who was to emigrate to San
Diego, used the back pages of this health guide to advertise his

"Home Treatment for Ladies," for which he made extravagant claims:
"It is designed for the very worst cases--cases in which the best
physicians and all other methods fail. It has frequently saved
patients from the terrors of the surgeon's knife, by curing them
after the surgeons had said that they could never get well without
an operation." The book is simplistic and folkloristic, retaining an outdated belief in phrenological signs (a broad chin was
supposed to denote amativeness), in the evils of masturbation
("slow but certain suicide"), and, surprisingly, in a double standard (English claimed that women were injured physically by extramarital sex since they would become pregnant, while men did not
suffer any but moral ill effects). Self-control for women is
stressed, but at the same time they are encouraged to develop their
sexuality. A companion volume was entitled The Doctor's Plain Talk
to Young Men.

783   EVANS, ELIZABETH EDSON. The Abuse of Maternity. Philadelphia:
      J.B. Lippincott, 1875. 129 pp.
         Equally concerned about abortion and eugenics, Elizabeth
      Evans believed in the efficacy of social purity and chastity as
      ideals for both men and women. Her view of women was traditional
      --"No woman can be considered as having completed her destiny until
      she has borne a child"--and procreation was to her the only justi-
      fication for sexual intercourse. Her view of women's sexuality
      served to support these ideas: "Excepting in rare and abnormal
      instances, the sexual desire in woman is weak, by reason of her
      training, compared to its degree in man; . . . if women had their
      own way in the matter this physical intercourse would take place
      at comparatively rare intervals, and only under the most favorable
      circumstances." Opposed on eugenic grounds to marriage between
      relatives or among the poor and diseased, Evans was firmly opposed
      also to abortion as a means of concluding unwanted pregnancy.

784   FOOTE, EDWARD BLISS. Medical Common Sense; Applied to the
      Causes, Prevention and Cure of Chronic Diseases, and Unhappiness
      in Marriage. Boston: Wentworth, Hewes & Co., 1858. 271 pp.
         E.B. Foote was a "medical and electrical therapeutist" who
      practiced at the popular spa, Saratoga Springs, New York. Medical
      Common Sense is equally divided between commentary on general health
      matters ("Over-coats made of the skins of buffaloes are extremely
      warm in cold climates in winter, and rubber coats in all climates
      in rainy weather") and more specific remarks on marriage and sexu-
      ality. Foote surveys marriage customs throughout the world and
      propounds various would-be scientific theories about the electrici-
      ty of the sexual organs, incorporating the phrenological system of
      the Fowlers as well as a belief in the four humors. To his credit,
      Foote viewed women's sexuality positively, although he had a rather
      unique argument in favor of limiting coital frequency: "To render
      chemical electricity active in copulation, sufficient time must
      elapse for the vagina to get clear of the neutralized fluid. As
      soda is insipid after the effervescent effect is over, so is the

alkali of the vagina dead and inactive after having been neutralized
by the acid of the male. Several days and sometimes weeks must
elapse, after one indulgence, before the secretions of the vagina
will become so purely alkaline as to be prepared for another ani-
mated combination with the acid of the male." He also advocated
the full participation of women in the economy, believing in "the
necessity of ladies throwing off their dependence on the coarser
sex," and even advocated women's right to choose and propose to
their husbands.

785 _____. Plain Home Talk about the Human System--the Habits of
Men and Women--the Causes and Prevention of Disease--Our Sexual
Relations and Social Natures; Embracing Medical Common Sense
Applied to Causes, Prevention, and Cure of Chronic Diseases--
the Natural Relations of Men and Women to Each Other--Society--
Love--Marriage--Parentage--Etc., Etc. New York: Wells & Coffin,
1870. 912 pp.
This enlarged version of Foote's Medical Common Sense retains
most of the author's ideas regarding electromagnetism, phrenology,
and women's rights in sexual relationships.

786 FOWLER, LORENZO NILES. The Principles of Phrenology and
Physiology Applied to Man's Social Relations. New York: L.N.
& O.S. Fowler, 1842. 135 pp.
Lorenzo and Orson Fowler, nineteenth-century America's best-
known phrenologists, published a series of highly popular mass-
market books describing how their "science" could be applied to
everyday life, freely shifting both text and illustrations from
one work to another. Thus the discussion of amativeness, the
Fowlers' code word for sexuality, is found in various forms throughout the brothers' work. In this volume, Lorenzo freely acknowledges
the existence of female sexuality, although he feels that men tend
to exhibit stronger impulses in this area than do women. He argues,
using a female illustration, that overdevelopment of the portion
of the cerebellum in which the amative faculty supposedly lay would
lead to increased and sometimes uncontrollable desire for the oppo-
site sex and urges simple living and parental guidance as means of
discouraging precocious development of this faculty. The book concludes with discussions of heredity and the evils of tight lacing.

787 FOWLER, ORSON S. Amativeness: Embracing the Evils and Remedies
of Excessive and Perverted Sexuality, Including Warning and
Advice to the Married and Single. New rev. ed. New York:
Fowler & Wells, 1889. 65 pp.
Amativeness appears to have been first published in 1844 as
a supplement to Love and Parentage (entry 788) and was frequently
reprinted thereafter. In this work, a more direct approach to the
discussion is taken than in some of the Fowlers' other works, and
bumps on the head take a decided back seat to prescriptive behavior
recommendations. Heterosexual relations leading to parenthood are
seen as an imperative, and readers are told that acquired physical

characteristics and states of mind existing at the time of conception may be passed on to offspring. Masburbation is decried, as is abortion, availability of the latter being seen as contributing to an increase in extramarital sexual activity.

788   _____. Love and Parentage, Applied to the Improvement of
Offspring: Including Important Directions and Suggestions to
Lovers and the Married Concerning the Strongest Ties and the
Most Momentous Relations of Life. New York: Fowler and Wells,
1844. 144 pp.
       Similar to the Fowlers' many other popular phrenological
works, Love and Parentage contains two chapters, on "reciprocity"
and "frequency," which present summary views on sexuality (in a
sense, of course, the entire book is about sexuality). Sexual
pleasure leading to reproduction is "the single legitimate object
of marriage," and Fowler looks askance at marriages that claim to
have been contracted for other reasons. Sounding like a nineteenth-
century version of Marabel Morgan, Fowler advises women to "yield
cheerfully and with a view to please him, or else the ultimate effect will be lost." Fowler notes that many women find sexual relations disagreeable, but urges them to submit, since that will
place their husbands under obligations of love and gratitude.
Men, likewise, are advised to promote desire and cultivate their
wives' erotic response: "Her coldness is your fault mainly. Almost any wife whose husband is not repugnant can be persuaded to
all the intensity of emotion necessary or desirable." As far as
frequency was concerned, Fowler felt that coitus could occur "as
frequently as is compatible with health, and the oftener the better," reserving to women the ultimate decision. "And if parents
would diminish their frequency so as to enhance ecstasy, they
would be incalculable gainers in the amount of pleasure experienced,
besides doubling, perhaps quadrupling, all the endowment of their
offspring." Begetting better babies through phrenology.

789   _____. Sexual Science; Including Manhood, Womanhood, and Their
Mutual Interrelations; Love, Its Laws, Power etc., Selection,
or Mutual Adaptation; Married Life Made Happy; Reproduction,
and Progenal Endowment, or Paternity, Maternity, Bearing,
Nursing, and Rearing Children; Puberty, Girlhood, etc.; Sexual
Ailments Restored, Female Beauty Perpetuated, etc., etc. as
Taught by Phrenology. Philadelphia: National Publishing Co.,
1870. 930 pp.
       A genial, if unscientific, folklore coupled with high roman-
ticism characterizes this later work of Orson Fowler. By this time
phrenology was taking a decided back seat to physiology, sentimentality, and pseudoscientific pronouncements. One example will
suffice: "The Female appoints the impregnating period. That woman
is intended to determine it, is proved by her having more passion
after her monthlies have cleared out her system, and induced vigorous action in these organs, than at any other time; therefore
Nature has adapted man to await her call without inconvenience, by

ordaining that this passion shall slumber on quietly till she
inspires passion in him by leading off in its manifestation. At
all events, it is worthless to him except when she does. You who
are unduly denied have only this redress to promote invitations."
Nevertheless, Fowler continued to enjoy popular appeal both as a
lecturer and writer.

790   GALBRAITH, ANNA M.   The Four Epochs of Woman's Life: A Study
       in Hygiene.   Philadelphia and London: W.B. Saunders, 1901.
       200 pp.
          Although Anna Galbraith intended this book to serve as a
       positive guide for newly or about to be married women, a pervasive
       negativism in her description of sexual relations would certainly
       have rendered her readers apprehensive about their new relation-
       ship: "There is always more or less suffering on the part of the
       wife at first. . . . Passion is presented to the young wife in so
       hideous a guise that it will take the utmost consideration of her
       husband afterward to enable her to completely overcome her repug-
       nance. . . . For the larger part of her married life she is either
       positively distressed by the apparent necessary demands of her hus-
       band upon her, and irresponsive to them, or kept to a cheerful re-
       sponse by a self-abnegation and regard for his comfort, not to say
       fear of his moral aberration, which is a positive drain upon her
       health and strength."   She advocated separate beds, separate rooms,
       continence as the best means of birth control, and separation from
       the husband as the last resort cure for sexual excitability.
       Galbraith, a graduate of Vassar College and the Woman's Medical
       College of Pennsylvania, was also the author of Hygiene and Physical
       Culture for Women.

791   GREENE, CHARLES A.   Build Well.   The Basis of Individual, Home,
       and National Elevation.   Plain Truths Relating to the Obligations
       of Marriage and Parentage.   Boston: D. Lothrop, 1885.   227 pp.
          This is a fairly typical marriage manual from the late nine-
       teenth century, with more emphasis on the dangers of masturbation
       and adultery than was usual in publications focusing on marriage.
       Although he was conservative on these issues and was a foe of
       abortion, Greene took a positive view of women's sexuality as a
       whole.   One of a growing number of sex writers who advocated greater
       sensitivity on the part of husbands to their wives' sexual needs,
       Greene recommended both the safe period and condoms as birth control
       measures, although he was critical of withdrawal as a technique.   He
       presented the following advice regarding female orgasm: "Sometimes,
       in the most favorable marriage, the wife feels little pleasurable
       sensation until the close of the conjugal act.   A careful retarding
       of it will, after a little time, lead to reciprocal enjoyment."
       The role of the clitoris, however, is never mentioned.   Intercourse
       during pregnancy is discouraged, but daily frequency otherwise is
       felt not to be harmful.

792   GUERNSEY, HENRY NEWELL.   Plain Talks on Avoided Subjects.

Philadelphia: F.A. Davis, 1882. 126 pp.

Plain Talks on Avoided Subjects was directly inspired by
William Acton's The Functions and Disorders of the Reproductive
Organs in Youth, in Adult Age, and in Advanced Life (entry 386).
Included are the typical warnings about servants introducing children to masturbation, and indeed, children are depicted as being
intensely sexual beings. Guernsey is equally concerned with both
sexes, and his ideas on appropriate women's behavior are fairly
reactionary. Despite the passage of several years since the debate
over E.H. Clarke's Sex in Education and its seeming resolution by
Mary Putnam Jacobi, Guernsey still maintained that puberty in girls
requires a focusing of energy on their physiological task rather
than their intellectual development and even recommended that
mothers read Clarke's work so as to give their daughters proper
guidance. But perhaps Guernsey (like Acton) is most notable for
his flat denial of women's sexuality (seemingly a contradiction
of his warnings about childhood sexuality and adolescent female
masturbation): "Young women have not, as a rule, any sexual pro-
pensity, or amorous thoughts or feelings." Guernsey has given us
yet another example of prescriptive social theory masquerading as
medical literature.

793   HALL, WINFIELD SCOTT, and JEANNETTE WINTER HALL. Sexual
       Knowledge, in Plain and Simple Language: Sexology or Knowledge
       of Self and Sex for Both Male and Female . . . Philadelphia:
       International Bible House, 1913. 320 pp.

Intended for use by parents in providing sex education to
their children, Sexual Knowledge was also written for a young adult
audience of about to be marrieds. Supporters of social purity
ideals, the Halls saw education as the cure for ignorance and vice.
Presenting separate sections on and for men and women, they focus
on reproductive physiology and a romantic idealization of motherhood, totally excluding information on sexual relations, venereal
disease, and similar "earthy" topics. Women are warned that masturbation (the only sexual activity directly mentioned) will wreck
their nervous systems, that exercise and baths during menstruation
are taboo, and that "every girl should have one inviolable rule of
relation to men--Hands off!" Surprisingly, and despite their moralistic piety, the Halls do advocate coeducational nudity in childhood as a means of learning sex differences.

794   HART, A.J. The Sex Ritual. Detroit: Physical Information
       Bureau, 1918. 199 pp.

Nineteenth-century myths predominate in this volume. Menstruation is called a sickness, women are characterized as having no
sexual desire until after marriage, and orgasm is defined as "im-
moderate excitement or action." Masturbation is decried, although
Hart notes that "very few girls are guilty of such abuse." Particularly offensive are unsubstantiated generalizations such as
this: "It is fairly accurate to state that the larger the showing
of mucous membrane in the lips, the greater is sex developed in the
particular individual."

795   HAYES, ALBERT H. <u>Physiology of Woman, and Her Diseases; Or,</u>
      <u>Woman, Treated of Physiologically, Pathologically, and</u>
      <u>Esthetically. With Eight Elegant Illustrative Pictures of</u>
      <u>Female Beauty</u>. Boston: Peabody Medical Institute, 1869. 345
      pp.
         Like many of his contemporaries, Albert Hayes prepared this
      work in order to promote business for his so-called medical insti-
      tute, as well as his cure-all for female complaints, the Yosemite
      Panacea. Hayes says nothing startling, although his allusions are
      often more literary than medical. There are the usual proscriptions
      against masturbation during adolescence and excessive intercourse
      during marriage (once every seven or ten days was enough), and
      Hayes's ideas are largely derived from those of other authors.
      He differs from other women's health writers, however, by includ-
      ing chapters on such subjects as beauty, where he displays a
      chauvinist attitude toward woman's role: "As long as the sex
      possesses [beauty], they can get along without the suffrage." In
      his views on prostitution, his scholarly sophistication left much
      to be desired: "Egypt of old was famous for harlots. Egyptian
      blood runs warm. Girls are nubile at ten. The religious festivals
      of ancient Egypt were full of sexual abominations." The influence
      of Acton is apparent as well: "There can be no doubt that sexual
      feeling in the female, is, in a majority of cases, in abeyance,
      and that it requires positive and considerable excitement to be
      roused at all; and, even if roused (which in many instances it
      never can be), is very moderate compared with that of the male."

796   HERROLD, MAUDE M. <u>Woman and Disease: A Collection of Facts for</u>
      <u>Women</u>. Kansas City, Mo.: published by the author, 1898. 374
      pp.
         A graduate of the Woman's Medical College of Pennsylvania,
      Herrold dedicated this book to "Vashti that Grand Queen of Persia,
      Who First Dared Defy the Injustice and Tyranny of a Sensual Hus-
      band," as well as to Abigail Adams, Elizabeth Cady Stanton, Susan
      B. Anthony, and Matilda Joslyn Gage. Imbued with the spirit of
      the divinity of woman, <u>Woman and Disease</u> discusses gynecological
      disorders, venereal disease, sexual excess, and other topics re-
      lating to women's sexuality. Herrold saw the emancipation of women
      as a precondition to the improvement of sexual relations. Her
      opinion of lesbianism, influenced by Krafft-Ebing, was strong:
      "Parents should be especially informed concerning the dangers of
      these evil infatuations which result from one person having a
      large amount of animal magnetism or 'snake attraction' victimizing
      those who possess weak wills or are ignorant of such diseased con-
      ditions existing." Herrold covers a lot of ground with comments
      on such diverse subjects as the use of hypnotism to induce women
      to submit to gynecological surgery and an American religious cult
      that reportedly worshiped "an image of the sexual organs as the
      women of India who are slaves to the Mohammedan creed are required
      to do."

797   HOLBROOK, MARTIN LUTHER. Marriage and Parentage. New York:
      M.L. Holbrook & Co., 1882. 185 pp.
          A treatise on so-called sanitary marriage and parentage,
      Marriage and Parentage presents eugenic views on how healthy chil-
      dren can be conceived and born. Holbrook condemns the use of to-
      bacco and corsets and calls for sexual intercourse for conception
      only when the prospective parents are at their physical peak. Sexu-
      al activity during pregnancy and lactation is tabooed, as is abor-
      tion.

798   _____. Physical, Intellectual and Moral Advantages of Chastity.
      New York and London: M.L. Holbrook and L.N. Fowler, 1894.
      120 pp.
          The title is a dead giveaway to the author's intent in this
      promotional tract, which also includes the text of "Alcohol and
      Unchastity," an address given by Holbrook at the World's Congress
      for Social Purity, as well as an appendix quoting numerous authori-
      ties to substantiate his views. Holbrook addressed his remarks
      equally to men and women, maintaining that sexual indulgence out-
      side of marriage (i.e., masturbation and prostitution) were un-
      natural and led to physiological bankruptcy. Excessive sexual
      relations in marriage were also unchaste. Using Socrates as the
      premier example of the beneficial effects of chastity, Holbrook
      promised his readers that chastity would lead to healthier children
      and a better world: "Indeed, it is the chaste men and women who
      to-day are moving civilization forward to its high destiny." Ever
      the practical adviser, Holbrook offered advice on attaining a
      chaste life, recommending as a start the purchase of his nutrition
      and cookery book, Eating for Strength.

799   HOLCOMBE, WILLIAM H. The Sexes Here and Hereafter. Philadelphia:
      J.B. Lippincott, 1869. 277 pp.
          A disciple of Emanuel Swedenborg, Holcombe believed in the
      inherent bisexuality of all things. This work is his attempt to
      popularize Swedenborg's ideas on "Conjugial Love which surpasses
      in beauty, purity, and practical value, anything hitherto known
      or imagined." Sex, love, and marriage express the nature of the
      deity, and even the letters of the alphabet are sexual, the vowels
      being feminine and the consonants masculine. Moreover, the sexual
      identities of men and women are continued into the hereafter. If
      such unions were perfect, war would cease, disease would disappear,
      and heaven would descend to earth.

800   HOLLICK, FREDERICK. The Marriage Guide, or Natural History of
      Generation; A Private Instructor for Married Persons and Those
      about to Marry Both Male and Female; In Every Thing Concerning
      the Physiology and Relations of the Sexual System and the
      Production or Prevention of Offspring--Including All the New
      Discoveries, Never Before Given in the English Language. New
      York: T.W. Strong, 1850. 428 pp.
          By the time the American News Company printed the "500th

edition" of Hollick's Marriage Guide in 1883, it had become one of the most popular marriage and sex manuals of its day. More or less a quack, Hollick claimed to have performed numerous clitoridectomies and similar genital surgery. He also used the book to sell mail order condoms at $9 per package ("which will last a long time") and to advertise the services of two masseurs whose specialty was "shampooing" the perineal and genital muscles. Illustrated with engraved line drawings, the Marriage Guide was unusually bold, if not semipornographic, in tone, probably accounting for its great popularity, although much of it is devoted to a discussion of reproductive physiology.

Hollick views female sexuality positively and acknowledges the role of the clitoris: "The intensity of the sexual orgasm apparently depends upon the perfection of its nervous organization." Interestingly, however, he also poses the possibility of a "superior" vaginal orgasm, perhaps the earliest American writer to do so. "I believe that sexual excitement is never known in its full intensity excepting when it is experienced in the neck of the Womb, it being always weak and partial when confined only to the Clitoris and Nymphae." Of special interest are his discussions of aphrodisiacs (including cannabis indica), contraception, and female orgasm ("in most females the orgasm is very difficult to be produced").

801 _____. The Origin of Life: A Popular Treatise on the Philosophy and Physiology of Reproduction, in Plants and Animals, Including the Details of Human Generation, with a Full Description of the Male and Female Organs. New York: Nafis & Cornish, 1845. 233 pp.; addenda.

The Origin of Life was one of many sex and health manuals by Frederick Hollick, a popular New York writer and lecturer whose works were translated into Spanish for the Cuban market. Much of the book is on reproductive physiology, but Hollick offers observations on sexual behavior as well. Women's sexual feelings were more intense than men's, although fewer women experienced them. Hollick felt that women should determine when sexual relations were appropriate for them, although he warned that marriage should not be delayed far past puberty. Masturbation was practiced more frequently by women because women had fewer outlets for intercourse than did men, and Hollick joined most of his contemporaries in condemning the practice, as well as the boarding schools where it was learned. As a matter of fact, Hollick was obsessed with masturbation, claiming that 99 percent of the population was addicted to it and that it led to more disease and suffering than all other causes combined. This is a typical Victorian mix of moralistic hokum and biological fact.

802 HOOKER, EDITH HOUGHTON. The Laws of Sex. Boston: Richard G. Badger, [1919?]. 373 pp.

A physician and founder of the Guild of St. George, a home for unmarried mothers in Baltimore, Edith Hooker was a firm advocate of the single standard. The Laws of Sex is an attack on promiscuity and such related problems as prostitution and venereal disease. Writing with a feminist perspective, Hooker had a clear grasp of such issues as the economic origin of prostitution and proposed, among other things, elimination of stigmas on illegitimacy and a system of maternity benefits for women during their childbearing years. Hooker reviews the history of marriage, prostitution, and American sex legislation and critiques methods for the control of venereal disease. She concludes that complete reform of economic, educational, and political systems, including full emancipation of women, is a prerequisite to achievement of equitable, ethical standards of sexual conduct for both sexes.

803   HOWARD, WILLIAM LEE. Facts for the Married. New York: Edward
      J. Clode, 1912.   161 pp.
         Facts for the Married was one of a series of books written
by Howard on sexuality and sexual hygiene. Patronizing in its
attitude toward women, it was intended primarily for the male
popular audience and consists of a series of "conversations" on
topics relating to marriage, sex, and reproduction. Howard's advice to men on wedding night conduct is typical: "Patience, a kiss
of comprehension, and the complete control of your animal instincts
will make you the idol she has so long subjectively worshipped."
Like many of his contemporaries, Howard believed that the desire
for motherhood was stronger in women than that of sexual desire
per se, and he even went so far as to say that women who did not
want children were sexually abnormal. He did, however, advocate
women taking an active role in determining the frequency and timing
of sexual relations, although he suggested that the best time was
three hours after dinner! Other subjects discussed by Howard were
the ill health of American women, prenatal influences, and the
danger of alcoholic beverages to prospective parents.

804   _____ . Sex Problems in Worry and Work. New York: E. J. Clode,
      1915.   204 pp.
         Sex Problems in Worry and Work reiterates many of the same
ideas found in Howard's Facts for the Married (entry 803)--the
dominance of the maternal instinct in women and the desirability
of chastity. Howard, however, is primarily concerned with the
role of sexual behavior and disturbances in causing worry and
nervousness, and Howard's cursory reading of Freud (including a
few references to his name) apparently led him to embrace the
theory that fears or neuroses "have a sexual basis dating from
early childhood." He felt strongly that sexual instinct could be
sublimated into works of creativity, or, in the case of women, into
acts of pseudomaternity, but warned that this could be diverted
into unhealthy channels: "One of the reasons we find many of the
authoresses [of romantic fiction] unmarried women and apparently
not attracted to the male sex is because they have used up their
sexuality in their work." Howard also picked up on certain contemporary trends, such as the attribution of sexual maladies to

160

thyroid and thymus disorders. In one instance Howard argued that such glandular imbalance was due to the system of educating girls along "male lines" during adolescence, resulting ultimately in women's colleges frequently containing women who lacked sex impulses, virtual "psychic eunuchs." This was an interesting variation on the ideas originally expressed by E.H. Clarke in Sex in Education and is indicative of the staying power of Clarke's theories, despite a lack of empirical proof.

805   INGERSOLL, ANDREW J. In Health. 4th ed., rev. Boston: Lee and Shepard, 1899. 261 pp.
      A wide range of religious viewpoints was represented in nineteenth-century sexuality literature, but few authors tried to make religion as much a part of sex as did A.J. Ingersoll. Operator of the Pinewood Sanitarium in Corning, New York, Ingersoll originally published In Health in 1877, basing the volume on his own experience and focusing on one overriding idea: "All sensation of sexual feeling should be committed or yielded to Christ." Ingersoll was somewhat vague about how this was to be accomplished, but he had no doubt about his method's efficacy. For example, the old question about women's incapacity during their menstrual periods was vanquished: "In all cases where women have received my religious views of this function, they perform physical or mental labor during these periods without any inconvenience." Generally, however, Ingersoll was a traditionalist in his views of women. God designed woman to be a wife and mother; wives should obey their husbands; hysteria was frequently caused by voluntary suppression of sexual life. Ingersoll believed that most sexual complaints and disorders of the female reproductive system were psychosomatic in origin and likewise could be cured by faith and prayer: "If woman had reverence for her sexual life, and faith in Christ, she would suffer but little in childbirth." Later editions of Ingersoll's book feature testimonials from the famous, including John Ruskin and John Greenleaf Whittier, but their numbers include no women.

806   JEFFERIS, BENJAMIN GRANT, and JAMES LAWRENCE NICHOLS. Search Lights on Health; Light on Dark Corners. 6th ed. Naperville, Ill.: J.L. Nichols, 1894. 429 pp.
      Search Lights on Health was only one of the titles by which this work was known. Others included Safe Counsel, Light and Life, and Know Thyself, all of them the popular products of Nichols, who printed and distributed them in various parts of the country in order to meet the demand generated by his mail-order audience. Search Lights is typical of the medical/sexual self-help literature of the time, taking a moralistic approach to topics such as masturbation and physical contact during courtship. In some areas, however, Jefferis and Nichols were more liberal than some of their colleagues. For example, intercourse during the early months of pregnancy was permissible (in moderation), and procreation was not the sole objective of conjugal relations. Women's wishes, especially those of new brides, regarding frequency of sexual relations

were to be respected, and in general the authors give women a much cleaner sexual bill of health than men. "Their sexual instinct is not so intensely developed, consequently women are not so inclined to injure themselves by excesses." Perhaps as a result of this belief, the authors include no instruction on promoting sexual pleasure in women. The book differs from some others of the period as well by including prescriptions for general behavior. Sections on such topics as letter writing, child abuse, and narcotics no doubt convinced readers that they were truly getting their money's worth by purchasing this volume.

807   KELLOGG, JOHN HARVEY. Ladies Guide in Health and Disease. Girlhood, Maidenhood, Wifehood, Motherhood. Des Moines, Iowa: W.D. Condit, 1883. 638 pp.

The popular medical works of J.H. Kellogg are a mainstay of nineteenth-century prescriptive literature and served for generations of Americans as a source of information about sex, diet, and general health. Kellogg's concern over what he perceived to be the increasing ill health of American women impelled him to write this book, which begins with a discussion of reproductive physiology and proceeds through the various stages of woman's life. The author's view of women's sexuality was hardly encouraging to sexual emancipationists: "The motherly instinct is without doubt the ruling passion in the heart of the true woman. The sexual nature of woman finds expression in this channel when her life is a normal one, rather than in the grosser forms of sexual activity." As might be expected, Kellogg was a foe of masturbation, the "soul-destroying vice" and root of ill health, but he did acknowledge the clitoris and labia minora to "constitute the chief seat of sensation in the sexual act." Among the other topics with which he deals: abortion, pregnancy, beauty, dress, and exercise.

808   _____. Plain Facts for Old and Young: Embracing the Natural History and Hygiene of Organic Life. New ed., rev. and enlarged. Burlington, Iowa: I.F. Segner, 1888. 644 pp.

This edition of Plain Facts was issued about midway in the volume's popular career, which began in 1877 with the appearance of Plain Facts about Sexual Life and continued until at least 1903. Because of its popularity, the book is still found frequently today in used book stores, and is especially noteworthy because of the nearly two hundred pages Kellogg devotes to his discussion of the evils of masturbation (compared to ten on continence and thirty-one on prostitution) and its telltale signs--bashfulness, love of solitude, and round shoulders. "Eating clay, slate-pencils, plaster, chalk, and other indigestible articles is a practice to which girls who abuse themselves are especially addicted." Kellogg's recommended cure was the application of carbolic acid to the clitoris.

In his favor, it must be said that Kellogg was a strong advocate of woman's right to control her own person and sexual activity. Nevertheless, the same folklore that pervades his

discussion of masturbation can be found throughout his chapters on
sexual relations in marriage. Acton is quoted to prove that women
are asexual by nature and Kellogg warns against intercourse during
menstruation and pregnancy. The book concludes with a discussion
of diseases of the reproductive system, as well as general health
hints. The intellectual heir of Sylvester Graham, Kellogg transformed his mentor's ideas into his own eclectic combination of
folklore, moralism, and medical information and misinformation.

809   LARMONT, MARTIN. Medical Adviser and Marriage Guide, Representing
      All the Diseases of the Genital Organs of the Male and Female.
      New York: published by the author, 1854. 332 pp.
      This popular manual written by a New York "physician" spe-
cializing in the treatment of venereal disease was still being reprinted in 1870. Of particular interest are the numerous drawings
of healthy and diseased organs and the case studies, which are
little more than advertising for Larmont's services, including
mail-order condoms at $5 per dozen. Larmont discusses the female
reproductive system and includes sections on nymphomania and masturbation in women, the latter supposedly responsible for a wide
range of female maladies including rickets, jaundice, mouth ulcers,
and even prostitution. Although he acknowledges the role of the
clitoris in providing sexual pleasure to women, Larmont's other
pronouncements on female sexuality are often far from enlightened
(yet, one hastens to add, typical of the time).

810   LEWIS, DIO. Chastity; Or, Our Secret Sins. Philadelphia:
      G. Maclean, 1874. 320 pp.
      Chastity was one of a series of popular health books written
by Dio Lewis, a temperance advocate and pioneer in the development
of physical education in the United States. A supporter of social
purity and economic self-sufficiency for women as means of ending
prostitution, Lewis also believed in women's right to control the
sexual aspects of marriage. This was an outgrowth of his theory
that the pivotal passion of woman was maternity, not sexuality
(the pivotal passion in men): "The average woman has so little
sexual desire that if licentiousness depended on her, uninfluenced
by her desire to please man or secure his support there would be
very little sexual excess." Lewis was also concerned that too
much sexual activity, as well as other forms of indulgence, would
weaken the chances of prospective offspring for healthy development.
Once monthly intercourse was his ideal, although his suggestion of
restraint for fourteen days following the completion of the menstrual cycle was hardly destined to yield the contraceptive assurance
that Lewis guaranteed. Chastity is particularly interesting because it draws together ideas from a number of popular reform
movements of the nineteenth century--temperance, dietary reform,
women's rights, social purity--and combines them into the doctrine
of sexual and personal self-control that Lewis hoped would be the
salvation of American civilization.

811   LONG, HARLAND WILLIAM. <u>Sane Sex Life and Sane Sex Living;</u>
<u>Some Things That All Sane People Ought to Know about Sex Nature</u>
<u>and Sex Functioning, etc.</u> Boston: R.G. Badger, 1919. 157 pp.
Frequently reprinted, Long's <u>Sane Sex Life</u> was, owing to
censorship problems, ostensibly directed to the medical profession,
although from its style and tone it is obvious that its real audience was intended to be the general public. A fairly elementary,
even folksy, sex and marriage manual, it begins with a discussion
of the male and female sexual systems which contains a modicum of
misinformation (pubic hair, for example, is alleged to confine an
electrical current, said to develop during coitus, to the vicinity
of the sex organs).
    Long advised husbands and wives to settle the question of
whether they would engage in intercourse for other than reproductive
reasons and criticized writers who espoused the procreation-only
view. Consideration on the wedding night is urged and suggestions
given for sexual technique. Simultaneous orgasm is "a consummation
that can never be excelled in human life," and semen is extolled
as "a most powerful stimulant to all the female sex organs, and to
the whole body of woman." Long also recommends petting as preparation for coitus and masturbation as a means for single women and
widows to "greatly improve their health."

812   LYMAN, ELIZA BARTON. <u>The Coming Woman; Or, the Royal Road to</u>
<u>Physical Perfection.</u> Lansing, Mich.: W.S. George, 1880. 355
pp. SL.
    In this general health guide, Lyman articulates her convic-
tion that women should have full control of their own bodies, including control over the frequency of sexual relations. Despite
this progressive outlook, she did maintain conventional beliefs
in other areas relating to sexuality, recommending rest during
beginning menstruation, decrying the "disaster" of masturbation,
and asserting that the temperaments and maternal influence, including "marking," could not be disregarded when contemplating
marriage and motherhood. Interestingly, in her chapter on the
reproductive system, she anticipated Kegel exercises by over
seventy years with her "series of voluntary contractions of the
muscles of the lower portion of the vagina," designed to tone the
vaginal walls and generally improve the support and control of the
system.

813   MacFADDEN, BERNARR ADOLPHUS. <u>Womanhood and Marriage: 53 Lessons</u>
<u>in Sex Hygiene Exclusively for Women.</u> New York: Physical
Culture Publishing Co., 1918. Unpaged.
    The Physical Culture Publishing Company was one of several
enterprises established by MacFadden to print and distribute his
popular health tracts on such subjects as constipation, hair care,
fasting, and walking. Reverence and idealization of woman and
motherhood typify MacFadden's work, and a wide range of topics,
from courtship to sterility, are covered. Traditional beliefs on
woman's nature prevail ("Woman is by nature negative, passive,

and, for this reason, is less easily stirred and can more readily control herself"), but women are to control the sexual relationship. MacFadden offers exercises for improving the bust ("The possessor of a good bust is found to be perfectly sexed and in every way suited for the bearing of healthy and vigorous children") as well as for realigning a displaced uterus. Much of the book is concerned with the social rather than sexual aspects of marriage.

814   MAREA, E. The Wife's Manual Containing Advice and Valuable Instruction for Married Women and Those Anticipating Marriage. n.p.: published by the author, 1896. 125 pp.
      This little book contains advice to women on such topics as the choice of a husband, marital happiness, pregnancy, birth control, and infant care. Considerable attention is paid to questions of sexuality and sexual behavior. Marea enunciates many of the commonly held beliefs of the nineteenth century: that woman's sexual appetite is smaller than a man's, that sexuality must be regulated and directed to proper ends, and that woman's mission on earth is to bear children. Sexual intercourse during pregnancy is called an "unnatural act," while masturbation and sexual excess lead to insanity, imbecility, and decay.

815   MAXWELL, MRS. W.H. A Female Physician to the Ladies of the United States: Being a Familiar and Practical Treatise on Matters of Utmost Importance Peculiar to Women. Adapted for Every Woman's Own Private Use. New York: published by the author, 1860. 111 pp.
      This popular work includes discussions of menstruation, menopause, leucorrhea, childbirth, and what Maxwell calls "premature delivery," a cleverly masked term for abortion. Maxwell, who claimed to have been practicing medicine for thirty years, had a private hospital in New York and, while obviously an abortionist, also exhibits genuine concern about women's health and the role of women physicians in their treatment. As might be expected, Maxwell argues in favor of abortion, claiming that it can save unmarried girls from prostitution. Like many of her contemporaries, she also speaks out on the dangers of masturbation.

816   MELENDY, MARY RIES. Perfect Womanhood for Maidens--Wives--Mothers; A Book Giving Full Information on All the Mysterious and Complex Matters Pertaining to Women. Chicago: Monarch, 1903. 448 pp.
      This popular sex and health guide for women bore several titles during its publishing history, including The Ideal Woman and Ideal Womanhood and Motherhood. Melendy, a homeopathic physician, presents information on such topics as sexual physiology, marriage, menstruation, childbirth, and abortion in addition to home health hints, first aid, infant care, and female beauty. Melendy's advice was typical of many late nineteenth- and early twentieth-century writers. Masturbation was "a source of misery, and even death," and abortion no less than murder. Melendy

believed in prenatal influence, although she also felt that a healthy environment could help to overcome the effects of unsound heredity.

817   ____. Sex Life the Pathway to Mental and Physical Perfection: The Twentieth Century Book of Sexual Knowledge. Philadelphia: National Publishing Co., 1914. 648 pp.
    Melendy's Sex Life was issued in a single volume with a shorter work, The Science of Eugenics and Sex Life, by Walter J. Hadden and Charles H. Robinson. Its publication history is somewhat cloudy, although it was reprinted at least once in 1927. Melendy was the author of a number of other popular health tracts, and this work is largely derivative from the work of other authors. Melendy was, however, one of the "new women" and included a chapter, "Influence of Woman in Public Affairs," in the midst of her "Special Warning to the Boy and Girl" (on the evils of masturbation) and advice on choosing a mate, chastity, and the change of life. Sex was the come-on, but Melendy gave her readers their money's worth, including a cure for rattlesnake bite as well as recipes for fig jelly and macaroni soup.

818   MILLER, ELI P. A Treatise on the Cause of Exhausted Vitality; Or, Abuses of the Sexual Function. New York: J.A. Gray & Green, 1867. 131 pp.
    Miller, whose many publications ranged from treatises on free trade to essays on Turkish baths, has written here a conventional work on the evils of masturbation, promiscuity, and "matrimonial excesses." Although the primary focus of the book is on the loss of "vital force" through the discharge of semen, Miller includes some references to the impact of masturbation and excessive sexual indulgence on women. He finds masturbation to be the cause of leucorrhea and a wide range of other diseases in women, with nervous exhaustion being the chief danger. He also warns about the danger of masturbation in little girls. His views are generally based on so-called divine and natural law and show little evidence of scientific analysis. Interestingly, he makes full use of the often discussed "Victorian" economic metaphors for sexual behavior. Other editions of the work appear under the title Vital Force: How Wasted and How Preserved.

819   MILLER, JOHN A. Femina, a Work for Every Woman. San Francisco: Femina Co., 1893. 422 pp.
    Originally published in 1891 as Home Treatment for Diseases of Women and Some Favorite Prescriptions, Femina was written for a popular audience and focused on the so-called inflammatory diseases of the female reproductive system. Miller was a believer in preventive medicine and attributed many of women's gynecological health problems to excessive intercourse, although he did not advocate coitus only for procreation. Opposed to women's stepping outside their biologically ordained maternal sphere, Miller generalized in traditional fashion about their sexuality: "Women, as a

rule, are more passive, less amorous and more chaste in thought and feeling than men." He also criticized excessive gynecological surgery and the poor quality of American medical education (a graduate of the University of California, Miller had also studied in Germany).

820   NAPHEYS, GEORGE H. The Physical Life of Woman: Advice to the Maiden, Wife and Mother. 6th ed. Philadelphia: G. Maclean, 1872. 322 pp.

   Philadelphia physician George Napheys's works on medical therapeutics, sex, and women's health were among the most widely read books of their type in late nineteenth-century America. And yet a close examination of The Physical Life of Woman shows it to have been full of bias, unscientific notions, and a pervading moralistic self-righteousness that tended to see sexual behavior in terms of right or wrong. Obviously, such points of view appealed to thousands of readers, giving them security—as long as they followed the correct path: traditional heterosexual intercourse, preferably with a mutual orgasm leading to conception, but not during menstruation, lactation, or the first five months of pregnancy if there was a tendency to miscarriage. Napheys believed in sexuality as a normal condition of women, so much so that he viewed single women as semipathological cases: "Deprived of the natural objects of interest, the sentiments are apt to fix themselves on parrots and poodles or to be confined within the breast and wither for want of nourishment." There was nothing good about polygamy: "The Mormons of Utah would soon sink into a state of Asiatic effeminacy were they left to themselves." And anything other than diminution of sexual desire after menopause should be viewed with alarm.

821   NICHOLS, MARY GOVE. Lectures to Ladies on Anatomy and Physiology. Boston: Saxton & Peirce, 1842. 300 pp.

   Mary Gove Nichols was a self-taught health lecturer and writer and sometime water-cure practitioner who was greatly influenced by Sylvester Graham. Female sexuality is discussed in the eleventh and twelfth lectures on the nervous system. She cautions against premature and excessive development of sexual instincts and like so many of her contemporaries warns that female masturbation may lead to leucorrhea, hysteria, consumption, and insanity. In this regard, she was directly influenced by Dr. Samuel Woodward's reports on his observations at Worcester, from which she quotes freely. Girls' boarding schools are seen as contributing to the problem, and Nichols also claims it to be a cause of nine out of ten cases of prostitution. Interestingly, there is no discussion at all of conventional heterosexual relations.

822   NOYES, JOHN HUMPHREY. Male Continence. Oneida, N.Y.: Oneida Community, 1872. 24 pp.

   John Humphrey Noyes, patriarch of the Oneida community, claimed to have discovered his system of male continence, or controlled sexual intercourse without ejaculation, in the 1840s. Of course, such techniques were not unknown prior to Noyes and were, indeed, practiced in many parts of the world. But by giving his ideas a quasi-religious justification and making them, along with eugenics, an integral part of his perfectionist communitarian philosophy, Noyes was better able to justify his philosophy to the nineteenth-century mind. Central to his theory was a separation between reproductive functions and organs and those governing purely sexual activities, a distinction not usually made by his contemporaries. He thus legitimated the exercise of purely spiritual conjugal union, with the condition that such union would not lead to propagation. Self-control on the part of the male partner was required, but Noyes claimed that none of his followers found the practice injurious. Indeed, women's pleasure was heightened, not only by the prolongation of intercourse itself, but also because male continence eliminated their fears of possible pregnancy and unwanted children. Significantly, Noyes includes no firsthand testimonials from women of the community as to the efficacy of the system, although he does include such material from men. Substantial portions of this tract are reprints of a shorter 1866 tract, a chapter from Noyes's The Bible Argument (1848), and a description of the community, originally published in the Woman's Journal, by Thomas Wentworth Higginson.

823   PANCOAST, SETH. The Ladies' Medical Guide and Marriage Friend. Philadelphia: published by the author, 1859. 584 pp.
    Much of Pancoast's Ladies' Medical Guide relates to such topics as reproductive anatomy and physiology, pregnancy, women's diseases, and beauty. His material on sexuality, while confined to a few chapters, includes some striking observations. Pancoast believed that women should have the right to control their own reproductive functions, since excessive childbearing was a major cause of woman's ill health. Sexual abstinence, however, was not normal, and his lengthy discussion of the clitoris, "the principal seat of the thrill or voluptuous sensation in the female," makes one wonder why the function of this organ was neglected by so many of his successors. Likewise, there is one of the earliest mentions of lesbianism ("the lustful embraces of women of each other . . . This revolting vice derived its name from the Island of Lesbos, where it was practiced by the celebrated poetess Sappho.") and a chapter on hermaphroditism. A chapter on woman's sphere, while emphasizing that the true role of woman is the home, advocates woman's emancipation from her inferior status, as well as educational and professional opportunities, opposing, however, suffrage and political activism. In addition to the text, this book, which was reprinted several times, includes a list of authors and books quoted and referred to, featuring everything from Paradise Lost to Acton's work on prostitution and the reproductive organs, an interesting source for tracing the influence and use of materials.

824   PHYSICIAN, A [pseud.]. Licentiousness and Its Effects upon

Bodily and Mental Health. New York: Wm. H. Graham, 1844. 102 pp.

This is a Grahamite antimasturbation/antilicentiousness tract. The author strongly advocates water cures for both men and women, as well as a vegetable diet. The author's female masturbation material appears to have been taken from the work of Mary Gove Nichols.

825 PITCAIRN, FREDERICK WILSON, and ELIZABETH J. WILLARD. Woman's Guide to Sexual Knowledge or What Every Woman Should Know. Philadelphia: National Publishing Co., 1906. 512 pp.

Typical of the popular health and sex books produced for the mass market, often for mail-order sales, by National and similar publishing houses, Woman's Guide to Sexual Knowledge covers a wide range of topics, including reproductive biology and physiology, pregnancy, home gymnastics, "modern methods of dressing the hair," and food for invalids. Written for a female audience, it warns of hasty consummation of marriage, advises that procreation is best accomplished in the morning, and recommends abstinence during menstruation and for two to three hours after eating. Otherwise, the authors genially comment that sexual behavior "will depend on age, habit, occupation, situation, climate, season, aliment, and numerous other moral, physical, and external influences, which are capable of modifying this function."

826 PULTE, JOSEPH HIPPOLYT. Woman's Medical Guide, Containing Essays on the Physical, Moral and Educational Development of Females, and the Homeopathic Treatment of Their Diseases in All Periods of Life, Together with Directions for the Remedial Use of Water and Gymnastics. Cincinnati: Moore, Anderson, Wilstach & Keys, 1853. 336 pp.

A homeopathic physician of Cincinnati, Pulte was best known for his Homeopathic Domestic Physician which, along with the Woman's Medical Guide, was frequently reprinted. Reacting against the nascent women's rights movement, Pulte continually argues in favor of woman's separate sphere, decrying the need for women's education. "The phrase 'emancipation of woman,' should never have been thought of; its very sound is a disgrace to language, the especial gift of the Creator." For someone so concerned about woman's appropriate role, Pulte says surprisingly little about her sexuality. Nymphomania is seen as a cause of masturbation, a reversal of common belief, while anaphrodisy, or frigidity, is dismissed quickly with the advice that women so affected should consult their physicians. Hysteria is also discussed, Pulte noting a decline in its frequency.

827 RECTOR, EDWARD L. Ethical Hygiene: Solid Facts Boiled Down. Six Live Books on the Laws of Health: Physical Hygiene, Mental Hygiene, Moral Hygiene, Sex Hygiene, Maternal Hygiene, and Social Ethics. Parkersburg, W.Va.: Purity Publishing Co., 1917. 259 pp.

A tract in the tradition of the purity movement, Ethical Hygiene contains substantial material on sexual ethics and behavior. Rector was especially concerned with the problem of venereal disease, which he claimed afflicted over 50 percent of the American people. His views on women's sexuality ranged from the reasonably enlightened ("All healthy girls will experience desires for sexual intercourse. Do not become alarmed and think such feelings indicate a depraved being") to the folkloristic (Masturbation "ruins the life and destroys the health of thousands of girls every year. . . . the girl usually grows into a roughly-built, coarse-featured, masculine woman"). Husbands are urged to exercise consideration and self-control for their wives's sake, but sexual technique and pleasure are bypassed altogether. Rector was also the author of a book on Christian salvation entitled Saved or Deceived.

828   RICHARD, S.Y. The Science of the Sexes or How Parents May Control the Sex of Their Offspring and Stock-raisers Control the Sex of Stock. 5th ed. Louisville, Ky.: Spining, 1879. 315 pp.
   The method for controlling sex that Richard advocated consisted of the woman lying on her left side after coitus if females were desired and on her right side if males were desired. Similar directional actions could be performed with the testicles, which, like the ovaries, were seen as having male (right) and female (left) parts. Richard was convinced that this system was infallible, but he also believed in a story about a woman, frightened by a rattlesnake during pregnancy, who gave birth to a snake-headed child. Intrigued by sexual and reproductive oddities, he also included some useful statistical and other charts summarizing published and other references to age at first menarche, cases of prolonged menstruation, and the like. He also quotes extensively from such authorities as Sims, Foote, and Storer.

829   ROBINSON, WILLIAM JOSEPHUS. Sex Knowledge for Women and Girls: What Every Woman and Girl Should Know. New York: Critic and Guide, 1917. 170 pp.
   Sex Knowledge is another variation on the themes so commonly addressed by Robinson: birth control, prevention of venereal disease, eugenics, and similar topics. Its similarity to Woman: Her Sex and Love Life (entry 832) is obvious, although it is much less detailed.

830   _____. Sexual Problems of Today. New York: Critic and Guide, 1912. 285 pp.
   One of many popular works on sexuality by Robinson, Sexual Problems of Today is a pastiche of short essays, some of them no longer than a paragraph. Robinson saw himself as a crusader against the ignorance of both physicians and patients and especially took up the cause of sexual rights for women. Sexual health was the basis of a happy home, but this would never occur as long as men insisted on impregnating wives unfit or undesirous of

childbearing, giving them venereal disease. Robinson railed against the seduction of young girls, as well as against the idea that women's sexuality disappeared with menopause. Proabortion and probirth control, Robinson was an outspoken prophet of many social changes not seen until the present women's movement.

831   ROBINSON, WILLIAM JOSEPHUS, ed. Sexual Truths Versus Sexual Lies, Misconceptions and Exaggerations. New York: Critic and Guide, 1919. 400 pp.
        Robinson apparently lifted the essays in this collection from other sources, but he does not acknowledge their points of origin. Many of them are by European writers, such as Magnus Hirschfeld, and topics covered relating to women include frigidity, abstinence, and female sexuality in general. Robinson has added some odd little touches, including brief articles ("Death during Intercourse," "False Accusation of Rape") and a letter from Benjamin Franklin on why old women are preferable to young for illict relations.

832   ROBINSON, WILLIAM JOSEPHUS. Woman: Her Sex and Love Life. New York: Critic and Guide, 1917. 411 pp.
        This general sex manual for women incorporates many of the ideas found in Robinson's other publications. Despite his belief in such progressive measures as liberal divorce, the availability of birth control measures, and the prevention of venereal disease, Robinson remained a traditionalist in many ways. Woman's sex instinct was seen as "finer, more spiritual, more platonic" than man's, while motherhood still remained the highest ideal: "We emphatically believe that couples who are in excellent health, who are of untainted heredity, who are fit to bring up children, and have the means to do so, should have at least half a dozen children." He did not believe in a single standard based on a premarital chastity ideal for men, nor did he see any harm in women faking orgasm. Among the other erroneous beliefs he perpetrated were the hereditary nature of homosexuality and masturbation as a cause of anemia and pimples. Woman was frequently reprinted and apparently enjoyed a wide readership.

833   ROOT, HARMON KNOX. The Lover's Marriage Lighthouse: A Series of Sensible and Scientific Essays on the Subjects of Marriage and Free Divorce, and on the Uses, Wants, and Supplies of the Spiritual, Intellectual, Affectional, and Sexual Natures of Man and Woman, etc. New York: published by the author, 1858. 511 pp.
        An illustration (one of fifty-eight in the book) on page 347 entitled "The Onanists and Their Child" is but one of the many treats in store for readers of this proselytizing tract for the cause of reform of marriage relations. Although his social ideas were far in advance of the time, other theories strike modern readers as slightly ridiculous: "I have found that the first step in the production of a new being, is the spiritual impregnation of

the male by the female through the organs of vision, by spirit-mating." On the other hand, Root derides the idea that the hymen is proof of virginity and suggests that sexual experience by women before marriage might be beneficial if it would prevent them from being locked into disastrous unions. Women are seen definitely as sexual beings, and Root warns of masturbation, incidentally including an early reference by name to the dildo. As a whole, the book is rather unorganized and eclectic in its presentation. Root also offered mail-order medical advice for one dollar, as well as Electro-Chemical Foot-bath and Vapor-bath treatments at his New York office.

834   RUTTLEY, JOHN H. Nature's Secrets and the Secrets of Women Revealed; Or How to Be Born and How to Live. San Francisco: published by the author, 1875. 210 pp.

The prescription of sexual behavior to ensure the production of sound, healthy offspring was the concern of many nineteenth-century writers in the medicosexuality field. Ruttley, an English-born San Francisco physician, held some of the more original, impractical views on this subject that one finds in the literature. A firm believer in the power of antenatal influence on the health and character of the child, he advocated sexual relations for procreation alone. Intercourse should be planned well in advance and required complete chastity for thirty to ninety days prior to the event, with total separation of husband and wife for one month. During this time, Ruttley recommended that the woman should leave home and go to some scenic spot in order to develop rapport with nature! When she returned, coitus should immediately occur in daylight "with the blinds thrown open." Of course, intercourse during pregnancy and lactation was also taboo. Weaning might occur at six weeks; if so, the child would be able in adult life to be sexually continent for sixty days and his or her child for ninety days. Two years, however, should intervene between birth and the next conception.

Ruttley also predicted dire consequences from masturbation, opposed abortion, alcohol, drugs, and tobacco, and recommended against eating pork and sausage (or cabbage more than twice a year). He also included a chapter, apparently intended to substantiate his theories, discussing the degeneracy of the British royal family and inserted some promotional hype for his Wafer for Female Weakness and Elixir of Life.

835   RYAN, MICHAEL. The Philosophy of Marriage, in Its Social, Moral, and Physical Relations, with an Account of the Diseases of the Genito-Urinary Organs Which Impair or Destroy the Reproductive Function, and Induce a Variety of Complaints; with the Physiology of Generation in the Vegetable and Animal Kingdoms; Being Part of a Course of Obstetric Lectures Delivered at the North London School of Medicine, Charlotte Street, Bloomsbury, Bedford Square. 3d ed. London: H. Bailliere, 1839. 388 pp.

An anti-Malthusian English physician, Michael Ryan was a moralist who was greatly disturbed by the prostitution, illegitimacy, pornography, and other public evidence of "immoral" sexuality that he saw around him. The Philosophy of Marriage was his attempt to explain sex and reproduction and to delineate the laws of nature that he believed should govern sexual behavior. His views on such topics as intercourse during pregnancy were ambiguous. On one hand, he felt that it "causes abortion, frustrates the view of nature and seriously injures the health or may destroy the life of the woman." Yet at the same time, he maintained that "moderate intercourse may be indulged in with caution and gentleness at all times." Masturbation in girls came in for close censure, as did so-called premature marriage, marriage late in life, or marriage when there was a disparity in age. Ryan is at times a romantic--"Marriage is a fairy land--the land of promise"--but he also views sexual intercourse as being solely for the propagation of the species. Abstinence or even thinking about contraception is contrary to nature. Ryan's sources range from folklore to his own clinical observations, making The Philosophy of Life a most eclectic tome.

836   SAVORY, GEORGE WASHINGTON. Marriage: Its Science and Ethics. Chicago: Stockham Publishing Co., 1900. 404 pp. LC.

Savory's Marriage is perhaps most notable for its reference to simultaneous orgasm: "The husband must learn how to call out the wife's passion to the full, while he restrains his own impetuosity till both can reach the orgasm or climax together, for then only can come that full delight in the ultimation of love by which superior children can be begotten." The primary emphasis on procreation rather than pleasure is not surprising.

Presenting a series of dialogues between a doctor, a pastor, and a married couple, Savory, a clergyman from San Jose, California, argues for spirituality and "soul union" in a monogamous marriage relationship. Husbands are advised not to be selfish in their passion: "Any embrace which is known to be unwelcome to the wife can be only a yielding to the animal and hence an embrace of lust." Abstinence is seen as the only acceptable means of birth control, and readers are assured that they can control the sex of offspring through the timing of intercourse at certain points in the menstrual cycle.

Although Savory incorporated extensive discussion of biblical references to marriage, he also recommended "the sexual gymnastics of the Egyptian dancing girls, practiced for ages with the result of robust health." He was also a promoter of vegetarianism: "Abolish beef and you abolish brutality, murder, sensuality between the sexes."

837   SCOTT, JAMES FOSTER. The Sexual Instinct: Its Use and Dangers as Affecting Heredity and Morals. Essentials to the Welfare of the Individual and the Future of the Race. New York: E.B. Treat, 1899. 436 pp.

Also published under the title Heredity and Morals as Affected by the Use and Abuse of the Sexual Instinct, this work was being reprinted as late as 1931, with minor revisions. Scott, a prominent Washington, D.C., physician, intended his book to be read by an audience of laymen, specifically cautioning that it was not intended for women and boys. An outspoken advocate of social purity, he was primarily concerned with the impact of extramarital male sexual indulgence on men as well as on their wives. Special emphasis is placed on the danger of sexual activity as a means of spreading venereal disease. The fourth chapter, "Woman and the Unmanliness of Degrading Her," contains Scott's clearest views on the nature of women's sexuality. Like many purity advocates and crypto-feminists Scott believed that woman, by virtue of her role as mother, belonged to a higher sphere than men. She was not devoid of sexual feeling, but her sexuality was transmuted by her role: "The sensual gratification which woman experiences in co-ition is normally not the chief pleasure, but to her the enjoyment of the act is the sum of the lustful satisfaction, plus the 'love touch,' plus the kisses and caresses, plus the feeling of confidence that her husband will fulfil his share of parental responsibility." Scott decried the double standard and advocated education as the means for women to gain the knowledge essential for political change and establishment of their equal rights. Other chapters dealt with prostitution, abortion, onanism (under which Scott grouped everything from withdrawal to bestiality), and the work of Krafft-Ebing on sexual perversion.

838 SHANNON, THOMAS WASHINGTON, and W.J. TRUITT. Personal Help for the Married. A Volume of Vital Facts for All Married and Marriageable Men and Women, Who Would Escape the Disastrous Consequences of Ignorance of the Laws of Sex and Heredity. Together with Counsel, Advice, Help and Instruction of Serious Importance to the Millions Who Have Suffered Pain, Remorse and Agony Due to Mistakes Which May Yet Be Corrected. Marietta, Ohio: S.A. Mullikin, 1918. 288 pp.

One of a "Personal Help" series directed at a working-class audience, this volume includes much material on reproduction, childbirth, heredity, and child rearing. It is in many senses a throwback to an earlier time. For example, Fowler (which one is unspecified) is cited on preferential age at marriage, and selection of a mate based on temperament is advocated. Male self-control is extolled, while the marriage night is described as a potentially traumatic experience for the bride. Homey homilies abound: "It is said that love enters through the nose. If that be true, it may well be said that love may be driven out through fetid, filthy feet." Acton's impact is felt in the following characterization: "The best mothers, wives and managers of households know little or nothing of the sexual pleasure. Love of home, children and domestic duties are the only passions they feel."

839 SOLOMON, SAMUEL. A Guide to Health; Or, Advice to Both Sexes,

in Nervous and Consumptive Complaints: With an Essay on the
Scurvy, Leprosy, and Scrofula, Also, on a Certain Disease,
Seminal Weakness, and a Destructive Habit of a Private Nature.
To Which Is Added, an Address to Parents, Tutors, and Guardians
of Youth, with Observations on the Use and Abuse of Cold Bathing.
New York: R. Bach, [1803]. 294 pp.

Samuel Solomon was a Liverpool "physician" whose Guide to
Health ran into many printings in both the United States and
England. It was hardly coincidental that almost every page contained testimony for his Cordial Balm of Gilead or his Anti-
Impetigines, patent medicines that were claimed to cure everything
from flatulence to blindness. One section addresses the question
of masturbation in women. Here Solomon was a bit fuzzy, implying
that this act required the same involvement of the vagina as heterosexual coitus. He also asserted that sexual relationships between
women were not uncommon, although he felt that they were often the
result of a hermaphroditism caused by an enlarged clitoris. The
balm was prescribed to cure all.

840   STALL, SYLVANUS. What a Young Husband Ought to Know.
      Philadelphia: Vir Publishing Co., 1897. 300 pp.

This is one of a series of sex education and marriage books
published by Vir and written by Stall, Mary Wood-Allen, and Emma
F.A. Drake. Christian theology permeates Stall's sexual philosophy.
His views on women adhered to the post-Acton view: "Wives seldom
seek the closer embraces of their husbands. They are generally
indifferent; often absolutely averse." Women had "finer nervous
sensibilities" than men and were destined to motherhood. Although
Stall joined many of his contemporaries in regarding sexual intercourse as a drain on life's vital force, he was not so rigid as to
believe that sex in marriage was only for procreation. It is interesting to note, however, that he gave the husband rather than
the wife control over deciding how much sex was enough: "Each
young husband must determine for himself and his wife when they
have reached the limit of moderations." He noted, however, that
the wife's wishes should be respected. Stall was opposed to abortion, recommended the use of the "safe period" form of birth control, and urged couples to abstain from sex during pregnancy.
Guernsey's Plain Talks and works of Eliza Bisbee Duffey are frequently cited.

841   STOCKHAM, ALICE B. Karezza: Ethics of Marriage. New rev. ed.
      Chicago: Stockham Publishing Co., 1903. 140 pp.

Readers familiar with John Humphrey Noyes's doctrine of male
continence will find much that is familiar in Alice Stockham's
Karezza. In fact, Stockham freely acknowledges her debt to Noyes
by quoting extensively from his works. Her own philosophy was more
heavily overlaid with a highly romantic spirituality and contained
specific instructions for the mental exercises necessary to imple-
ment Karezza (one recommendation was that reading of such authors
as Browning and Emerson should accompany meditation for several

days before conjugal union occurred). Nevertheless, the basic goals--elimination of unwanted pregnancy and waste of life's vital force--remained. Echoes of other themes common to many nineteenth-century sex writers are heard: the brutality of the wedding night when many brides were caught unaware, the power of maternal impressions to "brand" the character of an infant in the womb, and the notion that motherhood was the highest goal of woman's life.

842　　　　. Tokology: A Book for Every Woman. Rev. ed. Chicago: Sanitary Publishing Co., 1886. 373 pp.

Frequently reprinted up to 1916, Alice Stockham's Tokology was primarily designed as a guide to painless (or at least healthy) pregnancy. The revised edition differs from the 1883 original by including a chapter on regulating the sex of offspring, as well as testimonials from women readers of the earlier editions. Although Stockham believed in the primacy of the maternal instinct in women, she was highly critical of society's tendency to teach sexual repression to girls while extolling sexual license to boys. She believed that sex was for both procreation and pleasure, but her ideas on Karezza, or male continence (referred to here as "sedular absorption"), were not yet developed as they were to become in her later work. Indeed, Tokology contains a much stronger appeal for use of the safe period or even continence, and Stockman certainly believed that total continence should be the rule during pregnancy. Indeed, she downplays all physical imperatives: "The mind can rise superior to the body. . . . Control of appetite is the first step in human culture." Judging from the testimonials, her readers agreed with her.

843　TRALL, RUSSELL THACHER. Home-Treatment for Sexual Abuses. A Practical Treatise on the Nature and Causes of Excessive and Unnatural Sexual Indulgence, the Diseases and Injuries Resulting Therefrom, with Their Symptoms and Hydropathic Management. New York: Fowlers and Wells, 1853. 118 pp.

A disciple of Sylvester Graham, New York hydropathist R.T. Trall was an archenemy of masturbation, the subject of this tract. Using the economic metaphor of the body as a closed system, Trall saw the overall result of masturbation and excessive sexual indulgence as nervous and vital exhaustion. In women, the practice could lead to leucorrhea, nymphomania, prolapsed uterus, and uterine cancer. Cure, however, could be effected through proper exercise and diet, sufficient sleep, and a variety of hydropathic baths and internal administrations of water.

844　　　　. Sexual Physiology: A Scientific and Popular Exposition of the Fundamental Problems in Sociology. New York: Miller, Wood, & Co., 1866. 312 pp.

Numerous line drawings illustrate the biological principles of sex and reproduction with which much of this book deals, but psychological aspects of sexuality are not neglected. Women's orgasms, as well as their sexuality, are seen as normal functions, but Trall did not connect this with an emancipated view of woman's role, maintaining that her strongest desire was for maternity. He believed that procreation and pleasure were equally important as objects of sexual activity, and that by exercising control over sexual relations, women could in effect eliminate the need for birth control and abortion. Trall advocated weekly (or less frequent) coitus as optimum for the health of both parents and offspring. Woman's right to control sexual relations is a central idea in this popular manual.

845   WALKER, ALEXANDER. Intermarriage; Or the Mode in Which, and and the Causes Why, Beauty, Health and Intellect, Result from Certain Unions, and Deformity, Disease and Insanity, from Others. London: John Churchill, 1838. 442 pp.
       Although eugenics was not coined as a term until the late nineteenth century, interest in "scientific" breeding began much earlier. While Walker's primary objective was to put forth criteria for mate selection to ensure healthy offspring, he made numerous observations on all aspects of women's sexuality. Many of his ideas--that woman was ruled by her ovaries, that women masturbated as well as men--were shared by his contemporaries. Other observations were not so typical. His discussion, albeit brief, of infibulation and clitoridectomy among indigenous peoples indicates a possible link between the diffusion of anthropological observation of mutilation and the rise of sexual surgery in the mid nineteenth century. Likewise, his warning against "Sapphic tastes" indicates that intense female friendships were not always viewed as innocent, asexual relationships. To Walker, woman was definitely an active sexual being. This popular work was often reprinted in the United States, with a late English edition appearing in 1897.

846   WALLING, WILLIAM H. Sexology. Rev. and enlarged ed. Philadelphia: Puritan Publishing Co., 1904. 232 pp.
       In his introduction to the 1970 M & S Press reprint of Denslow Lewis's The Gynecologic Consideration of the Sexual Act, Marc Hollender observed that William H. Walling's Sexology and Satan in Society by Nicholas Francis Cooke (entry 772), which had first appeared in 1871, were virtually identical. An examination of the 1904 edition of Sexology reveals that Walling indeed plagiarized several chapters from the earlier work, including those on masturbation, education and training, and the physiology of marriage. In some cases, he condensed Cooke's chapters by omitting paragraphs; he also changed an occasional word or phrase. Walling did not, however, include Cooke's so-called apologia or his chapters on women's rights issues. Walling also added material, which may or may not have been original, on reproductive physiology, pregnancy, and child rearing. It is of some bibliographic interest to note that the 1904 edition of Sexology and the 1876 edition of Satan in Society were both reprinted in the 1974 Arno Press series, "Sex, Marriage and Society," the editors and publishers apparently being unaware of how closely the later work duplicated the earlier.

847 WELLS, SAMUEL R. Wedlock; Or, the Right Relations of the Sexes;
     Disclosing the Laws of Conjugal Selection, and Showing Who May
     and Who May Not Marry. New York: Samuel R. Wells, 1869. 238
     pp.
          Long-time associate of the Fowler brothers in various phren-
     ological and publishing enterprises, Samuel R. Wells presented in
     Wedlock a popular guide to courtship and marriage. Sexuality was
     not a major emphasis, although in a chapter on celibacy, Wells as-
     serted that sexual celibacy was not nearly so harmful to women as
     to men and was, indeed, highly preferable to being married to a
     brute or being a prostitute. His chief emphasis, however, was on
     legal conventions and social customs; one chapter instructed read-
     ers how to write love letters, and another reprinted several poems,
     presumably for use during the courtship process. Wells also dis-
     cussed questions of heredity, polygamy, and complex marriage and
     described marriage customs among indigenous people throughout the
     world.

848 WILCOX, DELOS FRANKLIN. Ethical Marriage: A Discussion of the
     Relations of Sex from the Standpoint of Social Duty. Ann Arbor,
     Mich.: Wood-Allen Publishing Co., 1900. 235 pp.
          An expert on municipal franchises and public utilities, D.F.
     Wilcox made only this one excursion into writing on sexuality and
     marriage. Leading to his ultimate conclusion, that continence
     within marriage and without would lead to the reform of society as
     a whole, Wilcox took the view that sex within marriage should only
     occur for purposes of procreation: "A married couple should have
     a definite program of procreation, and should confine their sexual
     unions strictly to its requirements." Even then Wilcox advocated
     restricting intercourse to single incidents, with intervals of at
     least one month in between, to determine if pregnancy had occurred.
     If it had, there should be no more coitus until the next child was
     desired. Since he took such a dim view of sex for pleasure's sake
     alone, it is hardly surprising that Wilcox opposed artificial birth
     control practices, including male continence. He was rather am-
     bivalent about women's sexuality, linking it to their desire for
     children: "Reason and experience . . . indicate that sexual inter-
     course at a time when conception is not likely is indifferent or
     positively distasteful to women." He was also firm in his belief
     that intercourse was not justifiable for male gratification alone.
     Underlying his philosophy was a belief in eugenics as a means of
     improving society. His ideas were documented by sources ranging
     from Plato to Swami Vivekenanda's Raja Yoga, obviously selected to
     prove his point. Ethical Marriage is of additional interest as an
     example of the link between Progressive-era political/economic
     thought and sexual reform.

849 WILLMAN, REINHOLD. Married Life: A Family Handbook. Chicago:
     J.S. Hyland, 1917. 430 pp.
          Intended as a general guide to all aspects of health in
     married and family life, Willman's work emphasizes sexuality and

sexual behavior. With its emphasis on religious authority and moralistic determinants of behavior, it hearkens back to the nineteenth century, demonstrating the nonlinear development of American popular sex literature. The influence of the Progressive era, however, is evinced by the emphasis Willman places on sexual hygiene and prevention of venereal disease. Women are seen as lacking in sexual desire, when compared to men, and the author notes that this leads to a slower reaction time during sexual relations. Sensual pleasure alone is not sufficient justification for sex, even in marriage, but Willman does recognize woman's ability to achieve orgasm. Birth control and abortion are called "unnatural acts."

850   WOOD-ALLEN, MARY. Marriage: Its Duties and Privileges. Chicago: Fleming H. Revell, 1901. 422 pp.

Fully half of this marriage manual is occupied with questions relating to pregnancy and baby care, an emphasis that leaves no doubt about Wood-Allen's ideas regarding woman's role in marriage. Yet Wood-Allen did not automatically believe in a subordinate role: "The man does not expect to lose his individuality in that of his wife, nor should she allow herself to be wholly merged in the individuality of her husband." Because she advocated personal freedom, Wood-Allen advocated consideration of separate beds and separate rooms, yet she also believed that "every true woman desires children."

Because of this role in maternity, the woman was to control sexual relations. Acton is extensively quoted to demonstrate the value of continence. Indeed, Wood-Allen advocated absolute continence except when procreation was desired and then only once a month in an atmosphere of utter solemnity.

851   WOODWARD, SAMUEL BAYARD. Hints for the Young in Relation to the Health of Body and Mind. Boston: G.W. Light, 1856. 65 pp.

Originally published in 1835 in the Boston Medical and Surgical Journal, Woodward's essay was gradually enlarged over several editions of which this appears to have been the last. Woodward, who was superintendent of the Worcester Lunatic Asylum in Massachusetts, was convinced that masturbation was a major cause of insanity and mental retardation, although probably more so in men than in women. Woodward outlines thirteen case histories, three of which were of women, in order to prove his theory. This is an excellent example of the tortuous grapplings of the nineteenth-century mind with the problems of causation.

852   WRIGHT, HENRY C. Marriage and Parentage; Or, the Reproductive Element in Man, as a Means to His Elevation and Happiness. Boston: Bela Marsh, 1855. 324 pp.

Marriage and Parentage is a statement of reformer Henry C. Wright's perfectionist philosophy. Wright believed that controlled reproduction coupled with true love marriages would result in an improved race of human beings redeemed from disease and misery. In the ideal marriage, not only would a deep spiritual love prevail, but sexual passion would always be subject to love. Women, because of their role in gestation, birth, and child rearing (Wright saw woman's ultimate design as being wife and mother), were to control the frequency and even quality of sexual relations. "The wife must decide how often, and under what circumstances, the husband may enjoy this passional expression of his love." As might be expected sex was only for procreation and was tabooed during gestation and lactation. Although this was not an unusual philosophy for the time, Wright's almost naive faith in the ultimate result of these prescriptions as well as his solid connections with the antislavery and other reform movements make this flowery work of more than incidental interest.

Prescriptive Literature, 1920 and After

An emphasis on sexual technique and women's sexual satisfaction characterized much of the prescriptive and advice literature appearing after World War I. To no small degree, this was made possible by increasing liberalization of legal attitudes regarding obscenity. Not only had the federal law forbidden the importation of certain types of "sexual" literature (Marie Stopes's Married Love (entry 921) was judged to be not obscene only in 1931), but individual states restricted the dissemination both of explicit sex information and of material relating to birth control as well.

From the 1930s on, popular marriage manuals such as the Dutch import Ideal Marriage by T.H. Van de Velde (entry 923), which included a detailed discussion of sexual technique, enjoyed a wide readership. It was not until the 1960s, however, that works began to appear--The Sensuous Woman (entry 876), The Joy of Sex (entry 865)--which challenged the premise that marriage was the only suitable basis for sexual relations. Reflecting the similar trend in medical and scientific research of separating reproductive and sexual functions in women, these new manuals achieved an over-the-counter frankness previously reserved for works sold in plain brown wrappers.

Other writers combined elements of tradition with new perspectives. Marabel Morgan's phenomenally successful The Total Woman (entry 905) advocated women's subordination to their husbands, while at the same time urging them to "be the seducer, not the seducee." Others, such as Max Exner (entry 870), were influenced by the sociological studies of sexual behavior that began to appear in the 1920s.

Regardless of the particular perspective of each author, however, certain ideas commonly found in pre-1920 prescriptive literature receive little, if any, notice. Chief among these is the concept of the asexuality of women. Rather, women's sexuality is seen typically as being qualitatively different from that of men, but nevertheless an active force. Writers such as John Francis Flynn (entry 873), who in 1931 maintained that many women never experienced sexual desire, seem, even for then, to be relics of a bygone era. Decisions regarding the appropriateness and frequency of sexual relations are, for the most

part, left up to the individual parties involved, although oral sexual
techniques, masturbation, and other variations on conventional heterosexual behavior still elicit varied opinions. Moralizing, however, has
definitely fallen by the wayside.

One should not however, equate such attitudes with a rise in feminist consciousness. David Reuben (entry 912) calls women "girls," while
"M" in The Sensuous Man (entry 900) assumes that feeling possessed is
an essential factor in woman's sexual well being. Only time will tell
whether the contemporary women's movement will have a lasting impact
on the way that men view women's sexuality.

853   ANDERSON, JACOB GRANT. Sex Life and Home Problems. Anderson,
      Ind.: Gospel Trumpet, 1921. 216 pp.
          Anderson, a clergyman, was home problems editor of the Gospel
      Trumpet, a weekly religious magazine, and incorporated letters he
      received from readers regarding domestic and sex problems in this
      volume. A general marriage guide, with an emphasis on moral phi-
      losophy, Sex Life and Home Problems focuses on the theme that un-
      satisfactory sexual relations in marriage will result in general
      difficulties in all aspects of domestic life. Anderson combined
      old and new ideas. While he believed in a single standard and in
      the importance of moral training and sex education for children,
      he also retained beliefs in the temperaments and in women as the
      guardians of sexual morality because of their spirituality and
      capacity for maternal love. Although his discussion of reproduc-
      tive biology is brief, he places greater emphasis on such topics
      as pregnancy, motherhood, and menopause. No prude, Anderson be-
      lieved in sex for pleasure as well as reproduction, although he
      recommended limiting sexual relations to only two incidents per
      month if possible.

854   ARDEN, THEODORE Z. A Handbook for Husbands and Wives. New
      York: Association Press, 1939. 47 pp.
          This short marriage manual contains more material suggesting
      values than one might expect from so brief a work. Sex is seen as
      the foundation of marriage, and intercourse is described as the
      end result of all affection in marriage, surely a male-biased view
      that fails to recognize women's needs for nonsexual affection.
      Arden is not, however, oblivious to the sexual differences between
      men and women, and comments on the diffuse nature of women's sexu-
      ality. Men are also advised not to force their passion upon women.
      Arden includes material on sexual physiology and technique as well
      as birth control, but comments, "No family is complete without
      children."

855   BERNARD, BERNARD. Sex Conduct in Marriage (The Art of Maintain-
      ing Love and Happiness in Marriage). Chicago: Health and Life,
      1922. 121 pp.
          Bernard, editor of Health and Life magazine, not only

published and sold popular health and sex literature through the mail, but for twenty-five cents would dispense personal advice ("Please fill in the following form . . .") to his readers. Sex Conduct in Marriage is generally simplistic in tone, extolling sexual relations as a sacred communion, condemning sexual excess as immoral, and urging sex education, particularly as a means of eliminating bride's trauma. Bernard also believed that many women never experience "the great joy and uplift of the full expression of their feminine functions" because of their ignorance and mis-conception of sex as immoral. An advocate of the diaphragm for contraception, Bernard called abortion a crime and believed that "a child conceived in passion will inherit a lustful tendency."

856   BIRCHALL, ELLEN F., and NOEL B. GERSON. Sex and the Adult Woman. New York: Gilbert, 1965. 237 pp.
        Birchall, a psychiatrist (Gerson was apparently a writer assisting her), recognized the conflicts being created for many women by the demands of the sexual revolution versus traditional morality. She proposes in this book ways and techniques to achieve mutual sexual satisfaction in men and women. Seeing major problems as ignorance, sexual inhibitions, and hostilities, she suggests self-analysis to determine one's "sex profile" and goals for change. Many of her ideas are rooted in Freudianism and reflect pre-women's movement culture. Birchall feels that women are too masculinized and advocates traditional gender roles for both sexes. She sees women as basically sexually passive (although with an ac-tive "indirect" sexuality) and claims that all of them "have in-dulged in prostitution fantasies" (no evidence given). "Above all, remember that woman's greatest satisfaction is being taken."

857   BIRD, LOIS F. How to Be a Happily Married Mistress. Garden City, N.Y.: Doubleday, 1970. 189 pp.
        How to Be a Happily Married Mistress is similar to Marabel Morgan's The Total Woman (entry 905), which was published two years later. Like Morgan, Bird, author of several books on sex and marriage, advocates a traditional role for woman, including structuring marital relationships to please men. Bird, like Morgan, also recommends variety in love making, with women playing an active role: "Anything but whips and wife swapping should be 'Let's go.'" Women are encouraged to be self-reliant in sexual arousal: "If you want to be turned on after you're in bed, you'd better start your motor running before you get there." To Bird, womanhood and female "biological destiny" are sources of joy.

858   BUTTERFIELD, OLIVER M. Sex Life in Marriage. Rev. ed. New York: Emerson Books, 1962. 192 pp.
        Butterfield's Sex Life in Marriage was one of the more popu-lar mid-century manuals. The first edition had run to twenty-two printings by 1962 when the revised edition was issued. Although its author was a Methodist clergyman, the book takes an extremely open-minded and relativistic approach to many questions such as

birth control, frequency of sexual relations in marriage, and cultural determinants of sexual behavior. Butterfield placed great emphasis on the importance of mental attitudes in determining sexual satisfaction, and although he discussed sex techniques and certain physiological problems, it was his belief that these are secondary to emotional and psychological questions in securing successful marriages. Like many of his peers, he believed in the efficacy of simultaneous orgasm, although he recognized the role of the clitoris in causing orgasms in women. Although the question of frequency rated an entire chapter, Butterfield said nothing about such areas as oral sex and venereal disease. His references at the end of each chapter are primarily to works published during the 1920s and 1930s.

859   CALDERONE, MARY S., and ERIC W. JOHNSON. The Family Book about Sexuality. New York: Harper & Row, 1981. 330 pp.
        This general sex education and information book is aimed especially at the young adult audience. Calderone, best known for involvement with SIECUS, and Johnson, a professional sex educator, are especially concerned with presenting factual, up-to-date information placed in a context of a responsible, unbiased value system. Sexist language is avoided, and flexibility of gender role and sexual behavior is stressed. There is little information on sexual technique per se, but much emphasis on family planning, the family's (the authors use the term loosely) role in developing sexuality, and sex education. In addition to the text, there are an encyclopedia of sexual terms for quick reference, reading lists, resource lists, and an index. Line drawings have been provided by Vivian Cohen.

860   CHARTHAM, ROBERT. Advice to Women. New York: New American Library, 1972. 128 pp.
        Chartham's primary purpose is to describe different sex techniques for men and women, with emphasis being placed on women's active sexual role being equally important as men's role in determining sexual satisfaction. There is an element of folklore in some of his assertions, such as that girls are introduced to masturbation through the action of bicycle saddles, and his attitudes toward the women's movement are far from enlightened. Written for the mass market, Advice to Women reflects the frankness that typified much of the sex literature of the early 1970s.

861   _____. Mainly for Wives. New York: Tower, 1964. 154 pp.
        Chartham is a popular English sex writer whose books are frequently reprinted in the United States. This is a general sex manual type of guide, ostensibly written for women, but actually unisex in approach. Chartham believes that women should play an active, assertive role in sexual relations and that both men and women are frequently ignorant of basic techniques of sexual expression, as well as of other sex-related areas, such as birth control. He discusses such topics as the anatomy of sex organs,

contraception, and sex positions. Generally there is little new information that is not contained in other works.

862 CHESSER, EUSTACE. Unmarried Love. New York: McKay, 1965. 177 pp.

Written for the unmarried population and with a definite slant toward youth, Unmarried Love expresses Chesser's philosophy that sexual behavior is largely a matter of individual preference. In particular, Chesser decries traditional sexual morality which seeks to impose a single mode of conduct as "right," maintaining that "no morality which denies or seeks to spoil sexual pleasure is credible today." He also feels that young people are often used as scapegoats by adults who project their own repressed desires on them. In addition to the extensive commentary on social questions of sexual behavior, there are three chapters on birth control, an "indispensable condition" to premarital intercourse, and material on sexual and love-making technique.

863 _____. Woman and Love. New York: Citadel Press, 1962. 175 pp.

Directed specifically to married women, Woman and Love provides advice on a wide range of topics, from mate selection to telling daughters about menstruation. Chesser is especially aware of many sources of conflict in contemporary marriage, such as selfishness in sexual relations and ignorance regarding differences in sexual attitudes and response between men and women. His basic philosophy is to not worry as long as both partners enjoy the relationship. He also feels, however, that compromise and accommodation are essential from both men and women.

864 CLARK, Le MON. Emotional Adjustment in Marriage. St. Louis: C.V. Mosby, 1937. 261 pp.

Written as a guide for physicians and their patients, Emotional Adjustment in Marriage is largely derived from other works, ranging from Krafft-Ebing to Katharine Bement Davis. There is some internal contradiction resulting from reliance on such diverse sources. The reader is told that "women in general are less intensely interested in expression of the sexual impulse." Yet, "woman desires and enjoys the sexual embrace as much as does man." Clark also believes that "temporary" homosexuality can be cured by fixing "one's attention upon the goal of complete heterosexual desire and heterosexual intercourse." Frigidity is fully discussed, a topic common to most marriage manuals of the period. Yet Clark criticizes the missionary position for providing inadequate clitoral stimulation and recommends abandoning the idea that passivity in women is natural or desirable. Other topics discussed in this book, which covers many more aspects of marriage than emotional adjustment, include sex education, birth control, and divorce.

865 COMFORT, ALEXANDER, ed. The Joy of Sex: A Cordon Bleu Guide

to Lovemaking. New York: Crown, 1972. 253 pp.

The best known of the sexual technique books to appear in the 1970s, The Joy of Sex and its sequel More Joy (entry 866) are an encyclopedia of information for improving heterosexual performance. Although Comfort's basic guidelines to readers, "Don't do anything you don't really enjoy," and "Find your partner's needs and don't balk them if you can help it," would indicate an attitude supporting total equality for women in questions of sexuality, this doesn't always carry over to discussions of social questions. Topics as diverse as bisexuality, aging, and vasectomy are grouped in a section entitled "Problems" (a problem?). Abortion, euphemistically called "termination," is blithely dismissed—"In a well-conducted sex life it shouldn't be necessary"--while women are given this advice regarding rape: "Don't get yourself raped--i.e., don't deliberately excite a man you don't know well, unless you mean to follow through." Many of the illustrations of women (such as those in the section on clothes) imply a sexual objectification of that sex which is not implied by the pictures of men. Why, for example, is bisexuality illustrated by a picture of two women lovers, accompanied by the caption, "Women seem to relate more easily to same-sex stimulation in a group scene, and women exciting each other are a turn-on for males."

866 _____. More Joy: A Lovemaking Companion to The Joy of Sex. New York: Crown, 1974. 220 pp.

This sequel to The Joy of Sex (entry 865) offers additional suggestions for varying heterosexual performance and sexual technique. It retains much of the sexism and other prejudicial biases of the initial volume.

867 DAVIS, MAXINE. Sexual Responsibility in Marriage. New York: Dial Press, 1963. 380 pp.

The author of several books on sex and health, including The Sexual Responsibility of Women (entry 868), Maxine Davis here presents a discussion of sexuality in the context of marriage. Incorporating the work of Masters and Johnson and other researchers, she also provides information on the cultural context of many of our ideas on "appropriate" sexual behavior. "It is essential . . . to eliminate the contradictions and inconsistencies of the past and to rebuild our moral and ethical interpretations." Davis argues particularly strongly for sex education, but she is not totally free from stereotyped views of women, maintaining that "motherhood is the primary female function" and that the maternal instinct is an innate characteristic of women.

868 _____. The Sexual Responsibility of Women. New York: Dial Press, 1956. 299 pp.

Popular and frequently reprinted during the late 1950s and early 1960s, this is a general guide for women to sexuality and sexual behavior in marriage. Davis, a journalist, deals with such topics as reproductive physiology, sex technique, hygiene, and related areas such as premenstrual tension and contraception. Although Davis urges women to adapt themselves sexually to their husbands, much of her material assumes a more prowoman stance. She advocates women's active sexuality, as well as the validity of the clitoral orgasm and urges women to assume equal responsibility with men for the achievement of sexual satisfaction.

869   EVERETT, MILLARD S. The Hygiene of Marriage. New York: Vanguard Press, 1932. 248 pp.
      Perhaps the most interesting feature of this marriage manual is the chapter on birth control clinics, which includes addresses and lists of officials and directors of major American clinics. This emphasis on birth control characterizes the book, which also discusses such topics as menstruation, venereal disease, marriage, childbirth, and sex technique. Everett had the support of such leaders in the field as Robert Latou Dickinson and Mary Ware Dennett in preparing this work, which grew out of materials used in a course at Central YMCA College in Chicago. Although Everett reflects the best available knowledge of the time, he still perpetuates several mistaken ideas, such as the "curability" of homosexuality and that "the orgasm resulting from clitoridal and vulvar stimulation is less complete than that which occurs when the vaginal reaction is also aroused."

870   EXNER, MAX JOSEPH. The Sexual Side of Marriage. New York: W.W. Norton, 1932. 252 pp.
      Differences in the sexual constitutions of men and women and adjustment problems resulting from them constitute the overall theme of this book, one of many written by Exner. Here he is especially concerned with the "negative cultural compulsions, ignorance and bungling methods" which jeopardize the attainment of satisfaction in marriage. Among the specific factors contributing to maladjustment he discusses are the denial of the sexual needs and rights of women and too "physical" an attitude toward sexual relations. Although he believes that sexual desire and behavior manifest themselves differently in men and women and that it is woman's nature to develop her sexual capacity gradually, he nevertheless feels that "ideal marriage" can be achieved. Exner is familiar with the sociological sex research being done at the time and incorporates the findings of such authors as Katharine Bement Davis and Gilbert Van Tassel Hamilton.

871   FIELDING, WILLIAM J. Sex and the Love-Life. New York: Dodd, Mead, 1927. 322 pp.
      This marriage manual deals with all aspects of the sexual life cycle in men and women. Fielding, who was heavily influenced by Havelock Ellis, believed that while women were sexually conservative and comparatively passive, they were also more erotic and emotional than men. Both men and women needed to realize the differences between their sexual natures and adapt accordingly. Frigidity, for example, was often not a fixed psychoneurotic

condition but "a state of apathy or repugnance to unsatisfactory sexual relations--unsatisfactory because the preliminary wooing and consideration which nature demands has never been forthcoming." Fielding did not refrain from prescribing specific behavior and advised his readers to limit intercourse to twice a week and to abstain during menstruation. He also included chapters on birth control, which he advocated, menopause, venereal disease, and sexual disorders.

872 FLOR, HOLLY MARIE [CAROLINE GORDON, pseud.]. The Beginner's Guide to Group Sex: Who Does What to Whom and How. New York: Drake, 1973. 143 pp.

Wife swapping, or group sex, was one aspect of the so-called sexual revolution of the late 1960s and early 1970s that lent itself readily to mass-market publications of the how-to variety. This particular effort is full of interesting details--most male swingers are Republicans, most females read McCall's--totally unsupported by documented evidence, and includes such material as questionnaires to test readers' swinging potential, a glossary of sexual terms, addresses of useful organizations, advice on technique, and so on. As the author notes, swinging is governed by the philosophy that "sex is a biological drive. It is nonaffectional in nature." Apparently based on practical experience as well as extensive knowledge of information sources, the book documents the existence of a menstrual taboo as well as sanctions favoring lesbian sexual practice in swinging.

873 FLYNN, JOHN FRANCIS. Love and Sex Life of Woman. Glendale, Calif.: published by the author, 1931. 184 pp.

Even in 1931, books were being written, like this one, that perpetuated the sexual ideology of the nineteenth century: "Many women never have any particular desire and the pleasure they receive is in the embrace of the one they love. Their ideals are much higher and more spiritual than a man's." Flynn's female readers were also urged not to share a bed with their husbands and to long for the "spiritual blissfulness" of motherhood. In addition to being a physician, Flynn was the proprietor of the Francis Face Food and Cleansing Cream Company, whose wares are advertised in the book.

874 FOLSOM, JOSEPH KIRK, ed. Plan for Marriage: An Intelligent Approach to Marriage and Parenthood, Proposed by Members of the Staff of Vassar College. New York: Harper & Brothers, 1938. 305 pp.

This collection of essays on various aspects of marriage is composed of material written by regular faculty members at Vassar College or teachers at its summer Institute of Euthenics. The essays were originally given as a series of lectures on marriage and family life at the college in 1937. Although some of the book deals with such subjects as household budgeting and working wives, there are also chapters on reproductive anatomy and physiology and "the medical basis of intelligent sexual practice."

875   FRANCIS, BERNARD. <u>Woman's Mysterious Influence over Man: Her</u>
      <u>Secret Powers and How to Use Them, Important Sex Information, etc.</u>
      San Francisco: Woman's Educational Publishing Co., 1920. 132 pp.
          Francis's primary objective in this book is to show women how
      to land a husband and, after that is done, how to keep him. Emphasis
      is placed on physical attributes: "Well formed, fully developed
      breasts . . . appeal to the masculine instinct, since they are
      usually the indications of a passionate nature." Some of Francis's
      observations on women's sexuality are fairly progressive--the im-
      portance of foreplay is recognized and menopause is seen as a normal
      function having no effect on woman's sexual behavior. In other
      areas, however, he is decidedly unenlightened: "There is a secre-
      tion given off by women during intercourse which is absorbed by the
      penis during the orgasm, and this secretion counteracts, to some ex-
      tent, the loss of the semen expended by the man. It is the lack of
      this secretion which makes masturbation so harmful. Francis also
      advocates women faking orgasms for the sake of marital stability,
      advising them to ask their friends how to do it!

876   GARRITY, JOAN TERRY [J., pseud.]. <u>The Sensuous Woman: The</u>
      <u>First How-to Book for the Female Who Yearns to Be All Woman.</u>
      New York: Lyle Stuart, 1969. 192 pp.
          One of the most popular sex technique books to emerge from
      the so-called sexual revolution, <u>The Sensuous Woman</u> reflects its
      pre-woman's movement origins in some of its generalizations about
      women's gender/sex roles and sexual behavior: "We were designed
      to delight, excite and satisfy the male of the species. <u>Real</u> women
      know this." "Married or not, men are going to continue looking [at
      other women], and a great number will sample women besides yourself.
      You may not like it, but you're going to have to live with it."
          Primarily, <u>The Sensuous Woman</u> is an assembly of techniques
      for attracting men and keeping them. Emphasis is placed on physi-
      cal aspects of sexuality, and women are advised to train like
      athletes for the act of love. Faking orgasm when necessary for
      inflating men's egos is encouraged, and women are given hints on
      a wide range of subjects, from bedroom fashions to how and where
      to meet men.

877   GREENBLAT, BERNARD R. <u>A Doctor's Marital Guide for Patients.</u>
      Chicago: Budlong Press, 1957. 88 pp.
          Intended to be distributed by physicians to their patients,
      this short marriage manual discusses reproductive biology and
      physiology, conception, and pregnancy, as well as social attitudes
      and sexual techniques. Greenblat emphasizes the importance of
      orgasm for women, but also discusses differences between male and
      female sexuality and how these can affect sexual response. Simul-
      taneous orgasm is lauded as a goal.

878   GRIFFITH, EDWARD FYFE. <u>Modern Marriage and Birth Control.</u>
      London: Gollancz, 1944. 255 pp.
          Originally published in 1935, <u>Modern Marriage</u> was entirely
      rewritten in 1944 to reflect scientific advances in contraception

and changing opinion in such areas as social psychology. Highly
popular in Britain, it covers such subjects as anatomy, physiology,
venereal disease, and sterility. Birth control procedures are
discussed in detail, although Griffith also recommends that married
couples should have children as soon as possible, with an optimum
family size of three or four offspirng. Indeed, his ideal is the
creation of stable family life. Griffith also comments on the
situation of single women, recommending that they read Laura
Hutton's The Single Woman (entry 1334), and offers a checklist of
conditions for attaining an ideal sex relationship in marriage.
An entire chapter is devoted to the hymen and methods for its
dilation.

879   GROVES, ERNEST RUTHERFORD. Marriage. New York: Henry Holt,
      1933. 552 pp.
      Groves's work has the distinction of being probably the first
text written for a college course on marriage and was based heavily
on its author's experience as instructor in such a course at Duke
University. Dealing with much more than sexuality, it incorporates
material on economic and domestic adjustment, pregnancy, child
rearing, and divorce. Chapters relating directly to sexuality include discussions of sex appeal, sex attitudes, heterosexuality,
sexual adjustment in marriage, and problems of the unmarried. The
dilemma of career-minded women in adjusting to housekeeping and
maternal responsibilities is also examined. Marriage is the most
detailed of Groves's works and in many ways serves as the foundation for his other books.

880   GROVES, ERNEST RUTHERFORD, and GLADYS HOAGLAND GROVES. Sex in
      Marriage. New York: Macaulay, 1931. 250 pp.
      Sex in Marriage, also published in slightly different form
as Sex Fulfillment in Marriage, was one of a number of books written by the Groveses in the sex, marriage, and family field. It
was a companion volume to Wholesome Marriage, which dealt with
social and financial aspects of the relationship. Critical of
society's taboos on open discussion of sexual topics, the authors
recommend self-analysis as a technique for placing one's own sexual attitudes in perspective. And what a contrast between the
Groveses' view that "the absence of sex from courtship is probably
a more dangerous symptom than extreme passion" and writers earlier
in the century who advocated a strict hands-off policy. Women are
urged, however, to take the lead in maintaining standards of sexual conduct, although the authors recognize that this is a mutual
responsibility. Sexual technique is discussed at some length, with
emphasis on mental attitude rather than physical explicitness.
Sexual problems common to marriage are described, and readers are
encouraged to seek solutions suited to their own situations. There
is also material on birth control.

881   GROVES, GLADYS HOAGLAND, and ROBERT A. ROSS. The Married Woman:
      A Practical Guide to Happy Marriage. New York: Greenberg, 1936.
      278 pp.

Gladys Hoagland Groves and her collaborator Robert A. Ross prepared this book as a guide for women contemplating marriage or experiencing problems in existing relationships. The authors' approach is informal and there is no documentation or list of references for further reading. Proceeding from courtship through marriage to "menopause and after," Groves and Ross are matter of fact in their discussion of sexual concerns: "Girls who have worried over masturbation are liable to fear lest they have ruined their chance at playing a satisfactory role as wife, when the fact that they have been driven by sex tension to seek relief in self-manipulation only goes to show that they are normally sexed, and need not dread being classed as frigid." Sexual problems, such as frigidity and extramarital relationships, are discussed. Menopause is seen as a semipathological state: "Mental obliquity, misunderstanding, and a feeling of being misunderstood may develop; mild manic symptoms sometimes are present."

882 HALCOMB, RUTH. Sex and the Single Ms. Chatsworth, Calif.: Books for Better Living, 1974. 189 pp.

Incorporating a feminist philosophy of individual choice, Sex and the Single Ms. focuses more on the quality and types of heterosexual relationships possible in a free love/free choice society than on sexuality per se. Emphasis is placed on the importance of new, self-defined roles for women. The comments on simultaneous and multiple orgasms are interesting: "Both men and women can learn to hold back their orgasms, but there aren't many reasons why women should do so even once they know how."

883 HAYDEN, JESSE F. The Art of Marriage: A Scientific Treatise. Rev. and enlarged ed. High Point, N.C.: Book Sales Agency, 1935. 221 pp.

A list of books recommended for further study found at the end of this volume includes such authors as Havelock Ellis, Margaret Sanger, and Bertrand Russell, and Hayden also provides page citations in the text to references taken from their works. Nevertheless, Hayden's own ideas in this marriage manual are often questionable. Sterilization of criminals, for example, is advocated, and the intensity of women's orgasms is seen as being in direct relation to the size of the clitoris and the "perfection of its nervous organization." Women are described as having a "naturally passive" nature. Hayden advocates prolonging intercourse to conserve "sex powers" by deferring orgasm and, as part of this sensual approach, recommends that a garlic and lard ointment be applied to selected portions of the male anatomy before coitus. Fortunately Hayden's ideas on some other topics, such as birth control, were more enlightened.

884 HOTEP, I.M. [pseud.]. Love and Happiness: Intimate Problems of the Modern Woman. New York: Alfred A. Knopf, 1938. 235 pp.

Hotep organizes his discussion around woman's sexual life cycle, examining contemporary options and offering his opinion on preferred behavior. He argues for better sex education that will enable unmarried girls to make moral decisions for themselves. And even though he opposes the repressive attitude so often espoused by the church, he still believes in the importance of virginity and premarital chastity. Nor does the doctor believe in open marriage, specifically criticizing Bertrand Russell's views on this subject. At the root of Hotep's philosophy is a limited perception of woman's role, evinced by the following statement: "There is many a girl in Bryn Mawr and Smith and Wellesley today who is going to pay dear for her Phi Beta Kappa key; perhaps someday she may even hurl it from her in wrath as an emblem of the education that unfitted her for marriage with a stodgy fellow whose mental horizon coincided with the confines of the market place."

885   HUTTON, ISABEL GALLOWAY EMSLIE. The Sex Technique in Marriage. New York: Emerson Books, 1932. 160 pp.
      Also published in England under the title The Hygiene of Marriage, this marriage manual offers practical advice for general readers on a variety of topics ranging from mate selection to menopause and birth control. Hutton, who was a physician practicing in London, advocated absolute continence for both men and women before marriage and took a traditional view of women's sexuality, arguing that women did not need to feel sexually attracted to their husbands since such feelings would certainly develop if they loved them. Hutton, however, advocates "sexual relations immediately after marriage" in order to relieve strain and to make women aware of their sexual feelings as soon as possible. The role of the clitoris in inducing orgasm is noted, and men are urged to be considerate of their wives, especially to ensure that they attain orgasm. Sterility and other sexual dysfunctions are discussed; the chapter on birth control focuses on circumstances where it is desirable rather than on specific contraceptive techniques.

886   JACKSON, DAVID P. The Story of Man and Woman: A Study of the Sexual Relationship in This Life and the Life to Come: Its Physiology, Psychology, Morals, and Theology. Philadelphia: Dorrance, 1923. 252 pp.
      Jackson's own interpretation of scripture dominates this discussion of religious justifications for and origins of love and marriage. Although some scientific material is introduced, the tone overall is undeniably fundamentalist. The book is divided into two sections. The first, longer part relates biblical incidents, such as the story of Adam and Eve, bearing on sexual relations between men and women, and contains Jackson's prescriptions for appropriate female sexuality: "A woman is not a complete human being except when joined with a man, in accordance with the Creator's arrangement by the wedded union, sexual intercourse and the birth of a child. . . . Unmarried persons are defective." Jackson also asserts that biblical creation took 42,000 years, that evolution is a false theory, and that "in Paradise Restored all women will be past the change of life." The second, shorter section of the book offers suggestions for child training and courtship.

887   JEE, JEAN C., PETER S. LEE, and DAVID Y. CHEN, comps. Building
       a Healthy Family. New York: Board of Education of the City of
       New York, Bureau for Health and Physical Education, 1975. 61
       pp. ISR.
           This dual-language Chinese-English sex education manual was
       prepared to meet the needs of the rapidly growing Chinese immigrant
       population in New York City. It does not deal with sexual tech-
       nique and emphasizes maintenance of Chinese cultural tradition,
       "even though much of the tradition may be considered by some people
       to be 'outdated' and 'outmoded' in this day and age." Reproductive
       physiology and birth control are emphasized. Masturbation is de-
       mythologized, although self-control is encouraged. Discussion of
       sexual pleasure is absent, giving heterosexual intercourse (there
       is no mention of homosexuality) a decidedly reproductive cast. A
       supplementary bibliography includes no Chinese-language materials,
       except for two films, a clear indication of the need for additional
       work in this and other new immigrant languages.

888   KAHN, FRITZ. Our Sex Life: A Guide and Counsellor for Everyone.
       Translated by George Rosen. New York: Alfred A. Knopf, 1939.
       459 pp.
           Kahn was a German physician concerned about the unhappiness
       and physical misery he saw being caused by sexual ignorance. Our
       Sex Life is primarily a sex manual rather than a marriage manual
       emphasizing social relationships. Kahn's focus is the physical
       and its consequences, and in addition to discussing physiology,
       sex technique, and sex hygiene, he includes chapters on contracep-
       tion, abortion, sterility, sexual dysfunctions, venereal disease,
       and prostitution. There is also a section on sexuality in children
       and adolescents. Kahn's view of female sexuality reflected a clas-
       sic point of view: "Just as a magnet is charged with power, a
       woman is charged with sexuality, so much so that it has become
       her second, or even better, her primary nature. . . . The entire
       life of a genuine, well-developed woman who has not been led astray
       by masculine desires [feminism?] is dedicated to the service of
       sexuality." Kahn also believed that homosexuality was only a vari-
       ation of love and much less to be abhorred than eating meat.

889   KELLER, DAVID H. 101 Personal Hygiene Questions and Answers.
       New York: Sexology, 1942. 64 pp.
           Some of the illustrations that grace Keller's Picture Stories
       (entry 890) are also found in this compendium of popular sex in-
       formation. Questions, presumably from readers of Sexology, cover
       a wide range of topics, including chastity belts, women's dreams,
       and masturbation in infants. Some of Keller's responses are sad
       indicators of the mores of the time: "I am very sorry; but I can-
       not give you any information by mail concerning methods to prevent
       conception, as this is forbidden by the laws of the United States."
       Other ideas are conventional and express Keller's philosophy of
       moderation: "In married life there should be some variation in the
       sexual relations. . . . But always there must be kept in mind that
       any practice which makes prominent any secondary type of love, at

the final expense of the first or procreative (child-producing) type, is dangerous and, in the outcome, it will not give complete satisfaction."

890   _____. Picture Stories of the Sex Life of Man and Woman. New York: Falstaff Press, 1946. 91 pp.
       David Keller, founding editor of Sexology magazine and science fiction writer, frequently wrote books and pamphlets on sex. Despite this one's cautionary warning on the flyleaf--"Intended for circulation among mature persons only"--the work consists mostly of such "sexy" pictures as two photos of cow ova and diagrams of injuries to the cervix, all in vivid black and white. This is of anatomical and physiological interest only.

891   _____. The Sexual Education Series. 10 vols. New York: Popular Book Corporation, 1928.
       This series, one of Keller's earliest forays into the sexuality field, consists of ten volumes covering topics ranging from sex education to infant care. In style it bears strong resemblance to the catch-all home health and sexuality compendiums so popular in the late nineteenth and early twentieth centuries. Keller, who was also well known as a writer of science fiction, went on to become first editor of Sexology magazine.

892   KELLY, G. LOMBARD. Sex Manual for Those Married or about to Be. Augusta, Ga.: Southern Medical Supply Co., 1945. 84 pp.
       One of the more popular sex-marriage manuals of the mid-twentieth century, Kelly's Sex Manual went through several editions, some with multiple printings, by 1953. It is also interesting that the 1953 edition had several subeditions: one for physicians, one for marriage counselors, and a third for Catholics (omitting material on birth control). Kelly discusses a wide range of topics, emphasizing, as a rule, an active perception of women's sexuality: "In this day and time, any writer who doubts the existence of a strong sexual impulse in the average woman simply has not had any sexual experience with normal women." His most interesting comments, however, are on clitoral versus vaginal orgasm. He stresses unequivocally the reality of only the clitoral orgasm and includes this statement to support his view: "Two Austrian physicians (Hitschmann and Bergler) lay great stress upon what they call the vaginal orgasm. They go so far as to claim that any woman, no matter how passionate she is, who cannot attain orgasm in normal intercourse, but requires massage of the clitoris, is frigid. It is no doubt true that the more sensitive the vagina, the more apt a woman is to reach the climax on her own, but the orgasm is in the clitoris and not in the vagina, which has no genital corpuscles to perceive it."

893   KORDEL, LELORD. Lady, Be Loved! Cleveland: World, 1953. 209 pp.
       It should come as no surprise that this book appeared at the time when the feminine mystique was at its height in the United

194

States. Kordel wrote it to tell women what men want, which is a feminine, dainty (one of his favorite words) spouse who does her utmost to appeal sexually to her husband and to satisfy him. Women's faults are described in great detail, and Kordel is especially concerned about dirt and smell (the influence of Van de Velde is apparent here, as it is elsewhere, such as in Kordel's touting of simultaneous orgasm), as well as constipation, which has "wrecked more marriages than frigidity has."

So-called aphrodisiacs, such as celery, asparagus, and artichokes, are recommended, and equal ignorance is displayed in the following comment about tampons: "When tampons become saturated, they are no longer absorptive, but merely act as plugs to stop drainage, and the unabsorbed blood backs up in the vagina and uterus." The information in this book is far from accurate, yet it does reflect not an atypical current of thought of the time.

894   LAWS, JUDITH LONG. "A Feminist Review of the Marital Adjustment Literature: The Rape of the Locke." Journal of Marriage and the Family 33, no. 3 (August 1971):483-516.

     An obtuse writing style obscures the analysis in this critique of marital adjustment literature and research. Laws argues that studies show a low level of methodological sophistication and rely too much on traditional marriage concepts as the norm. One section of the article deals with sexuality and sexual adjustment, reviewing material published between 1953 and 1970. A bibliography of material cited in the text includes 168 items.

895   LAZARSFELD, SOFIE. Rhythm of Life: A Guide to Sexual Harmony for Women. Translated by Karsten and E. Pelham Stapelfeldt. New York: Greenberg, 1934. 329 pp.

     This translation of Wie die Frau den Mann Erlebt, a work originally published in Leipzig and Vienna, affords readers an opportunity to compare European and American marital advice literature. Based on the author's experience with a Vienna marriage and life counseling service, the book incorporates case material as well as correspondence with the counseling service. Freudian and Adlerian psychological and psychoanalytic theory is incorporated, as are anthropological findings. Lazarsfeld calls for full equality between men and women, beginning in childhood, as being the key to sustained sexual harmony throughout life.

896   LEGMAN, GERSHON. Oragenitalism: Oral Techniques in Genital Excitation. New York: Julian Press, 1969. 319 pp.

     Julian Press, now an imprint of Crown, was formerly one of the largest publishers of books in the sex and erotica field in the United States. This work by Gershon Legman, who was perhaps best known for Love and Death and the Rationale of the Dirty Joke, is a detailed discussion of techniques of oral-genital sex, "the most fervent gesture of love and adoration possible between a man and a woman." Legman notes that the proscription of this activity is largely related to its connection to male homosexuality and lesbianism, as well as to animal sexual behavior, which has, in some areas, resulted in its legal prohibition with punishments of up to twenty years in prison. This is a reissue of a work originally published by Legman in 1940, with much additional material on specific practices.

897 LEVINE, LENA. The Doctor Talks with the Bride. New York: Planned Parenthood Federation of America, 1945. 16 pp. ISR.

A general introduction to marriage and sex, this pamphlet deals with such subjects as the hymen, the nature of heterosexual intercourse, technique, and contraception. Some of the old stereotypes are perpetuated: "Nature, having made the male the aggressor, the initiator, the hunter, has also equipped him for the task, the prime essential for which is early awakening of desire. The female, on the other hand, was equipped for flight. She was the one to be wooed, and, to assure perfect interfunction of two such individuals, nature gave to the female a slowly awakening desire." Simultaneous orgasm is lauded as the norm, and Levine sees the clitoris primarily as active in foreplay, rather than as the seat of the orgasm itself.

898 LISWOOD, REBECCA. A Marriage Doctor Speaks Her Mind about Sex. New York: E.P. Dutton, 1961. 192 pp.

Liswood, a physician and marriage counselor, wrote this book as an aid to married couples in dealing with sexual behavior and possible sex problems in their relationships. She is concerned with dispelling myths and misconceptions, but many of her own biases pervade her advice. Thus, while she believes in clitoral orgasm and downplays the importance of simultaneous orgasm, she also advocates psychiatric treatment for "transforming" homosexuals into heterosexuals, as well as traditional gender roles: "As a girl grows older she should share the home planning as well as the homemaking duties with her mother." Among the other topics Liswood discusses are birth control, sex education, stages in marital relationships, and emotional aspects of marriage, with emphasis on the importance of communication.

899 LOWRY, EDITH BELLE. Herself: Talks with Women Concerning Themselves. Chicago: Forbes, 1920. 221 pp.

This health guide for women stresses reproductive and sexual functions. In some respects, Lowry embraces conventional views that seem ironic given her own career as a physician and writer. She warns of the dangers of puberty: "The girl at this age should not attempt to accomplish as much work or study as the boy does." Woman's role is to be a wife and mother: "All women naturally desire to have children. If they do not, they are the victims of false ideas or of fear." Masturbation results in a "ruined nervous system and a weakened character." At the same time, she called for sex education, more physical exercise for women, and more responsible attitudes and laws relating to marriage. Although she believed that sexual relations were for much more than mere procreation, she took a dim view of any kind of sexual involvement outside of marriage. Lowry also discussed such health concerns as pregnancy, constipation, hemorrhoids, and nervousness.

900   M [pseud.]. The First How-to Book for the
       Man Who Wants to Be a Great Lover. New York: Lyle Stuart, 1971.
       253 pp.
           As might be expected, a book on male sexual technique such
       as this one should contain substantial information on women's sexu-
       ality. Although much emphasis is given to a description of tech-
       niques to increase women's sexual pleasure, the most striking thing
       about the book is its inherent sexism. It assumes that women will
       probably be passive (things are done to women, not with them) and
       submissive. "When you enter a woman she feels possessed--a neces-
       sary factor to her sexual well-being." Folkloristic touches in-
       clude the idea that women are "hung up" about breast size. On the
       positive side, the author dispels the old taboo about sex during
       menstruation, although he does admit that certain sexual techniques
       might best be avoided at that time.

901   MacFADDEN, BERNARR ADOLPHUS. Woman's Sex Life. New York:
       MacFadden, 1935. 152 pp.
           Woman's Sex Life appears to be an adaptation of some of
       MacFadden's earlier work; certainly his emphasis on womanly purity
       and the dangers of love making is more typical of the Progressive
       era than of 1935. Although MacFadden believes that women should
       control the sexual relationship, he also maintains that procreation
       is the central purpose of sexual activity. Masturbation may cause
       frigidity or worse: "The mind and soul are tainted and dwarfed
       through its insidious influence." Half of the book is devoted to
       discussions of birth control, sterility, menstrual disorders, and
       "female complaints."

902   McKEEVER, W.H. [WILLIAM ARCH] et al. The Science of Living.
       Cincinnati: S.A. Mullikin, 1924. 1240 pp.
           Guidance of children and youth in matters relating to sex
       and marriage is the dominant theme of this book, which includes
       material on such related subjects as pregnancy and venereal dis-
       ease. While The Science of Living is, in format, strikingly similar
       to nineteenth- and early twentieth-century health and sex compendi-
       ums, there are some innovations, such as a chapter on sex and psy-
       choanalysis, which mangles Freud for the masses: "Have not Freud
       and his followers emphatically shown that the repression of the
       sex impulse, as in a life of rigid continence, will injure body,
       mind, and character? Yes, unless the physical desire is tran-
       scended." Tradition triumphs, however, and women are extolled to
       seek the "ideal womanhood" of marriage and motherhood, and both
       sexes are urged to exert self-control: "Unengaged young people,
       under no conditions, should engage in hugging and kissing. Even
       in the engaged state these social relations are not necessary for
       expressing love between lovers and they are not essential to bliss-
       ful courtship."

903   MASTERS, WILLIAM H., and VIRGINIA E. JOHNSON. The Pleasure Bond:
       A New Look at Sexuality and Commitment. Boston: Little, Brown,
       1975. 268 pp.

Keeping physical attraction and sexual pleasure alive are
the best ways to ensure a successful marriage free from sexual
dysfunction. Yet, as Masters and Johnson point out in The Pleasure
Bond, false assumptions about sexuality and male/female roles often
prevent marriage from being effective and often lead to painful
stress and conflict. Incorporating dialogues from several sympo-
siums held with lay people in 1971-72, Masters and Johnson discuss
such issues as the double standard, second marriages, swinging,
extramarital sex, and the bugaboo, "work before pleasure." Stress-
ing the importance of compromise, communication, and conciliation,
the authors do not refrain from articulating what might be considered ethical or moral viewpoints. This is a clear departure
from their other, clinically oriented work, but is probably easier
for the general public, the intended audience, to understand.

904   MEAKER, SAMUEL RAYNOR. A Doctor Talks to Women: What They
      Should Know about the Normal Functions and Common Disorders of
      the Female Organs. New York: Simon and Schuster, 1954. 231 pp.
      Although Meaker emphasizes medical aspects of the female re-
productive system, commentary on sexual behavior and attitudes is
also introduced. Menopause is treated as a normal event, not oc-
casioning any change in women's sexual desire or sex appeal, while
menstruation is called "a recurring nuisance." Meaker dismisses
the idea of inherent frigidity, maintaining that most so-called
cases are due to inept sex technique on the part of the male, a
situation that can be overcome by education and counseling. He
does, however, acknowledge "subnormal sex desire," which "occurs
with remarkable frequency in certain types of women who show other
evidences of being neurotic, unsocial, or emotionally lopsided.
Among these are the mercenary gold-digger, the overly aggressive
champion of women's rights, the fanatic upholder of the ideal of
virginity, the businesswoman in frantic competition with men, and
the housewife obsessed with dust-chasing."

905   MORGAN, MARABEL. The Total Woman. Old Tappan, N.J.: Fleming
      H. Revell, 1973. 192 pp.
      Keystone of the phenomenally successful "Total Woman" empire,
Marabel Morgan's magnum opus represents the so-called Christian
current of contemporary writing on women's sexuality, one that is
often overlooked by analysts of the literature. The entire book
is about gender role within the context of marriage, and three
chapters deal specifically with sex. Morgan, of course, advocates
women's subordination to their husbands, but within the context her
attitudes toward sexuality are a far cry from the would-be puri-
tanical, sex-only-for-procreation school. Women are exhorted to
an active sexuality--"Be the seducer, not the seducee"--and sex is
seen primarily as pleasure rather than as a means of reproduction.
"God devised sex for our pleasure. . . . Sex was going strong before sin ever entered the world." Morgan places great importance
on women's orgasms and maintains that "anything goes" as far as
sex in marriage is concerned.

906   NAISMITH, GRACE. Private and Personal. New York: David McKay, 1966. 272 pp.
      A general sex information book for women, Private and Personal reflects its author's knowledge of scientific sex research and is generally free from prejudicial stereotyping and preaching. Naismith emphasizes the importance of naturalness in sexual behavior; masturbation is normal in a child's development, just as is sexual activity after menopause. Among the topics covered are birth control, cancer detection, sex education, venereal disease, and reproductive biology. Especially interesting is the chapter on the American male's fascination (near-fetishism, Naismith calls it) with women's breasts.

907   NELSON, JANET FOWLER, in collaboration with MARGARET HILLER. Marriages Are Not Made in Heaven. New York: Woman's Press, 1939. 158 pp.
      Written to be used as a text by discussion groups sponsored by the YWCA and similar organizations, this book deals with a variety of issues having an impact on sexual behavior and marital satisfaction. It is surprisingly innovative in several areas. Not only does it discuss the history of social and familial relations utilizing the concept of patriarchy, but it also includes a chapter on homosexuality (most rare in a marriage manual!) which tacitly advocates acceptance of homosexuality as a viable alternative. Crushes are described as "a stage of development." Sexual desire is seen as part of a broader context of love and emotional commitment, while a "mutually satisfying sex experience" becomes a requisite for a satisfactory marriage. Petting is frowned upon because it can make conventional intercourse, "the completest kind of expression," an anticlimax, yet too much self-control is equally bad because of its tendency to inhibit sexual expression even in marriage.

908   NIEMOLLER, ADOLPH FREDERICK. Feminine Hygiene in Marriage. New York: Harvest House, 1938. 155 pp.
      Concern with cleanliness and health as they relate to the female reproductive system are the primary concerns of this prescriptive manual for women. Niemoller devotes considerable attention to the discussion of the functioning of the reproductive system and the processes of menstruation, pregnancy, and menopause. He describes techniques for alleviating menstrual discomfort, discrediting such "remedies" as ovarian extracts and other patent drugs. Chapter 7, "The Hygiene of Menstruation," is a unique discussion of sanitary napkins, tampons, and other devices for absorbing menstrual flow, while another chapter explores the ins and outs of douching. Niemoller is not reluctant to make suggestions to his readers for the improvement of their sex lives. Separate bedrooms, for example, are recommended, for then "each union becomes a new courtship and conquest, not a mere taking advantage of one's 'rights.'" "And the wife must always remember that as a woman's natural sexual capacity is greater than a man's, she should therefore never encourage him to efforts beyond his strength, for to do so is one of the surest methods of bringing on impotency in him."

909   PEDERSEN, VICTOR COX. <u>The Woman a Man Marries: An Analysis of</u>
      <u>Her Double Standard</u>. New York: George H. Doran, 1927. 276 pp.
      Pederson directs this book to a female audience, especially
to those who think it is virtuous to not enjoy sexual relations in
marriage. "No marriage ever has been or ever will be happy unless
it rests upon a normal physical basis and a sense of the equality
in the sexual bond between man and woman." Within this context,
Pedersen advocates a traditional role for woman, claiming that her
marital difficulties are caused not only by a lack of knowledge
regarding sexual functions, but by a variety of adverse social
conditions, including feminism. This political philosophy has
produced a breed of masculine women, a tendency not to be encouraged.
"Physicians in general are convinced that the more intellectually
positive members of this group are those who make up the inner
circle of the feminist movement. They often find their sexual
expression in nothing but the discussion of sexual problems."
While it may be rather simplistic to call Pedersen a misogynist,
one can only wonder whether he had women's best interests at heart.

910   PODOLSKY, EDWARD. <u>Post-War Sex Problems and How to Solve Them</u>.
      New York: Cadillac, 1946. 48 pp. ISR.
      In this pamphlet, Podolsky deals in a question-and-answer
format with various topics associated with returning servicemen
and servicewomen after World War II. Topics discussed include
frigidity, venereal disease, and hastily contrived marriages
(Podolsky felt that these had especially been entered into by "un-
worthy, cool, calculating, scheming" women). The postwar baby boom
was certainly encouraged by statements such as this: "Children
stabilize a marriage. The veteran should have children as soon
after marriage as possible."

911   _____. <u>Sex Today in Wedded Life</u>. New York: Simon, 1942.
      240 pp.
      Podolsky was one of the mid-twentieth century's most prolific
writers of popular literature on sex. Here he covers such topics
as sexual technique, sexual dysfunction, pregnancy, and sex in later
life. There is a lot of hokum here: "Strongly-sexed women have
large nostrils, while the sharp-pinched nose goes with the sexually
weak or indifferent." Podolsky does, however, acknowledge woman's
innate sexuality and asserts that much so-called frigidity is
caused simply by faulty technique. Among the interesting features
of this book is a diagram of chastity belts on page 126. Too often,
however, Podolsky simply perpetuates old myths and stereotypes:
"Masturbation must be regarded as an important factor in the development of mental diseases."

912   REUBEN, DAVID R. <u>Any Woman Can! Love and Sexual Fulfillment</u>
      <u>for the Single, Widowed, Divorced . . . and Married</u>. New York:
      David McKay, 1971. 364 pp.
      The question-and-answer format used by Reuben in <u>Everything</u>
<u>You Wanted to Know about Sex . . .</u> is used once more in this sex

and marriage guide for single, widowed, and divorced women. Emphasis should be placed on the word marriage, for Reuben is convinced that this is the ultimately desirable state for women. Elaborate instructions are given for how to catch a husband, along with advice in such areas as sex technique, abortion, birth control, and male sexual problems. Reuben retains much of the old biological destiny viewpoint: "From the instant of conception onward, the primary thrust of every woman's being is to be fertilized, to conceive, and to reproduce. No force on earth can stand in her way." There is much inherent sexism as well in the author's persistent use of the word girl, although he is also conscious that women's conceptions of their own sexuality are often determined by misinformation provided by men. Ironically, this book is a case in point.

913   ROBIE, W.F. Rational Sex Ethics: A Physiological and
       Psychological Study of the Sex Lives of Normal Men and Women,
       with Suggestions for a Rational Sex Hygiene Together with
       Further Investigations. Boston: Richard G. Badger, 1920. 351;
       333 pp.
       This is a one-volume edition of Robie's Rational Sex Ethics
and Rational Sex Ethics, Further Investigations, which originally
appeared in 1916 and 1919, respectively. Robie was superintendent
of the Pine Terrace Sanitarium in Massachusetts. Motivated to study
the sexuality of "normal" men and women, he prepared a questionnaire
and solicited responses to it, as well as personal interviews, from
friends, patients, and others. Although his survey methods were
rather eclectic, he managed to collect several hundred sex and case
histories for both men and women, many of which are printed in these
two volumes.
       Robie was also well read in the literature of sexology and
even attempted an empirical critique of Freud's sexual theory of
the neuroses. His chief crusade, however, was for the "normaliza-
tion" of masturbation, which he saw as much less of an evil than
use of prostitutes and yet something almost universally criticized
in popular sex education literature.
       Although he did not favor women's suffrage, Robie did believe
in a full sexuality for women, advocating instruction to them regarding the normality and importance of sexual relations in marriage. Sex technique was not neglected. The total result of both
works, however, is rather diffuse, the sex and case histories being
perhaps the most useful and reliable parts of the material.

914   ROSENBAUM, VERYL. Being Female: Discovering and Enjoying Your
       Physical, Emotional, and Sexual Nature. Englewood Cliffs, N.J.:
       Prentice-Hall, 1973. 192 pp.
       Rosenbaum, a psychoanalyst, employs Freudian theories of
woman's psychosexual development in this discussion of woman's role.
She treats such topics as the female body, orgasm, romance, and
marriage in a combination of jargony theory (there is a lot of talk
about "anal" versus "genital" personalities) and cases drawn presumably from her own practice. Her assertions are not based on
empirical evidence, and at times they raise more than a few serious

doubts in the mind of the reader. For example, "The vaginal orgasm is a fact, and the difference between the two kinds of female orgasms is profound. All orgasms feel good but vaginal orgasms are much better. . . . Some genital women I know experience vaginal orgasms in dreams, while reading a moving love poem, or while looking at a scene of beauty." And she concludes, with pride, "I could not have written this book unless I felt that I had attained a state of genitality myself."

915   ROSSITER, FREDERICK MAGEE. The Torch of Life: A Key to Sex Harmony. New York: Aventine Corporation, 1932. 214 pp.
      Rossiter, an English physician, was one of many authors preparing sex and marriage manuals during the 1920s and 1930s. The Torch of Life is somewhat unique in that it reprints the entire text of the biblical Song of Solomon. Avoiding material on contraception, venereal disease, and variant sexual behavior, Rossiter focuses on physical aspects of sexual relations. There is, however, a certain amount of genial hokum. Sex hormones are called "mystical secretions" and are given far-ranging abilities indeed: "A man or a woman with well-formed eyebrows, especially at the outer angle, usually has plenty of thyroid and may be supposed to have plenty of sex hormones." Men are encouraged to aim at pleasing women rather than themselves and even to wear silk if it is necessary for a woman's pleasure.

916   SANGER, MARGARET. Happiness in Marriage. New York: Brentano's, 1926. 321 pp.
      Margaret Sanger wrote many books on birth control, sexuality, and social issues during her career. While Woman and the New Race (entry 198) perhaps best articulates the social reform underpinnings of her birth control philosophy, Happiness in Marriage is more directly concerned with sexuality and sexual relationships, ranging from advice on courtship to discussions of impotence and frigidity. Sanger's courtship advice is fairly conservative and often has a highly romantic aura, although it is sometimes realistically direct: "One indispensable truth the engaged girl must remember: the fiance's breath, odor, touch, embrace and kiss must be pleasing to her. If they are not, if there is an impulsive or instinctive emotional or physical recoil, then under no circumstances should the engagement be prolonged." As in her other works, Sanger viewed women as being ultimately responsible for playing an active, controlling role in sexual relationships. Unfortunately for many women, Sanger urges the almost impossible simultaneous orgasm--"A preliminary failure does not mean that success may not be eventually attained." She concludes with a discussion of birth control.

917   STONE, HANNAH, and ABRAHAM STONE. A Marriage Manual: A Practical Guidebook to Sex and Marriage. New York: Simon and Schuster, 1952. 301 pp.
      Originally published in 1935, the Stones' Marriage Manual was reprinted twenty-nine times and was translated into several foreign languages. Hannah Stone died in 1941, but this completely

revised edition, which appeared in 1952, still bears her name. Incorporating the research of such investigators as Kinsey and Dickinson, this final edition also draws upon the clinical experience of the Margaret Sanger Research Bureau, of which Abraham Stone was director, and of the Marriage Consultation Center at the Community Church.

The guide deals almost exclusively with sexual aspects of marriage, including such topics as reproductive biology, reproduction, family planning, and sexual dysfunction. One addition to this revised edition is a chapter on "happiness in marriage." A question-and-answer format is maintained in each chapter, and additional readings are suggested.

918   STONE, LEE ALEXANDER. An Open Talk with Mothers and Fathers.
       Kansas City: Burton Publishing Co., 1920. 117 pp.
       Stone presents arguments opposing promiscuity because of its relationship to venereal disease and argues in favor of compulsory sterilization on eugenic grounds: "The states that have passed laws providing for the destruction of the procreative powers of criminals and degenerates have taken a long step forward in race progression." More unique is his attack on Katharine Bement Davis, whose Factors in the Sex Life of Twenty-Two Hundred Women (entry 951) is one of the classic studies of women's sexuality. Stone criticized what he interpreted to be harsh policies during her tenure at the New York State Reformatory for Women: "Professional reformers of her type are a menace to their sex. They are the ones who keep constantly before the eyes of man 'The Woman Tempted Me' lie. The woman reformer should know something of the joys of motherhood. Such knowledge would make her more humane." Note that the foreword to the volume was written by General Leonard Wood, one-time military governor of Cuba and, in the 1920s, governor general of the Philippines.

919   _____. Sex Searchlights and Sane Sex Ethics: An Anthology of
       Sex Knowledge. Chicago: Science Publishing Co., 1922. 747 pp.
       Lee Alexander Stone was a physician and prolific writer on sex hygiene, who shared many of the views of William J. Robinson. In fact, Robinson's works are advertised in the end leaves of this book. There is little new information in this general guide to sex and related subjects, such as sex education and venereal disease. Rather, it is more interesting as a social document in its forthright espousal of contraception (a cartoon illustration shows a woman labeled "Truth" holding a placard reading "Birth control means health, happiness, perfect children") and sex education: "It should be possible and practicable to devise a method of sex instruction whereby the ideas of the most advanced educators could be presented by motion pictures." Don Chilcote's illustrations and cartoons (octopi labeled "Syphilis" and "Gonorrhea" grasp human victims in one choice example) as well as photographs of leading sex reformers and sex-related conditions are of special interest. There is even a section of poetry ("The Women Who Walk," "The Worn Out Woman," etc.), a glossary, and a bibliography.

920   STOPES, MARIE CHARLOTTE CARMICHAEL. Enduring Passion: Further
      New Contributions to the Solution of Sex Difficulties, Being
      the Continuation of Married Love. New York: G.P. Putnam's
      Sons, 1931. 181 pp.
         Publication of this sequel to Stopes's Married Love (entry
      921) came hot on the heels of U.S. District Court Judge John M.
      Woolsey's 6 April 1931 decision that Married Love was not obscene.
      Here Stopes presents her often highly original solutions to a
      variety of marital sexual problems, such as excessive demands,
      sterility, and frequency of relations. Ideas such as "the only
      justification of marriage is the mutual need for and the mutual
      enjoyment in sex union," and her claim that sexual harmony can
      overcome all other difficulties and differences in marriage makes
      one skeptical of the validity of her other theories. Her criticism
      of lesbianism says more about her infatuation with prostatic fluid
      and hormone extracts than about love between women: "Lesbian love
      . . . can never supply the actual physiological nourishment, the
      chemical molecules produced by the accessory glandular systems of
      the male." Needless to say, scientists disputed this claim.

921   ____. Married Love: A New Contribution to the Solution of
      Sex Difficulties. New York: Eugenics Publishing Co., 1931.
      170 pp.
         Part of the fame of Married Love stems from its having been
      the subject of an obscenity trial in 1931 (United States v. One
      Obscene Book Entitled Married Love, 48 F. 2nd 821 [1931]). Written
      by Marie Stopes, one of the early twentieth century's best-known
      birth control advocates, it attempts to diagnose the causes for
      the many unhappy marriages the author saw around her and in her
      practice. At the root of the problem, Stopes felt, was men's and
      women's ignorance of "sex tides," monthly or bimonthly periods when
      women were more receptive to sexual activity than at other times.
      By regulating intercourse to take account of these cycles, marital
      happiness could be attained. Stopes offered other suggestions as
      well: variation of sexual position, separate bedrooms and modesty
      to maintain an aura of romance, and full sex education for both
      men and women prior to marriage. She was especially firm in her
      belief in the necessity for women's orgasms: "To have had a mod-
      erate number of orgasms at some time at least, is a necessity for
      the full development of a woman's health and all her power."

922   STRECKER, EDWARD A., and VINCENT T. LATHBURY. Their Mothers'
      Daughters. Philadelphia: J.B. Lippincott, 1956. 255 pp.
         Psychiatrists Strecker and Lathbury took a traditional
      Freudian attitude toward women's roles and sexuality in this would-
      be advice book for mothers. Seeing woman's main function as giving
      birth to and raising children, they blamed faulty maternal child-
      rearing patterns for a wide range of adult "faults," from schizo-
      phrenia to frigidity and even feminism. Antifeminist to the core,
      they related the case history of one such woman whom they succeeded
      in "curing" of her malady: "An intelligent woman who came to us

as a pronounced feminist, has made much progress. Her dress, her manner and attitude toward males have become gratifyingly feminine. She is almost a woman." One highlight of the book is a ninety-item questionnaire intended to be taken by readers. "Correct" answers are given, yes or no, at the end of the book. Yes was correct for this one: "Do you think that the biological function of women, particularly the bearing and rearing of children, is more important than having a career?"

923   Van de VELDE, THEODOOR HENDRIK. Ideal Marriage, Its Physiology
      and Technique. Translated by [Frances Worsley] Stella Browne.
      New York: Random House, 1930. 322 pp.
         One of the most popular twentieth-century sex manuals, Ideal
      Marriage was the work of T.H. Van de Velde, a Dutch gynecologist.
      Its emphasis on sexual physiology (150 pages) and physical sex
      technique distinguish it from many of its contemporaries and make
      it a direct ancestor of such works as The Joy of Sex. Van de Velde,
      however, was still a traditionalist in many respects. For example,
      the book was directed specifically to the medical profession and
      "married men, for they are naturally educators and initiators of
      their wives in sexual matters." Literary and folkloristic sources
      are freely utilized, and the author devotes special attention to
      the importance of odors and the achievement of simultaneous orgasm.

924   _____. Sex Efficiency through Exercises: Special Physical
      Culture for Women, with 480 Cinematographic and 54 Full-page
      Illustrations. London: Heinemann, 1933. 163 pp.
         The photographic material, including a section of "flicker
      films," distinguishes this work of the writer of the ever popular
      Ideal Marriage (entry 923). Van de Velde presents instructions
      for exercises that are designed to increase women's potential for
      active participation in heterosexual intercourse and to assist in
      controlling voluntary muscular action in the act of birth. It is
      interesting that in his introduction Van de Velde indicates that
      Ideal Marriage was prepared for a male audience, whereas this book
      is directed to women. In reality, were sex manuals such as Ideal
      Marriage read only by men?

925   _____. Sex Hostility in Marriage: Its Origin, Prevention, and
      Treatment. Translated by Hamilton Marr. New York: Covici,
      Friede, 1931. 350 pp.
         One of a series of books by Van de Velde on sexuality and
      marriage, Sex Hostility examines the origins of sexual aversion
      and antagonism in marriage. Much of the Dutch doctor's argument
      is predicated on his belief that mental as well as physical dif-
      ferences between men and women are innate, natural, and biological-
      ly determined, rather than culturally acquired. Woman's emotions
      govern her, just as man's intellect does him. Characterized by
      impulsiveness and susceptibility, "the range of the woman's con-
      scious mind is smaller than that of the man." Moreover, as a result
      of her physiology, woman is dependent on man, and her "unnatural"

strivings to assert her own power are a frequent cause of strife. Van de Velde feels that once the basic male/female differences are recognized antagonism can be avoided through appropriate choice of a marriage partner, insight and flexibility, and use of skillful erotic technique. Professional therapy is only the last resort.

926   WILSON, ROBERT A. Feminine Forever. New York: M. Evans, 1966. 224 pp.
        In the nineteenth century, it was not uncommon for authors of popular medical works to include advertising for their services as part of their narrative. The presence of such a sales pitch in this book, however, coupled with a decidedly polemical tone, should give readers more than sufficient clues regarding Dr. Wilson's true intentions. Feminine Forever has the somewhat dubious distinction of being the book that promised to end menopause forever. Sexist to the core, it advocated estrogen-progestin treatment as a menopause preventive, menopause being viewed with horror and disgust by Wilson as a pathological condition leading to loss of sexual vitality and function. To him, woman was solely a sexual creature. Wilson's own credentials, which were substantial, gave credence to his views, which were supported in a laudatory foreword by Robert Greenblatt, chair of the endocrinology department of the Medical College of Georgia: "Like a gallant knight he has come to rescue his fair lady not at the time of her bloom and flowering but in her despairing years; at a time of life when the preservation and prolongation of her femaleness are so paramount." Wilson glibly dismisses arguments that estrogen use may induce cancer and reveals a great deal in one chapter where he describes the "frightful experience" of seeing menopause transform his mother into a pain-racked, petulant invalid. One can only pity the women (and men) who bought Wilson's message and believed promises such as this one: "Tomorrow's woman, far more so than any of her forebears, may realize the ultimate mission of her sex: to broaden the role of love as an operative agent in human affairs."

927   WOLBARST, ABRAHAM L. Generations of Adam. New York: Newland Press, 1930. 355 pp.
        Also published by Grosset and Dunlap as Healthy Sex Life, Generations of Adam is a general guide to sex and some allied subjects, such as venereal disease. Wolbarst is especially concerned with overturning theological notions that sex should be equated with sin, maintaining that false morality is responsible for most sex problems. Although his emphasis is on male sexuality, because it is "far more urgent and boisterous" than that of women, there is ample material on women. One interesting observation of Wolbarst's, substantiated by contemporary embryological theory, is that the female is the original of the two sexes.

928   WOOD, LELAND FOSTER. Harmony in Marriage. New York: Round Table Press, 1939. 122 pp.
        Wood discusses various components of marital harmony,

including finances, the home situation, and conflict resolution.
One chapter is on "physical harmony," Wood's euphemism for sex.
Sex in marriage is seen as an expression of affirmation of love and
the family ideal. Patience on both sides is counseled, and stress
is placed on mutual communication and adjustment. There is also a
discussion of sexual problems, such as frigidity.

929　WRIGHT, HELENA. The Sex Factor in Marriage. New York:
　　　Vanguard Press, 1931. 122 pp.
　　　　　A London gynecologist, Helena Wright originally published
The Sex Factor in Marriage in England. Because of its explicitness
(for the time) in its discussion of sex technique, its clearance by
U.S. Customs for admission to the United States was considered
somewhat of a landmark. Wright was especially concerned with the
sexual response of women and emphasized the importance of clitoral
stimulation in the achievement of orgasm. She perceived, however,
a basic difference in the mechanism of male and female physical
satisfaction: "She needs arousing; he needs relief." Sexual relationships, however, were both a mental and physical union, and
sex itself a sacrament of life. Wright evinced a traditional attitude toward marriage, maintaining that married life was incomplete
without children; her focus, however, was on happy parenthood rather than just maternity.

Behavior and Attitudes: Surveys and Other Studies

Beginning in the late nineteenth century with the work of such pioneers as Robert Latou Dickinson (entries 953, 954) and Clelia Duel Mosher (entry 985), researchers on sexuality have been collecting aggregate data documenting women's sexual attitudes and behavior in the United States. Working as individuals, often with no firm methodology or consistent strategy for data collection, these forerunners of Alfred C. Kinsey and Shere Hite nevertheless recognized the need for hard facts at a time when subjective opinions too often passed for scientific proof.

By the 1920s, advances in social science methodology and the provision of institutional bases for support of survey operations gave a new dimension to sex research. Katharine Bement Davis's Factors in the Sex Life of Twenty-Two Hundred Women (entry 951), although not without its flaws, set new standards for this kind of work and clearly demonstrated the feasibility of gathering information on sexual behavior from the general population. By the time that Alfred C. Kinsey began his monumental studies of sexual behavior in men and women in the late 1930s, survey research in this field was winning increasing acceptance among the American population. His Sexual Behavior in the Human Female (entry 975), published in 1953, became a best-seller.

The 1970s saw the initiation of yet another generation of surveys, undertaken in part as a response to the public's increased desire for factual sex information, itself an outgrowth of the so-called sexual revolution and the rise of laboratory-based sex research. No survey however, has shown itself to be totally free from methodological problems, and users of these studies should be cautious in accepting the conclusions of their authors.

In addition to structured surveys, researchers studying women's sexual attitudes and behavior have also gathered data from limited populations, interviews with individuals, correspondence, and case records. Some studies of sexual behavior have clearly been written for commercial purposes and display little if any documented, verifiable information. Still other works focus on the evaluation and criticism (usually negative) of previous research; an extreme example of this genre is Edmund Bergler and William S. Kroger's Kinsey's Myth of Female Sexuality (entry 935).

Although the items listed in this section often include material on specific populations, such as lesbians and older women, studies included in the chapters dealing with those groups focus more closely on them.

930   ADAMS, CLIFFORD ROSE. An Informal Preliminary Report on Some Factors Relating to Sexual Responsiveness of Certain College Wives. State College, Pa.: n.p., 1953. 65 pp.
          Adams's purpose in preparing this study was to measure and determine the interrelationship of marital happiness, sexual adjustment, and sexual responsiveness of wives. A group of 214 women, part of a larger group previously involved in another study at the Pennsylvania State College, was selected to receive a questionnaire. From the 186 respondents, 150 were selected by Adams for statistical analysis, with an additional breakdown into the 50 "highest" scorers as sexually responsive and the 50 "lowest" as unresponsive. These two groups are used throughout the report as the basis for comparative analysis. Information is provided on a wide range of subjects including birth control practice, frequency, foreplay, and orgasm. One must question, however, Adams's findings in the latter area since the questionnaire defines climax (as it calls it) as a "feeling of satisfaction." This is an interesting study, but one wonders about the validity of the sample and method.

931   BAHM, ROBERT MICHAEL. The Influence of Non-sexual Cues, Sexual Explicitness and Sex Guilt on Female's Erotic Response to Literature. Ph.D. dissertation, University of Massachusetts, 1972. 105 pp.
          Summarizing previous studies and ideas on women's response to erotica, Bahm then describes his methodology for examining the influence of sexual versus nonsexual (affection, romance, etc.) cues, sexual explicitness, and sex guilt on sexual arousal in females. His test subjects were 288 female psychology students at the University of Massachusetts, each of whom was asked to report her response to eight erotic stories (actually all variants on a common theme). Bahm found that "non-sexual cues previously regarded as influencing sexual arousal in females do not significantly affect sexual arousal." Bahm's generalizations, however, since they relate to a limited, distorted sample, should be used with caution, especially when he relates them to conclusions by other researchers drawn from much broader samples and using different techniques.

932   BARBACH, LONNIE, and LINDA LEVINE. Shared Intimacies: Women's Sexual Experiences. Garden City, N.Y.: Anchor Press/Doubleday, 1980. 360 pp.

Linda Levine, a Washington, D.C., sex therapist, and Lonnie Barbach, author of <u>For Yourself</u> and <u>Women Discover Orgasm</u>, interviewed 120 women for this popular account of women's creative solutions to sexually related problems as well as their positive experiences. The authors have tried to represent the range of opinions offered by their subjects and do not espouse one particular point of view. In addition to sexual technique, the topics covered include communication with the sexual partner, sexual dysfunction, pregnancy and sexuality, parenting and sexual behavior, sex education, and the aging process. There is a short bibliography.

933   BARTELL, GILBERT D. <u>Group Sex: A Scientist's Eyewitness Report on the American Way of Swinging</u>. New York: Wyden, 1971. 298 pp.

Three years of research went into this account of group sex by an anthropology professor at Northern Illinois University. Interviews were conducted by Bartell, his wife, and female graduate students and secretaries, working as twosomes and visiting swinging parties and setting up other informant situations. The inherent sexism of the practice is revealed in statements such as this: "As male swingers see it, they live according to the <u>Playboy</u> style. In their ads they offer, in effect, exchange objects in the form of nude photographs of their partners." Although there is no overt feminist consciousness in Bartell's conclusions, his thesis that swinging is an acting out of male sexual needs based largely on fantasies retained from adolescence is susceptible to a feminist interpretation. His research methods appear, at the least, to be rather casual.

934   BELL, ROBERT R. <u>Premarital Sex in a Changing Society</u>. Englewood Cliffs, N.J.: Prentice-Hall, 1966. 182 pp.

Concerned with the juxtaposition of attitudes, values, and behavior, whose evolution is by no means synchronous, Bell reviews literature examining the changing nature of premarital sex in American society. He reaches four main conclusions: (1) there is no evidence that rates of premarital coitus have been increasing; (2) values have changed since World War II to the extent that more girls accept premarital coitus with an emotional involvement; (3) premarital chastity does not affect marital adjustment; and (4) premarital sexual values and behavior are significantly related to differences in social class, education, race, and religion. Bell's historical survey of American sexual mores is simplistic and sometimes inaccurate, as in the area of bibliographic citations. At times he relies exclusively on the research of only a small number of authors, such as Kinsey et al. on behavior.

935   BERGLER, EDMUND, and WILLIAM S. KROGER. <u>Kinsey's Myth of Female Sexuality: The Medical Facts</u>. New York: Grune & Stratton, 1954. 200 pp.

Bergler and Kroger worked themselves up into a semihysterical fever pitch in this virulent attack on the work of Alfred C. Kinsey.

Their primary criticism was that no "normal" person would voluntarily give information for such a study and, moreover, that unconscious factors would distort the information that was given.
"The self-selected groups of neurotics comprising Kinsey's volunteers . . . misused Kinsey's interviews to bribe their consciences
because of their respective neuroses." Certainly Bergler and
Kroger were not alone in their questioning of Kinsey's sampling
and statistics, but much of their antagonism stemmed not from
empirical distortion but from their defensiveness toward Kinsey's
skepticism about psychiatry and psychoanalytic theory. One idea
they found especially hard to accept was Kinsey's view of female
orgasm (later demonstrated in the laboratory by Masters and Johnson):
"What Kinsey describes as normal is the well-known picture of the
neurotic, vaginally frigid woman."

Their own "proof," however, is rather flimsy; rather than
present diverse views, letting readers draw their own conclusions,
Bergler and Kroger cite other critics of Kinsey as well as other
authors whose views support their own. Moreover, much of the book
is simply a reworking of material found in Bergler's Neurotic
Counterfeit-Sex. The authors conclude that Kinsey's work has done
more harm than good: "Kinsey's statistics may be used by neurotics
as full 'scientific' confirmation of their own 'counterfeit-sex.'"
And, one might add, as a basis for demonstrating that the ideas of
psychiatrist Bergler may actually do more harm than good.

936   BLEDSOE, ROBERT J. Female Sexual Deviations and Bizarre
       Practices. Los Angeles: Sherbourne, 1964. 138 pp.
       Bledsoe, a novelist, obviously prepared this paperback for
the commercial "sexploitation" market. Case histories are admittedly concocted, and although respected theorists are occasionally
cited, the overwhelming emphasis is on the descriptive narrative
of the cases. Bledsoe does not attempt to place the material in
any kind of perspective (father-daughter incest is given equivalent
coverage with mother-son, as if the former could even be considered
a "female" sex practice in most cases). The short bibliography
aims at intellectual respectability by including such works as J.
Huizinga's The Waning of the Middle Ages and the Kinsey female volume.

937   BROMLEY, DOROTHY DUNBAR, and FLORENCE HAXTON BRITTEN. Youth and
       Sex: A Study of 1300 College Students. New York: Harper and
       Brothers, 1938. 303 pp.
       Bromley and Britten were journalists who set out to study
what they perceived to be radical changes, developed since World
War I, in the sexual behavior and mores of American college students. Their information was derived from a combination of interviews and questionnaires involving 1,364 students in 46 colleges
and universities. On the basis of their findings, women students
were classified into six groups: virgins, wait-for-marriage, loving, experimenters, sowers of wild oats, and homosexually inclined,
each of which is discussed in s separate chapter. There was little

statistical analysis, and the authors were not concerned with the statistical validity of their sample; most questionnaires were distributed by an informal network of students paid ten cents for each return that Bromley and Britten received bearing their initials. Some of their assertions and conclusions, such as this one--"Out-and-out homosexuality appears to enjoy less éclat than it did a decade or so ago when a few campus leaders in several of the larger women's colleges made it something of a fad"--might provide interesting subjects for further study. Other conclusions, such as their comparisons with the Katharine Bement Davis study, are questionable, owing to the great differences between the composition of the two sample populations and research methodology.

938 BRY, ADELAIDE. The Sexually Aggressive Woman. New York: Peter H. Wyden, 1975. 181 pp.

   Bry, a Philadelphia psychotherapist, gathered material for this book by posting notices and placing ads in newspapers, reading "Psychologist, gathering material for book, seeks interviews with sexually aggressive women." What she presents here are a series of interviews with these women. "The one common denominator seems to be that each has acknowledged her own sexual desires and has given herself permission to express them." Bry does offer some analysis in which she links sexual aggressiveness in women to a refusal to be bound by cultural traditions of "correct" sexual behavior for women, and links this sexual aggressiveness to cultural changes, such as those brought about by the women's movement.

939 BURGESS, ERNEST WATSON, and PAUL WALLIN. Engagement and Marriage. Philadelphia: J.B. Lippincott, 1953. 819 pp.

   Between 1936 and 1946, Burgess and Wallin collected data on 1,000 engaged and 666 married couples for this study of the factors making for success and failure in marriage. Several chapters relate directly to sexual attitudes and behavior and deal with such topics as premarital sexual relations. Engagement and Marriage is especially useful because the authors summarize the findings, including statistics, from earlier research (Davis, Terman, etc.) and compare this material with their own data. Variables such as religious affiliation, age, and education are tested.

   Engagement and Marriage differs from some studies of this type in its exploration of attitudes of those subjects who do not engage in certain behaviors, such as premarital intercourse. This material is covered by excerpts from interviews, as well as statistics. One significant conclusion of Burgess and Wallin was that a large proportion of husbands and wives experienced problems of sexual adjustment, which decreased the amount of sexual satisfaction in marriage. Most often this was due to a divergence between men and women in their attitudes toward sexual intercourse and the frequency of their desire for it.

   In addition to their statistical and narrative presentations, the authors include a bibliography and a facsimile of their self-scoring "Marriage Prediction Schedule," used to determine the probability of success in marriage.

940 CANNON, KENNETH L., and RICHARD LONG. "Premarital Sexual
     Behavior in the Sixties." Journal of Marriage and the Family
     33, no. 1 (February 1971):36-49.
          This review article summarizes research on premarital sexual
     behavior published in the 1960s. It provides a useful overview of
     research during that period.

941 CAULDWELL, DAVID OLIVER. Unusual Female Sex Practices. New
     illustrated ed. Inglewood, Calif.: Banner, 1966. 215 pp. LC.
          Typical of the "nonfiction" generated for the sexploitation
     market, this collection of five essays incorporates case histories,
     interviews, and poor quality illustrations. The essays deal with
     voyeurism, incest, teenage seductresses, female pedophilia, and
     wife swapping. One should ask, however, how much real difference
     there is between this material and that which was often presented
     in professional journals as scientific, objective research.

942 CHARTHAM, ROBERT. What Turns Women On. New York: Ballantine
     Books, 1974. 207 pp. ISR.
          Students of mid-twentieth-century writing on sex are well
     aware of the effect of the so-called sexual revolution on the
     language and content of nonfiction works. This can be seen, for
     example, in comparing this work to some of Chartham's earlier writ-
     ings, such as Mainly for Wives. What Turns Women On is a book
     about sex fantasies of women and details responses from 119 American
     and 79 British women, selected from Chartham's files and from re-
     sponses to an appeal in Forum, the sex magazine. It is long on
     description and short--very short--on analysis. Completely hetero-
     sexual in viewpoint, its most interesting (from a nonfantasy point
     of view) section is the introduction wherein Chartham describes
     his personal history and background, including his association
     with Forum magazine.

943 CHESSER, EUSTACE. Sex and the Married Woman. New York:
     G.P. Putnam's Sons, 1969. 286 pp.
          Chesser, the English author of the popular Love without Fear,
     utilizes the work of Masters and Johnson and other contemporary
     researchers, as well as his own experiences as a physician, mar-
     riage counselor, and psychologist, in this study of women's sexual
     relationships from the honeymoon to menopause. He believes that
     women's single biggest sexual problem is the guilt caused by an
     upbringing that does not promote sane and healthy attitudes toward
     sex, thereby turning it into a "problem." He is a radical regard-
     ing marriage, which he does not believe in unless children are
     desired: "Any attempt to divide the body into zones which can
     only be entered if we hold the passport of marriage, or which we
     are forbidden to cross even with a passport, is ridiculous and com-
     pletely illogical." He also discounts ideas of maternal instinct
     as being sheer myth.
          Chapters deal with such subjects as contraception, orgasm,
     menopause, and sexual techniques. There are also ten short

interviews with women on what they had expected of marriage and what they got out of it, line drawings, a bibliography, and an index.

944   CHIDECKEL, MAURICE. Female Sex Perversion: The Sexually Aberrated Woman as She Is. New York: Eugenics Publishing Co., 1935. 331 pp.

It will come as no surprise to readers of this book that Dr. Chideckel's literary career included fiction as well as personal memoirs and popular medical works. Not that Female Sex Perversion was billed as fiction--it wasn't--but Chideckel's approach and style exhibit more than a few flights of the imagination. Even the chapter titles--"Celia, the History of a Sex Pervert," "Homosexuality: Surging Forces at Work," and "Sadism and Masochism as a Well Paying Business"--give clues regarding the author's intent. There are even what can only be described as prurient illustrations. Passages such as the following, in a chapter on exhibitionism, are typical and are indicative of the author's underlying moral rigidity: "Any relaxation from the standard of purity, any emancipation from prevailing ethics, spells moral and social decline. Universal license does not make better men and women. Nudism is not only hypocrisy with a new sort of mimicry, but sexual perversion in the form of exhibitionism. A colony of nudists is a colony of sex perverts." And so, for that matter, according to Chideckel, is just about everyone else.

945   _____. The Single, the Engaged and the Married. New York: Eugenics Publishing Co., 1936. 268 pp.

Focusing on women, Chideckel divides this popular account into three sections: love, courtship, and marriage. His purported goal is to provide factual knowledge about sexuality in order to facilitate the development of satisfactory marriages. Many of his ideas, however, reflect conventional stereotypes. Women are seen as being more emotional than men, yet capable of greater self-control, refinement, and repression of their sexuality. Chideckel, a physician, claimed to have surveyed and studied various populations of women, such as virgins and unmarried women, but he also incorporated material from such researchers as Katharine Bement Davis. He also summarizes cases that he has treated, and several chapters deal with sexual maladjustments of various types. His beliefs in the necessity for women submitting to men and in the normality of the vaginal, as opposed to clitoral, orgasm, are reflected in his "treatments." One young woman, for example, was taught, over many months, "to develop a desire for normal coitus, and to allow sensations of the clitoris to die out. Results were brilliant." Despite his self-assurance, Chideckel was sometimes sloppy in his documentation. F.W. Stella Browne is referred to in the text as W.F. Stella, while the scant list of "authorities consulted" includes such citations as "Works of Dr. Dickinson and Miss Laura Beam" and "Works of German, Russian and French sexologists."

946   CLARK, ALEXANDER L. A Study of Factors Associated with Wives'
      Sexual Responsiveness. Ph.D. dissertation, Stanford University,
      1960. 123 pp. ISR, LC.
          In a survey of 602 couples, data were gathered for this
      analysis of the relation of social and social-psychological factors
      to variations in wives' sexual responsiveness as measured by re-
      ports of their frequency of orgasm. Variables tested included
      religious affiliation, religiosity, character of marital relations,
      length of marriage, personality factors, health, and the sexual
      performance of husbands. Clark also includes a review of related
      studies. Unfortunately, his use of the orgasm as the sole measure
      of sexual responsiveness in women works to bypass other components
      of female sexual response and gives this work and the articles that
      resulted from it a male-defined bias not atypical of much of the
      pre-women's movement research in this area.

947   CLOYD, JERALD W. "The Market-Place Bar: The Interrelation
      between Sex, Situation, and Strategies in the Pairing Ritual
      of Homo Ludens." In Sexuality: Encounters, Identities, and
      Relationships, edited by Carol Warren, 33-52. Beverly Hills,
      Calif.: Sage Publications, 1977.
          One of the phenomena of the so-called sexual revolution has
      been the development of singles bars catering primarily to young
      people interested in "meeting and possibly having sexual encounters
      with persons of a similar orientation." Cloyd, a sociologist,
      studied eleven bars to gather the data for this study. He found
      that differences in socialization led men and women to have differ-
      ent motives in bar behavior: "Barroom behavior is usually charac-
      terized by an asymmetrical goal orientation between the sexes, with
      the female interested in getting to know the male per se, and the
      male getting to know the female in order to score [have sex]."
      This difference is often seen in the modes of interaction and
      tactics undertaken in the bar situation, which Cloyd describes.

948   COCHRAN, WILLIAM G., FREDERICK MOSTELLER, and JOHN W. TUKEY.
      Statistical Problems of the Kinsey Report on Sexual Behavior
      in the Human Male. Washington, D.C.: American Statistical
      Association, 1954. 338 pp.
          This report was prepared at the request of the National
      Research Council's Committee for Research in Problems of Sex, the
      major source of Kinsey's funding, to provide a response to critical
      questions on statistical methodology raised by reviewers of Kinsey's
      report on male sexual behavior. Despite this focus, the study has
      important implications for evaluating the Kinsey female volume and
      other sex research that purports to have studied a representative
      sample of the population, drawing more or less "universal" conclu-
      sions from the responses of that sample. Of particular interest
      is Appendix B (pp. 153-219), prepared by W.O. Jenkins of the
      University of Tennessee. This appendix compares the Kinsey method-
      ology with that used on nine previous sex studies in the United
      States, including Katharine Bement Davis's Factors in the Sex Life

of Twenty-Two Hundred Women (entry 951) and Dickinson and Beam's
The Single Woman (entry 953).

949   CONNOR, JOHN W. "Family Bonds, Maternal Closeness, and the
       Suppression of Sexuality in Three Generations of Japanese
       Americans." Ethos 4, no. 2 (Summer 1976):189-221.
       One of the few studies relating to sexuality in nonblack
American minority groups, this article is based on data gathered
from three generations of Japanese-Americans in Sacramento,
California. The data were compared with data gathered from a
Caucasian control group. Connor found that certain aspects of the
traditional Japanese family, such as high dependency needs, closeness to the mother, and suppression of sexuality, continued to function in Japanese-Americans, even those of the third generation.

950   CUBER, JOHN F., with PEGGY B. HARROFF. The Significant
       Americans: A Study of Sexual Behavior among the Affluent.
       New York: Appleton-Century, 1965. 204 pp.
       Cuber and Harroff based their book on interviews with 437
upper-middle-class men and women between the ages of thirty-five
and fifty-five. Most of them were married, and all of them were
economically and socially successful. The authors do not indicate
how the people were located and selected, nor do they present any
statistics on responses, attitudes, or behavior patterns. The result is a diffuse work with many quotations from the interviews,
whose only conclusions seem to be that (1) there is great diversity
in patterns of marital and sexual relationships and (2) most people
believe in traditional Judeo-Christian monogamy, but practice a
much less rigorous pattern of sexual behavior.

951   DAVIS, KATHARINE BEMENT. Factors in the Sex Life of Twenty-Two
       Hundred Women. New York: Harper, 1929. 430 pp.
       Undertaken by the Bureau of Social Hygiene, the Rockefeller-
supported organization of which Katharine Bement Davis was general
secretary, this study remained, until Kinsey's female volume appeared in 1953, the most complete survey of the sexual attitudes
and behavior of American women. It remains of key importance to
historians and, at the time it was published, was unique in its
aim of analyzing conditions among "normal" women, as opposed to
the psychiatric and other atypical cases usually cited by the authorities of the time.
       Actually it is two different studies, each of which utilized
a different questionnaire. The first group studied were married
women; out of 10,000 contacted, 1,073 finally responded. A second
group of 10,000 unmarried women yielded 1,200 replies. Neither
group, however, was typical of the population as a whole--the unmarried women were all college graduates--and this skewing of the
sample no doubt had an impact on the content of the responses.
       Although the completed study did not appear until 1929, the
actual survey began around 1921 (Davis is not clear on this) with
the married women's survey, the single women being surveyed around

1924. This should be borne in mind by researchers trying to correlate the age of respondents, or year of birth, with the pattern of response. Moreover, since participation in the study was voluntary, after initial contact, additional response patterning may have occurred in this regard.

Factors is, nevertheless, a highly useful study. Aside from the data it gathered, it clearly demonstrated the feasibility of conducting a survey on sexual behavior among the general public and of receiving thoughtful responses to questions covering a wide range of subjects: masturbation, homosexuality, sexual pleasure in marriage, and sex education, to name a few. Although the statistical analysis of the data often makes for turgid reading, the study is enlivened by narrative "case" studies, voluntarily submitted by the respondents. Davis and the other authors are also remarkably free from moralizing conclusions and judgments of their material.

The study's findings cover many areas: the relationship between masturbation and pleasurable sexual relations in marriage, the periodicity of sexual desire, the general lack of sex education from reliable sources, and the correlation of personal happiness to sexual behavior. The unmarried women's questionnaire included a section entitled "Opinion," which asked for subjective responses to ethical questions, and a chapter is devoted to a summary of these. Appendices deal with the question of why women requesting the questionnaire failed to answer it and the relative merits of the questionnaire and personal interview methods for eliciting useful information. Unfortunately, neither questionnaire is reprinted in full, nor is adequate summary information given on the demographic composition of the survey populations, both respondent and nonrespondent. Nevertheless, this is an important work which cannot be bypassed by any student of the field.

952   De MARTINO, MANFRED F. The New Female Sexuality: The Sexual
       Practices and Experiences of Social Nudists, "Potential" Nudists,
       and Lesbians. New York: Julian Press, 1969. 236 pp.
       De Martino, a psychology faculty member at Onondaga Community College in Syracuse, used questionnaires and standard personality inventories in this study of sexuality in 102 female nudists and 73 "potential" nudists. In addition, he also presents data on "potential" nudists who are lesbians and a group of women members of Mensa, the high IQ organization. Additional fieldwork was done at the Empire Haven nudist camp in Monrovia, New York. There is some sloppiness in research technique (we are, for example, never given a clear definition of a "potential" nudist), and De Martino tends to quote directly from questionnaire responses without giving any statistical analysis of what the responses might mean both comparatively and as a whole.

953   DICKINSON, ROBERT LATOU, and LURA BEAM. The Single Woman: A
       Medical Study in Sex Education. Baltimore: Williams & Wilkins,
       1934. 469 pp.

This is a difficult book to use, both because of its organization and the manner in which the data comprising it were assembled. Beginning in 1883 (or 1890, according to A Thousand Marriages [entry 954]), Dickinson, who is perhaps best known for his skill as a medical illustrator and his involvement in the birth control movement, began gathering case histories, some with details of sexual experience, the remainder without such material, of women seen in his gynecological practice. In 1931, the first full-scale work based on this material was prepared by writer Lura Beam and called A Thousand Marriages. The Single Woman, also written by Beam from Dickinson's records, is a continuation of that work and should be used in conjunction with it, since A Thousand Marriages details many points of methodology relating to both studies, points not printed separately in the later book.

The Single Woman includes material from 1,078 cases: 350 histories with details of sexual experience, and two control groups without such details, one with 300 cases and the other with 428 (material relating to the control groups, however, is relegated to a separate section of the book). The book is organized into four broad sections: health, sexuality, creative problems, and interpretation, with smaller subject breakdowns including such varied topics as daydreams, virginity, and religion and art. Lesbianism is included and is defined as "a transient attempt to re-create life by love for the same sex with or without a specifically sexual consummation."

Because the cases came to Dickinson because of their suffering from some sort of gynecological disturbance, be it an infection, suspected pregnancy, or whatever, there is no reason to expect them to replicate characteristics of the female population as a whole. An even more serious problem in using the data, however, is the study's using data from the entire fifty-year period covered by the cases (1883-1933) as if they were static. No attempt is made to chart change or differences over time or in circumstance, except for one chapter comparing 1895 data with 1930 data.

954 _____. A Thousand Marriages: A Medical Study of Sex Adjustment. Baltimore: Williams & Wilkins, 1931. 482 pp.
This pioneering study of women's sexual behavior in the United States was the work of Robert Latou Dickinson, one of the leading advocates of birth control in the early twentieth century (Lura Beam was a writer brought in to cast Dickinson's data into publishable form). A gynecologist, Dickinson began in 1890 (or in 1883, according to The Single Woman [entry 953]) to gather information about the sex histories of his patients, primarily white urban middle- and upper-middle-class women. While 1,200 histories were gathered, only the 900 relating to married women were analyzed for this report, along with a control group of 200, for whom Dickinson had general case histories, but no sex histories. The average case was observed for seven years, and sample uncompleted and completed history forms are included in appendices.

Smaller groups with such characteristics as being newly

married or suffering from dysfunction were separated from the whole for more detailed analysis or discussion, and the subjects covered range from autoeroticism to demographic data. Nevertheless, the study has serious problems. Since Dickinson did not precede data collection with any sort of research design or plan, there is no guarantee of consistency, and lapses in fundamental data occur. Moreover, it is noted that certain information was "masked" to disguise patients' identities. Some statistical summaries include data for only part of the sample (figures on orgasm in coitus, for example, are reported for only 442 cases). And especially frustrating to historians is the failure to note when the cases were recorded or to chart any change over time, a condition that surely is of importance when dealing with data spanning nearly fifty years.

955   EHRMANN, WINSTON W. Premarital Dating Behavior. New York: Henry Holt, 1959. 316 pp.

Questionnaires and interviews were used to gather information for this study of premarital heterosexual activity among 1,157 male and female college students between 1946 and 1953. Ehrmann's discussion of his research methodology is extensive and demonstrates the effort that went into assuring the accuracy of the research. Much of the book is statistical in nature, but Ehrmann does excerpt some interview materials and compares his findings with those of other sex researchers. Among his conclusions, he found that female partners were responsible for exerting control over the sexual behavior allowed in the relationship and that female sexual expression was primarily related to being in love and the degree of intimacy perceived in the role. Male sexuality, on the other hand, was far less romantic and relatively unrelated to the quality of the relationship. Thus, Ehrmann concluded that there were distinct male and female subcultural differences in youth culture with respect to dating and sex.

956   FLEMING, KARL, and ANNE TAYLOR FLEMING. The First Time. New York: Simon and Schuster, 1975. 319 pp.

This is a compilation of recollections by twenty-eight famous personalities, telling how they lost their virginity. Thirteen of the subjects are women, including Maya Angelou, Alice Roosevelt Longworth, and Mae West. "We came to the end of the book with the feeling that fundamentally the introduction to sex is about as complicated and difficult an experience as it has always been, and that certainly 'the first time' remains an emotional, guilt-ridden, bewildering and not wildly erotic moment." The First Time deals with much more than simple loss of virginity, providing additional information about the entire sexual milieu in which the subjects grew up and had their initial sexual experiences. Based on taped interviews, this is a valuable book, documenting an aspect of life usually omitted from more formal biographies.

957   FREEDMAN, H. Super Marriage; Super Sex. New York: Ballantine

Books, 1974. 213 pp. ISR.

This is a clearly commercial product which describes the sexual experiences of more than one hundred people from around the world, but primarily from the United States and Britain. "Diverse in their sexual variety and ingenious in their techniques, the descriptions of their most intimate relations are explicit and rich in detail." Selected from letters written to Forum magazine between 1968 and 1974, the descriptions are rather consistent in style throughout, suggesting heavy editing. Arrangement is topical by type of sexual activity, and the focus is primarily heterosexual, although lesbian and bisexual incidents are reported. There is also a discussion of marriage alternatives.

958   FREEDMAN, MERVIN B. The College Experience. San Francisco: Jossey-Bass, 1967. 202 pp.

This study of the college experience and its impact on the lives of students was conducted over a fifteen-year period, making extensive use of data from Vassar College, as well as from Stanford, the University of California, Mills College, and San Francisco State University. One section of the book deals with sexuality and reports on tests conducted with three Vassar classes and interviews with forty-nine students. Freedman found that attitudes toward sex became more liberal during the college years, but that on the whole students' attitudes and behavior were characterized by restraint rather than license. A second part of the sexuality section traces changes in student sexual attitudes and behavior during the twentieth century, discussing other studies of college women and men.

959   FRIDAY, NANCY. Forbidden Flowers: More Women's Sexual Fantasies. New York: Pocket Books, 1975. 324 pp.

A sequel to My Secret Garden (entry 960), Friday's first book of women's sexual fantasies, Forbidden Flowers is divided into two sections: "Where Do Sexual Fantasies Come From?" and "The Uses of Sexual Fantasy," concerning the role that fantasies play in women's lives. Friday notes a difference in the quality of the fantasies in the two books: "While I would characterize the majority of fantasies in Garden as various strategies women had devised to handle or disarm sexual guilt, the fantasies I have collected for this book are much more characterized by pleasure and guiltless exuberance." The selections are hardly representative of women as a whole, however--the average age of respondents was twenty-two--and Friday's system of voluntary submissions is bound to skew the sample. Sensibly, Friday does not attempt to make unfounded generalizations but lets the letters speak for themselves.

960   _____. My Secret Garden: Women's Sexual Fantasies. New York: Trident Press, 1973. 361 pp.

My Secret Garden was Nancy Friday's first collection of women's sexual fantasies and presents fantasies contributed by about four hundred women, many of whom responded to advertisements placed by Friday in newspapers and magazines. The book is roughly organized by fantasy type, and Friday's commentary is interspersed between the fantasy texts. She draws few conclusions, although her ideas about women's erotic images of other women are interesting. These fantasies, she believes, are projections of how the fantasizer feels about herself and that fantasizers are seeking from these women what they don't get from male lovers in reality. Friday distinguishes, however, between these and genuine lesbian fantasies, several of which are included (the difference lies in the woman's _real_ sexual object choice while fantasizing).

961   FRIEDMAN, LEONARD J. Virgin Wives: A Study of Unconsummated Marriages. London: Tavistock, 1971. 161 pp.
        Despite its somewhat sensational title, Virgin Wives is a serious study summarizing a seminar in the treatment of unconsummated marriages sponsored by the Family Planning Association, the British equivalent of Planned Parenthood. Ten women physicians participated in the seminar, which was led by Michael Balint, a noted British psychotherapist (the author was not a participant in a direct sense, but was an active observer at seminar meetings). During the course of the study, 1958-61, one hundred cases, some of which are presented in detail here, were discussed by the seminar, whose members estimated that about seven hundred of this type were seen in all. Post-women's movement readers will observe many stereotypical, Freudian-based assumptions throughout the study. A statement on page 117, for example, equates abhorrence of heterosexual intercourse with the hatred of being a woman and a denial of femininity. Laying these objections aside, however, the study demonstrates the efficacy of short-term psychotherapy in helping patients consummate their marriages. It should be noted that patient participation was purely voluntary. There is a summary chapter with statistics on the one hundred cases, and Friedman is open about discussing the methodological shortcomings of the study. Historians of sexuality will find the chapter summarizing previous discussions of unconsummated marriages in the professional literature of particular interest.

962   GEBHARD, PAUL H., and ALAN B. JOHNSON. The Kinsey Data: Marginal Tabulations of the 1938-1963 Interviews Conducted by the Institute for Sex Research. Philadelphia: W.B. Saunders, 1979. 642 pp.
        This volume presents statistics derived from case history data, 1938-63, gathered by Alfred C. Kinsey and the Institute for Sex Research. Much of the material appears here for the first time, being omitted from the two Kinsey reports and other institute studies. The authors explain the methodology used in preparing this report as well as in conducting the original interviews and include a chronology of key points in the history of interview collection, including names of organizations and locations of populations surveyed. "We have cleaned our samples, more accurately processed the data, and have made new tabulations. These may be compared with our previous-

ly published material so that the extent of prior error may be estimated and suitable qualifications and corrections made."

963   GEDDES, DONALD PORTER, ed.   An Analysis of the Kinsey Reports
      on Sexual Behavior in the Human Male and Female.   New York:
      E.P. Dutton, 1954.   319 pp.
         Desipte its title, the primary focus of this anthology of
      essays is the Kinsey female volume (entry 975), which appeared in
      September 1953.   Sixteen authors representing a wide range of in-
      tellectual disciplines and viewpoints have contributed original
      articles critiquing aspects of Sexual Behavior in the Human Female.
      Millicent McIntosh, president of Barnard College, expresses her
      concern about the effect of Kinsey's reports on young people, while
      Herbert Hyman and Paul B. Sheatsley appraise Kinsey's research
      methodology.   Editor Geddes also reprints some of the reviews and
      criticism of the male volume which appeared after its publication
      in 1948.

964   GHURYE, GOVIND SADASHIV.   Sexual Behaviour of the American
      Female.   Bombay, India: Current Book House, 1956.   173 pp.
         Primarily a summary of the reports of Kinsey, Davis, Terman,
      Dickinson, and a few other American sex researchers, Sexual Behaviour
      of the American Female does not present any new research findings.
      It is interesting, however, in demonstrating the reception of
      American sex research abroad.   Some of Ghurye's criticisms of
      Kinsey, such as the failure to present adequate statistics, were
      remedied by subsequent Institute for Sex Reserach publications.
      His persistent characterization of female orgasm, however, as "a
      doubtful and mysterious entity," perhaps displays his own cultural
      bias as much as it does the vagaries of existing knowledge regard-
      ing this phenomenon.

965   GITTELSON, NATALIE.   The Erotic Life of the American Wife.   New
      York: Delacorte, 1972.   380 pp.
         Natalie Gittelson traveled throughout the United States to
      talk with women about their marriages and attitudes toward sex.
      She found a pattern of alienation between husband and wife in many
      cases.   Some of this tension was due to the women's movement, while
      other causes included the availability of abortion and birth con-
      trol and a growing acceptance of lesbianism, all of which broadened
      women's sexual alternatives.   Gittelson concluded that although
      there is no single formula for a successful marriage, good marriages
      seem to be characterized by an intense life of both the body and the
      mind.

966   GREENE, GAEL.   Sex and the College Girl.   New York: Dial Press,
      1964.   256 pp.
         This loosely structured journalistic report is based on
      scholarly research, as well as 614 interviews conducted at 102 col-
      leges and universities in the United States.   Greene does not indi-
      cate how the campuses or students were selected, although some of

the material was gathered by eighteen female student "reporters" in response to a request for volunteers. Men as well as women were interviewed. Alhtough Greene found wide variation in attitudes and behavior, she also found a real trend toward sexual freedom, including pressure to lose one's virginity. Despite their coolness, however, students were ill-informed about contraception and on more than one occasion displayed false bravado about their sexual experience. Greene is not moralistic, but she does conclude: "Sex is not a problem. But the abuse and misuse of sex creates genuine tragedy that college deans and counselors have finally warned us we can no longer ignore."

967   HAMILTON, GILBERT Van TASSEL. A Research in Marriage. New York: A. & C. Boni, 1929. 570 pp.
    In this study of one hundred married men and one hundred married women, Hamilton attempted to answer the question of whether marriage is a faulty institution or whether marital problems lie in the psychological baggage that men and women bring with them to marriage. His subjects did not comprise a scientifically constructed sample and were, for the most part, upper-middle-class New York City residents under the age of forty. Hamilton prepared question cards, incorporating as many of Katharine Bement Davis's survey questions as possible, with 372 questions for women who had been pregnant, 357 for those who had not, and 334 for men. His respondents were given these in Hamilton's office, and he then took down, presumably in shorthand, their responses, word for word. The questions themselves are quite complete, though sometimes worded in leading ways, and include queries on such topics as childhood sex education, sexual technique, and sex daydreams.
    Hamilton, who was a Freud-influenced psychiatrist, concluded that bad teaching and negative parental and societal attitudes during childhood had a definite negative impact on adult sexuality. Yet his attempt to find direct correspondence between adult patterns and childhood experience seems somewhat strained.
    The book's strength lies in its tabular presentation of the survey question responses in the respondents' own words. Some of Hamilton's specific conclusions are susceptible to broader interpretations: "Of the 46 women who are inadequate as to orgasm capacity, 20 had been diagnosed at one time or another in their lives as more or less seriously psychoneurotic. . . . Only one of the 54 women who could have orgasms with reasonable frequency had ever been regarded as psychoneurotic."

968   HAMILTON, GILBERT Van TASSEL, and KENNETH MACGOWAN. What Is Wrong with Marriage. New York: Albert and Charles Boni, 1930. 319 pp.
    Using Hamilton's A Research in Marriage (entry 967) as a base, Kenneth Macgowan, who is best known for his theatrical career, paraphrased and simplified that work for general audiences. In some cases, he asked new questions of the material, occasionally returning to the original case files. This is not an uncommon

practice in sex research, cf. the Brechers' An Analysis of Human Sexual Response or Money and Tucker's Sexual Signatures, both popularizations of more complex research reports. Macgowan, however, even includes a chapter summarizing the popularization. For serious researchers, the original version is probably the more desirable source.

969   HIMELHOCH, JEROME, and SYLVIA FLEIS FAVA, eds. Sexual Behavior in American Society: An Appraisal of the First Two Kinsey Reports. New York: W.W. Norton, 1955. 446 pp.
       This collection of essays includes material written especially for this volume, as well as reprints of previously published articles, some of them from Social Problems, the journal edited by Himelhoch. Topics discussed range from methodology through the impact of Kinsey's work on college student behavior to its relationship to the law. Especially useful is a 260-item bibliography of books, pamphlets, editorials, and articles relating to the Kinsey reports.

970   HIRSCH, ARTHUR HENRY. The Love Elite: The Story of Woman's Emancipation and Her Drive for Sexual Fulfillment. New York: Julian Press, 1963. 281 pp.
       Arthur H. Hirsch received a Ph.D. from the University of Chicago and until 1933 chaired the history department at Ohio Wesleyan University. Author of such works as The Huguenots of Colonial South Carolina, his interest became focused on sex in his later years.
       The Love Elite is purported to be based on 120,000 personal letters, "thousands of interviews and conversations," and other material. It is obvious, however, that the letters and interviews were either only fantasies in Hirsch's mind or were solicited by him. Some of his examples border on the ridiculous, such as Dorothy Jean, "stoop-shouldered, thin and too short, she had a peculiar animal-like gait." Dorothy Jean, who was the governess of a retarded, twelve-year-old deaf mute, found fulfillment on a park bench.
       Hirsch believed that sexual intimacy in or out of marriage was the chief characteristic of the women of the so-called love elite. Yet he also retained a firm belief that "it is in becoming a mother that a woman fulfills her destiny—the destiny of her physical body and of her spiritual self." The Love Elite is little more than a compilation of sexual incidents. It is Hirsch himself who provides the interest for the researcher.

971   HITE, SHERE. The Hite Report: A Nationwide Study on Female Sexuality. New York: Macmillan, 1976. 438 pp.
       Shere Hite, an independent New York–based sex researcher, conducted this study in order to determine how women feel about their sexuality. Opinion oriented rather than statistical in focus, The Hite Report is based on 3,000 questionnaire returns from a canvassing of more than 100,000 United States women between 1972 and

1974. Four different questionnaires were used during the course of the study, the final one containing fifty-eight multipart questions. What statistics Hite does present are drawn from the 1,844 responses to the first three questionnaires. The study has sometimes been criticized because of internal inconsistency in the questionnaire format as well as skewing of the sample population (a large percentage of the respondents came from feminist populations and there was no effort to construct a population reflecting the demographic characteristics of the American female population as a whole).

Incorporating selections from the narrative replies of the survey subjects, the book proceeds through discussions of masturbation, orgasm, intercourse, clitoral stimulation, lesbianism, sexual slavery, the sexual revolution, older women, and a concluding chapter on "a new female sexuality." Hite believes that in the past men have defined female sexuality in terms of their own sexual objectives, resulting in a mechanical pattern of sexual behavior revolving around male erection, penetration, and orgasm. She believes that more diverse and diffuse response patterns are desired by women and are desirable for them as well. She calls for fundamental rethinking of mass society's notions about women's sexuality.

972 HITE, SHERE, ed. Sexual Honesty by Women for Women. New York: Warner Paperback Library, 1974. 294 pp. ISR.
Two years before Shere Hite's report on female sexuality (entry 971) was published, she compiled this preliminary work, which presents verbatim replies from forty-five out of the two thousand responses to her survey she had received by that time. Hite also reprinted the texts of the three versions of the questionnaire she used. Aside from a brief introduction, there is no analysis of the findings, making this book a real commercial quickie. Because it does, however, reproduce responses in toto, it is useful for those analyzing the more complete 1976 report.

973 HOTVEDT, MARY E. Family Planning among Mexican-Americans of South Texas. Unpublished paper, Sangamon State University, 1976. Unpaged. ISR.
This book-length manuscript reports on fieldwork done in Hidalgo County, Texas, in the Rio Grande Valley during 1970 and 1971. Hotvedt devotes considerable space to providing an overview of the cultural history and sociology of the area and its Mexican-American population. Among the topics relating to women's sexuality that are discussed are chastity, the sexuality of single women, and sexual behavior in marriage. "In general . . . orgasm did not seem to be the goal of lovemaking for women. The rewards seemed more to be a feeling of love, passion or intensity, and indulgence of sexual sensations although not necessarily to orgasm."

974 HUNT, MORTON. The Affair: A Portrait of Extra-Marital Love in Contemporary America. New York: World, 1969. 317 pp.
Describing patterns of extramarital behavior among white

middle-class Americans, Morton Hunt takes the position that the ultimate effect of each affair depends on the total set of circumstances surrounding the relationship. He believes that in characterizing affairs' patterns, the degree of emotional intimacy and involvement of the two partners is the most important criterion.

Hunt's findings are based on 360 questionnaire responses, 91 taped interviews with people involved in affairs, interviews and discussions with psychologists, psychiatrists, and other professionals, and miscellaneous primary and secondary sources. He is concerned only with conventional heterosexual relationships and excluded homosexual and incestuous affairs, experiences with prostitutes, and such sexual activities as rape and masturbation. Much of the book consists of first-person descriptions of what went on during the affairs. Despite the use of the questionnaire, no statistics are presented, and the text of the survey form is not reprinted.

975   KINSEY, ALFRED C., et al. Sexual Behavior in the Human Female. Philadelphia: W.B. Saunders, 1953. 842 pp.

In July 1938, Alfred C. Kinsey, an Indiana University biologist whose previous work had focused on the gall wasp, embarked on a study that would eventually culminate in publication of perhaps the two best-known works on human sexual behavior ever written: Sexual Behavior in the Human Male, which was published in 1948, and Sexual Behavior in the Human Female, which appeared in 1953. Although Kinsey originally undertook the work on his own, largely in response to student needs for accurate sex information, the project was supported from 1941 by grants from the National Research Council's Committee for Research in Problems of Sex. The Institute for Sex Research at Indiana University continues the work begun by its founder to this day.

Sexual Behavior in the Human Female includes narrative and statistical analyses of case histories reported by 5,940 white females prior to 1950. Another 1,849 women representing black and prison populations were surveyed, but were not included in the statistics for this report, although Kinsey and his collaborators noted that these cases had influenced their thinking. All individuals surveyed were members of social, professional, or other groups used to initiate contact by the survey team. The Kinsey population is neither random nor representative of the American female population as a whole. Moreover, totals in calculations, as is noted in the introductory section on scope and method, often fall short of 5,940, owing to a variety of factors, including inapplicability of questions to subjects and respondents refusing to reply. In addition to the case histories gathered via personal interviews, the research team utilized other research on mammalian and human sexuality (cited in footnotes and bibliography), as well as diaries, correspondence, photographs, and other source materials collected by the institute or provided by subjects. The thoroughness of Kinsey's approach has yet to be emulated by his successors in this field.

Following the introductory material on the background and methodology of the study, the report is organized into two sections. The first summarizes findings on types of sexual activity among women under the following headings: preadolescent sexual development, masturbation, nocturnal sex dreams, premarital petting, premarital coitus, marital coitus, extramarital coitus, homosexual responses and contacts, and total sexual outlet. The second section compares male and female findings in the areas of anatomy and physiology of sexual response and orgasm, psychologic factors and neural mechanisms of sexual response, and hormonal factors in sexual response.

The comparative section on men and women is based on data as diverse as observation of other mammalian species and retrospective case history reports. Some data are from tests done specially for this study by five gynecologists on 879 women. Interestingly, Kinsey's conclusions from these findings anticipated the post-Masters and Johnson clitoral/vaginal orgasm controversy by more than a dozen years: "Some of the psychoanalysts and some other clinicians insist that only vaginal stimulation and a 'vaginal orgasm' can provide a psychologically satisfactory culmination to the activity of a 'sexually mature' female. It is difficult, however, in the light of our present understanding of the anatomy and physiology of sexual response, to understand what can be meant by a 'vaginal orgasm.'"

Sexual Behavior in the Human Female is not without its faults. Sample composition is one. Statistical validity is another, although the volume benefited from criticism in this area that followed publication of the male report. Perhaps a greater problem is Kinsey's decision to use incidences leading to orgasm, the same indicator used in the male report, as the measure of sexual activity. Kinsey was aware of the difficulty, given the diffuse quality of female sexual response, but chose not to venture into an attempt at developing an alternative mode of measurement.

Kinsey's work should be used cautiously, if possible in conjunction with some of its postpublication criticism. Nevertheless, it remains a benchmark by which other studies may be evaluated. Others may use larger, more representative samples, and, certainly, many are more readable, but in its overall motivation and approach Sexual Behavior in the Human Female continues to remain in a class by itself.

976   KOPP, MARIE E. Birth Control in Practice: Analysis of Ten Thousand Case Histories of the Birth Control Clinical Research Bureau. New York: Robert M. McBride, 1934. 290 pp.
     Margaret Sanger's Birth Control Clinical Research Bureau furnished the cases on which this report is based. Three basic areas are analyzed: economic and social conditions of patients, physical factors, and indicators of contraceptive need and effectiveness. The physical factors section includes a survey of the sexual behavior of the cases, including such topics as frequency of intercourse and experience of orgasm. The text and statistical tables are preceded by a methodological discussion.

977 LANDIS, CARNEY, et al. Sex in Development: A Study of the
Growth and Development of the Emotional and Sexual Aspects of
Personality Together with Physiological, Anatomical, and Medical
Information on a Group of 153 Normal Women and 142 Female
Psychiatric Patients. New York: Paul B. Hoeber, 1940. 329 pp.
    One of many projects in human sexuality sponsored by the
Committee for Research in Problems of Sex of the National Research
Council, Landis's study sought to determine whether deviations and
distortions in sexual development are of primary importance in the
etiology of neuroses and psychoses. A research population of 295
women, fifteen to thirty-five years of age, was selected. It consisted of 109 single and 44 married women who had never been under
psychiatric care and 101 single and 41 married women who were patients in a mental hospital. Interviews, questionnaires, psychiatric case histories, and physical examinations were used to gather
evidence.
    Landis and his colleagues found that "normality" had a much
wider range of developmental variations than had been thought.
"Those women who had good general adjustment usually had a good
sex adjustment in marriage." The patient group had a poorer record
of marital adjustment than the nonpatients, and many of the patients
reported adverse home conditions in early childhood. Different
types of patients (depending on their diagnosis) exhibited some
differences in psychosexual development patterns, but on the whole
the study concluded that "the pattern of psychosexual development
prior to the onset of the psychosis was practically indistinguishable from the pattern of development of the normal individual."
Interview forms and questionnaire form question texts are reprinted,
as are several statistical summaries.

978 LeBARON, JOSEPH. Sex Life of the American Prostitute. North
Hollywood, Calif.: Brandon House, 1962. 159 pp.
    Typical of commercially motivated sex literature, Sex Life
of the American Prostitute, despite its title, relates more to
sociology than sexuality. LeBaron's information is not documented,
although his "cases" seem to focus on New York City. The chapter
on the semiprostitute foreshadows some of the concerns of the
women's movement of the late 1960s and early 1970s: "If any woman
who sells or barters the pleasure of her body is a prostitute, then
those girls whose marriages are motivated solely by material considerations, or those wives who hold out on their connubial favors
until they are promised a new dress, a fur coat or some other
luxury, are members of the prostitute group."

979 LIBBY, ROGER W., and ROBERT N. WHITEHURST, eds. Renovating
Marriage: Toward New Sexual Life-Styles. Danville, Calif.:
Consensus, 1973. 366 pp.
    Renovating Marriage presents a collection of essays, a few
of them reprints from periodicals and books, discussing the range
of marital and sexual life-style options currently available as
alternatives to traditional, monogamous, sexually exclusive

marriage. As the editors point out, most of the chapters deal with the upper-middle-class, WASP, heterosexual context, although the ideas are applicable to a wide range of other ethnic, sexual, and social groups. Of particular interest are Roger W. Libby, "Extra-marital and Co-marital Sex: A Review of the Literature"; Pepper Schwartz, "Female Sexuality and Monogamy"; and Jessie Bernard, "Infidelity: Some Moral and Social Issues."

980 LONDON, LOUIS SAMUEL. Sexual Deviations in the Female: Case Histories of Frustrated Women. Rev. ed. New York: Julian, 1957. 172 pp.

A Freudian, London believed that all psychiatric problems were rooted in sexual disturbances. Sixteen cases running the gamut from "obsessional thinking of white slavery" to "nymphomania with vampirism" are presented here, as well as a lengthy discussion en-titled "Lesbian Love in a Schizoid Manic." The cases are presented in a simplistic, sensational manner, and there is little effort on the part of London to give the material any kind of broader perspective. The following passage is typical: "Besides her sadomasochism she resorted to kleptomaniac acts, and would steal cookies in bakeshops (symbolic of sex). She had castration ideas (cutting off her hand) which portrayed masturbation guilt. . . . Her thoughts were continually of sexual relations and of being pursued by brutal men. Since she was southern, many colored men appeared in her day connections and thoughts of these seeped into her conscience from her unconscious cravings."

981 McDERMOTT, SANDRA. Female Sexuality: Its Nature and Conflicts. New York: Simon and Schuster, 1970. 223 pp.

Also published as Studies in Female Sexuality, Female Sexuality is based on interviews with 250 English women. Fourteen interviews have been reprinted in full, while the remainder have been excerpted for use in chapters relating to knowledge of sexu-ality, morality, love, marriage, orgasm, lesbianism, sexual varia-tions, and masturbation. The book was obviously written for the popular market; there are no footnotes, bibliography, or index, and the interviews read like fantasy material.

982 MacDONALD, ARTHUR. Abnormal Woman, a Sociologic and Scientific Study of Young Women, Including Letters of American and European Girls in Answer to Personal Advertisements. Washington, D.C.: published by the author, 1895. 189 pp.

MacDonald was an anthropological criminologist who was with the U.S. Bureau of Education from 1892 to 1904. At the time he prepared this book, he was as yet unmarried. His alleged purpose was to study "abnormality," that is, conditions varying from the normal. To achieve this goal, he placed ads in the personal col-umns of major United States and European newspapers inviting cor-respondence. This book prints his replies. MacDonald followed up some of the correspondence with additional letters and even personal visits to measure the women's nervous system--" to see whether their nervous condition may possibly be one of the causes of their answering a 'personal.'"

983   MORSE, BENJAMIN. Sexual Behavior of the American College Girl.
       New York: Lancer, 1963. 174 pp.
       Written for the nonfiction "sexploitation" market, Sexual
Behavior of the American College Girl presents case histories pur-
porting to show the variety of "different individuals reacting in
different fashion to fundamentally different circumstances." It
should be noted, however, that there is considerably more commentary
by the author (who bills himself as a physician and counselor) than
in most other books of this type. One chapter is entitled "Special
Problems of the College for Women"--"Sexually 'wild' girls are not
such a rare commodity in these colleges as one might think"--while
others deal with such subjects as petting, lesbianism, marriage,
and pregnancy.

984   _____. The Sexually Promiscuous Female. Derby, Conn.:
       Monarch, 1963. 158 pp.
       Another of the Monarch panoply of supposedly accurate, non-
fiction studies of sexual behavior in the United States, The
Sexually Promiscuous Female includes such chapters as "The Coeducational Narcissist," "The Frustrated Spinster," and "The Nymph and
Society." Morse offers a modicum of analysis, but his primary
function is to present the narrative "case studies" with which all
Monarch products are replete. One only wonders how many readers
regarded them as real, compared to those who were aware that the
reality was probably only a marketing illusion.

985   MOSHER, CLELIA DUEL. The Mosher Survey: Sexual Attitudes of
       45 Victorian Women. Edited by James MaHood and Kristine Wenburg.
       New York: Arno Press, 1980. 469 pp.
       MaHood and Wenburg have compiled, edited, and to some extent
reconstructed the responses of Clelia Duel Mosher's forty-five
women subjects to her questionnaires on sexuality, work done between
1892 and 1920. Based on originals in the Stanford University
Archives, this typescript edition includes both questions and answers, as well as a preface describing Mosher's methods and an introduction by Carl Degler. Of the survey's respondents, 70 percent
were born before 1870, making this an unparalleled source for the
study of late nineteenth- and early twentieth-century female sexuality. Material can be found on such subjects as frequency of
sexual relations and knowledge of sexual physiology before marriage.
Biographical profiles of the subjects and general health information relating to them and their families are also included. This
is a primary source; the editors do not attempt to interpret
Mosher's data.

986   OLIVER, BERNARD J., Jr. Sexual Deviation in American Society:
       A Social-Psychological Study of Sexual Non-conformity. New
       Haven: College-University Press, 1967. 256 pp.

In this simplistic monograph, Oliver defines sexual deviation as general sexual nonconformity. He believes that such nonconformity should be studied and understood in order to be prevented. Among the so-called deviations he discusses are rape, prostitution, homosexuality, incest, nonmarital sexual relations, masturbation, and frigidity. For the most part, Oliver simply extracts information from other authorities such as Kinsey. His indiscriminate citation of such questionable "sources" as Monarch and Lancer paperbacks indicates his inability to distinguish between valid and suspect authorities and data.

987 RAINWATER, LEE, and KAROL K. WEINSTEIN. And the Poor Get Children. Chicago: Quandrangle, 1960. 202 pp.
A study sponsored by the Planned Parenthood Federation of America, And the Poor Get Children is based on a sample of forty-six men and fifty women. The overall focus of the research was on "the psycho-social factors involved in family planning and contraceptive use by working class men and women." Data on sexual relations and attitudes were gathered, a difference between this study and most others on contraception. Despite its many methodological problems, the study succeeds in deomnstrating the relationship of economic and social conditions to women's sexual attitudes and behavior. One key conclusion was that there is a definite correlation between successful implementation of contraceptive practices and sexual "success" and satisfaction among women.

988 SCHAEFER, LEAH CAHAN. Women and Sex: Sexual Experiences and Reactions of a Group of Thirty Women as Told to a Female Psychotherapist. New York: Pantheon Books, 1973. 269 pp.
Schaefer originally presented this study as a thesis at Columbia University in 1964. It is based on interviews with thirty white, middle-class, married women between the ages of twenty-five and forty, all of whom at some time had been in psychotherapy. Dealing with childhood through adult life, Schaefer focuses on early sexual memories, menstruation, and expectations and experiences of initial intercourse and orgasm. Each interview took twelve hours. Among Schaefer's findings: none of the women reported receiving realistic sex instruction; there was almost total negative reaction to the concept of parental intercourse; and how orgasm is experienced seemed to be learned rather than automatic. Some of her other findings tend to contradict Freudian views of women's sexuality. Schaefer's preliminary questionnaire and interview guide are printed in full.

989 STAPLES, ROBERT, ed. The Black Family: Essays and Studies. Belmont, Calif.: Wadsworth, 1971. 393 pp.
Reprints of several essays relating to black sexuality and sexual behavior are included in this anthology. Authors represented, in addition to Staples, include E. Franklin Frazier, David Heer, Ira Reiss, and Kenneth Clark. None of the selections dealing directly with sexuality was written by a woman, and since they appeared

originally in the 1950s and 1960s, they do not benefit from a
feminist perspective.

990   STAPLES, ROBERT. The Black Woman in America: Sex, Marriage,
       and the Family. Chicago: Nelson-Hall, 1973. 269 pp.
           "The Sexual Life of Black Women" is the chapter in this mono-
       graph by sociologist Robert Staples that relates most directly to
       sexuality, although other chapters on such topics as marriage and
       prostitution also contain relevant information. An examination of
       Staples's "sources," however, leads one to question the validity of
       some of his generalizations. For example, a commonly cited source
       on the history of black sexuality, E. Franklin Frazier's "Sex Life
       of the African and American Negro" from Ellis and Abarbanel's
       Encyclopedia of Sexual Behavior, is itself lacking in source docu-
       mentation, except for a general bibliography. Or consider state-
       ments such as this: "When a Black woman is petitioned by a Black
       man for sexual relations, she is virtually defenseless." Black
       women deserve better, especially better research, with conclusions
       based on facts rather than undocumented generalizations.

991   _____. The World of Black Singles. Contributions in Afro-
       American and African Studies, no. 57. Westport, Conn.:
       Greenwood Press, 1981. 259 pp.
           Unlike Staples's earlier book on black women, which was based
       entirely on secondary materials, Black Singles includes information
       from four hundred questionnaires, as well as one hundred interviews
       with black, college-educated singles between the ages of twenty-
       five and forty-five in the San Francisco Bay area, conducted be-
       tween 1975 and 1979. Most of the respondents were women. Several
       chapters relate to sexuality and sexual behavior. Like The Black
       Woman, this work often contains generalizations undocumented by
       empirical data. As Staples notes, "We believed that understanding
       black singlehood was more important than methodological rigor."

992   STRAKOSCH, FRANCES M. Factors in the Sex Life of Seven Hundred
       Psychopathic Women. Utica: State Hospitals Press, 1934. 102
       pp.
           Strakosch, who prepared this study as a Ph.D. dissertation
       in psychology at Columbia University, gathered her research data
       from case histories in the files of the New York State Psychiatric
       Institute and Hospital. This secondhand approach may have resulted
       in some subjective interpretations on her part, and this was proba-
       bly also the case with the original preparers of the case documents.
           After transferring the information to check sheets, which
       could be used for statistical tabulation, Strakosch compared her
       findings with those of four previously published works: Davis's
       study of 2,200 women (entry 951), G.V. Hamilton's A Research in
       Marriage (entry 967), and Dickinson and Beam's A Thousand Marriages
       (entry 954) and The Single Woman (entry 953). Elements studied in-
       cluded autoeroticism, premarital relationships, homosexuality, mari-
       tal adjustment and the reaction to marital coitus, sexual fantasies,

and love affairs. Strakosch found that basically the sexual behavior patterns among the so-called psychopathic women (actually
a population hospitalized for a wide range of mental illnesses)
and the normals in the other studies were identical, the one major
difference being in marital adjustment. She concluded that "in
general, our results lend no support to the hypothesis that overt
expressions of the sex drive bear a relationship to the psychotic
or psychoneurotic personality."

993   STYCOS, JOSEPH MAYONE. Family and Fertility in Puerto Rico.
      New York: Columbia University Press, 1955. 332 pp.
          Although this monograph focuses on marriage, fertility, and
      contraception, several chapters include material on sexuality,
      sexual behavior, and related topics, such as the complex of vir-
      ginity in courtship. Data were gathered from interviews with seventy-
      two heterosexual working-class couples living in different locations
      on the island, but the documentation indicates that a wide variety
      of other materials were consulted. Stycos's work is especially
      striking in its demonstration of the role of child-rearing prac-
      tices and other cultural factors in determining adolescent and
      adult patterns of sexuality. The volume also includes statistical
      charts, an extensive methodological discussion, and a bibliography
      of 115 citations.

994   TAVRIS, CAROL, and SUSAN SADD. The Redbook Report on Female
      Sexuality: 100,000 Married Women Disclose the Good News about
      Sex. New York: Delacorte Press, 1977. 186 pp.
          In October 1974, Redbook published a questionnaire on women's
      sexuality and received more than 100,000 replies from readers in
      response. The close-ended questions were designed by Temple
      University sociologist Robert R. Bell. Authors Tavris and Sadd,
      both of whom have Ph.D.s in social psychology, analyzed the results,
      incorporating a computer analysis of a random sample of 2,278 re-
      plies.
          Because of the size of the respondent population, as well as
      its approximation to the national United States profile in such
      areas as religious and political beliefs, the authors feel that
      their study is more representative of the female population as a
      whole than other surveys, such as those of Kinsey and Hite. This
      assertion may be questioned, however. For example, while nation-
      wide only 46 percent of the female population (according to the
      authors) was 34 or younger in 1974, 77 percent of their respondents
      were. Likewise, the authors included only married and remarried
      women, excluding single, divorced, and widowed women from their
      conclusions. Such exclusion would certainly affect findings in
      such areas as lesbian sexual behavior and masturbation.
          The authors' conclusions include the following: the stronger
      a woman's religious beliefs the more satisfied she is likely to
      feel about her sex life; premarital sex has little effect on sex
      in marriage; the majority of young women have heterosexual rela-
      tions before marriage; most wives under forty enjoy oral sex.

Tavris and Sadd frequently cite other sex studies and include an interesting discussion on the question of volunteer bias among respondents to sex surveys. The Redbook Report, however, is not the last word in women's sex surveys, and its conclusions should be subjected to further analysis and testing before they are accepted as being representative of American women as a whole.

995   TERMAN, LEWIS MADISON. Psychological Factors in Marital
       Happiness. New York: McGraw-Hill, 1938. 474 pp.
       Terman, a Stanford University psychologist, and his colla-
borators examined three major groups of variables--personality, background, and sexual adjustment--in this assessment of factors associated with marital happiness and unhappiness. Although a total of 2,484 subjects were involved in all aspects of the investigation, most of the research involved 792 middle- and upper-middle-class couples living in southern and central California. Aided by grants from the National Research Council's Committee for Research in Problems of Sex, Terman and his associates concluded that sexual compatibility played no more important a role in determining happiness in marriage than did the other, nonsexual factors.
       There were, however, some specific findings relating to sex, and these are discussed in chapters 10, 11, and 12. Happy subjects as a rule were more likely to have been given frank answers to childhood questions about sex, and their premarital attitudes reflected neither disgust nor "eager, passionate longing." Complaints relating to orgasm (usually the woman's) and frequency of coitus accounted for more than half of all sexual complaints. In addition to these obvious variables, the study also examined such factors as premarital sexual experience and contraceptive practice. Findings are often compared with those of other researchers, such as Katharine Bement Davis. There are numerous statistical charts and tables.

996   WALKER, LENORE E. The Battered Woman. New York: Harper & Row,
       1979. 270 pp.
       It could reasonably be argued that the entire issue of woman battering has strong sexual overtones. This is certainly clear in Walker's chapter on sexual abuse, which this feminist psychologist sees as an integral part of the battering syndrome. Based on interviews with over 120 women, Walker's findings include that the battered woman's sexual relationship with her partner "contributes to her victimization in that the loving behavior is the reinforcer, which keeps her hoping that the next time will be better," that the women held generally traditional attitudes toward sexuality, and that sexual abuse, esepcially unusual, kinky sex practices, was common. Other material on sexuality in the book includes a section on incest.

997   WITTELS, FRITZ. The Sex Habits of American Women. New York:
       Eton, 1951. 189 pp.
       Perhaps the most interesting features of this mass-market

paperback are the statistical charts, which attempt to merge data gathered by such researchers as Terman, Davis, and Dickinson into one depiction, such as charts entitled "Contrasts in Adolescent Sexual Development" or "How Many Practiced Auto-eroticism?" Statistically, of course, such merging is suspect, but the concept is an interesting one. Wittels's text is largely derivative and reflects his Freudian background. "Normal women wish to have children." Spinsters "are not interested in sexual life, or pretend not to be. They live for pets, for aimless women's clubs."

998   WOLFE, LINDA. The Cosmo Report. New York: Arbor House, 1981.
      416 pp.
      The questionnaire on which this report is based was prepared by the editors of Cosmopolitan magazine, where it appeared in the January 1980 issue. Comprised of 79 questions, it elicited 106,000 responses from the magazine's women readers, and a preliminary article summarizing the findings appeared in October 1980. The only other survey of this scale, Redbook's 1975 study of 100,000 women, had included material only on married women, while Cosmopolitan included women of all marital/affectional statuses. Wolfe freely acknowledges that the respondents, most of whom fall into the eighteen to thirty-four age group, may not represent American women as a whole, but she is also aware of the impossibility of conducting such a massive study using any other technique than self-selection and its implicit skewing.
      The presentation of the material is particularly clear. The questionnaire is reprinted in full, there is an appendix of computer-generated statistical tables, and major statistically based findings relating to each question area precede Wolfe's narrative discussion. Wolfe's material often compares Cosmopolitan's findings with those of other researchers, such as Kinsey, and offers excerpts from respondents' own narrative replies. Among the study's conclusions: although half the women were content with the sexually freer atmosphere characterizing the contemporary period, the remainder thought that the sexual revolution had gone too far and that women were being used as pawns by men, a situation resulting in women's engaging reluctantly in sexual activities in an effort to maintain a relationship that might otherwise founder.

999   _____. Playing Around: Women and Extramarital Sex. New York:
      William Morrow, 1975. 248 pp.
      Traditionally, as Linda Wolfe shows in the early parts of this book, women's participation as active partners and initiators in adulterous relationships has been rigidly tabooed. With the decline of the double standard and the rise of sexual freedom, not only is this attitude changing, but adultery has been replaced by extramarital sex, a term with fewer negative connotations. Although Wolfe surveys the literature and history of women who engaged in these relationships, the bulk of this work consists of interviews with women engaged in extramarital relationships. She talked with sixty-six women, about half of whom are included here, classified

236

into three main categories: women who stayed traditionally married but had affairs, women whose marriages broke up, and women who engaged in various forms of experimental marriage. Readers should reflect on an unarticulated common thread running through this subject: the idea that women derive their sense of satisfaction and worth from someone outside themselves.

1000   WOLFF, CHARLOTTE. Bisexuality: A Study. Rev. and expanded ed. London: Quartet Books, 1979. 262 pp.
       The revised edition of Bisexuality includes autobiographical material and an essay on differences between bisexuality and androgyny not found in the original edition. Wolff's basic view of bisexuality, that it "is the root of human sexuality, and the matrix of all bio-psychical reactions, be they passive or active," remains. Reviewing theories of bisexuality, both biological and psychological, she also discusses differences between gender identity and sexual orientation. Wolff believes that the "natural" human condition is a mixture of both male and female gender identities in the same person, but that society encourages the development of single-role stereotypes.
       The empirical bases for her conclusions are interviews, autobiographical statements, and questionnaires from seventy-five self-identified bisexual men and seventy-five similar women. Statistics, as well as transcripts of interviews, are presented. Wolff concludes by advocating societal reorientation to human sexuality rather than compartmentalization into various orientations.

1001   ARAFAT, IBTIHAJ SAID, and BETTY YORBURG. "Drug Use and the Sexual Behavior of College Women." Journal of Sex Research 9, no. 1 (February 1973):21-29.

1002   B., A. [pseud.]. "In the Margaret Louisa Cafeteria of the Y.W.C.A." Medical Critic and Guide 25, no. 4 (April 1922): 133-35.

1003   BAILEY, FLORA L. "Some Sex Beliefs and Practices in a Navaho Community." Papers of the Peabody Museum of American Archaeology and Ethnology 40, no. 2 (1950):1-108.

1004   BALL, JAU DON, and HAYWARD G. THOMAS. "A Sociological, Neurological, Serological and Psychiatrical Study of a Group of Prostitutes." American Journal of Insanity 74, no. 4 (April 1918):647-66.

1005   BARCLAY, ANDREW M. "Sexual Fantasies in Men and Women." Medical Aspects of Human Sexuality 7, no. 5 (May 1973):205-16.

1006   BELL, ROBERT R. "Comparative Attitudes about Marital Sex among Negro Women in the United States, Great Britain and Trinidad." Journal of Comparative Family Studies 1, no. 1 (Autumn 1970): 71-81.

1007   BELL, ROBERT R., and SHELLI BALTER. "Premarital Sexual Experiences of Married Women." Medical Aspects of Human Sexuality 7, no. 11 (November 1973):111–23.

1008   BELL, ROBERT R., and PHYLLIS L. BELL. "Sexual Satisfaction among Married Women." Medical Aspects of Human Sexuality 6, no. 12 (December 1972):136–44.

1009   BELL, ROBERT R., and JAY B. CHASKES. "Premarital Sexual Experience among Coeds, 1958–1968." Journal of Marriage and the Family 32, no. 1 (February 1970):81–84.

1010   BLAZER, JOHN A. "Married Virgins––a Study of Unconsummated Marriages." Journal of Marriage and the Family 26, no. 2 (May 1964):213–14.

1011   BOND, H. "Note of the Post Mortem Examination of a Female Who Committed Suicide Almost Immediately after Coitus." American Journal of Medical Sciences 13 (1833):403.

1012   BRISSETT, DENNIS, and LIONEL S. LEWIS. "Guidelines for Marital Sex: An Anlysis of Fifteen Popular Marriage Manuals." Family Coordinator 19, no. 1 (January 1970):41–48.

1013   BROWN, JULIA S. "A Comparative Study of Deviation from Sexual Mores." American Sociological Review 17, no. 2 (April 1952):135–46.

1014   CLARK, ALEXANDER L., and PAUL WALLIN. "The Accuracy of Husbands' and Wives' Reports of the Frequency of Marital Coitus." Population Studies 18, no. 2 (November 1964):165–73.

1015   CLARK, Le MON. "A Further Report on the Virginity of Unmarried American Women." International Journal of Sexology 6, no. 1 (August 1952):27–32.

1016   _____. "A Report on the Virginity of American Unmarried Women." International Journal of Sexology 4, no. 3 (February 1951):166–69.

1017   CLAUSEN, JOHN A. "Biological Bias and Methodological Limitations in the Kinsey Studies." Social Problems 1, no. 4 (April 1954):126–33.

1018   COOPER, JEFF. "Free Love in the Far North: Sex among the Eskimos." Sexology 41, no. 1 (August 1974):39–42.

1019   "A Curious Case [a chastity preserver]." In Fourth Annual Report of "Helmuth House," 41 East 12th Street, From September 15th, 1889, to June 15th, 1890, 14–15. New York: John C. Rankin, Jr., 1890. NLM.

1020   DENFIELD, DUANE, and MICHAEL GORDON. "The Sociology of Mate Swapping; Or the Family That Swings Together Clings Together." Journal of Sex Research 6, no. 2 (May 1970):85-100.

1021   ELLIS, ALBERT. "From the First to the Second Kinsey Report." International Journal of Sexology 7, no. 2 (November 1953): 64-72.

1022   _____. "Questionnaire Versus Interview Methods in the Study of Human Love Relationships." American Sociological Review 12, no. 5 (October 1947):541-53; 13, no. 1 (February 1948):61-65.

1023   _____. "Sexual Promiscuity in America." Annals of the American Academy of Political and Social Science 378 (July 1968):58-67.

1024   _____. "A Study of the Love Emotions of American College Girls." International Journal of Sexology 3, no. 1 (August 1949):15-21.

1025   FIASHE, ANGEL. "Sex in the Slums." Medical Aspects of Human Sexuality 7, no. 9 (September 1973):88-111.

1026   FREEMAN, HARROP A., and RUTH S. FREEMAN. "Senior College Women: Their Sexual Standards and Activity, Part 1, Dating: Petting-Coital Practices." Journal of the National Association of Women Deans and Counselors 29, no. 3 (Spring 1966):136-43.

1027   GLENN, NORVAL D., and CHARLES N. WEAVER. "Attitudes toward Premarital, Extramarital, and Homosexual Relations in the United States in the 1970's." Journal of Sex Research 15, no. 2 (May 1979):108-18.

1028   GOLDFIELD, MICHAEL D., and IRA D. GLICK. "Self-Mutilation of the Female Genitalia: A Case Report." Diseases of the Nervous System 31, no. 12 (December 1970):843-45.

1029   HARITON, EVONNE BARBARA. "The Sexual Fantasies of Women." In The Female Experience, edited by Carol Tavris, 33-38. Del Mar, Calif.: Communications/Research/Machines, 1973.

1030   HARITON, EVONNE BARBARA, and JEROME L. SINGER. "Women's Fantasies During Sexual Intercourse: Normative and Theoretical Implications." Journal of Consulting and Clinical Psychology 42, no. 3 (June 1974):313-22.

1031   HARVEY, O.L. "The Institutionalization of Human Sexual Behavior; a Study of Frequency Distributions." Journal of Abnormal Psychology 29, no. 4 (January-March 1935):427-33.

1032   _____. "A Note on the Frequency of Human Coitus." American Journal of Sociology 38, no. 1 (July 1932):64-70.

1033   HENTON, COMRADGE L. "Nocturnal Orgasm in College Women: Its
       Relation to Dreams and Anxiety Associated with Sexual Factors."
       Journal of Genetic Psychology 129, 2d half (December 1976):
       245–51.

1034   HOLLENDER, MARC H. "Women's Coital Fantasies." Medical Aspects
       of Human Sexuality 4, no. 2 (February 1970):63–70.

1035   HOUSER, J.A. "Raped by Ghosts." Medical Brief 36, no. 10
       (October 1908):552.

1036   HYMAN, HERBERT H., and JOSEPH E. BARMACK. "Sexual Behavior in
       the Human Female." Psychological Bulletin 51, no. 4 (July
       1954):418–32.

1037   HYMAN, HERBERT H., and PAUL B. SHEATSLEY. "The Kinsey Report
       and Survey Methodology." International Journal of Opinion and
       Attitude Research 2, no. 2 (Summer 1948):183–95.

1038   JACKSON, ERWIN D., and CHARLES R. POTKAY. "Precollege Influences
       on Sexual Experiences of Coeds." Journal of Sex Research 9, no.
       2 (May 1973):143–49.

1039   JAMES, ALICE, and RUTH PIKE. "Sexual Behavior of Couples Receiv-
       ing Marriage Counseling at a Family Agency." Journal of Sex
       Research 3, no. 3 (August 1967):232–38.

·1040 JAMES, JENNIFER, and JANE MEYERDING. "Early Sexual Experience
       as a Factor in Prostitution." Archives of Sexual Behavior 7,
       no. 1 (January 1978):31–42.

1041   JAMES, WILLIAM H. "The Distribution of Coitus within the Human
       Intermenstruum." Journal of Biosocial Science 3, no. 2 (April
       1971):159–71.

1042   _____. "The Reliability of the Reporting of Coital Frequency."
       Journal of Sex Research 7, no. 4 (November 1971):312–14.

1043   JOHNSON, VIRGINIA E., and WILLIAM H. MASTERS. "Plain Talk for
       Women Who Lie about Sex." Redbook 141, no. 5 (September 1973):
       76–77+.

1044   KEHOE, ALICE B. "The Function of Ceremonial Sexual Intercourse
       among the Northern Plains Indians." Plains Anthropologist:
       Journal of the Plains Conference 15, no. 48 (1970):99–103.

1045   KEPHART, WILLIAM M. "Sexual Activity of Divorced Women."
       Medical Aspects of Human Sexuality 7, no. 10 (October 1973):
       146–60.

1046   KERCKHOFF, ALAN C. "Social Class Differences in Sexual

Attitudes and Behavior." Medical Aspects of Human Sexuality 8, no. 11 (November 1974):10-31.

1047   KING, KARL; JACK O. BALSWICK, and IRA E. ROBINSON. "The Continu-ing Premarital Sexual Revolution among College Females." Journal of Marriage and the Family 39, no. 3 (August 1977):455-60.

1048   KIRKPATRICK, CLIFFORD, and THEODORE CAPLOW. "Courtship in a Group of Minnesota Students." American Journal of Sociology 51, no. 2 (September 1945):114-25.

1049   LANDIS, JUDSON T. "The Women Kinsey Studied." Social Problems 1, no. 4 (April 1954):139-42.

1050   LANDIS, JUDSON T., THOMAS POFFENBERGER, and SHIRLEY B. POFFENBERGER. "The Effects of First Pregnancy upon the Sexual Adjustment of 212 Couples." American Sociological Review 15, no. 6 (December 1950):767-72.

1051   "Letter from a Father to His Coed Daughter (and Five Reactions to the Psychosexual Advice It Offers)." Medical Aspects of Human Sexuality 6, no. 12 (December 1972):152-62.

1052   LEVER, JANET, and PEPPER SCHWARTZ. "Man and Woman at Yale." Sexual Behavior 1, no. 7 (October 1971):13-24.

1053   LEVINGER, GEORGE. "Husbands and Wives Estimates of Coital Frequency." Medical Aspects of Human Sexuality 4, no. 9 (September 1970):42-57.

1054   LICHTENSTEIN, PERRY M. "The Fairy and the Lady Lover." Medical Review of Reviews 27, no. 8 (August 1921):369-74.

1055   LONG, J.W. "Report of a Case of Sexual Perversion Simulating Hydrophobia." Richmond Journal of Practice 10, no. 3 (March 1896):76-79.

1056   MAHONEY, E.R. "Gender and Social Class Differences in Changes in Attitudes toward Premarital Coitus." Sociology and Social Research 62, no. 2 (January 1978):279-86.

1057   MILLER, WARREN B. "Sexual and Contraceptive Behavior in Young Unmarried Women." In Psychosomatic Obstetrics and Gynecology, edited by David D. Youngs and Anke A. Ehrhardt, 211-38. New York: Appleton-Century-Crofts, 1980.

1058   MORRIS, NAOMI M. "The Frequency of Sexual Intercourse During Pregnancy." Archives of Sexual Behavior 4, no. 5 (September 1975):501-7.

1059   MORRIS, NAOMI M., and J. RICHARD UDRY. "Periodicity in Sexual

Behavior in Women." Medical Aspects of Human Sexuality 5, no. 4 (April 1971):140-51.

1060 O'NEILL, GEORGE C., and NENA O'NEILL. "Patterns in Group Sexual Activity." Journal of Sex Research 6, no. 2 (May 1970):101-12.

1061 RAINWATER, LEE. "Some Aspects of Lower Class Sexual Behavior." Journal of Social Issues 22, no. 2 (April 1966):96-108.

1062 REICH, LOUIS H., and THOMAS WEHR. "Female Genital Self-Mutilation." Obstetrics and Gynecology 41, no. 2 (February 1973):239-42.

1063 ROBINSON, IRA E.; KARL KING, and JACK O. BALSWICK. "The Premarital Sexual Revolution among College Females." Family Coordinator 21, no. 2 (April 1972):189-94.

1064 RUPPEL, HOWARD J. "Sex and Social Class." Sexual Behavior 3, no. 2 (February 1973):14-18.

1065 SCHIMEL, JOHN L. "The Fallacy of Equality in Sexual Relations." Medical Aspects of Human Sexuality 3, no. 8 (August 1969):15-24.

1066 _____. "57 Reasons a Wife May Decline Sex." Sexual Behavior 1, no. 1 (April 1971):67-70.

1067 _____. "Sexual Behavior as Communication." Medical Aspects of Human Sexuality 4, no. 12 (December 1970):8-17.

1068 SCHROEDER, THEODORE. "Incest in Mormonism." American Journal of Urology and Sexology 11, no. 10 (October 1915):409-16.

1069 SHOPE, DAVID F. "The Orgastic Responsiveness of Selected College Females." Journal of Sex Research 4, no. 3 (August 1968):206-19.

1070 SOLBERG, DON; JULIUS BUTLER, and NATHANIEL N. WAGNER. "Sexual Behavior in Pregnancy." New England Journal of Medicine 288, no. 21 (24 May 1973):1098-1103.

1071 THOMAS, DAVID. "More about Chastity Devices." International Criminal Police Review 189 (June-July 1965):180-81.

1072 TOLLISON, C. DAVID; JOSEPH G. NESBITT, and J.D. FREY. "Comparison of Attitudes toward Sexual Intimacy in Prostitutes and College Coeds." Journal of Social Psychology 101 (April 1977):319-20.

1073 TOLOR, ALEXANDER, and PAUL V. DiGRAZIA. "Sexual Attitudes and Behavior Problems During and Following Pregnancy." Archives of Sexual Behavior 5, no. 6 (November 1976):539-51.

1074   UDRY, J. RICHARD, and NAOMI M. MORRIS. "Distribution of Coitus
        in the Menstrual Cycle." Nature 220, no. 5167 (9 November 1968):
        593-96.

1075   "Viewpoints: Do Marriage Manuals Do More Harm Than Good?"
        Medical Aspects of Human Sexuality 4, no. 10 (October 1970):
        50-63.

1076   WAHL, CHARLES WILLIAM. "The Psychodynamics of Consummated
        Maternal Incest: A Report of Two Cases." Archives of General
        Psychiatry 3, no. 2 (August 1960):188-93.

1077   "What Do You Think Is Erotic? 10 Women Explain What Turns Them
        On . . ." MS. 7, no. 5 (November 1978):56-57; 80.

1078   ZACHARIAS, LEONA; WILLIAM M. RAND, and RICHARD J. WURTMAN. "A
        Prospective Study of Sexual Development and Growth in American
        Girls: The Statistics of Menarche." Obstetrical and Gyneco-
        logical Survey 31, no. 4 (April 1976):325-37.

Children and Adolescents: Behavior and Prescription

Throughout much of the nineteenth century, sex information directed to younger female audiences was limited either to diatribes against the evils of masturbation or to discussion of the physiological process of menstruation. By the early twentieth century, not only was a broader approach to the subject of childhood and adolescent sexuality being taken, but sex education materials aimed at parents urged that even small children be given an introduction to the concept of reproduction (albeit through the use of flower and bird analogies).

E.G. Lancaster's "The Psychology and Pedagogy of Adolescence" (entry 1104), published in 1897, while not focusing specifically on sexual behavior did survey teenage attitudes on questions of love and friendship. By 1920, when Phyllis Blanchard published The Adolescent Girl (entry 1081), research into adolescent sexual attitudes and behavior was becoming commonplace. Given impetus by the work of G. Stanley Hall and Sigmund Freud, such studies were supplemented by the rise of a new variety of prescriptive literature aimed at the teenage audience, which dealt directly with such questions as petting, same-sex crushes, and venereal disease.

Research on sexuality in infancy and childhood has been less evident. One pioneering work was Albert Moll's The Sexual Life of the Child (entry 1108), first published in England in 1912. Other studies have examined such topics as the sexual abuse of children and children's ideas about sexuality. Much of the work has come from the context of psychoanalytic theory and practice rather than from the observation or examination of actual behavior and conscious attitudes.

Concern about pregnancy among unmarried teenagers has influenced the direction of much of the survey work being done with this age group, such as that of John Kantner and Melvin Zelnik (entries 1102, 1128, 1129). Prescriptive literature from the nineteenth century to the present has assumed various attitudes toward this problem ranging from the hands-off extremism of many social purity advocates to the recommendations of contemporary writers who accept the reality of adolescent sexual activity, urging that young people be provided with the information and means to apply contraceptive techniques.

The double standard has been clearly in evidence in much of the writing about and for this age group. Sexual activity was, and still is, used to define girl delinquents, but not boys of the same age. Moreover, gender-role stereotypes abound in much of the advice literature directed to the female adolescent group. Only within the past decade have writers such as Sol Gordon (entry 1096) begun to indicate that motherhood may not be the ultimate goal of every girl.

1079   ADKINS, GRACE REESE. The Sex Life of Girls and Young Women. Cincinnati: Standard Publishing Co., 1919. 191 pp.
        This sex education manual for young women begins with a discussion of the reproductive system of the flower, proceeds to the female reproductive system, and describes sexual intercourse in the blandest of terms: "When a husband and wife desire to have children, the penis of the male is inserted in the vagina of the female, and a quantity of semen is ejected." When she does describe sexual pleasure, it is obvious that she doesn't expect much of it to be felt by women: "Even in later married life, the thrill is generally more pronounced in the male than in the female; although, in the security of the home, conscious of the approval of the laws of God and man, the wife learns to find a very sweet and tender satisfaction in this union with the husband to whom she has given her heart's love." Young unmarried women are advised not to let men touch them and to encourage them to exercise self-control. In an interesting feminist touch, Adkins also admonishes girls that flirting and sentimentalism can have a disastrous effect on their education. Dancing is condemned as leading to immorality, and there are chapters devoted to prostitution, venereal disease, marriage, and motherhood.

1080   BAUER, WILLIAM WALDO, and FLORENCE MARVYNE BAUER. Way to Womanhood. Garden City, N.Y.: Doubleday, 1965. 112 pp.
        This sex education book for teenage girls takes moral positions on a number of issues, such as abortion (characterized as murder) and "irregular" sexual activities, such as masturbation, which the Bauers feel are "wrong" because they violate "the fundamental experience of the race through many centuries." Motherhood is called the "supreme function of womankind," although the Bauers concede that it is possible to combine marriage and career. Other topics on which the authors offer their opinions include reproductive biology, menstruation, pregnancy, dating, selection of a marriage partner, and use of tobacco and alcohol.

1081   BLANCHARD, PHYLLIS. The Adolescent Girl: A Study from the Psychoanalytic Viewpoint. New York: Moffat, Yard, 1920. 242 pp.
        G. Stanley Hall wrote the preface to this published version of Blanchard's 1919 Clark University doctoral dissertation. Although Blanchard was only twenty-five at the time, she had already engaged in serious study of the theories of Freud, Adler, and Jung,

246

as well as myriad other philosophers and analysts, and to a certain
degree, this book is a summary of their ideas on adolescent girls,
especially in the area of sexuality. There is a certain naive
charm about many of Blanchard's statements: "An elaborate set of
the sexual symbolisms which most frequently occur in . . . erotic
dreams has been worked out by the psychoanalysts, and is probably
more or less universally applicable, although it is far from being
the all-inclusive content of the dream psyche which was at first
claimed for it." Blanchard's research technique was often casual
--she interviewed her friends and others sent to her by friends--
but her cases are descriptive of a variety of conscious and unconscious sexual feelings. The Adolescent Girl was reprinted
several times during the 1920s. In 1930 Blanchard and Carlyn
Manasses prepared a sequel, New Girls for Old (entry 1082), which
is much more sociologically oriented than this work.

1082   BLANCHARD, PHYLLIS, and CARLYN MANASSES. New Girls for Old.
        New York: Macaulay, 1930. 281 pp.
        In some ways a continuation of Blanchard's The Adolescent
Girl (entry 1081), New Girls for Old examines the changes affecting
young women since World War I. To a large degree, it is the discussion of the replies to a questionnaire returned by 252 college
and working women, ages fifteen to twenty-six; the questionnaire
text and other statistics are included in an appendix. Several
chapters of the book relate to sexuality and include such topics
as petting, premarital sex, and sex education. Blanchard and
Manasses are decided liberals, especially compared to writers such
as Max J. Exner (entry 1094). Regarding petting, for example, they
state that it is good preparation for marriage and not injurious
"unless indulged in to such an extent that it interferes with the
necessary regimen in respect to food, rest and sleep." Similar
attitudes prevail on such subjects as masturbation and lesbianism.

1083   BREWER, JOAN SCHERER. "A Guide to Sex Education Books: Dick
        Active, Jane Passive." Interracial Books for Children Bulletin
        6, nos. 3 and 4 (1975):1+.
        Joan Scherer Brewer of the staff of the Institute for Sex
Research at Indiana University surveyed sex education titles recommended for young children by public and school librarians in
Bloomington, Indiana, as well as books available in the library
of the institute. She found that sexist stereotypes abounded and
that "life styles other than those of traditional middle-class,
white, heterosexual America are disparaged either explicitly or by
omission." She also found that the books were antihumanist and
described socially determined differences between the sexes as if
they were biological in origin.

1084   BURGESS, ANN WOLBERT, et al. Sexual Assault of Children and
        Adolescents. Lexington, Mass.: Lexington Books, 1978. 245 pp.
        A sensitive, thoughtful, and sometimes disturbing book,
Sexual Assault deals with a serious hidden social problem. While

the victims of child and adolescent sexual assault may be male or female, the perpetrators of the act are invariably male. Therefore, the material here is of relevance for female sexuality in showing male attitudes toward girls, especially as sex objects, and in documenting the psychosexual impact of assaults on the young female victim. Topics discussed include rape, incest, counseling, and legal processes.

1085   BUTMAN, JEAN, and JEAN KAMM. The Social, Psychological and
       Behavioral World of the Teen-age Girl. Ann Arbor: University
       of Michigan Center for Research on Utilization of Scientific
       Knowledge, 1965. 158 pp. ISR.
            The primary goal of Butman and Kamm's study was to understand
       illicit pregnancy and its causation among teenage girls by investi-
       gating a variety of social and cultural factors in pregnant and
       nonpregnant populations. Their subjects, who were studied in the
       early 1960s, were found in two school districts in the Midwest.
       Methodology included use of questionnaires and interviews. Among
       the areas relating directly to sexual behavior that were studied
       were standards of cross-sex relations, involvement in relationships,
       and sources of sex information. A black/white racial differentia-
       tion is maintained throughout the study, in addition to the preg-
       nant/nonpregnant one. Extensive statistics and tables complement
       the narrative.

1086   CLARKE, EDWIN LEAVITT. Petting: Wise or Otherwise? New York:
       Association Press, 1938. 31 pp.
            Similar to Max Exner's petting pamphlet (entry 1094), this
       is somewhat livelier in tone, employing a dialogue among two young
       people and a husband-wife pair of physicians. The arguments, how-
       ever, that petting can easily go too far and that nonsexual quali-
       ties are more important bases for sustained relationships remain
       the same. There is additional material here on abortion, single
       motherhood, and venereal disease. A tacit expectation exists in
       much of the material--that male sexual desire is stronger than
       women's and therefore in much greater need of control than that
       of females.

1087   CORNER, GEORGE WASHINGTON. Attaining Womanhood: A Doctor Talks
       to Girls about Sex. 2d ed., rev. and enlarged. New York:
       Harper, 1952. 112 pp.
            One of the key figures in the development of the scientific
       study of sex in the United States, Corner prepared this teenage
       sex education manual as a companion to a similar work for boys.
       Originally published in 1939, it covers such topics as reproductive
       biology, standards of sexual behavior, and venereal disease. De-
       spite his background, Corner held traditional views of woman's
       sociosexual role. Women were sexually "receptive" rather than
       "aggressive," and only "under the sway of love" was sexual desire
       developed. Biology, as usual, was still destiny: "Because of the
       special tasks Nature has imposed upon women, and the social customs

that have grown up about human life to protect the reproduction of the race, women are biologically destined and socially trained to do practically all their life's work in intimate association with others."

1088   CUTRIGHT, PHILLIPS. "The Teenage Sexual Revolution and the Myth of an Abstinent Past." Family Planning Perspectives 4, no. 1 (January 1972):24-31.
    Comparing data gathered between 1940 and 1968, Cutright concludes that rising illegitimacy rates among teenage girls are due not to increased sexual activity but to improved health conditions leading to increased fecundity (ability to conceive) and increased ability to avoid spontaneous abortion. He also offers some observations about nineteenth-century age at menarche and its relation to attitudes of that time regarding teenage female sexual behavior.

1089   DENNETT, MARY WARE. The Sex Education of Children: A Book for Parents. New York: Vanguard Press, 1931. 195 pp.
    According to Christopher Lasch, Margaret Mead's Growing Up in New Guinea had a substantial influence on Dennett's ideas in this book. A well-known suffrage, birth control, and sex education advocate, Dennett believed that concepts of sex learned in early childhood had a profound and perhaps irreconcilable impact on later sexual attitudes and behavior. Particularly harmful were ideas of sexuality that characterized it as fearful, shameful, and dangerous. The key to change lay in parents educating their children. Dennett embraced modern views of masturbation as "the best available choice" in some circumstances and cautioned parents against relying on the advice of family physicians, who might be ill-informed on sexual matters. Appendices include a discussion of sex physiology, a reprint of an article on sex language by Walter Overton, and sketches of some sexually maladjusted individuals. There are also a "mother's letter" on masturbation and a short annotated bibliography.

1090   DRAKE, EMMA FRANCES ANGELL. The Daughter's Danger: Prize Paper to Girls Sixteen and Upwards. Philadelphia: Vir, 1905. 51 pp. LC.
    In a semihysterical tone, Drake warns of the dangers of love and in straying from the path of purity. As she notes, "when a woman loses her purity she has lost it all." Girls are warned to avoid dancing, the theater, and provocative dress. They may take cold baths before bedtime, but should refrain from sweets and mustard.

1091   EDDY, GEORGE SHERWOOD. Sex and Youth. Garden City, N.Y.: Doubleday, Doran, 1928. 338 pp.
    Sex and Youth was written for young adults and also appeared in a special pamphlet edition for students, which deleted much material on marriage appearing in the larger volume. Eddy, like many sex writers of his generation, was disturbed by the adverse impact that ignorance and forced repression had on people's sexual

happiness. In particular, he recognized that delaying marriage and sexual relationships far beyond the time when sexual maturity was reached created tension and behavior dilemmas for youth. Petting and masturbation are discussed, and while Eddy appeals to his readers' sense of individual responsibility there is no doubt that he is on the side of self-control. Eddy also devoted chapters to selection of marriage partners, marital problems, and contraception, concluding with a section of questions and answers selected from open forums conducted with students throughout the country.

1092 ELLIOTT, GRACE LOUCKS. Understanding the Adolescent Girl. New York: Henry Holt, 1930. 134 pp.
       Designed to provide guidance to parents, teachers, and youth leaders and based on the experience of the Y.W.C.A. and similar organizations, Understanding the Adolescent Girl contains material on sexuality incorporating the findings of Phyllis Blanchard and Katharine Bement Davis and similar writers of the 1920s. Elliott discusses periodicity in monthly behavior linked to hormone levels and the need for sex education, stressing the importance of responsible commitment and the ultimate goal of marriage. There is a detailed discussion of same-sex crushes, which "may 'fix' the sex response . . . to women instead of to men, so that they do not fall in love and marry." Masturbation is described as a symptom of immaturity, a practice that may make marital relations difficult, and something for which "creative activities and relationships" (presumably nonsexual) should be substituted.

1093 ELLIOTT, GRACE LOUCKS, and HARRY BONE. The Sex Life of Youth. New York: Association Press, 1929. 142 pp.
       Based on the work of the Commission on Relations between College Men and Women of the Council of Christian Associations, The Sex Life of Youth reports on the findings of this study group which met during the year 1927–28. Interpreting its findings "in the light of fundamental Christian principles," the group criticized both scientific (i.e., pathological) treatises and motion pictures for skewing campus sexual attitudes. Prescriptive rather than empirical, the book includes chapters on such topics as masturbation, petting (defined to include all physical contact between sexes, including holding hands and a good-night kiss!), and marriage.

1094 EXNER, MAX J. The Question of Petting. New York: Association Press, 1932. 22 pp.
       Prepared and distributed by the American Social Hygiene Association and the National Council of the Young Men's Christian Association, this pamphlet originally appeared as an article in the March 1926 issue of Association Men. Taking a moralistic view, Exner defines petting as "promiscuous play-at-love" and "a low order of love." He feels that it overstimulates mere physical urges, "blinding one to the more essential personal qualities and the more subtle harmonies which are required for a life-long companionship and enduring happiness."

1095   FRISBIE, CHARLOTTE JOHNSON. Kinaalda: A Study of the Navaho
        Girl's Puberty Ceremony. Middletown, Conn.: Wesleyan University
        Press, 1967. 437 pp.
            This anthropological study is the result of fieldwork con-
        ducted among the Navaho in 1963. It also incorporates previous
        studies, observations, and field notes. Kinaalda is the name of
        the ceremony conducted when a Navaho girl reaches puberty, a multi-
        day event which is part of the cultural tradition of the tribe.
        While Frisbie focuses on the conduct of the ceremony itself (she
        even simulates the "score" of the music used), she includes col-
        lateral information regarding the Navahos' attitude toward menstru-
        ation and woman's sexual function.

1096   GORDON, SOL. The Sexual Adolescent: Communicating with
        Teenagers about Sex. North Scituate, Mass.:   Duxbury Press,
        1973. 206 pp.
            Originally prepared as a report to the Commission on Popula-
        tion Growth and the American Future under the title Family Planning
        Education for Adolescents, The Sexual Adolescent was written for
        both professional and lay audiences, but especially for parents.
        Gordon is concerned with both consequences and communication, the
        consequences of unwanted pregnancy, abortion, and venereal disease,
        and communication as a means of preventing them. Gordon dispels
        the myth that sex education leads to increased sexual activity;
        parents are urged to play the primary role in sex education.
            While contraception, abortion, and venereal disease are
        Gordon's chief concerns, he also discusses the roles of religion
        and ethics in fostering responsible sexual behavior. His views on
        women and sexuality in general promote individual choice within a
        context of responsibility. Few authors are so intent on dispelling
        stereotypes, as shown by statements such as this: "Motherhood is
        not inevitable and desirable for every girl. Some people can lead
        more fulfilling lives without children than with them. The tradi-
        tional concept that every girl must have a baby should not be sup-
        ported by parents and educators." Gordon supplements the text with
        extensive references, a resource list, and a glossary of anatomical
        and equivalent slang terms. An appendix prints the principal recom-
        mendations of the Commission on Population Growth and the American
        Future.

1097   GOTTLIEB, BERNHARDT STANLEY. What a Girl Should Know about Sex.
        Indianapolis: Bobbs-Merrill, 1961. 190 pp.
            Gottlieb gets off to a good start with direct, frank discus-
        sions of the reproductive and sexual organs, menstruation, sexual
        activity, and pregnancy. Informal in tone and incorporating much
        conversational dialogue, Gottlieb attempts to answer the questions
        most frequently asked by girls during the course of his medical
        practice. His generally progressive attitudes regarding sexual
        behavior ("Masturbation is a way of learning about the sexual feel-
        ings which you will experience in marriage") take a different turn
        in his chapters on women's gender role. "The Eternal Feminine,"

for example, describes typical women as subjective, intuitive, self-effacing, and passive. Motherhood is an integral part of marriage and not just from the perspective of rearing children, for every husband "expects his wife to take on many of the tasks that his mother performed. . . . In her mind she accepts the role of mother-liness to her husband." Gottlieb also differentiated between cli-toral and vaginal orgasm.

1098   GREGORY, SAMUEL. Facts and Important Information for Young Women, on the Subject of Masturbation; With Its Causes, Prevention, and Cure. Boston: George Gregory, 1845. 66 pp.
       Gregory, at this time a popular lecturer on health subjects, was to found the Boston Female Medical School (later New England Female Medical College) in 1848. Facts and Important Information was a highly popular work that sold more than ten thousand copies in its first year of publication, perhaps because it was one of the few works on masturbation specifically aimed at a female audi-ence. Gregory's intent was clearly moralistic, and his arguments were derived largely from works such as Woodward's Hints for the Young, Mary Gove Nichols's Lectures, and Tissot's Onanism. Gregory presents the standard antimasturbation arguments. His emphasis on cultivation of girls' intellect through the study of science as a preventive measure is rather original and serves as an interesting clue in determining the reasons for his interest in the medical education of women.

1099   GROUP FOR THE ADVANCEMENT OF PSYCHIATRY. Sex and the College Student: A Developmental Perspective on Sexual Issues on the Campus; Some Guidelines for Administrative Policy and Under-standing of Sexual Issues Formulated by the Committee on the College Student. Report No. 60. New York: Group for the Advancement of Psychiatry, 1965. 129 pp.
       Recognizing that changing patterns of sexual mores and be-havior were having a major impact on college campuses, the members of the Committee on the College Student of the Group for the Advance-ment of Psychiatry prepared this report. Their sources included interviews with deans and counselors, printed rules and regulations from the institutions, professional literature, and case histories and recollections from the experience of committee members. The report is divided into four parts which discuss (1) psychoanalytic theories on the development and integration of sexuality into the personality, (2) sexual activity on campuses, (3) college attitudes and regulations, and (4) guidelines for dealing with sexual issues on the campus.
       A traditional Freudian perspective is assumed; the theoreti-cal section displays no consciousness that male and female develop-ment may be drastically different or related to differing cultural norms. Value judgments and subjective conclusions abound: "Whether recognized or not, female homosexuality, like male homosexuality, has important components of exploitive, sadistic, masochistic, and other patterns of destructive or self-destructive behavior." Or,

"the need of men to confirm their sexual capacity has long been recognized. Sexual proficiency and the achievement of satisfaction by women has also been recognized as important." The suggestions of the committee, however, are quite liberal and sensible, calling primarily for improved sex education and counseling as well as minimization of moralistic reactions by school administrators to student behavior. Readers should be alert for signs of sexist bias, as in the discussion of faculty-student relationships where it is assumed that the student is always female.

1100   HALL, WINFIELD SCOTT, and JEANNETTE WINTER HALL. Girlhood and Its Problems: The Sex Life of Woman. Philadelphia: John C. Winston, 1919. 233 pp.

Girlhood and Its Problems contains material in some cases identical with that found in the Halls' Sexual Knowledge. Focusing on reproductive and general health, the authors advocate a traditional role for women: "Every normal young woman wishes to be a home-builder,--a wife and mother." Rest, refraining from exercise, and absence from school are advocated for young women during menstruation. Sexual behavior is dealt with indirectly--a hands-off policy toward men is advocated, and continence during pregnancy and for three months after birth is recommended. The Halls also discuss eugenics, which they perceive as a necessary solution to the urban social conditions they saw as threatening the home. Their belief even extended to an advocacy of state control over reproduction.

1101   JENSEN, GORDON D. Youth and Sex; Pleasure and Responsibility. Chicago: Nelson-Hall, 1973. 156 pp.

A pediatrician and psychiatrist, Jensen prepared this book for a teenage audience. It covers such topics as anatomy, petting, contraception, and sexual variations. Jensen does not moralize, and his references to "boys and girls" make it clear that he is addressing (realistically, one might add) sexually active teenage readers. Sexual technique is discussed, and the illustrations, both photos and drawings, are realistic. Emphasis is placed on the normality of individual variations. Although the book is indexed, there are no suggestions for further reading. A second edition appeared in 1979.

1102   KANTNER, JOHN F., and MELVIN ZELNIK. "Sexual Experience of Young Unmarried Women in the United States." Family Planning Perspectives 4, no. 4 (October 1972):9-18.

This article provides a summary report on a study of 2,839 white and 1,401 black, never-married teenage girls. Information regarding their sexual experience was gathered through interviews conducted in 1971 by the Institute for Survey Research of Temple University. The article includes numerous tables and graphs illustrating variable correlations, usually in simple percentage terms. Kantner and Zelnik place special emphasis on knowledge (or lack of knowledge) about conception and birth control.

1103   [KIDD, MARY.] <u>Growing Up; A Book for Girls by a Catholic Woman</u>
        <u>Doctor</u>. New York: Benziger Brothers, 1939. 47 pp.
            Although <u>Growing Up</u> went through nine printings by 1946, only
        two copies--at Gonzaga University and at the Institute for Sex
        Research--are readily traceable through standard bibliographic
        sources. Written specifically for Catholic teenage girls, it
        focuses on the reproductive and mothering aspects of the marriage
        relationship; references to the clitoris and birth control are ab-
        sent, although the author concedes that sex should be pleasureable.
        Men's "passions" are seen as being stronger than women's, necessi-
        tating self-control on both sides. There is an interesting three-
        page discussion of the supposed danger of same-sex crushes: "All
        intelligent, understanding people have realized by now, that girls
        who <u>habitually</u> indulge in 'crushes' are late in growing up and in
        developing the natural tendency of women to be attracted by the
        male sex." Religious justifications for opinions are used whenever
        possible.

1104   LANCASTER, E.G. "The Psychology and Pedagogy of Adolescence."
        <u>Pedagogical Seminary</u> 5, no. 1 (July 1897):61-128.
            An early survey of adolescent attitudes and behavior, this
        study, while prepared by Lancaster, a fellow at Clark University,
        utilized a questionnaire designed by G. Stanley Hall. He received
        827 responses, apparently from throughout the United States, but
        it is not clear how the sample was selected. Although no direct
        questions on sexual behavior were asked, there were some on love
        and friendship, which reveal a high rate of same-sex attraction:
        3 males and 46 females out of 91 respondents to this section.
        Lancaster also calls for education in sex hygiene, but limits
        girls' education in this area to information on menstruation.

1105   LATIMER, CAROLINE WORMELEY. <u>Girl and Woman: A Book for Mothers</u>
        <u>and Daughters</u>. New York and London: D. Appleton, 1910. 331 pp.
            <u>Girl and Woman</u>, which included an introduction by Howard A.
        Kelly, was reprinted several times between 1910 and 1926. A gen-
        eral guide to health during puberty, it includes a chapter on "sexu-
        al knowledge" as well as material on menstruation, reproduction, and
        "moral disturbances." Latimer was a firm proponent of sex educa-
        tion, and her comments on that subject might well be heeded today:
        "Innocence does not depend upon ignorance of sexual things, nor
        even upon ignorance of evil; it is a quality inherent in all healthy
        young minds, and if it is sullied or lost through a knowledge of
        sexual matters it is because these facts are not presented as they
        should be,--with simple directness as part of nature's scheme of
        life."

1106   MARTINSON, FLOYD M. <u>Infant and Child Sexuality: A Sociological</u>
        <u>Perspective</u>. St. Peter, Minn.: Book Mark, 1973. 146 pp. ISR.
            Martinson, a sociologist who taught for many years at Gustavus
        Adolphus College in Minnesota, privately published this work after
        it was rejected by twenty-nine publishers who were apparently

afraid to handle a taboo subject. It is actually a very useful summary of existing information and incorporates a wide range of data in addition to previously published material: over one thousand sex histories of college students gathered by Martinson, interviews with two hundred single mothers, case material from six Upper Midwest communities, and some interview notes done by Alfred C. Kinsey with two-to-five-year-olds. The book is divided into three sections dealing with birth to three years, three to seven years, and eight to twelve years of age. There are both a bibliography and an index. Boys and girls are given roughly equal amounts of space, although there is a decided tendency to group all children together in the analysis rather than trying to establish sex- or gender-based differences.

1107   MILLER, BENJAMIN F.; EDWARD B. ROSENBERG, and BENJAMIN L. STACKOWSKI. Masculinity and Femininity. Boston: Houghton Mifflin, 1971. 120 pp.
　　　Prepared as a text for high school students, this book deals with far more than simply gender roles, although they are discussed, with emphasis on their changing nature over time. Generally Miller, Rosenberg, and Stackowski are up to date in their discussion of such topics as dating, reproduction, and contraception and emphasize the role of individual responsibility in decision making. Some of the book's strengths lie in its freedom from prescribed male/female role behavior, including the selection of drawings and photos depicting both blacks and whites. In some areas, however, the authors are not as well informed as they might be. Prostitution is seen as an exclusive female "profession," while a section on homosexuality places undue stress on the threat of seduction of the young. A 1976 edition neglects to correct some obsolete material, such as that describing abortion as illegal. Each chapter is accompanied by a reading list, but those items included are of uneven quality. It would be useful to know how many schools adopted this book as a standard text.

1108   MOLL, ALBERT. The Sexual Life of the Child. Translated by Eden Paul. London: George Allen, 1912. 339 pp.
　　　German sexologist Albert Moll's works frequently appeared in translation in both English and American editions. The Sexual Life of the Child, originally published in Leipzig in 1908, attempted to present a comprehensive view of children's sexuality. It is especially interesting as an early critique of some of the theories of Sigmund Freud and his followers. Moll felt that Freud had erred in endowing many childhood actions (such as thumb sucking) with sexual attributes and also believed that he had greatly overestimated their role in disease causation. Moll, however, did not deny the importance of childhood sexuality: "The experiences of childhood, which have not as yet any relationship with sexual life, are nevertheless of great significance in relation to the subsequent upbuilding of the sexual life, and above all in relation to the development of the psychosexual sentiments." While he acknowledged

that much less information was available about girls than boys,
Moll nevertheless attempted to give equivalent coverage to both
sexes.

Among the specific topics with which he dealt were the structure of the sexual organs, sexual differentiation, stages of psychosexual development, masturbation, pedophilia, and sex education.
Case histories, not all of them pathological in nature, are used as
illustrations. Moll's references indicate that he was as familiar
with the works of such English and American authorities as Sanford
Bell and Havelock Ellis as he was with his Continental colleagues.
While some moralizing occurs (conventional monogamous heterosexuality, for example, is the only "normal" form of sexual expression),
the book attempts to make use of empirical evidence whenever possible.

1109   PARKER, VALERIA HOPKINS. For Daughters and Mothers.
        Indianapolis: Bobbs-Merrill, 1940. 138 pp.
        This general guidance manual for teenage girls and their
mothers contains considerable material on such topics as reproduction and dating behavior. Parker is generally conservative. Not
only does she disapprove of petting, but she advises girls to avoid
heavy exercise, including swimming, during menstruation. Although
both the male and female reproductive systems are described, sexual
intercourse is referred to merely as "close physical union which
may end in parenthood," hardly an enlightening description. Self-
control is stressed.

1110   PATTON, EDWIN FRITZ. Introduction to Motherhood. South Pasadena,
        Calif.: Commercial Textbook Co., 1938. 137 pp.
        One of the most striking characteristics of sex education
literature is the extent to which it also serves to inculcate notions of "normal" gender roles in the minds of its readers. The
title Introduction to Motherhood leaves no doubt as to its author's
intentions (his companion volume for boys was entitled Introduction
to Manhood). Such statements as this one on page 15 clinch the
argument: "Good motherhood-providing the world with fine sons and
daughters--is the highest goal, the finest achievement, and at the
same time the most satisfying experience in a woman's life." Almost total emphasis is placed on reproduction, and half of the book
is devoted to child rearing. The dangers of venereal disease are
discussed, but the closest Patton ever comes to describing the
mechanics of heterosexual intercourse is the following: "The
natural consequences of love . . . are physical caresses, which,
with repetition, grow gradually more and more intimate until the
point of actual context of sexual organs is reached." The vulva
is defined as "the structures surrounding the outer opening of the
vagina," the latter euphemistically referred to as the birth canal.
The clitoris is never mentioned. The book was designed, according
to the introduction, as a text for junior and senior high school
students. Patton also recommended that mothers read it aloud once
a year to their six-to-nine-year-olds. One wonders.

1111   POMEROY, WARDELL B. <u>Girls and Sex</u>. New York: Delacorte Press,
        1969. 159 pp.
           A sequel to Pomeroy's <u>Boys and Sex</u>, <u>Girls and Sex</u> is based on
        his work at the Institute for Sex Research, as well as additional
        information gathered from groups of high school girls in New York
        and New Jersey. Pomeroy was assisted by professional writer John
        Tebbel.
           A sex education book designed to be read by teenage girls,
        <u>Girls and Sex</u> emphasizes behavior, discussing such subjects as
        dating, petting, orgasm, heterosexual intercourse, pregnancy, mas-
        turbation, and homosexuality. Stress is placed on the development
        of responsible, realistic attitudes as well as differences in sexu-
        al attitudes and behavior between boys and girls. Although Pomeroy
        freely comments on what he considers to be appropriate behavior, he
        does not engage in preaching moral pieties. He also recognizes
        that teenagers and their parents are likely to have divergent views
        on some subjects. His ability to see the validity of the girl's
        perspective makes this somewhat different from other works of the
        same type.

1112   REISS, IRA L. <u>The Social Context of Premarital Sexual Permis-
        siveness</u>. New York: Holt, Rinehart and Winston, 1967. 256 pp.
           High school and college students as well as a national adult
        sample were surveyed in this study of attitudes toward premarital
        sexual behavior. Five main variable areas were tested: (1) general
        background; (2) family characteristics; (3) dating experiences and
        love conceptions; (4) perceived permissiveness of parents, peers,
        and close friends; and (5) sexual behavior and guilt reactions.
        A total of 2,734 responses were evaluated. Among Reiss's conclu-
        sions: "The high permissiveness of youngsters today is an unin-
        tended consequence of parental approval of the participant-run
        courtship system." And, "Unless the male-female roles in the family
        become identical it is likely that male and female sexuality will
        continue to differ." In addition to the text, Reiss includes sev-
        eral appendices, the full text of the three survey questionnaires,
        and a 250-item bibliography.

1113   RICE, THURMAN BROOKS. <u>How Life Goes On and On: A Story for
        Girls of High School Age</u>. Chicago: American Medical Association,
        1933. 39 pp.
           This is an extremely sexist sex education tract, written by
        Thurman B. Rice, an Indiana University Medical School professor,
        who distinguished himself later in the decade by his fervent oppo-
        sition to the work of Alfred C. Kinsey. Rice believed in one role
        for women--"The Best Career of All--Motherhood"--and attempts to
        support this view with the following story: "On one occasion my
        wife, who has five children, was lamenting the fact that she was
        'getting nowhere' and was envious of a woman of her age who had
        attained some fame as a bacteriologist. The bacteriologist was
        growing and working with bacteria in culture tubes; my wife was
        growing and working with human lives in a home. Who had the more
        important work?" Who, indeed?

1114   RUBIN, ISADORE, and LESTER A. KIRKENDALL, eds. <u>Sex in the</u>
        <u>Adolescent Years: New Directions in Guiding and Teaching Youth</u>.
        New York: Association Press, 1968. 223 pp.
            Prepared for parents and counselors, this collection of
        essays, with only a few exceptions, consists of material originally
        appearing in the Parent-Guidance section of <u>Sexology</u> magazine.
        Much of the material is by Kirkendall or Rubin, and only one woman
        author is represented. Several of the essays relate specifically
        to topics involving adolescent females: menstruation, premarital
        sex, and pregnancy. Others deal equally with both sexes.

1115   SCHAUFFLER, GOODRICH CAPEN. <u>Guiding Your Daughter to Confident</u>
        <u>Womanhood</u>. Englewood Cliffs, N.J.: Prentice-Hall, 1964. 208
        pp.
            Schauffler was a gynecologist of thirty years' experience
        who wrote this book for mothers and teenage daughters. It deals
        with such topics as reproductive biology (female organs only),
        menstruation, boy-girl relations, pregnancy, and venereal disease.
        Schauffler's neglect of the male side of sexuality may stem from
        his overall conservatism. He does not believe in "permissiveness
        for teenagers and even feels that masturbation is "not quite normal."
        Much of his conservatism appears to be due to his experience with
        unwanted teenage pregnancies, the result of sexual permissiveness.

1116   SHEPHERD, MRS. E.R. <u>For Girls: A Special Physiology; Being a</u>
        <u>Supplement to the Study of General Physiology</u>. New York: Fowler
        & Wells, 1882. 214 pp. LC.
            A pioneer sex education book, <u>For Girls</u> was written for the
        ten to twenty-one age group. An unwavering advocate of a corset-
        free female form, Shepherd believed that the body must be developed
        to the same degree as the mind for perfect health. The uterus she
        called "the controlling structure of woman," and indeed, it is that
        organ whose health she stresses more than any other. Physical and
        mental exertions, modes of dress, and so on, are evaluated in terms
        of their supposed effect on uterine health. There are many items
        of interest here, including her description of menstrual napkins
        and comments on masturbation: "So great a change takes place in
        the eye, the face, the skin, the muscles, the temper, the mind, and
        the actions, from loss of blood and by nervous irritation, that no
        person need hope to conceal this habit from others." One can only
        wonder at the effect of Shepherd's comments on her young readers.

1117   SHULTZ, GLADYS DENNY. <u>Letters to Jane</u>. Rev. ed. Philadelphia:
        J.B. Lippincott, 1960. 222 pp.
            Originally published in the late 1940s, <u>Letters to Jane</u>, a
        collection of "correspondence" between a mother and daughter and
        some of the daughter's college friends on various aspects of sexu-
        al behavior, was updated by its author to reflect changes in sexu-
        al mores that occurred in the United States during the 1950s. De-
        spite this revision, Shultz remained a traditionalist regarding
        woman's role. Marriage and children are still the pathway to

"fulfillment as women. . . . if you miss these, you will have missed the biggest thing of all." Girls are admonished to control the extent of sexual expression and moral standards in relationships, and the existence of the double standard is excused by such comments as "it is much more difficult for a man to live up to his ideals than for a girl, even when he has them." Shultz also notes that men are subjected to more temptations than women. Despite this, she still advises marriage as a prerequisite for sexual relations and also offers advice on how to meet unattached men.

1118   SMITH, NELLIE MAY. <u>The Mother's Reply: A Pamphlet for Mothers</u>.
        New York: American Social Hygiene Association, 1914. 20 pp.
        Intended as a guide for mothers of children between the ages of four and thirteen, this pamphlet uses a large number of bird analogies to describe reproduction and sexual behavior. Although the information in the first chapter is intended for use with both boys and girls, later chapters describing the growth of babies in the womb and the process of menstruation are for girls only. Smith advocates surrounding all of this information with a web of secrecy: "We do not talk about the coming of the baby or of the monthly period as we do about other things. These things are private and only to be talked about with Mother. . . . I am sure, now that Mother has told you all these things, you will not talk about them to any one else." The purity perspective is also emphasized: "No girl who thinks of her body as sacred will allow a boy to handle her, or kiss her, even in fun or in a game."

1119   SORENSON, ROBERT C. <u>Adolescent Sexuality in Contemporary</u>
        <u>America: Personal Values and Sexual Behavior, Ages Thirteen to</u>
        <u>Nineteen</u>. New York: World, 1973. 549 pp.
        This study of how and why adolescents behave as they do sexually is based on information from 200 interviews and 411 questionnaires obtained from a nationwide sample. One really wonders about the validity of such a small number of responses for what purports to be a comprehensive study. Laying aside such reservations, however, the study, which used separate questionnaires for boys and girls, was quite exhaustive and revealing in its findings. For example, only 25 percent of the respondents had been given birth control information by their parents, while an even smaller number, 16 percent, asked their parents for advice about sexual matters often. The questionnaire texts and 530 tables summarizing questionnaire responses are included. Sorenson concludes with three recommendations: stop denigrating beginning sexual activities (i.e., petting); avoid emphasizing male and female stereotyped roles in sex relations; and emphasize sex techniques in sex education classes.

1120   SPERRY, LYMAN BEECHER. <u>Confidential Talks with Young Women</u>.
        Chicago: Revell, 1893. 137 pp.
        Lyman Beecher Sperry was a popular health writer and lecturer who was one of the primary explorers of the present Glacier National

Park region of the Montana Rockies. In this work, which has a
counterpart volume for young men, Sperry presents many of the ideas
that have come to be associated with the stereotype of Victorian
sexuality. It is especially interesting that nowhere does he discuss the external genitalia or their role in producing sexual pleasure, even though he is highly critical of masturbation, defining
it as exciting or rubbing of the sex organs. One wonders if his
readers thought he referred to rubbing the vagina, uterus, or
ovaries, since these are the only organs he mentions by name.
Sperry was not opposed to women's education, but he firmly believed
that "the bearing and rearing of children is the God ordained work
of woman." Even though he never discussed sexual intercourse, except a vague reference to "proper contact with the male" in his
section on marsupials, he nevertheless felt compelled to warn his
readers about its potential dangers: "Personal contact--like
sitting close to each other or holding a hand--is more than a matter
of questionable propriety; . . . such affectionate personal contact
arouses the sexual organs and is apt to produce conditions of physical excitement and mental weakness which may finally lead to dis-
honor and disgrace." No wonder some young women believed they
could become pregnant from a kiss!

1121   STEINHARDT, IRVING DAVID. Ten Sex Talks to Girls (14 Years and
       Older). Philadelphia and London: J.B. Lippincott, 1914. 193
       pp.
          Originally given as a series of lectures at the Hebrew
       Educational Society of Brooklyn, the essays in this volume were
       also printed in the New York Medical Journal. Subsequently revised
       (though only minimally) and reissued in 1939, Ten Sex Talks was a
       companion to a similar volume for boys. Steinhardt discusses
       anatomy, physiology, menstruation, general hygiene, and so on.
       Some of his views are decidedly old-fashioned, such as that mastur-
       bation will lead to the insane asylum or an early grave. He also
       cautions girls against lying in one another's arms and warns that
       swimming pools are carriers of gonorrhea.

1122   SUEHSDORF, ADIE, ed. Facts of Life for Children. Indianapolis:
       Bobbs-Merrill, 1954. 96 pp.
          Prepared by the Child Study Association of America, this sex
       education primer for adults has been frequently revised and re-
       printed under the title What to Tell Your Children about Sex. A
       question-and-answer format is used, and there is an index of ques-
       tions. Sex-role stereotyping is present. For example, in response
       to the little girl's question, "Will I have a baby, too?" parents
       are advised, "Simply tell them, 'When you grow up you'll get mar-
       ried and have babies.'" Women are depicted as passive in sexual
       intercourse, and the missionary position is described as the stan-
       dard, with simultaneous orgasm the desired goal. A section on
       "Problems" includes a discussion of homosexuality, prostitution,
       venereal disease, and abortion.

1123   VENER, ARTHUR M., and CYRUS STEWART. "Adolescent Sexual Behavior
        in Middle America Revisited: 1970-1973." Journal of Marriage
        and the Family 36, no. 4 (1974):728-34.
            This is a follow-up survey of the same school system used by
        the authors for a 1969 study (entry 1124). Although Vener and
        Stewart found significant increases in coitus for fourteen- and
        fifteen-year-olds of both sexes, they are cautious in assuming
        that this indicates any long-run increase in adolescent sexual ac-
        tivity. They also suggest that general permissiveness regarding
        all forms of social behavior leads to increased sexual activity.

1124   VENER, ARTHUR M.; CYRUS S. STEWART, and DAVID L. HAGER. "The
        Sexual Behavior of Adolescents in Middle America: Generational
        and American-British Comparisons." Journal of Marriage and the
        Family 34, no. 4 (1972):696-705.
            In this study of sexual behavior among 4,220 diverse high
        school students in three Michigan towns in 1969, the authors com-
        pare their data to that of earlier studies both in the United States
        and Great Britain. They conclude that since World War II there
        has been no evidence to indicate a significant increase in sexual
        intercourse among teenagers. Vener, Stewart, and Hager note, how-
        ever, that lack of precisely equivalent data, especially on girls,
        biases their conclusions, just as earlier studies may have been
        skewed by internal biases.

1125   VINCENT, CLARK E. Unmarried Mothers. New York: Free Press,
        1961. 308 pp.
            A variety of factors relating to unmarried mothers are ana-
        lyzed in this study of 1,000 California women and a control group
        of 200 single, never pregnant women. Although the bulk of the
        book deals with such subjects as socioeconomic status, psychology,
        and adoption, the first section explores attitudes toward "illicit
        sexual behavior" held by society and the subjects of the study.
        Vincent found that the women's attitudes reflected a wide range
        of opinion, but all of them were faced with the dilemma of recon-
        ciling society's contradictory attitudes toward nonmarital sex and
        pregnancy out of wedlock. There is an extensive bibliography.
        Vincent also includes questionnaire texts and a series of proba-
        bility tables.

1126   WILLIAMS, MARY McGEE, and IRENE KANE. On Becoming a Woman.
        New York: Dell, 1959. 159 pp.
            This general guide to behavior during the teenage years was
        written specifically for the teenage female market. The authors
        cultivate the feminine mystique at an early age with chapters such
        as "How to Get--and Keep--Boys Interested" and "It's Not Too Soon
        to Dream of Marriage." A chapter on crushes is surprisingly open-
        minded: "The violent crush which almost every teenage girl ex-
        periences toward some older woman is usually not worth worrying
        about." The sex information offered is vague. Heterosexual inter-
        course is alluded to but never really described, while masturbation

is bypassed altogether. Nevertheless, girls are warned against
petting and premarital intercourse. One wonders if the authors
assumed their readers knew a great deal before they ever opened
this book.

1127   WOOD-ALLEN, MARY [and SYLVANUS STALL]. What a Young Woman
        Ought to Know. Philadelphia: Vir, 1898. 264 pp.
        One of the popular Self and Sex Series, What a Young Woman
Ought to Know is a general health and hygiene manual dealing with
far more than sexuality. Wood-Allen, however, does include some
information on the subject, discussing menstruation and menstrual
hygiene, the importance of chastity and proper behavior, and her
ideas on the sacredness and holiness of sex. She was moralistic
and physiologically fuddled in her appraisal of novel reading:
"Romance reading by young girls will, by . . . excitement of the
bodily organs, tend to create their premature development, and the
child becomes physically a woman months, or even years before she
should."
        Masturbation was equally dangerous, and Wood-Allen invoked
the old warnings against its causing insanity and a tendency toward
repetition of the habit in children of the victim. "The only
natural method of arousing a recognition of sexual feeling is as
God has appointed in holy marriage." Wood-Allen also warned against
sentimental friendships between adolescent girls: "They are a weak-
ening of moral fiber, a waste of mawkish sentimentality, they may
be even worse. Such friendship may degenerate even into a species
of self-abuse that is most deplorable."
        Never discussing the physiological details of heterosexual
intercourse, Wood-Allen nevertheless railed against the dangers of
venereal disease. Her extreme social purity position and advocacy
of eugenics mark her as a typical advocate of Progressive-era theories on appropriate sexual attitudes and behavior. Later editions
of the book do not carry Stall's name as co-author.

1128   ZELNIK, MELVIN, and JOHN F. KANTNER. "Sexuality, Contraception
        and Pregnancy among Young Unwed Females in the United States."
        In U.S. Commission on Population Growth and the American Future,
        Research Reports, Volume 1, Demographic and Social Aspects of
        Population Growth, edited by Charles F. Westoff and Robert Parke,
        Jr., 355-74. Washington, D.C.: Government Printing Office,
        1972.
        Kantner and Zelnik's studies of teenage sexuality and related
topics are of some interest because of their conscious efforts to
include respondents from all racial groups in their research population. Their decision here, however, to use a simple black/white
age-ordered dichotomy in presenting their findings not only ignores
the possibility of significant differences among Caucasians, native
Americans, Asian-Americans, and others grouped under the "White"
category but also bypasses other determinants of sexuality and
sexual behavior, such as economic status, level of education, and
religious affiliation. Although Kantner and Zelnik acknowledge

this exclusion, it still does nothing to remedy what common sense tells us is a simplistic, distorted, and even racist method of research and presentation.

1129   ZELNIK, MELVIN; JOHN F. KANTNER, and KATHLEEN FORD. Sex and Pregnancy in Adolescence. Beverly Hills, Calif.: Sage Publications, 1981. 272 pp.
      Sex and Pregnancy in Adolescence summarizes the findings of 1971 and 1976 surveys in this area conducted by the authors, and adds other material relating to a 1979 survey. Although much of the material was previously published in journal articles, the authors here attempt to provide more background analysis of causes of patterns of premarital sex, contraceptive use, and pregnancy-related behavior among the fifteen- to nineteen-year-old women who were surveyed. The black/white racial dichotomy (which lumps other nonwhite groups with whites) used by the authors in their earlier studies is maintained throughout. The lack of an index or list of statistical tables (of which there are many) makes this a some-what difficult book from which to obtain specific information. There is a bibliography.

1130   ABBOTT, F.W. "The Education of Youth upon Matters Sexual." Massachusetts Medical Journal 15, no. 5 (May 1895):197-205; no. 6 (June 1895):251-58; no. 7 (July 1895):293-99; no. 8 (August 1895):340-44.

1131   ABBOTT, MRS. T. GRAFTON. "Sex Problems of the Adolescent Girl-- As Seen from the Parental Point of View." Journal of Social Hygiene 19, no. 5 (May 1933):251-62.

1132   ABERNATHY, THOMAS J., Jr., et al. "A Comparison of the Sexual Attitudes and Behavior of Rural, Suburban and Urban Adolescents." Adolescence 14, no. 54 (Summer 1979):289-95.

1133   ABERNETHY, VIRGINIA. "Sexual Knowledge, Attitudes & Practices of Young Female Psychiatric Patients." Archives of General Psychiatry 30, no. 2 (February 1974):180-82.

1134   ADAMS, PAUL L. "Late Sexual Maturation in Girls." Medical Aspects of Human Sexuality 6, no. 3 (March 1972):50-75.

1135   APERT, E. "The Question of Sex in Infantile Medicine." American Journal of Urology and Sexology 12, no. 8 (August 1916):365-74.

1136   BAKWIN, HARRY. "Erotic Feelings in Infants and Young Children." Medical Aspects of Human Sexuality 8, no. 10 (October 1974): 200-215.

1137   BARNES, EARL. "Feelings and Ideas of Sex in Children." Medico-Legal Journal 11, no. 1 (1893):25-31.

1138   BARNETT, MARJORIE C. "Vaginal Awareness in the Infancy and
        Childhood of Girls." Journal of the American Psychoanalytic
        Association 14, no. 1 (January 1966):129–41.

1139   BEEKMAN, FENWICK. "Precocious Maturity in Girls, with Report
        of a Case." Archives of Pediatrics 32 (January 1915):4–19.

1140   BENDER, LAURETTA, and ABRAM BLAU. "The Reactions of Children
        to Sexual Relations with Adults." American Journal of
        Orthopsychiatry 7, no. 4 (October 1937):500–518.

1141   BENDER, LAURETTA, and ALVIN E. GRUGETT. "A Follow–Up Report on
        Children Who Had Atypical Sexual Experience." American Journal
        of Orthopsychiatry 22, no. 4 (October 1952):825–37.

1142   BLUMGART, LEONARD. "The Sexual Life of the Child." In
        Proceedings of the International Conference of Women Physicians,
        vol. 3, The Health of the Child, 90–105. New York: Woman's
        Press, 1919.

1143   BRENMAN, MARGARET. "Urban Lower–Class Negro Girls." Psychiatry:
        Journal of the Biology and Pathology of Interpersonal Relations
        6, no. 3 (August 1943):307–24.

1144   BROWN, FRED. "Sexual Problems of the Adolescent Girl."
        Pediatric Clinics of North America 19, no. 3 (August 1972):
        759–64.

1145   BROWN, SELMA. "Clinical Illustrations of the Sexual Misuse of
        Girls." Child Welfare 58, no. 7 (July–August 1979):435–42.

1146   BRUNSWICK, ANN. "Adolescent Health, Sex and Fertility."
        American Journal of Public Health 61, no. 4 (April 1971):711–29.

1147   BURGESS, ANN WOLBERT, and LYNDA LYTLE HOLMSTROM. "Sexual Trauma
        of Children and Adolescents." Nursing Clinics of North America
        10, no. 3 (September 1975):551–63.

1148   CHENEY, C.O. "Sex Conflict in Adolescents." Archives of
        Pediatrics 37 (October 1920):628–31.

1149   CHILDERS, A.T. "Some Notes on Sex Mores among Negro Children."
        American Journal of Orthopsychiatry 6, no. 3 (July 1936):442–48.

1150   CLEAVES, MARGARET. "Education in Sexual Hygiene for Young
        Working Women." Charities and the Commons 15, no. 21 (24
        February 1906):721–24.

1151   _____. "Education in Sexual Physiology and Hygiene." Woman's
        Medical Journal 18, no. 11 (November 1908):221–26.

1152   DAVENPORT, FRANCES ISABEL. Adolescent Interests: A Study of
        the Sexual Interests and Knowledge of Young Women. Archives of
        Psychology, no. 66. New York: n.p., 1923. 62 pp.

1153   DAVIS, OZORA S., and EMMA F. ANGELL DRAKE. The Parents' Guide
        or Where Do Babies Come From. Atlanta and Naperville, Ill.:
        J.L. Nichols, 1917. 307 pp.

1154   DEVEREAUX, GEORGE. "The Psychology of Feminine Genital Bleeding:
        An Analysis of Mohave Indian Puberty and Menstrual Rites."
        International Journal of Psycho-analysis 31, pt. 4 (1950):237-57.

1155   DWYER, JOHANNA T. "Psychosexual Aspects of Weight Control and
        Dieting Behavior in Adolescents." Medical Aspects of Human
        Sexuality 7, no. 3 (March 1973):82-114.

1156   FANTIS, EDWOOD L. "Homosexuality in Growing Girls." Sexology
        2, no. 6 (February 1935):348-50.

1157   FINKELSTEIN, RUTH. "Program for the Sexually Active Teenager."
        Pediatric Clinics of North America 19, no. 3 (August 1972):
        791-94.

1158   FRAIBERG, SELMA. "Some Characteristics of Genital Arousal and
        Discharge in Latency Girls." Psychoanalytic Study of the Child
        27 (February 1973):439-75.

1159   GADPAILLE, WARREN J. "Adolescent Sexuality--A Challenge to
        Psychiatrists." Journal of the American Academy of Psychoanalysis
        3, no. 2 (April 1975):163-77.

1160   _____. "Adolescent Sexuality and the Struggle over Authority."
        Journal of School Health 40, no. 9 (November 1970):479-83.

1161   _____. "A Consideration of Two Concepts of Normality as It
        Applies to Adolescent Sexuality." Journal of the American
        Academy of Child Psychiatry 15, no. 4 (Autumn 1976):679-92.

1162   GAGNON, JOHN H. "Female Child Victims of Sex Offenses."
        Social Problems 13, no. 2 (Fall 1965):176-92.

1163   GIBBENS, TREVOR CHARLES NOEL, and JOYCE PRINCE. Child Victims
        of Sex Offences. London: Institute for the Study and Treatment
        of Delinquency, 1963. 24 pp.

1164   GOLDSMITH, SADJA, et al. "Teenagers, Sex and Contraception."
        Family Planning Perspectives 4, no. 1 (January 1972):32-38.

1165   GOULD, MIRIAM C. "The Psychological Influence upon the
        Adolescent Girl of the Knowledge of Prostitution and Venereal
        Disease." Social Hygiene 2, no. 2 (April 1916):191-205.

1166   GREENACRE, PHYLLIS. "Special Problems of Early Female Sexual
       Development." Psychoanalytic Study of the Child 5 (1950):122-38.

1167   HAINES, C.T. "Unusual Sexual Neurosis in an Infant."
       Hahnemannian Monthly 59 (October 1924):598-601.

1168   HARRISON, DANNY; WALTER H. BENNETT, and GERALD GLOBETTI.
       "Attitudes of Rural Youth toward Pre-marital Sexual Permissive-
       ness." Journal of Marriage and the Family 31, no. 4 (November
       1969):783-87.

1169   HATTENDORF, KATHARINE WOOD. "A Study of the Questions of Young
       Children Concerning Sex: A Phase of an Experimental Approach
       to Parent Education." Journal of Social Psychology 3, no. 1
       (February 1932):37-65.

1170   HUFFMAN, JOHN W. "The Sexually Precocious Girl." Medical
       Aspects of Human Sexuality 1, no. 4 (December 1967):12-17.

1171   HURLOCK, E.B., and E.R. KLEIN. "Adolescent Crushes." Child
       Development 5, no. 1 (March 1934):63-80.

1172   JOHNSON, WARREN R. "Awakening Sexuality of Girls." Sexual
       Behavior 3, no. 3 (March 1973):3-6.

1173   KEISER, SYLVAN. "A Manifest Oedipus Complex in an Adolescent
       Girl." Psychoanalytic Study of the Child 8 (1953):99-107.

1174   KEISER, SYLVAN, and DORA SCHAFFER. "Environmental Factors in
       Homosexuality in Adolescent Girls." Psychoanalytic Review 36,
       no. 3 (July 1949):283-95.

1175   KREITLER, HANS, and SHULAMITH KREITLER. "Children's Concepts
       of Sexuality and Birth." Child Development 37, no. 2 (June
       1966):363-78.

1176   LIEBERMAN, FLORENCE. "Sex and the Adolescent Girl: Liberation
       or Exploitation." Clinical Social Work Journal 1, no. 4 (Winter
       1973):224-43.

1177   _____. "Sexual Liberation and the Adolescent Girl." Birth and
       the Family Journal 2, no. 2 (Spring 1975):51-56.

1178   McCRANIE, MARTHA. "Misuse of Sex by the Adolescent Girl."
       Journal of the Medical Association of Georgia 57, no. 4 (April
       1968):159-63.

1179   MADDOCK, JAMES W. "Sex in Adolescence: Its Meaning and Its
       Future." Adolescence 8, no. 31 (Fall 1973):325-42.

1180   MANNING, WILLIAM R. "A Method of Approach in Teaching Sex

Ethics to Girls and Young Women." Proceedings of the Second Pan American Scientific Congress 10, sec. 8, pt. 2 (1917):618-34.

1181 MERRILL, JAMES A. "Examining the Young Girl and the Virgin Woman." Medical Aspects of Human Sexuality 2, no. 7 (July 1968): 37-42.

1182 MILLER, E.H. "Puberty; Its Benefits and Dangers." Journal of the Missouri State Medical Association 2, no. 11 (May 1906): 731-37.

1183 MILLER, PATRICIA Y., and WILLIAM SIMON. "The Development of Sexuality in Adolescence." In Handbook of Adolescent Psychology, edited by Joseph Adelson, 383-407. New York: John Wiley & Sons, 1980.

1184 MIRANDE, ALFRED M. "Reference Group Theory and Adolescent Sexual Behavior." Journal of Marriage and the Family 30, no. 4 (November 1968):572-77.

1185 MONEY, K.E. "Physical Damage Caused by Sexual Deprivation in Young Females." International Journal of Women's Studies 1, no. 5 (September-October 1978):431-37.

1186 MORRIS, ROBERT T. "Circumcision in Girls." International Journal of Surgery 25, no. 5 (May 1912):135-36.

1187 OSOFSKY, HOWARD J. "Adolescent Sexual Behavior: Current Status and Anticipated Trends for the Future." Clinical Obstetrics and Gynecology 14, no. 2 (June 1971):393-408.

1188 PAUL, EDEN. "The Sexual Life of the Child." Medical Critic and Guide 24, no. 3 (March 1921):87-103.

1189 PRATT, E.H. "Circumcision of Girls." Journal of Orificial Surgery 6, no. 9 (March 1898):385-92.

1190 REITER, EDWARD O., and HOWARD E. KULIN. "Sexual Maturation in the Female: Normal Development and Precocious Puberty." Pediatric Clinics of North America 19, no. 3 (August 1972):581+.

1191 RENSHAW, DOMEENA C. "Sexuality in Children." Medical Aspects of Human Sexuality 5, no. 10 (October 1971):63-74.

1192 SADGER, J. "The Sexual Life of the Child." Journal of Sexology and Psychanalysis 1, no. 4 (July 1923):337-48; no. 5 (September 1923):486-99; no. 6 (November 1923):579-90.

1193 SCHILLER, PATRICIA. "Effects of Mass Media on the Sexual Behavior of Adolescent Females." In Technical Report of the Commission on Obscenity and Pornography, vol. I, 191-95. Washington, D.C.: Government Printing Office, 1971.

1194   SCHNEIDER, GEORGE T., and WILLIAM L. GEARY. "Vaginitis in
        Adolescent Girls." Clinical Obstetrics and Gynecology 14, no.
        4 (December 1971):1057-76.

1195   "Sexual Hygiene for Young Women." St. Louis Medical Review,
        n.s. 4, no. 2 (February 1910):41-44.

1196   SMITH, GERALDINE FRANCES. "Certain Aspects of the Sex Life of
        the Adolescent Girl." Journal of Applied Psychology 8, no. 3
        (1924):347-49.

1197   SPIEGEL, NANCY TOW. "An Infantile Fetish and Its Persistence
        into Young Womanhood: Maturational Stages of a Fetish."
        Psychoanalytic Study of the Child 22 (1967):402-25.

1198   STEINHORN, AUDREY I. "Lesbian Adolescents in Residential
        Treatment." Social Casework 60, no. 8 (October 1979):494-98.

1199   TAUSSIG, FREDERICK J. "The Contagion of Gonorrhea among Little
        Girls." Social Hygiene 1, no. 3 (June 1915):415-22.

1200   THORNBURG, HERSCHEL D. "Age and First Sources of Sex Information
        as Reported by 88 College Women." Journal of School Health 40,
        no. 3 (March 1970):156-58.

1201   TOWNE, ARTHUR W. "Young Girl Marriages in Criminal and Juvenile
        Courts." Journal of Social Hygiene 8, no. 3 (July 1922):287-
        305.

1202   TSAI, MAVIS; SHIRLEY FELDMAN-SUMMERS, and MARGARET EDGAR.
        "Childhood Molestation: Variables Related to Differential
        Impacts on Psychosexual Functioning in Adult Women." Journal
        of Abnormal Psychology 88, no. 4 (August 1979):407-17.

1203   WAGNER, NATHANIEL; BYRON FUGITA, and RONALD PION. "Sexual
        Behavior in High School: Data on a Small Sample." Journal of
        Sex Research 9, no. 2 (May 1973):150-55.

1204   WALTERS, PAUL A. "Promiscuity in Adolescence." American Journal
        of Orthopsychiatry 35, no. 4 (July 1965):670-75.

1205   WEISS, JOSEPH. "A Study of Girl Sex Victims." Psychiatric
        Quarterly 29, no. 1 (January 1955):1-27.

1206   WILE, IRA S. "The Sex Problems of Youth." Journal of Social
        Hygiene 16, no. 7 (October 1930):413-27.

Masturbation and Nymphomania

No two topics better demonstrate the vagaries of public and professional attitudes toward women's sexuality than do masturbation and nymphomania. Universally condemned by nineteenth-century writers who saw it as the cause of a wide variety of ailments ranging from acne to insanity, masturbation has achieved a new post-Masters and Johnson respectability as a sex therapy technique to aid in overcoming orgasmic dysfunction. Often joined in a symbiotic relationship to nymphomania --some writers argued that masturbation caused nymphomania, others that nymphomania caused masturbation--the practice has assumed a variety of names--onanism, autoeroticism (or Havelock Ellis's version, autoerotism), self-abuse--over the past couple of hundred years.

According to the Oxford English Dictionary, the term nymphomania came into general usage in the early nineteenth century and denoted "a feminine disease characterized by morbid and uncontrollable sexual desire." Diagnoses of nymphomania were often based on highly subjective preconceptions of what constituted "normal" levels of female sexual desire and activity, and heroic measures, such as clitoridectomy (also used in cases of masturbation), were not unknown as "cures." Along with its male counterpart satyriasis (a.k.a. Don Juanism), nymphomania continues to be discussed in both professional and popular literature.

Aside from what they tell us about ideas regarding the etiology of disease, writings on masturbation and nymphomania have implications for the study of how society and the medical profession view broader issues, such as women's autonomy, assertiveness, and independence from stereotyped gender roles. Although some historical analysis of these topics has already occurred, additional studies are needed, particularly those that would place attitudes toward masturbation and nymphomania in the wider context of male definition and control of female sexuality and identity.

MASTURBATION

1207   ALIBERT, JEAN LOUIS MARIE. Onanism. Paris: Medical Library,

1900. 95 pp. ISR.

Alibert (1766-1837) and Samuel Tissot were early critics of masturbation whose work had lasting impact. This translation includes material on both men and women, freely incorporating folklore as fact. Alibert beleived that there were three types of masturbation in women: vaginal, clitorian, and clitorian bestial, the latter employing the services of poodles and other small dogs especially trained for the purpose. Other instruments of stimulation, all graphically described, ranged from carrots to the ubiquitous sewing machine treadle. The usual dire results--wasting away, insanity, and so on--were predicted.

1208　　　　. Self Abuse among Women. New ed. Paris: [Popular Medical Library of Hygiene, 1920]. 88 pp. ISR.

During the 1920s, the so-called Popular Medical Library of Hygiene (a.k.a. Medical Library) issued English translations, loosely edited, of the works of Jean Louis Marie Alibert. Their obvious motive was profit, for the firm also offered a "collection of 5,000 original and varied views of nude women in all attitudes, prints on bromide and citrate paper." This particular volume is a reworking of the female sections of Onanism (entry 1207) with some additions. It is generally, however, the same mixture of folklore and medical misinformation.

1209　ELLIS, HAVELOCK. "Auto-erotism: A Study of the Spontaneous Manifestations of the Sexual Impulse." In Studies in the Psychology of Sex, vol. 1, pt. 1, 161-283. New York: Random House, 1936.

Ellis did not equate autoerotism with masturbation. Rather, he used the term to designate all forms of sexual excitement in which there was no "other," either person or object, as the external stimulus. That Ellis chose to include it along with modesty and periodicity as a prolegomena to the further study of sex psychology was indicative of his judgment that it was a universal characteristic of human sexual behavior. Unfortunately, Ellis's consistent inability to assess the probable validity of his evidence, a difficulty seen throughout his work, led him to make such assertions as "the banana seems to be widely used for masturbation by women." Ellis includes material on hysteria in this essay, even utilizing "the results of a psychological investigation carried on in America by Miss Gertrude Stein among the ordinary male and female students of Harvard University and Radcliffe College."

1210　GOODELL, WILLIAM. "Masturbation in the Female." Medical Bulletin 6, no. 10 (October 1884):225-27.

A professor of gynecology at the University of Pennsylvania medical school, Goodell believed that masturbation was physically dangerous and could result in so-called congestion of the ovaries, leading to uterine hemorrhage. In chronic cases, such as the one discussed in this article, it should be classified as a disease. Goodell treated the case in question with applications of potassium bromide and cantharidial collodion to the external genitalia. The patient, however, continued the practice. Extending his observations to women as a whole, Goodell warned that masturbation was practiced extensively in boarding and public schools, noting, however, that the majority of women were less inclined to engage in the practice than men. Women's greater ability for endurance during masturbation, however, meant that those who did practice it carried it to a much greater extent than did their male counterparts.

1211 KELLY, G. LOMBARD, et al. Female Masturbation. New ed. Inglewood, Calif.: Banner, 1966. 192 pp. LC.
    A collection of essays on female masturbation, this book includes selections by several well-known writers on sexuality, including Kelly, Albert Moll, and J. Richardson Parke. The publishers do not indicate from which of the authors' works these selections were taken, nor are unsuspecting readers told that in some cases the material dates at least to the first decade of the twentieth century, if not earlier. There is also some doubt about the authenticity of the selections; the Moll essay cites Kinsey (1953), even though Moll was deceased by the time that Kinsey's female volume was published!

1212 MARCUS, IRWIN M., and JOHN J. FRANCIS, eds. Masturbation from Infancy to Senescence. New York: International Universities Press, 1975. 502 pp.
    This anthology of essays written primarily by psychiatrists is intended "to view masturbation in terms of its broad psychodynamic significance throughout development." While males and females are given roughly equal coverage, several essays focus exclusively on women: "Genital Self-stimulation in Infant and Toddler Girls" by James A. Kleeman, "Significance of Masturbation in Female Sexual Development and Function" by Virginia L. Clower, and "Women's Use of Fantasy During Sexual Intercourse" by Marc H. Hollender. An aura of Freudianism pervades the book, and the editors provide a useful summary essay describing the evolution of developmental views of masturbation. There are also a number of detailed bibliographies, chiefly of relevant psychoanalytic literature.

1213 MEAGHER, JOHN FRANCIS WALLACE. A Study of Masturbation and Its Reputed Sequelae. New York: William Wood, 1924. 69 pp.
    By 1936, when the third edition of A Study of Masturbation was issued, Meagher had expanded his original work to 149 pages. Although this first edition purportedly incorporates the ideas of two hundred sources on the subject, a total lack of reference citation, other than by author's name, makes further tracing, in most cases, difficult. Needless to say, the methodology of many of these sources is suspect, as are some of Meagher's own conclusions, such as that most women masturbate without any erotic feeling being involved and do not achieve orgasm as a result of this activity.

In both men and women, Meagher sees masturbation as representing a failure of psychosexual development and, if it is habitual, a problem to be cured through education and sublimation. He did, however, feel that any problems it created were mental and moral, rather than physical, in their effect.

1214   Onania; Or, the Heinous Sin of Self-Pollution, and All Its Frightful Consequences, in Both Sexes, Considered. 10th ed. Boston: John Phillips, 1724. 175 pp.
        Onania originally appeared in England in the early 1700s and was reissued in many English and American editions. The one cited here is available as part of an Arno Press reprint series published in 1974. Most of the antimasturbation arguments of the nineteenth century originated here. The anonymous author, for example, argues that in women masturbation is a cause of leucorrhea, bad complexion, hysteria, and consumption, conditions that Calhoun in his 1858 Report also attributed to the "solitary vice." In addition to masturbation material, this edition also includes a discussion, in the form of a letter to a woman reader, of the role of sex in marriage; numerous "testimonial" letters from readers are found throughout the book. Onania is an excellent example of the artificial creation of an anxiety-producing problem (masturbation) by an "authority" in order to lead an audience toward some sort of behavior change, in this case, denial of sexual satisfaction through autonomous action.

1215   TISSOT, SAMUEL A. Treatise on the Diseases Produced by Onanism. New York: Collins & Hannay, 1832. 113 pp.
        Tissot's work on masturbation was first published in Latin in 1758 and subsequently appeared in many French- and English-language editions until at least 1870. This New York edition, translated by an anonymous physician, was reprinted in an Arno Press series in 1974 and includes an appendix apparently written by the translator. Throughout his treatise, Tissot cites the writings of various authorities, displaying some ambivalence about Onania, whose cases and medical/scientific arguments he accepts, but whose theological and moral suasion he rejects. In his material on women, Tissot reiterates the symptoms described in Onania --hysteria, digestive disorders, leucorrhea--and adds such variants as elongation of the clitoris, nymphomania, and rickets. He observes that masturbation may lead to an indifference to heterosexual intercourse and even links masturbation to lesbianism (souillure clitoridienne), noting the connection between passionate female/ female friendship and sexual behavior.

1216   WAKELY, ROBERT T. Woman and Her Secret Passions, Containing an Exact Description of the Female Organs of Generation, Their Uses and Abuses. Together with a Detailed Account of the Causes and the Cure of the Solitary Vice. New York: n.p., 1846. 108 pp.
        The semipornographic tone of many of the cases discussed in this work, as well as its title and twenty-five-cent sales price,

would seem to indicate a profit-oriented motivation for its publication, even though author Wakely was not using it to advertise cures or services. Regardless of its origin, Woman and Her Secret Passions strikes the twentieth-century reader as being "modern" on several counts. First, although it condemns masturbation, there is virtually no appeal to divine law, biblical injunction, or similar arguments; the problem is one of physiology, sex education, and self-control. Second, women's sexuality is seen as a positive force that requires physical expression, but not necessarily for reproduction alone. Third, ideas such as the clitoris being the source of women's sexual pleasure and frigidity being caused by male incompetence rather than female predisposition are articulated. Of some interest are the story of "M.B.," who is seduced by her boarding-school friend Fanny (a classic association of masturbation and lesbianism) and the example of "D.A.," who masturbated while fantasizing about having intercourse with a young man of her acquaintance. It is, of course, moot whether this is fact or fiction. But the same question might be asked about many of the cases presented in nineteenth-century writing on sex.

1217   ARAFAT, IBTIHAJ SAID, and WAYNE L. COTTON. "Masturbation Practices of Males and Females." Journal of Sex Research 10, no. 4 (November 1974):293-307.

1218   BEGUS, SARAH, and MARY JANE LUPTON. "Masturbation: Loving Yourself." Women: A Journal of Liberation 5, no. 3 (1978):4-7.

1219   BIGELOW, HORATIO R. "An Aggravated Instance of Masturbation in the Female." American Journal of Obstetrics and Diseases of Women and Children 15, no. 2 (April 1882):436-41.

1220   BLOCH, A.J. "Clitoridectomy as a Cure for Masturbation in a Child Two and One-Half Years Old." Transactions of the Louisiana State Medical Society (1894):333-34.

1221   _____. "Sexual Perversion in Female." New Orleans Medical and Surgical Journal, n.s. 22, no. 1 (July 1894):1-7.

1222   BRADY, ELLIOTT T. "Masturbation, with Illustrative Cases and Remarks." Virginia Medical Monthly 18, no. 4 (July 1891):256-60.

1223   BRILL, A.A. "Masturbation; Its Causes and Sequelae." American Journal of Urology and Sexology 12, no. 5 (May 1916):214-22.

1224   BURDEM, F.A. "Self-pollution in Children." Massachusetts Medical Journal 16, no. 8 (August 1896):337-47; no. 9 (September 1896):385-94.

1225   CASTELLANOS, J. "Summary Prepared from French Journals." Southern Journal of Medical Sciences 1 (November 1866):495-96.

1226   CHAPMAN, J. MILNE. "On Masturbation as an Etiological Factor
        in the Production of Gynic Diseases." American Journal of
        Obstetrics and Diseases of Women and Children 16, no. 5 (May
        1883):449-58; 578-98.

1227   CLIFFORD, RUTH. "Development of Masturbation in College Women."
        Archives of Sexual Behavior 7, no. 6 (November 1978):559-74.

1228   COLBY, C.D.W. "Mechanical Restraint of Masturbation in a Young
        Girl." Medical Record 52, no. 6 (7 August 1897):206.

1229   COOPER, E.S. "Removing the Clitoris in Cases of Masturbation
        Accompanied with Threatening Insanity." San Francisco Medical
        Press 3, no. 9 (January 1862):17-21.

1230   CUSHING, E.W. "Melancholia; Masturbation; Cured by Removal of
        Both Ovaries." Journal of the American Medical Association 8,
        no. 16 (16 April 1887):441.

1231   DOWN, J., and H. LANGDON. "Influence of Sewing Machine on
        Female Health." New Orleans Medical and Surgical Journal 20
        (November 1867):359-60.

1232   EASTMAN, J.S. "Cure of Masturbation in a Woman by Neurectomy."
        Medical News 63, no. 7 (12 August 1893):174.

1233   ELLISON, EVERETT M. "A Case of Long-Continued Masturbation in
        a Girl, Cured by Fright." New Orleans Medical and Surgical
        Journal 74, no. 3 (September 1921):160-65.

1234   EYER, ALVIN. "Clitoridectomy for the Cure of Certain Cases of
        Masturbation in Young Girls." International Medical Magazine
        3, no. 4 (May 1894):259-62.

1235   FEDERN, PAUL. "Masturbation." Journal of Sexology and
        Psychanalysis 2, no. 3 (May 1924):251-66.

1236   FISHER, LOUIS. "Onanie Infantum; Clitoridectomy; Recovery."
        Archives of Pediatrics 16, no. 5 (May 1899):356-58.

1237   FREEMAN, ROWLAND G. "Circumcision in the Masturbation of
        Female Infants." Transactions of the American Pediatric Society
        26 (1914):57-60.

1238   FRIEDJUNG, JOSEPH K. "Masturbation in Young Children." Journal
        of Sexology and Psychanalysis 2, no. 2 (March 1924):119-22.

1239   GADPAILLE, WARREN J. "Brief Guide to Office Counseling:
        Masturbation in Preadolescent Girls." Medical Aspects of Human
        Sexuality 8, no. 9 (September 1974):179-80.

1240   GEER, JAMES H., and JOAN D. QUARTARARO. "Vaginal Blood Volume
        Responses During Masturbation." Archives of Sexual Behavior 5,
        no. 5 (September 1976):403-14.

1241   GELEERD, ELISABETH R. "The Analysis of a Case of Compulsive
        Masturbation in a Child." Psychoanalytic Quarterly 12, no. 4
        (October 1943):520-40.

1242   GRANT, HENRY M. "Sex Problems in Children; with Particular
        Reference to Masturbation." Northwest Medicine 25, no. 8
        (August 1926):432-26.

1243   GREEN, FRANK K. "A Contribution to the Literature of Youthful
        Manustupration." Pediatrics 25, no. 1 (January 1913):9-20.

1244   GRIFFITH, J.P.C. "Two Cases of Thigh Friction in Infants."
        Archives of Pediatrics 16, no. 5 (May 1899):331-33.

1245   HAINES, J. "Case of Onanism in a Child Five Years Old."
        Western Medical-Chirurgical Journal 1 (1850):330-33.

1246   HARLEY, MARJORIE. "Masturbation Conflicts." In Adolescents:
        Psychoanalytic Approach to Problems and Therapy, edited by
        Sandor Lorand and Henry Schneer, 51-77. New York: Paul B.
        Hoeber, 1961.

1247   HIMEL, AUGUSTIN J. "Some Minor Studies in Psychology with
        Special Reference to Masturbation." New Orleans Medical and
        Surgical Journal 60, no. 6 (December 1907):439-52.

1248   HITSCHMANN, EDWARD. "A Contribution to the Subject of Mastur-
        bation." Medical Critic and Guide 25, no. 4 (April 1922):127-32.

1249   HOWARD, WILLIAM LEE. "Masturbation among Women." Medicine 12,
        no. 1 (January 1906):35-38.

1250   _____. "Masturbation in the Young Girl a Cause of Acquired
        Sexual Perversion." Pediatrics 15, no. 5 (May 1903) :
        274-76.

1251   HUTCHISON, ALICE M. "Masturbation in Young Women." Lancet 2
        (26 December 1925):1350.

1252   JACOBI, ABRAHAM. "Masturbation in Childhood, etc.; a Clinical
        Lecture." Archives of Pediatrics 7, no. 4 (April 1890):281-86.

1253   _____. "On Masturbation and Hysteria in Young Children."
        American Journal of Obstetrics and Diseases of Women and Children
        8, no. 4 (February 1876):595-606; 9, no. 2 (June 1876):218-38.

1254   KAUFMAN, BERNARD. "A New Method of Diagnosticating Masturbation in Girls." New York Medical Journal 98, no. 16 (18 October 1913):772.

1255 KIERNAN, JAMES G. "A Medico-Legal Phase of Auto-eroticism in Women." Alienist and Neurologist 31, no. 3 (August 1910):329-38.

1256 KRAUSS, WILLIAM C. "Masturbational Neurosis." Transactions of the Medical Society of New York (1901):287-91.

1257 LAMPL-De GROOT, JEANNE. "On Masturbation and Its Influence on General Development." Psychoanalytic Study of the Child 5 (1950):153-74.

1258 LANPHEAR, EMORY. "Excessive Masturbation in a Young Female." Alienist and Neurologist 16, no. 4 (October 1895):463-65.

1259 LEVINE, MILTON. "Pediatric Observations on Masturbation in Children." Psychoanalytic Study of the Child 6 (1951):117-24.

1260 LUKIANOWICZ, N. "Imaginary Sexual Partner: Visual Masturbatory Fantasies." Archives of General Psychiatry 3, no. 4 (October 1960):429-49.

1261 McCULLY, S.E. "Masturbation in the Female." American Journal of Obstetrics and Diseases of Women and Children 16, no. 8 (August 1883):844.

1262 MALAMUD, WILLIAM, and G. PALMER. "The Role Played by Masturbation in the Causation of Mental Disturbances." Journal of Nervous and Mental Disease 76, no. 3 (September 1932):220-33; no. 4 (October 1932):366-79.

1263 MAPES, CHARLES C. "Anent the Pathogenesis, Symptomatology and Treatment of Masturbation." Urologic and Cutaneous Review 22, no. 4 (April 1918):223-27.

1264 _____. "Anent the Prevalence and Effects of Manustupration; A Semi-Critical Review." Urologic and Cutaneous Review 22, no. 3 (March 1918):147-55.

1265 _____. "A Contribution to the Literature of Manustupration, with Especial Reference to the Infantile Type." American Medicine, n.s. 19, no. 9 (September 1924):533-38.

1266 "Masturbation." Boston Medical and Surgical Journal 27, no. 6 (14 September 1842):102-8.

1267 MILLER, C.B. "Masturbation." American Practitioner 15 (May 1877):281-86.

1268 OBERNDORF, C.P. "Some Phases of Autoeroticism." New York Medical Journal 110, no. 19 (8 November 1919):756-60.

1269   ONUF [ONUFROWICZ], B. "On the Role of Masturbation, Especially
        as Applied to Some Psychoses." Urologic and Cutaneous Review 21,
        no. 10 (October 1917):562-70.

1270   PAPIN, T.L. "Case of Masturbation; Clitoridectomy." Missouri
        Clinical Record 1 (1874-75):121.

1271   PERRY, E.M. "Masturbation: Its Significance, Cause and Treat-
        ment." Texas State Journal of Medicine 27, no. 7 (November
        1931):505-8.

1272   PRYOR, J.H. "A Case of Excessive Masturbation in the Female,
        with an Unusual Method of Performance." Buffalo Medical and
        Surgical Journal 22, no. 1 (August 1882):62-65.

1273   RACHFORD, B.K. "Pseudomasturbation in Infants." Archives of
        Pediatrics 24, no. 8 (August 1907):561-89.

1274   REICH, ANNIE. "The Discussion of 1912 on Masturbation and Our
        Present-day Views." Psychoanalytic Study of the Child 6 (1951):
        80-94.

1275   ROBERTSON, J.W. "Relation Existing between the Sexual Organs
        and Insanity with Especial Reference to Masturbation." Pacific
        Medical Journal 41, no. 9 (September 1898):513-19.

1276   ROCKWELL, ALICE JONES. "A Study of Probable Causal Factors of
        Masturbation in a Girl of 6 Years." Psychological Clinic 18,
        no. 8 (January 1930):236-41.

1277   ROHLEDER, HERMANN. "Sexual Education as a Measure against
        Masturbation." Urologic and Cutaneous Review 33, no. 2
        (February 1929):86-89.

1278   SACHS, HANNS. "Masturbation." Journal of Sexology and
        Psychanalysis 2, no. 4 (July 1924):387-92.

1279   SADGER, J. "Masturbation and Its Treatment." Journal of
        Sexology and Psychanalysis 1, no. 1 (January 1923):29-50.

1280   "Sexual Survey #9: Current Thinking on Masturbation." Medical
        Aspects of Human Sexuality 12, no. 4 (April 1978):72-73.

1281   SMITH, E.H. "Masturbation in the Female." Pacific Medical
        Journal 46, no. 2 (February 1903):76-83.

1282   STEKEL, WILHELM. "Disguised Onanism (Masked Masturbation)."
        American Journal of Urology and Sexology 14, no. 7 (July 1918):
        289-307.

1283   STERN, ADOLF [ADOLPH]. "Masturbation; Its Role in the Neuroses."
        American Journal of Psychiatry 9, no. 6 (May 1930):1081-92.

1284   STORER, HORATIO ROBINSON. "On Self-Abuse in Women; Its Causa-
        tion and Rational Treatment." Western Journal of Medicine 2
        (1867):449-57.

1285   STRASSER, AUGUST ADRIAN. "Masturbation in Childhood." Medical
        Record 67, no. 24 (17 June 1905):934-37.

1286   STURGIS, FREDERICK R. "The Comparative Prevalence of Masturba-
        tion in Males and Females." American Journal of Dermatology
        and Genito-Urinary Disease 11, no. 9 (September 1907):396-400.

1287   ____. "Male and Female Masturbation and Their Prevalence."
        American Journal of Dermatology and Genito-Urinary Disease 14,
        no. 3 (March 1910):122-26.

1288   TAIT, LAWSON. "Masturbation; a Clinical Lecture." Medical News
        53, no. 1 (7 July 1888):1-3.

1289   TALMEY, BERNARD SIMON. "Sexual Problems of Today with a Case
        of Hysterical Insanity Caused by Excessive Masturbation." New
        York Medical Journal 97, no. 21 (24 May 1913):1084-88.

1290   TAUSK, VICTOR. "Masturbation." Journal of Sexology and
        Psychanalysis 2, no. 2 (March 1924):122-44.

1291   TOWNSEND, CHARLES W. "Thigh Friction in Infants under One Year
        of Age." Archives of Pediatrics 13, no. 11 (November 1896):
        833-36.

1292   W. [pseud.] "Remarks on Masturbation." Boston Medical and
        Surgical Journal 12, no. 6 (18 March 1835):94; 109; 138.

1293   WEST, J.P. "Masturbation in Early Childhood." Cleveland Medical
        Gazette 10, no. 9 (July 1895):415-19; 437-42.

1294   WINTER, JOHN S. "Self-abuse in Infancy and Childhood."
        American Journal of Obstetrics and Diseases of Women and Children
        45, no. 6 (June 1902):828-34.

1295   WITTELS, FRITZ. "Sexual Abstinence and Masturbation." American
        Journal of Urology and Sexology 12, no. 4 (April 1916):145-52.

NYMPHOMANIA

1296   ELLIS, ALBERT, and EDWARD SAGARIN. Nymphomania: A Study of the
        Over-Sexed Woman. New York: Gilbert Press, 1964. 255 pp.
            Ellis and Sagarin distinguish between nymphomania and simple
        promiscuity. True nymphomania, they claim, has four characteris-
        tics: lack of control, continuous need, compulsivity, and self-
        contempt. The authors' approach is light and relies on case

literature, sometimes incorporating dated, questionable authorities (Krafft-Ebing, Lombroso, etc.) as definitive proof. There does, however, appear to be an underlying thread of serious intent (sources, for example, are documented). Certainly the concept of nymphomania as it appears in psychological literature and the popular imagination is one that, along with its companion frigidity, merits historical research and analysis.

1297   The Over-Sexed Woman. St. Louis: Dios Chemical Co., 1951. 23 pp. ISR.
    "Written by a Registered Physician for the Medical Profession," this pamphlet is a sales pitch for Neurosine, a bromide compound produced by the Dios Chemical Company. The preparation was to be used in cases of nymphomania to provide sedation so that "the physician can gradually eliminate the aggravating aphrodisiacal influences from her environment and remove their etiological effects." Not content, however, with just this recommendation, the learned author also recommended it for masturbation, seasickness, alcoholic excitement, and constipation. The interesting thing about this pamphlet, aside from its general quackery, is the evidence it shows of how pharmaceutical firms use a sexual sales pitch to their physician clients. Neurosine, whatever its faults or merits, was simply a sedative, with no relation to nymphomania, masturbation, or other sexual "ills."

1298   PODOLSKY, EDWARD, and CARLSON WADE. Nymphomania. New York: Epic, 1961. 64 pp. ISR.
    Part of the Epic "Sexual Behavior Series," Nymphomania defines its subject as insatiable, uncontrollable sexual desire. The authors review various views of the subject, concluding that its causes include latent female homosexual desires, inability to have an orgasm, and a "strong" father fixation. Podolsky and Wade recommend relief for the condition through achievement of a clitoral orgasm, use by the male partner of coitus reservatus, or through sublimation of desire. There are several photo illustrations from films which, one supposes, are meant to depict the "condition," but they don't appear to show anything of the sort, being, in most cases, simply pictures of couples embracing.

1299   CHUNN, WILLIAM PAWSON. "A Case of Nymphomania." Maryland Medical Journal 18 (10 December 1887):121.

1300   FLAXMAN, NATHAN. "Nymphomania--a Symptom--Part I." Medical Trial Technique Quarterly (Mundelein) 19 (Fall 1972):183-95.

1301   _____. "Nymphomania--a Symptom--Part II: Psychoses." Medical Trial Technique Quarterly (Mundelein) 19 (Winter 1973):305-16.

1302   FREDERICK, CARLETON C. "Nymphomania as a Cause of Excessive Venery." American Journal of Dermatology and Genito-Urinary Disease 11, no. 10 (October 1907):458-60.

1303   HOR AND SPRAGUE [no first names]. "Nymphomania." Boston Medical and Surgical Journal 25, no. 4 (1 September 1841):61.

1304   LAMSON, HERBERT D. "Human 'She-wolves.'" International Journal of Sexology 6, no. 3 (February 1953):168-71.

1305   LEVITT, EUGENE E. "Nymphomania." Sexual Behavior 3, no. 3 (March 1973):13-17.

1306   LYDSTON, GEORGE FRANK. "Sexual Perversion, Satyriasis and Nymphomania." Medical and Surgical Reporter 61, no. 11 (14 September 1889):281-85.

1307   McCARY, JAMES LESLIE. "Nymphomania: A Case History." Medical Aspects of Human Sexuality 6, no. 11 (November 1972):192-210.

1308   MILLS, CHARLES K. "A Case of Nymphomania, with Hystero-epilepsy and Peculiar Mental Perversions, the Results of Clitoridectomy and Oophorectomy; the Patient's History as Told by Herself." Philadelphia Medical Times 15, no. 15 (18 April 1885):534-40.

1309   MOORE, JAMES E. "Nymphomania Cured by Hysterectomy." American Journal of Obstetrics and Diseases of Women and Children 39, no. 4 (October 1896):554-55.

1310   PARVIN, THEOPHILUS. "Nymphomania and Masturbation." Medical Age 4, no. 3 (10 February 1886):49-51.

1311   PAYNE, R.L. "A Case of Nymphomania." Medical Journal of North Carolina 2 (April 1859):569-70.

1312   PHILLIPS, L.M. "Nymphomania--Reply to Questions." Cincinnati Medical Journal 10, no. 7 (July 1895):467-71.

1313   POLAK, JOHN OSBORN. "A Case of Nymphomania." Medical News 71, no. 10 (4 September 1897):301.

1314   SHAINESS, NATALIE. "Nymphomania and Don Juanism." Medical Trial Technique Annual 19 (1973):1-6.

1315   STEWART, WILLIAM S. "A Remarkable Case of Nymphomania, and Its Cure." Transactions of the American Association of Obstetricians and Gynecologists 2 (1889):260-61.

1316   SUTCLIFFE, J.A. "Excision of the Clitoris in a Child for Nymphomania." Indiana Medical Journal 8, no. 3 (September 1889): 64.

1317   WALTON, JOHN TOMPKINS. "Case of Nymphomania, Successfully Treated." American Journal of the Medical Sciences, n.s. 33 (1857):47-50.

Lesbians

Pejorative descriptions of lesbians did not appear in the literature about women's sexuality until the late nineteenth century, when
sexologists, such as Richard von Krafft-Ebing and Havelock Ellis, attempted to define as pathological the ways in which women love other
women. Prior to that time, despite occasional references to Sappho
and her followers, writers such as William Rounseville Alger (entry
1320) had stressed the spiritual qualities of women's friendships.
The new definitions, often based on male models of homosexual behavior,
created a stereotyped image of lesbians as man-hating, masculine mis-
fits, outcasts of society whose sexual preference rendered them sick,
if not actually dangerous.

Such images, typically based on folklore or, at best, on the
atypical cases seen in psychiatric treatment, persisted into the post-
World War II era. Homosexuality was included in the American Psychiatric
Association's nomenclature of mental diseases. The lack of objective
behavioral and psychological data on lesbians helped to perpetuate the
old ideas.

The 1970s, however, saw a revolution in writing and thinking about
lesbians. Their consciousness raised by the gay rights and women's
movements, lesbians began to see the positive political implications
of their chosen life-style and to counter biased stereotypes with descriptions of their world as it really was. Sidney Abbott and Barbara
Love's Sappho Was a Right-On Woman (entry 1318) and Del Martin and
Phyllis Lyon's Lesbian/Woman (entry 1342) were but two of the many
books to offer this new perspective. The APA decided that homosexuality was no longer a mental illness, and new psychological, sociological,
and historical studies provided for the first time a realistic appraisal
of the lesbian situation. Theorists grappled with the meaning of the
term itself, arguing that older definitions equating lesbianism with
female homosexuality in a model derived from male behavior failed to
recognize qualitative differences in women's attitudes and experience.

Although many contemporary writers, such as E.M. Ettore (entry
1330), have rejected even references to older, stereotyped sources and
ideas in their work, knowledge of these views and the methods their

originators and advocates used to deny the integrity of lesbians and their sexual/affectional preference can serve a valid intellectual function. History may not always repeat itself, but our chances of preventing its happening are much greater if we understand how and why the past was the way it was.

1318   ABBOTT,SIDNEY, and BARBARA LOVE. Sappho Was a Right-On Woman: A
        Liberated View of Lesbianism. New York: Stein and Day,1973.251 pp.
        Abbott and Love take a feminist political approach to their
discussion of lesbianism. Maintaining that lesbianism is a question of identity more than sexual behavior per se, they begin their
book with a description of the guilt, deception, self-hatred, and
alienation that characterized lesbians prior to the rise of the
contemporary feminist and gay liberation movements. In their view,
the heterosexist assumptions of society have made lesbianism a
"crime" of rejection of sex-role stereotypes as much as of sexuality. The second section of the book links the political ideology
of lesbianism (freedom from confining sex roles) to that of feminism. "The lives of Lesbians provide an example of Feminist theory
in action." Of particular historical interest is their documentation of the controversy during the late 1960s and early 1970s in
NOW and other feminist organizations over acknowledgement of and
support for lesbians and questions relating to sexual preference.

1319   ADAIR, NANCY, and CASEY ADAIR. Word Is Out: Stories of Some
        of Our Lives. New York: Dell; San Francisco: New Glide
        Publications, 1978. 337 pp.
        Twenty-six lesbians and gay men are interviewed in this book
adaptation of a successful film documentary. The filmmakers set
out to present as wide a range of individuals as possible in an
effort to dispel many of the stereotypes that have grown up around
lesbians and gay men. The addition of photographs from the film
gives a broader dimension to the authors' intent, and demonstrates
that there is no one physical appearance that marks a person as
being gay. The biographical material presented in the interviews
is useful historically, for there are very few firsthand accounts
of what it felt like to be gay in the pre-1970s straight world.

1320   ALGER, WILLIAM ROUNSEVILLE. The Friendships of Women. Boston:
        Roberts Brothers, 1868. 416 pp.
        The Friendships of Women might well be called a classic of
lesbian lore, for it has served as a source for many contemporary
analysts of lesbian history and culture. Alger's main purpose in
this highly romantic paean to female friendship was to demonstrate
the value of friendship in women's lives, especially as a substitute for often disappointing sexual passion or love. Most of the
book is a chronicling of noteworthy friendships of women throughout
history and literature. Alger devotes considerable space to discussing such woman-woman relationships as those of Marie Antoinette
and the Princess Lamballe and Eleanor Butler and Sarah Ponsonby,
the Ladies of Llangollen, but the book by no means includes only

same-sex relationships.

This is in many respects a remarkable book, not the least for its total avoidance of questions of sexual activity among female friends, a fact that was already being noted by some of the writers on sexuality of this time. While Alger claimed not to be espousing relationships based on gushy sentimentality, passages such as this, describing schoolgirl friendships, leave no doubt about his views on the emotional core of women's relationships: "Keener agonies, more delicious passages, are nowhere else known than in the bosoms of innocent school-girls, in the lacerations or fruitions of their first consciously given affections."

1321   BECKER, HAROLD K. "A Phenomenological Inquiry into the Etiology of Female Homosexuality." Journal of Human Relations 17, no. 4 (1969):570-80.

Becker attempts to mask his lack of knowledge by casting his arguments in a turgid style: "A summation of biological factors relative to homosexuality attacks the rudiments of a biological predisposition toward the behavior." Freud, Caprio, and folklore are sources on which the author relies.

1322   BELL, ALAN P., and MARTIN S. WEINBERG. Homosexualities: A Study of Diversity among Men and Women. New York: Simon and Schuster, 1978. 505 pp.

Sponsored by the Institute for Sex Research of Indiana University, Homosexualities reports on a survey of black and white, male and female homosexually oriented people in the San Francisco Bay area undertaken in 1969-70. The female sample included 675 white lesbians and 110 black lesbians. A heterosexual comparison group matched with the homosexual population in terms of race, age, sex, and so on, was also recruited.

Each chapter analyzes some aspect of the respondents' sexual and social behavior, with men and women being treated separately. Extensive statistical tables are presented, as is a discussion of the research methodology employed. This is an interesting study to compare with the survey of Karla Jay and Allen Young (entry 1335).

1323   BERGLER, EDMUND. Homosexuality: A Disease or a Way of Life? New York: Hill and Wang, 1956. 302 pp.

Bergler devotes only one chapter to lesbians in this book, accounting for this sparse treatment by noting that lesbianism "has the identical prognosis and treatment prerequisites" as male homosexuality. It has its origin in an unresolved masochistic conflict with the mother of earliest infancy and is characterized by tension and pathological jealousy. Overall, Bergler characterizes both male and female homosexuality as neurotic distortions of the personality and claims that psychiatric-psychoanalytic treatment can effect successful cures. Three lesbian cases from Bergler's practice are cited as evidence.

1324   BLUMSTEIN, PHILIP W., and PEPPER SCHWARTZ. "Lesbianism and
       Bisexuality." In Sexual Deviance and Sexual Deviants, edited
       by Erich Goode and Richard R. Troiden, 278-95. New York:
       William Morrow, 1974.
           Blumstein and Schwartz based their article on interviews with
       150 men and women in Seattle, New York, Chicago, San Francisco, and
       a few other locations during 1973-75. All interviewees had had more
       than incidental sexual experience with members of both sexes. Using
       the Kinsey heterosexual-homosexual rating scale, respondents de-
       scribed various modes of bisexual behavior as the behavior related
       to sexual identification and sociosexual community sanctions. One
       conclusion: individuals often fail to organize their sexual lives
       coherently or consistently, yet the public, as well as psychiatrists,
       psychoanalysts, and other professionals, are trained to think only
       in terms of hetero- and homosexual polarities.

1325   BROOKS, VIRGINIA R. Minority Stress and Lesbian Women.
       Lexington, Mass.: Lexington Books, 1981. 219 pp.
           An extremely sophisticated analysis of the minority status
       of lesbian women in the United States, Minority Stress and Lesbian
       Women concludes that "low socioeconomic status and self-perceived
       public visibility as a lesbian woman" are stress producers, although
       the 675 lesbian respondents experienced more stress from being wom-
       en than from being lesbian. Brooks found less stress among those
       women who had been exposed to feminist ideology and who viewed wom-
       en, especially lesbian women, as a reference group. "With the
       enormous range of diversity that exists among lesbian women in re-
       lation to beliefs and value systems, socioeconomic status, age,
       race, and other variables, it would appear that the psychological
       well-being of this minority would be best served by a focus on the
       common need for civil rights in the political arena and on the com-
       mon need for group affiliation in the social arena." Especially
       useful are Brooks's reviews of theoretical literature and previous
       empirical research, although her ideas sometimes have a tendency to
       get lost in the detailed arguments and references. This book is
       prolesbian and feminist in perspective.

1326   CAPRIO, FRANK S. Female Homosexuality: A Psychodynamic Study
       of Lesbianism. New York: Citadel Press, 1954. 334 pp.
           For many years Caprio's Female Homosexuality was the standard
       psychiatric monograph in the field. Caprio based it on the work of
       other authorities (Mantegazza, Ellis, Freud), his own cases gathered
       over an eighteen-year period, an unspecified "fact-finding investi-
       gation," and "my miscellaneous travels," including a 1952-53 round-
       the-world trip that apparently included a stop at a Havana brothel.
       Accounts of lesbianism in "confession" magazines are also cited as
       "fact."
           Caprio's characterization of lesbians as childish and imma-
       ture in their emotional life, doomed to unhappiness, unstable and
       neurotic, and victims of a deep-seated neurosis reflected the
       stereotyped ideas of the psychiatric profession in the early 1950s

(the foreword to Female Homosexuality was written by Karl M. Bowman, a past president of the American Psychiatric Association). There is a decidedly prurient quality to much of his material, as in this description of his visit to a lesbian bar in California: "Following the dance the two walked behind a partition in the direction of the ladies' room. Here they could be seen embracing, kissing and fondling each other's breasts." Caprio also believed that lesbians "can be cured if they are earnest in their desire to be cured."

1327   CARPENTER, EDWARD. The Intermediate Sex: A Study of Some
       Transitional Types of Men and Women. London: George Allen &
       Unwin, 1908. 175 pp.
       The Intermediate Sex reprints the chapter by the same name
from Love's Coming-of-Age (entry 138) and introduces additional
material, such as an appendix of quotations from sexologists
(Ulrichs, Moll, Ellis, etc.) about the question of homosexuality.
Carpenter's overwhelming emphasis is on relationships between men,
a not uncommon slant of much of the material written on homosexuality during the past century and certainly evinced in Carpenter's
appendix to this volume. In the portions of the work that do contain material on women, Carpenter attempts to distinguish, when
appropriate, between the character of women's as opposed to men's
relationships. Thus he calls attention to what he sees as a rise
in homoerotic relationships among women accompanying the women's
rights movement and the encouragement that strong friendships receive in girls' schools, contrasting this to the pejorative manner
in which such relationships among boys are treated. He also distinguishes between relationships with emotional love as their primary component and liaisons formed for mere sexual gratification.
On the whole, however, Carpenter is disappointing in his lack of
attention to women.

1328   CORY, DONALD WEBSTER [pseud.]. The Lesbian in America. New
       York: Citadel, 1964. 288 pp.
       A sequel to Cory's The Homosexual in America, this popular
account by a homosexual author deals with a wide range of subjects
relating to lesbians in the United States. Much of the material,
such as that on butch/femme role playing, bar life, and "cures,"
seems to be dated, although it reflected lesbian culture and concerns at the time the book was written. Although Cory was familiar
with much of the psychiatric and literary material available on the
subject, providing a short bibliography in the field, his interview
material and general conclusions are undocumented. The book's introduction by Albert Ellis is self-serving and antilesbian. Ellis
believed that many lesbians were "covertly or overtly psychotic,"
having been "born sick." He claimed to be able to cure homosexual
people of their "antiheterosexuality" without affecting their "prohomosexuality." One wonders why Cory included an introduction with
such a message, which certainly does little to help Cory or his
lesbian subjects. Perhaps he had no say in the matter.

1329   ELLIS, HAVELOCK. "Sexual Inversion." In Studies in the
       Psychology of Sex, vol. 2, pt. 2, 1-391. New York: Random
       House, 1936.
          Originally published in a German-language translation in
       Leipzig in 1896, "Sexual Inversion" was the first volume to appear
       of what would become the Studies in the Psychology of Sex. Ellis
       distinguished inversion from simple homosexuality. Inversion, he
       maintained, was "sexual instinct turned by inborn constitutional
       abnormality toward persons of the same sex," whereas homosexuality
       included "all sexual attractions between persons of the same sex."
       Thus, he distinguished between a given, inborn condition and a be-
       havior determined by social or emotional conditions.
          Reflecting the availability of information, Ellis devotes
       most of this work to a consideration of men and often ranges far
       afield from Europe and the United States. He reviews previous
       research in the area by Krafft-Ebing, Hirschfeld, and others. A
       chapter on "Sexual Inversion in Women," while not notable for the
       veracity of its conclusions ("For the most part feminine homosexu-
       ality runs everywhere a close parallel course to masculine homo-
       sexuality and is found under the same conditions"), presents some
       interesting case histories, as well as myriad references to little-
       known sources. Particularly striking is Ellis's equation of les-
       bianism with bisexuality and "masculine temperament." While im-
       precise and misleading when viewed from a present-day perspective,
       it is important to recognize how blurred the distinction was in
       the late nineteenth century between sexual preference and gender
       role. Moreover, in Ellis, we see clear pejorative connotations
       being given to the passionate friendships between women which, as
       Lillian Faderman has shown, were so accepted a part of the female
       world in the earlier years of that century.
          An appendix, "The School Friendships of Girls," gives a de-
       tailed description of "flames," "raves," "spoons," and similar
       phenomena.

1330   ETTORE, E.M. Lesbians, Women and Society. London and Boston:
       Routledge & Kegan Paul, 1980. 208 pp.
          In her acknowledgements, Ettore sets the tone for this book
       when she writes, "If lesbianism says anything in contemporary so-
       ciety, it says 'no' to the misuse of power." Thus Ettore sees her
       work as a political statement, even to the point of eliminating
       most psychoanalytic, psychiatric, and psychological sources from
       her bibliography, because they "perpetuated the idea that lesbian-
       ism was an abnormality, a psychological sickness, a disease, etc.
       Thus, I would not continue to perpetuate these misconceptions."
       Although Ettore and the individuals she studies are English, many
       of her sources come from the American lesbian and feminist move-
       ments. Very prowoman and prolesbian, Ettore writes with a feminist
       but not separatist perspective.

1331   FREEDMAN, MARK. Homosexuality and Psychological Functioning.
       Belmont, Calif.: Brooks/Cole, 1971. 124 pp.

Incorporating material from his doctoral dissertation, "Homosexuality among Women and Psychological Adjustment," Freedman criticizes those who attempt to apply concepts of "health" and "illness" to the analysis of homosexuality. Particularly useful is the chapter "Psychological Adjustment and Normality," which discusses the diverse definitions of what is "normal." Freedman opts for a definition of normality as both adjustment to the environment and adjustment to oneself in terms of individually perceived needs. Another chapter compares the results of standard personality inventories administered to eighty-one members of the Daughters of Bilitis and sixty-seven heterosexual females. Freedman found that there were no significant differences in psychological adjustment between the two groups of women. In fact, the lesbian group functioned significantly better in certain areas than the control group of straight women.

1332　GUNDLACH, RALPH H., and BERNARD F. RIESS. "Self and Sexual Identity in the Female: A Study of Female Homosexuals." In New Directions in Mental Health, edited by Bernard F. Riess, vol. 1, 205-31. New York: Grune & Stratton, 1968.
　　　Gundlach and Riess studied a population of 460 women. Of these, 234 were self-identified as heterosexual in orientation, and 226 were self-identified lesbians, all members of the Daughters of Bilitis. The authors note that this was the largest lesbian population studied to that time. All the women were given a 500-item questionnaire, and the results were compared with those of a study of 206 gay and straight men. Although there were some key differences between the men and women that no doubt affected the comparative findings between the sexes (all the men, for example, were undergoing psychotherapy), the similarity in composition between the heterosexual women and their counterpart lesbian group was carefully structured. There were many more similarities than differences between the two groups of women, so much so that they were almost indistinguishable. The authors concluded that "homosexuality among women in our society seems unrelated to the establishment of feminine identity."

1333　HENRY, GEORGE WILLIAM. All the Sexes: A Study of Masculinity and Femininity. New York: Rinehart, 1955. 599 pp.
　　　So-called sexual maladjustment and variation are the themes of this work, which amplifies the material in Henry's Sex Variants. Believing that "sexual maladjustment and immaturity underlie almost all emotional disorders," Henry uses case records to identify types of variation and maladjustment, including everything from homosexuality to unusual dreams and fantasies. This labeling and description form the basis for broad generalizations, which often have no connection with fact. Recent research, for example, has disproved such conclusions as "All that has been said with reference to homosexual men applies equally well to women," or "There are probably few [middle-aged lesbians] who do not wish that they had been able to conform to the more usual pattern of sharing a home with a

husband and children." Despite its length, this impressionistic, subjective work has no footnote documentation or even a bibliography.

1334   HUTTON, LAURA. The Single Woman and Her Emotional Problems.
       Baltimore: William Wood, 1935. 151 pp.
            Laura Hutton's outspoken attitudes on masturbation and les-
       bian relationships must have shocked many of her readers. Not only
       did Hutton, a London physician, believe that sexuality inevitably
       would play a part in any intense emotional relationship between
       women, but she maintained that love was always more important than
       questions of so-called morality. As for masturbation: "Let the
       orgasm come, by whatever means is easiest, as quickly as possible,
       and turn with ease of mind and increased energy to the matter you
       have in hand."
            Nevertheless, Hutton believed that sublimation of sexual
       energy into other ambitions and activities, such as religion, was
       preferable to overt expression. Her general ambivalence can be
       seen, however, in her reluctance to advise her readers further
       than to simply be aware of the alternatives, and their consequences,
       of emotional and sexual expression in single life.

1335   JAY, KARLA, and ALLEN YOUNG. The Gay Report: Lesbians and Gay
       Men Speak Out about Sexual Experiences and Lifestyles. New York:
       Summit Books, 1979. 816 pp.
            This extensive survey of lesbian and gay male life-styles and
       sexuality and the problems relating thereto includes responses
       from 962 women and 4,329 men in the United States and Canada. Two
       separate questionnaires were used, but although lesbian and gay
       male material is presented in separate chapters, it is still pos-
       sible to chart similarities and differences between the two sexes.
       Because there are significant differences in many areas, the authors
       have not attempted to depict a single gay continuum. Their find-
       ings are presented statistically, as well as in narrative excerpts
       from the survey responses. The Gay Report is a welcome alternative
       to most studies of lesbians and gay men which examine special,
       atypical populations.

1336   KLAICH, DOLORES. Woman + Woman: Attitudes toward Lesbianism.
       New York: Simon and Schuster, 1974. 287 pp.
            In this highly readable social and cultural history of les-
       bianism, Dolores Klaich strives to present what she sees as an
       accurate portrayal of the full dimension of the lesbian situation.
       Condemning society's distorted identification of lesbians by their
       sexual and affectional preference alone, she shows how this one-
       sided, prejudiced view has worked to suppress awareness of the many
       other aspects of lesbian existence. The roles of nineteenth-century
       theorists (such as Krafft-Ebing), Freud, and more contemporary sex
       research in defining lesbian behavior for society are discussed.
       Klaich contends, however, that although most of these researchers
       and writers present only one side of the picture, one cannot say
       that lesbian activists are any more objective or reflective of the

wide range of lesbian behavior and attitudes.

In the second section of the book, Klaich examines some historical figures, among them Sappho, Natalie Barney, and Radclyffe Hall, whose lesbianism was integrated into their writing and who had an impact on the nonlesbian culture of their time. She concludes with a discussion of contemporary social and political questions, based on responses to a survey of lesbians throughout the United states. The book also contains three extensive interviews, footnotes, and a bibliography.

1337 LANER, MARY RIEGE. "Media Mating II: 'Personals' Advertisements of Lesbian Women." Journal of Homosexuality 4, no. 1 (Fall 1978):41-61.

Laner compares characteristics in the wording of advertisements placed in the Wishing Well, a lesbian contact magazine, with similar advertisements in other publications placed by homosexual and heterosexual men and heterosexual women.

1338 LEWIS, SASHA GREGORY. Sunday's Women: A Report on Lesbian Life Today. Boston: Beacon Press, 1979. 217 pp.

Lewis has relied heavily on Charlotte Wolff's Love between Women (entry 1359), Alan Bell and Martin Weinberg's Homosexualities (entry 1322), and an unpublished report by Marilyn Fleener presented to a meeting of the Western Social Science Association in 1977. She also interviewed about two dozen lesbians, but gives no indication as to how they were chosen. The result is a diffuse, sometimes impressionistic account, focusing on the so-called lesbian "subculture in hiding," and more contemporary lesbian community developments, such as the problem Lewis calls "lesbian fascism."

1339 LIVINGOOD, JOHN M., ed. National Institute of Mental Health Task Force on Homosexuality Final Report and Background Papers. Rockville, Md.: National Institute of Mental Health, 1972. 79 pp.

In September 1967, the National Institute of Mental Health appointed a fifteen-member task force of nationally known behavioral, medical, legal, and social scientists "to review carefully the current state of knowledge regarding homosexuality in its mental health aspects and to make recommendations for Institute programming in this area." Only one of those appointed, Evelyn Hooker, was a woman. The background papers, which were not included in an initial 1969 report, contain little specifically on women; the task force clearly recognized that few studies of lesbians had been made and that more were needed. The group recommended that NIMH establish a center for the study of sexual behavior, but this suggestion has, regrettably, never been implemented.

1340 MAGEE, BRYAN. One in Twenty--A Study of Homosexuality in Men and Women. London: Secker & Warburg, 1966. 192 pp.

In order to counteract the lack of information on lesbians he found in producing two British television documentaries on homosexualtiy, Magee tries to pay equal attention to both men and women in this book. He only partly succeeds, for while he does devote one-third of the book specifically to lesbians, the intro- ductory third, which provides an overview, is largely weighted to- ward men. Moreover, despite a basically sympathetic attitude, Magee persists in calling homosexuality "abnormal." Equally distorting (although perhaps not for the context of the 1960s) is his emphasis on butch/femme role playing, his digression into a discussion of bisexuality in the lesbian section, and such generalizations as this one about lesbian households: "The atmosphere is one of ob- sessional concern for the details of behaviour and the trivialities of everyday life."

1341   MARMOR, JUDD, ed. Sexual Inversion: The Multiple Roots of
       Homosexuality. New York: Basic Books, 1965. 358 pp.
       This collection of original essays includes only two relating directly to women: Cornelia B. Wilbur's "Clinical Aspects of Fe- male Homosexuality" and May E. Romm's "Sexuality and Homosexuality in Women." Wilbur does not offer much empirical evidence to sup- port her basically negative views, other than some vague references to cases. Nevertheless, she freely advances such generalizations as "The female child destined to be a homosexual looks upon her mother with hostility and rebellion." Or, "Female homosexual patients are usually compulsively preoccupied with sexuality in general and with sexual practices in particular." Romm repeats the error: "Homosexuals of both sexes are human beings who have given up hope of ever being accepted by their parents and by the society in which they live. They are basically unhappy because normal family life with the fulfillment in having children can never be within their reach. The label 'gay' behind which they hide is a defense mechanism against the emptiness, the coldness, and the futility of their lives."

1342   MARTIN, DEL, and PHYLLIS LYON. Lesbian/Woman. San Francisco:
       Glide Publications, 1972. 283 pp.
       Del Martin and Phyllis Lyon, founders of the pioneer lesbian organization, the Daughters of Bilitis, present a realistic picture of lesbian life in the United States prior to 1972. Based on their own experiences and contacts as women, lesbians, and activists, Lesbian/Woman is particularly strong in its depiction of how so- ciety has worked against lesbians at every turn, creating an ob- stacle course which they must pass through simply in order to sur- vive as human beings. In their discussion of such topics as religious attitudes, psychiatric theory and treatment, and military persecution, the authors clearly demonstrate the hypocrisy, injus- tice, and sheer ignorance that permeate these fields, causing them to condemn lesbians simply on the grounds of their sexual prefer- ence.
       Much has changed since 1972, primarily because of pressure from the feminist and gay rights movements, yet Martin and Lyon's account serves to remind us that lesbians, and indeed other minority

groups, are only as free as white male society and its institutions permit them to be. Lesbians may never return to the constraints of butch/femme relationships, but the compulsory heterosexuality that continues to permeate American culture erects barriers, however subtle, and conveys messages indicating that somehow women who love and identify with other women are less than okay. Only through the strength that they derive from other women, to which Martin and Lyon's book gives testimony, will they be able to survive.

1343   MASTERS, WILLIAM H., and VIRGINIA E. JOHNSON. Homosexuality in
       Perspective. Boston: Little, Brown, 1979. 450 pp.
       This study of psychophysiologic aspects of homosexual sexual functioning has as its overall goal provision of information to aid in therapy for homosexual sexual dysfunctions: "A homosexual man or woman who is sexually dysfunctional or dissatisfied is entitled to evaluation and treatment with the same clinical objectivity currently accorded the sexually dysfunctional heterosexual individual."
       Preclinical work for this project began in 1957, with clinical observation running from 1968 to 1977. Eighty-two lesbians were studied, along with gay men and two heterosexual comparison groups. Perhaps the most revealing aspect of the research was not so much its physiologic findings as its demonstration of how arbitrary and misleading it can be to pigeonhole individuals into either/or, hetero-/homosexual categories for the purposes of scientific study.
       There is an extensive bibliography and some statistical data. Homosexuality in Perspective is much more focused on interpersonal dynamics than was its predecessor Human Sexual Response, making one apprehensive about its skewed research population, as well as the "physiologic" approach to the study of sexual behavior.

1344   MORSE, BENJAMIN. The Lesbian: A Frank, Revealing Study of
       Women Who Turn to Their Own Sex for Love. Derby, Conn.:
       Monarch, 1961. 142 pp.
       "You will meet them all here. . . . A dozen of them, each one abnormal in her own special way, each a social and sexual outcast, each an individual example of something gone wrong. . . . The girls and women herein discussed are real girls and women. The names are fiction." Need more be said?

1345   MOSES, ALICE E. Identity Management in Lesbian Women. New York:
       Praeger, 1978. 118 pp.
       Moses studied eighty-one self-identified lesbian women from California (88 percent of the total), Ohio, and New York in this analysis of how lesbians manage day-to-day interactions with others. She also provides an overview of deviance theory, labeling theory, and identity management.
       Moses found that the women in the sample experienced concern about being identified as lesbians when around straight people who did not know they were lesbians. This usually necessitated some

sort of "management" of the situation, an example being passing as straight if this was seen as the optimal behavior. Nevertheless, the author found that most of the sample felt that "being lesbian is their choice and that the choice is a good one, for all its inevitable difficulties." The text is supplemented by a copy of the questionnaire, data tables, and a bibliography.

1346   PONSE, BARBARA. Identities in the Lesbian World: The Social Construction of Self. Contributions in Sociology, no. 28. Westport, Conn.: Greenwood Press, 1978. 226 pp.

Ponse analyzes the process by which lesbian identities are explained, constructed, maintained, and changed in the context of secrecy, stigma, and politics. Her material was gathered from interviews with seventy-five women and from a wide range of other sources. Ponse is especially interested in describing the range of emotional and sexual relationships and orientations that might be defined as lesbian and utilizes labeling theory in her analysis. Ponse adopts a loose definition of lesbians as "women who love women" or "women-related women." There are a glossary, notes, and a bibliography, but few statistics, making it difficult for the reader to know how typical Ponse's subjects might be in relation to other lesbians.

1347   POTTER, La FOREST. Strange Loves: A Study in Sexual Abnormalities. New York: Dodsley, 1933. 243 pp.

Potter, a New York physician, paints a vivid picture of his perception of the homosexual and lesbian threat to American civilization. Although men receive more attention than women, there is still ample material on lesbians, characterized by Potter as creatures with "atrophied breasts, infantile ovaries, a baritone voice, and a pair of hips like a gigolo." He felt that most lesbianism resulted from an early resentment of female gender roles, although he also felt that astrological factors might play a role, "when Libra, with its decidedly masculine element, overbalances the decidedly feminine characteristic of Venus." Parents were warned that "the girl who, after the menstrual cycle has been definitely established, still gets a thrill out of swinging a pick and shovel, or carrying fifty pound stones around to build a wall with, will bear watching." The feminist movement was also blamed. Psychoanalysis was touted as the best means for a "cure."

1348   QUERLIN, MARISE. Women without Men. New York: Dell, 1965. 174 pp.

Originally published in France in 1953, Women without Men was billed on its cover by the publisher as being "the first real contribution on the subject [of lesbianism] since the works of Freud and Helen [sic] Deutsch." Obviously it wasn't, and it's just as well, since Querlin's "array of causative factors--heterosexual anxiety, seduction, persistent mother attachment, adolescent instability, unresolved father fixation, male envy, revenge and self-mortification fantasies, and voyeuristic and exhibitionistic tendencies--" are more the product of an active imagination than of statistically valid empirical research involving the lesbian population as a whole. Nevertheless, this at times semifictional narrative is introduced as being "a remarkable, timely and clinically accurate book on a poorly illumined subject." Readers seeking brighter illumination should search elsewhere.

1349   RICH, ADRIENNE. "Compulsory Heterosexuality and Lesbian Existence." Signs 5, no. 4 (Summer 1980):631-60.
        In this essay, Rich argues that compulsory heterosexuality has developed as a political institution which serves as the primary means of perpetuating and enforcing male dominance over women. Women's tacit acceptance of the heterosexual norm has been, historically, a condition for their survival, but questioning of institutionalized heterosexuality by women is a major step toward their real liberation. Women need to embrace, define, and describe the underlying lesbian continuum of their lives and resist and reject pejorative, ahistorical, clinical definitions, prescriptions, and male behaviors which only serve to maintain oppressive heterosexuality. This is an important theoretical work by a leading lesbian/feminist poet and writer.

1350   ROBERTIELLO, RICHARD C. Voyage from Lesbos: The Psychoanalysis of a Female Homosexual. New York: Citadel, 1959. 253 pp.
        Dr. William V. Silverberg, Robertiello's psychoanalytic supervisor, in his introduction to this case study indicates a fundamental misconception in the psychoanalytical treatment process as it existed at that time: the analyst's predilection for dichotomizing lesbians into simplistic butch/femme types, leading to a categorization of psychodynamics according to type. Robertiello sees lesbianism as a compulsive illness caused by traumatic childhood experiences. "Most homosexuals are unhappy, suffering people" is followed by "Most homosexuals are fine, upstanding, moral and productive people." It is hard to see how the two can go so easily together, and Robertiello is seemingly unaware of the inherent contrariety of these two statements.
        Equally revealing are Robertiello's references to his twenty-nine-year-old client as a "girl." Although at the time of her initial visit she expressed no desire to change her sexual pattern, the client was gradually led, through dream interpretation by Robertiello, to see her unconscious wish to become heterosexual. "She came to realize that her basic wish, like the wish of any woman, was for a man." After four years the client broke off the analysis for several months, but then "made the change" and returned to her analyst. "She renounced her homosexual contacts and began living a completely heterosexual life. This didn't mean there weren't still problems, but at least they weren't strong enough to maintain the homosexuality."

1351   ROSEN, DAVID H. Lesbianism: A Study of Female Homosexuality. Springfield, Ill.: Charles C. Thomas, 1974. 123 pp.

Rosen reviews literature on lesbianism and includes new material based on his study of twenty-six women, all members of the Daughters of Bilitis. His findings support his view that homosexuality should not be classified as a psychiatric disorder. Evelyn Hooker, in her introduction, suggests that future researchers should ask, "What variables in personality, developmental history, and the cultural milieu of the individual lead to a healthy vs. a non-healthy homosexual pattern of life?"

1352 SAGHIR, MARCEL T., and ELI ROBINS. Male and Female Homosexuality: A Comprehensive Investigation. Baltimore: Williams & Wilkins, 1973. 341 pp.

Saghir and Robins divided this study into two sections, one dealing with male homosexuals, the other with women. In their study of lesbians they interviewed fifty-seven gay women, with forty-four straight women being used as a control group. Most of the lesbians were members of the Daughters of Bilitis, the lesbian organization, and were not part of either a patient or a prison population. The interviews, which were at least three hours long, covered such topics as childhood-adolescent characteristics, psychosexual response, sexual practices, heterosexual activity, psychopathology, family relationships, and group sociology. Saghir and Robins are critical of many previous studies of gay people, especially those dealing with psychopathology. Their basic conclusion is that there are significant behavior differences between homosexual men and lesbians: "The homosexual woman looks first for a relationship and usually establishes a relationship prior to any sexual activity." With the homosexual man, sex usually precedes establishment of a relationship.

1353 [SIM, F.L.] "Forensic Psychiatry. Alice Mitchell Adjudged Insane." Memphis Medical Monthly 12, no. 8 (August 1892):377-428.

Alice Mitchell of Memphis, Tennessee, who slashed the throat of her lover Freda Ward on the streets of that city, provided the 1890s with a sensational glimpse of sexual and affectional variation. This account of Mitchell's trial focuses on the role of heredity in determining Mitchell's condition. Yet is is also apparent that the nature of the Mitchell-Ward relationship was of far less concern as evidence of insanity ("There has been submitted to this court no evidence of sexual depravity") than the startling violence of the murder itself. The notoriety of the crime and the willingness of writers on lesbianism to grasp at any shred of evidence, however distorted and atypical, led this case to become a favorite stereotyped example of "true" lesbian behavior in much subsequent literature. Sim's account is based on court transcripts, newspaper stories, and depositions.

1354 SISLEY, EMILY L., and BERTHA HARRIS. The Joy of Lesbian Sex: A Tender and Liberated Guide to the Pleasures and Problems of a Lesbian Lifestyle. New York: Crown, 1977. 223 pp.

Although Sisley and Harris disavow any connection of their book's ideas with those of The Joy of Sex, they have certainly capitalized on that book's success, recognition, and format. Their introduction makes their own politics clear, however: "Heterosexual reality includes the female orgasm by accident only. . . . Heterosexual reality for men is sexual, for women it is largely reproductive."

Sisley and Harris believe that lesbian sexuality is non-economic in origin, pleasurable, and a transaction between equals, and although they are concerned primarily here with physical aspects of lesbian relationships, they also cover such topics as civil rights, closets, and consciousness raising. Sometimes the authors wax romantic: "Lesbian eyes cruise: they can give a stranger's body an instant's worth of intimacy as effective, for some, as a night's worth of lovemaking." Most of their advice, however, is practical and realistic. In addition to the text, there is a bibliography of fiction and nonfiction books, periodicals, articles, and other materials.

1355   STEKEL, WILHELM. The Homosexual Neurosis. Translated by James
        S. Van Teslaar. Boston: Richard G. Badger, 1922. 322 pp.
        Psychoanalyst Stekel is typical of many writers on lesbians in his equation of their situation to that of male homosexuals: "The life histories of homosexual women differ from those of males only in the fact that occasionally there seems present a certain yearning for children, as if the child could bring about release from the passion and a new state of bliss. Beyond that the urlind shows the same psychogenesis as the urning." Equally typical is his presentation of questionable evidence (digests of case records) to support his claim. One woman, whose female friend appeared to be seducing her husband, is diagnosed as being "jealous of her woman friend because she herself is in love with the friend." Indeed, jealousy of other women is often interpreted by Stekel as being indicative of lesbianism. It should be noted, however, that despite the vagaries of his scientific method Stekel believed in the abandonment of moral and legal sanctions against homosexuals. Nevertheless, he characterized lesbians and the men who formed the bulk of his cases as "perpetual infants," victims of a regressive neurosis.

1356   TANNER, DONNA M. The Lesbian Couple. Lexington, Mass.:
        Lexington Books, 1978. 142 pp.
        A sociologist, Tanner, who is not a lesbian herself, collected data for this study between 1972 and 1975. The twenty-four women involved were in couple relationships, lived in the Chicago area, and ranged in age from twenty to thirty-five. Each woman was interviewed in depth for from four to eight hours.

Tanner provides an overview of previous research, writing, and theorizing on lesbians. Her own contribution includes material in such areas as coming out, formation and maintenance of the couple relationship, types of relationships, and interaction with the gay community. She includes a bibliography as well as her question outline for the interviews, a welcome addition and a feature usually omitted by most authors of interview-based studies.

1357 VIDA, GINNY, ed. Our Right to Love: A Lesbian Resource Book. Englewood Cliffs, N.J.: Prentice-Hall, 1978. 318 pp.
        Produced in cooperation with Women of the National Gay Task Force, this collection of essays and personal statements, most of them original to this volume, deals with the totality of lesbian experience, especially its dimensions as an emotional and political expression. An underlying goal of the book is to replace destructive traditional stereotypes of lesbians with "the positive alternatives: our warmth and fulfillment, the health of loving one's equal, lesbianism as an active choice (as distinghished from 'arrested development,' for example), and so on." One section is devoted to sexuality, and discusses technique, experiences, and problems. There is also an extensive bibliography and resource list of organizations, bookstores, media, and so on, throughout the United States and Canada.

1358 WOLF, DEBORAH GOLEMAN. The Lesbian Community. Berkeley: University of California Press, 1980. 212 pp.
        Originally prepared as a Ph.D. dissertation in anthropology at the University of California, Berkeley, The Lesbian Community focuses on the mutual influences of feminism and lesbianism in the San Francisco lesbian community between 1972 and 1975. Sexual behavior is only incidentally treated, Wolf's emphasis clearly being the social and political dimensions of the research population. This 1980 paperback edition contains new material not found in the initial 1979 hardback printing. The book is an honest, straightforward, unprejudiced account and is a welcome antidote to materials not blessed by those virtues.

1359 WOLFF, CHARLOTTE. Love between Women. New York: Harper & Row, 1972. 303 pp.
        For this study, German-trained, London-based psychiatrist Charlotte Wolff obtained questionnaire responses from 108 lesbians and 123 heterosexual controls and autobiographies and interviews with the lesbians. This is not, however, primarily a statistical study, although Wolff presents the results of twenty-eight tabulations. Rather, working from the basis of Freudian theory of sexuality, Wolff postulates her own theory of lesbianism.
        Although Wolff tries to be both objective and sympathetic, she creates as many new stereotypes as she dispels. For her, emotional incest with the mother is the essence of lesbianism; indeed, her focus is on the emotional rather than the sexual side of eroticism. She claims (on what basis cannot be determined) that lesbians are "open to any sexual stimulation." Despite this, she sees these women as affected by a "tinge of tragedy," resulting from "the impossibility of complete sexual fulfillment, and particularly childlessness."

Like many writers with a psychiatric bent, Wolff confuses
gender role and sexuality. While she contends that lesbianism is
a question of gender identity, she also believes that bisexuality
is "the one and only way to achieve equality and progress in human
as well as love relationships." This idea, colored by her belief
in the so-called anatomical bisexuality of woman, is not clearly
expressed here, although Wolff's later book on the subject attempts
to dispel this basic inconsistency. One must, of course, continue
to ask to what degree one's theories influence the ultimate con-
figuration of and interpretation of the findings.

1360 WYSOR, BETTIE. The Lesbian Myth. New York: Random House,
      1974. 438 pp.
      Bettie Wysor claims to offer a new view of lesbianism in
this book, but she largely fails to achieve her goal. She explores
biblical, psychological, genetic, anthropological, and literary
ideas about homosexuality and lesbianism. There is an uncomfort-
able emphasis on material relating to male homosexuals or homosexuality in general (usually male oriented), rather than information
specifically about lesbians. Much of the book merely summarizes
the work of others. For example, Wysor relies heavily on the work
of Jeannette Foster in her chapter on literature. There is no attempt to relate feminist consciousness to lesbianism. Wysor also
includes transcriptions of several group discussions among lesbians
held in New York City in 1971 and 1972.

1361 ALBRO, JOYCE C., and CAROL TULLY. "A Study of Lesbian Life-
      styles in the Homosexual Micro-culture and the Heterosexual
      Macro-culture." Journal of Homosexuality 4, no. 4 (Summer
      1979):331-54.

1362 BARAHAL, HYMAN S. "Female Transvestism and Homosexuality."
      Psychiatric Quarterly 27, no. 3 (1953):390-438.

1363 BARKER, WILLIAM S. "Two Cases of Sexual Contrariety." St.
      Louis Courier of Medicine and Collateral Sciences 28, no. 4
      (April 1903):269-71.

1364 BASS-HASS, RITA. "The Lesbian Dyad: Basic Issues and Value
      Systems." Journal of Sex Research 4, no. 2 (May 1968):108-26.

1365 BENE, EVA. "On the Genesis of Female Homosexuality." British
      Journal of Psychiatry 3, no. 478 (September 1965):815-21.

1366 BERNSTEIN, IRVING C. "Homosexuality in Gynecologic Practice."
      South Dakota Journal of Medicine 21, no. 3 (March 1968):33-39.

1367 BIEBER, TOBY. "The Lesbian Patient." Medical Aspects of Human
      Sexuality 3, no. 1 (January 1969):6-12.

1368   BRODY, MORRIS W. "An Analysis of the Psycho-sexual Development of a Female—with Special Reference to Homosexuality." Psychoanalytic Review 30, no. 1 (January 1943):47-58.

1369   CALIFA, PAT. "Lesbian Sexuality." Journal of Homosexuality 4, no. 3 (Spring 1979):255-66.

1370   CAULDWELL, D.O. "Lesbian Love Murder." Sexology 16, no. 12 (July 1950):773-79.

1371   CLATWORTHY, NANCY M. "Lesbians: A Comparison of Two Groups." Criminologica 5, no. 1 (May 1967):41-46.

1372   COMSTOCK, T. GRISWOLD. "Alice Mitchell, of Memphis; a Case of Sexual Perversion or 'Urning' (a Paranoiac)." New York Medical Times 20, no. 6 (September 1892):170-73.

1373   COTTON, WAYNE L. "Social and Sexual Relationships of Lesbians." Journal of Sex Research 11, no. 2 (May 1975):139-48.

1374   CRONIN, DENISE M. "Coming Out among Lesbians." In Sexual Deviance and Sexual Deviants, edited by Erich Goode and Richard R. Troiden, 268-77. New York: William Morrow, 1974.

1375   De FRIES, ZIRA. "A Comparison of Political and Apolitical Lesbians." Journal of the American Academy of Psychoanalysis 7, no. 1 (January 1979):57-66.

1376   _____. "Pseudohomosexuality in Feminist Students." American Journal of Psychiatry 133, no. 4 (April 1976):400-404.

1377   EISINGER, A., et al. "Female Homosexuality." Nature 238, no. 5359 (14 July 1972):106.

1378   ELLIS, ALBERT. "The Effectiveness of Psychotherapy with Individuals Who Have Severe Homosexual Problems." Journal of Consulting Psychology 20, no. 3 (June 1956):191-95.

1379   FORD, CHARLES A. "Homosexual Practices of Institutionalized Females." Journal of Abnormal and Social Psychology 23, no. 4 (January-March 1929):442-48.

1380   FREEDMAN, MARK. "Homosexuality among Women and Psychological Adjustment." Ph.D. dissertation, Case Western Reserve University, 1967. 124 pp.

1381   FROMM, ERIKA O., and ANNA S. ELONEN. "Projective Techniques in the Study of a Case of Female Homosexuality." Journal of Projective Techniques 15, no. 2 (June 1951):185-230.

1382   GILBERT, J. ALLEN. "Homosexuality and Its Treatment." Journal of Nervous and Mental Disease 52, no. 4 (October 1920):297-322.

1383   HAY, RALPH. "Mannish Women or Old Maids." Know Yourself 1, no. 2 (July 1938):76-81.

1384   HEDBLOM, JACK H. "Social, Sexual and Occupational Lives of Homosexual Women." Sexual Behavior 2, no. 10 (October 1972): 33-37.

1385   HIDALGO, HILDA A., and ELIA HIDALGO CHRISTENSEN. "The Puerto Rican Lesbian and the Puerto Rican Community." Journal of Homosexuality 2, no. 2 (Winter 1976-77):109-21.

1386   HOPKINS, JUNE H. "The Lesbian Personality." British Journal of Psychiatry 115, no. 529 (December 1969):1433-36.

1387   _____. "Lesbian Signs on the Rorschach." British Journal of Projective Psychology and Personality Study 15, no. 2 (December 1970):7-14.

1388   HOWARD, WILLIAM LEE. "Effeminate Men and Masculine Women." New York Medical Journal 71 (5 May 1900):686-87.

1389   _____. "Psychical Hermaphroditism; a Few Notes on Sexual Perversion, with Two Clinical Cases of Sexual Inversion." Alienist and Neurologist 18, no. 2 (April 1897):111-18.

1390   _____. "Sexual Perversion." Alienist and Neurologist 17, no. 1 (January 1896):1-6.

1391   JENSEN, MEHRI SAMANDARI. "Role Differentiation in Female Homosexual Quasi-Marital Unions." Journal of Marriage and the Family 36, no. 2 (May 1974):360-67.

1392   KAYE, HARVEY E., et al. "Homosexuality in Women." Archives of General Psychiatry 17, no. 5 (November 1967):626-34.

1393   KELLY, JANIS. "Sister Love: An Exploration of the Need for Homosexual Experience." Family Coordinator 21, no. 4 (October 1972):473-75.

1394   KEMPH, JOHN P., and ERNA SCHWERIN. "Increased Latent Homosexuality in a Woman During Group Therapy." International Journal of Group Psychotherapy 16, no. 2 (April 1966):217-24.

1395   KENYON, FRANK EDWIN. "Female Homosexuality--a Review." In Understanding Homosexuality: Its Biological and Psychological Bases, edited by John A. Loraine, 83-119. New York: American Elsevier, 1974.

1396   _____. "Reports on Female Homosexuality, IV and V." British Journal of Psychiatry 114, no. 516 (November 1968):1337-50.

1397   KIERNAN, JAMES G.   "Perverted Sexual Instinct."   Chicago Medical
        Journal and Examiner 48, no. 3 (March 1884):263-65.

1398   _____.   "Psychological Aspects of the Sexual Appetite."
        Alienist and Neurologist 12, no. 2 (April 1891):188-217.

1399   _____.   "Responsibility in Sexual Perversion."   Chicago Medical
        Recorder 3 (May 1892):185-210.

1400   _____.   "Sexual Perversion and the Whitechapel Murders."
        Medical Standard 4, no. 4 (December 1888):171-72.

1401   KREMER, MALVINA W.   "Brief Guide to Office Counseling: Lesbian
        Patients."   Medical Aspects of Human Sexuality 8, no. 10
        (October 1974):219-20.

1402   KREMER, MALVINA W., and ALFRED H. RIFKIN.   "The Early Develop-
        ment of Homosexuality: A Study of Adolescent Lesbians."
        American Journal of Psychiatry 126, no. 1 (July 1969):91-96.

1403   LIDZ, RUTH WILMANNS, and THEODORE LIDZ.   "Homosexual Tendencies
        in Mothers of Schizophrenic Women."   Journal of Nervous and
        Mental Disease 149, no. 2 (August 1969):229-35.

1404   McCAGHY, CHARLES A., and JAMES R. SKIPPER, Jr.   "Lesbian Behavior
        as an Adaptation to the Occupation of Stripping."   Social
        Problems 17, no. 2 (Fall 1969):262-70.

1405   McINTOSH, MARY.   "The Homosexual Role."   Social Problems 16, no.
        2 (Fall 1968):182-92.

1406   MacKINNON, JANE.   "The Homosexual Woman."   American Journal of
        Psychiatry 103, no. 5 (March 1947):661-64.

1407   McMURTRIE, DOUGLAS C.   "Legend of Lesbian Love among North
        American Indians."   Urologic and Cutaneous Review 18, no. 4
        (April 1914):192-93.

1408   _____.   "Manifestations of Sexual Inversion in the Female;
        Conditions in a Convent School, Evidence of Transvestism, Un-
        conscious Homosexuality, Sexuality of Masculine Women, Masturba-
        tion under Homosexual Influences, Indeterminate Sexuality in
        Childhood."   Urologic and Cutaneous Review 18, no. 8 (August
        1914):424-26.

1409   _____.   "Principles of Homosexuality and Sexual Inversion in
        the Female."   American Journal of Urology and Sexology 9, no. 3
        (March 1913):144-53.

1410   _____.   "Sexually Inverted Infatuation in a Middle-aged Woman."
        Urologic and Cutaneous Review 18, no. 11 (November 1914):601.

1411 _____. "Some Observations on the Psychology of Sexual Inversion in Women." American Journal of Urology and Sexology 9, no. 1 (January 1913):38-45.

1412 MANN, EDWARD C. "Morbid Sexual Perversions as Related to Insanity." Virginia Medical Semi-Monthly 3, no. 2 (22 April 1898):46-50.

1413 _____. "The Trial of Josephine Mallison Smith." Alienist and Neurologist 14, no. 3 (July 1893):467-77.

1414 "Marriages between Women." Alienist and Neurologist 23, no. 4 (November 1902):497-99.

1415 OBERSTONE, ANDREA KINCSES, and HARRIET SUKONECK. "Psychological Adjustment and Life Style of Single Lesbians and Single Hetero- sexual Women." Psychology of Women Quarterly 1, no. 2 (Winter 1976):172-88.

1416 OHLSON, E. LAMONTE, and MARILYN WILSON. "Differentiating Female Homosexuals from Female Heterosexuals by Use of the MMPI." Journal of Sex Research 10, no. 4 (November 1974):308-15.

1417 OSMAN, SHELOMO. "My Stepfather Is a She." Family Process 11, no. 2 (June 1972):209-18.

1418 OTIS, MARGARET. "A Perversion Not Commonly Noted." Journal of Abnormal Psychology 8, no. 2 (June-July 1913):113-16.

1419 PARDES, HERBERT; JORGE STEINBERG, and RICHARD C. SIMONS. "A Rare Case of Overt and Mutual Homosexuality in Female Identical Twins." Psychiatric Quarterly 41, no. 1 (January 1967):108-33.

1420 PEPLAU, LETITIA A., et al. "Loving Women: Attachment and Autonomy in Lesbian Relationships." Journal of Social Issues 34, no. 3 (Summer 1978):7-27.

1421 "Perverted Sexual Instinct." Medical Record 26, no. 3 (19 July 1884):70.

1422 PODOLSKY, EDWARD. "'Homosexual Love' in Women," Popular Medicine 1, no. 6 (February 1935):373-76.

1423 RIESS, BERNARD F.; JEANNE SAFER, and WILLIAM YOTIVE. "Psycho- logical Test Data on Female Homosexuality: A Review of the Literature." Journal of Homosexuality 1, no. 1 (Fall 1974): 71-85.

1424 ROBERTIELLO, RICHARD C. "Clinical Notes: Results of Separation from Iposexual Parents During the Oedipal Period, a Female Homo- sexual Panic." Psychoanalytic Review 51, no. 4 (Winter 1964-65): 670-72.

1425   SCHAFER, SIEGRID. "Sexual and Social Problems among Lesbians."
        Journal of Sex Research 12, no. 1 (February 1976):50-69.

1426   _____. "Sociosexual Behavior in Male and Female Homosexuals:
        A Study in Sex Differences." Archives of Sexual Behavior 6,
        no. 5 (September 1977):355-64.

1427   SHAW, J.C., and G.N. FERRIS. "Perverted Sexual Instinct."
        Journal of Nervous and Mental Disease 10, no. 2 (April 1883):
        185-204.

1428   SHELLEY, MARTHA. "Lesbianism." In The Radical Therapist,
        edited by Jerome Agel, 169-72. New York: Ballantine Books,
        1971.

1429   SHUFELDT, R.W. "Dr. Havelock Ellis on Sexual Inversion."
        Pacific Medical Journal 45, no. 4 (April 1902):199-207.

1430   SIMON, WILLIAM, and JOHN H. GAGNON. "Femininity in the Lesbian
        Community." Social Problems 15, no. 2 (Fall 1967):212-21.

1431   _____. "The Lesbians: A Preliminary Overview." In Sexual
        Deviance, edited by John H. Gagnon and William Simon, 247-82.
        New York: Harper & Row, 1967.

1432   SOCARIDES, CHARLES W. "The Historical Development of Theoretical
        and Clinical Concepts of Overt Female Homosexuality." Journal of
        the American Psychoanalytic Association 11, no. 2 (April 1963):
        386-414.

1433   _____. "Theoretical and Clinical Aspects of Overt Female Homo-
        sexuality." Journal of the American Psychoanalytic Association
        10, no. 3 (July 1962):579-92.

1434   STOLLER, ROBERT J., et al. "A Symposium: Should Homosexuality
        Be in the APA Nomenclature." American Journal of Psychiatry 130,
        no. 11 (November 1973):1207-16.

1435   STONE, WALTER N.; JOHN SCHENGBER, and F. STANLEY SEIFRIED. "The
        Treatment of a Homosexual Woman in a Mixed Group." International
        Journal of Group Psychotherapy 16, no. 4 (October 1966):425-33.

1436   SWANSON, DAVID W. "Clinical Features of the Female Homosexual
        Patient; a Comparison with the Heterosexual Patient." Journal
        of Nervous and Mental Disease 155, no. 2 (August 1972):119-24.

1437   THOMPSON, NORMAL L.; BOYD R. McCANDLESS, and BONNIE R. STRICKLAND.
        "Personal Adjustment of Male and Female Homosexuals and Hetero-
        sexuals." Journal of Abnormal Psychology 78, no. 2 (October
        1971):237-40.

1438   THOMPSON, NORMAN L., et al. "Parent-child Relationships and
        Sexual Identity in Male and Female Homosexuals and Heterosexu-
        als." Journal of Consulting and Clinical Psychology 41, no. 1
        (August 1973):120-27.

1439   "Viewpoints: Is Homosexuality Pathologic or a Normal Variant
        of Sexuality?" Medical Aspects of Human Sexuality 7, no. 12
        (December 1973):10-26.

1440   "When Women Love Other Women: A Frank Discussion of Female
        Homosexuality." Redbook 138, no. 1 (November 1971):84-85+.

1441   WILSON, MARILYN L., and ROGER L. GREENE. "Personality Charac-
        teristics of Female Homosexuals." Psychological Reports 28,
        no. 2 (1971):407-12.

1442   WINNER, ALBERTINE L. "Homosexuality in Women." Medical Press
        218, no. 10 (3 September 1947):219-20.

1443   WISE, P.M. "Case of Sexual Perversion." Alienist and
        Neurologist 4, no. 1 (January 1883):87-91.

1444   WITTENBERG, RUDOLPH. "Lesbianism as a Transitory Solution to
        the Ego." Psychoanalytic Review 43, no. 3 (July 1956):348-57.

1445   ZUCKER, LUISE J. "Mental Health and Homosexuality." Journal
        of Sex Research 2, no. 2 (July 1966):111-25.

Other Special Populations

In addition to lesbians, the literature on women's sexuality distinguishes several other populations, which, owing to their special circumstances, have been separated from the female population as a whole for purposes of analysis and treatment. Theorists could certainly debate the ethics of this separation, which assumes certain standards of politically compulsory heterosexual performance as a norm, but the fact remains that such distinctions do occur.

Historically, older women at the age of menopause and beyond have been diversely characterized and counseled by the medical profession and nonmedical advisers. Some, such as Emma F.A. Drake (entry 1447), saw menopause as an end to women's active sexual lives, a time fraught with danger for their physical and mental well being. Edward Podolsky (entry 1451), writing in the 1930s, maintained that sexual desire in women often increased after menopause, and might be channeled into such directions as kleptomania or exhibitionism. More recent writers have taken a more rational approach to the subject, and there has even been one book-length study of sexual behavior in older people, The Starr-Weiner Report on Sex and Sexuality in the Mature Years (entry 1453).

Works dealing with the sexual behavior and problems of mentally and physically disabled women range from self-help literature, such as the guides prepared by the United Ostomy Association, to studies of the impact of particular disabilities on sexual functioning. Implicit in much of this material is a recognition that disabled people have the same right to lead sexually fulfilling lives as do individuals without disabilities.

Studies of women prisoners and girl delinquents fall into two categories. First, there are those, such as the works of Rose Giallombardo (entries 1494, 1495) and Alice Propper (entry 1502) on women's prison populations, which attempt to define and describe the dimensions of sexuality in institutionalized populations. A second type of investigation examines the causes of so-called delinquent sexual behavior among girls and women. Edith Abbott and Sophonisba P. Breckinridge's The Delinquent Child and the Home (entry 1492) is a classic of this genre and, like many studies of this type, documents

305

the double standard that still leads to the criminalization of girls'
--but not boys'--sexual and sex-related behavior.

Transsexuals and other individuals with sexual identity problems
are the final group included in this section. Still an area of controversy, transsexualism has been criticized by such feminist writers
as Janice Raymond (entry 1535), who sees it as a scheme fostered by
the medical establishment to perpetuate gender-role stereotyping and
women's oppression. Less controversial perhaps are the efforts to as-
sign sexual identities to individuals with blurred or confused genetic
and endocrinological configurations. Regardless of its focus, work in
this field has major implications for the definition of women's gender-
role and psychosexual functioning.

OLDER WOMEN

1446   BEALE, G. COURTENAY. Woman's Change of Life. New York:
       Self-Science Institute, 1934. 164 pp.
           Beale, like many writers on menopause, sees it as a quasi-
       pathological condition, necessitating vigilance over both mental
       and physical health. A "normal" amount of sexual activity during
       adult life is seen by Beale as the best preparation for a trouble-
       free menopause. He warns women with little or no sexual experience
       as well as those given to sexual excess that they may expect to
       suffer inordinately. Sexual excess, Beale also believes, may
       hasten the menopause.
           Another theory the author supports is that menopause throws
       woman's sexual life into total disarray. Most women experience
       "just about the time when the great change looms bodefully near,
       an Indian summer of desire, a renewed longing for love and its
       physical satisfactions." This is an excellent example of meno-
       pausal folklore masquerading under the guise of science.

1447   DRAKE, EMMA FRANCES ANGELL. What a Woman of Forty-five Ought
       to Know. Philadelphia: Vir, 1902. 211 pp.
           One of the popular Self and Sex Series written by Drake, Mary
       Wood-Allen, and Sylvanus Stall, What a Woman of Forty-five Ought to
       Know dealt with menopause. Noting that physicians had long taken
       the erroneous view that the menopause was a crisis, Drake maintained
       that it should have no more effect on a healthy woman than the pas-
       sage from childhood to puberty. Given this view, it is rather
       ironic that Drake emphasized the role of nervousness, weariness,
       hot flashes, sweating, and so on, in characterizing this time of
       woman's life and even devoted a chapter to changes in the hair,
       teeth, and eyes. She advocated cessation of sexual activity and,
       in a chapter for husbands, noted "The physical has had its day.
       . . . While it is a physical loss to you, it is a positive harm
       to your wife," assuming that women would feel no sexual desire
       during or after menopause. She also believed that sexual excess
       as demanded by husbands in earlier life would have an adverse

impact during menopause, as would the practice of contraception or the procurement of abortions.

1448 GALLICHAN, WALTER MATTHEW. The Critical Age of Woman. London: T. Werner Laurie, 1920. 160 pp.

The artificiality of modern civilization, coupled with a general ignorance of sexual matters, has led to the perception of menopause as a time of danger to woman's mind and body. Gallichan maintained that such a threat could be alleviated by education and especially adherence to the laws of sexual periodicity during woman's premenopausal years. Yet this work contains certain contradictions. Gallichan at one point argues that women do not exhibit as much sexual desire as men, claiming later that the intensity of erotic desire is equal in both sexes. Menopause is ostensibly a normal function, yet he goes into great detail about various mental aberrations supposedly occurring at that time. Certainly, there is no ultrafeminism in a statement such as this: "The mind and body of a normal woman cry out literally for sex love and maternity."

1449 HUTTON, ISABEL GALLOWAY EMSLIE. The Hygiene of the Change in Women (the Climacteric). London: William Heinemann, 1936. 110 pp.

This popular account, by the author of The Hygiene of Marriage, was based on European and American sources, but includes no documentation. Hutton's main purpose is to dispel much of the ignorance and fear that typify women's thinking about menopause. She presents a thorough discussion of the physiology of the entire menstrual cycle, which she regards as neither an illness nor a pathological condition. Hutton discusses sexuality in relation to both the menstrual period and menopause. While not recommending intercourse during the period for esthetic reasons, she denies that the practice is harmful. Hutton sees no reason for an alteration in sexual behavior during or after menopause and observes that women can continue intercourse with orgasm to an indefinite age. She also provides extensive suggestions on personal hygiene and health care.

1450 KAUFMAN, SHERWIN A. The Ageless Woman: Menopause, Hormones and the Quest for Youth. Englewood Cliffs, N.J.: Prentice-Hall, 1967. 191 pp.

This well-written, popular account takes a fairly conservative, yet common sense approach to questions of hormonal deficiency and estrogen replacement and is in sharp contrast to the Feminine Forever type of proselytizing for eternal youth through estrogen. Kaufman is particularly concerned with distinguishing between menopausal problems that are definitely caused by hormonal and other physiological changes and other conditions that are more likely to be culturally determined. One chapter is devoted to atrophic vaginitis, a thinning and drying of vaginal tissues which may lead to painful intercourse. An extensive bibliography includes both historical and contemporary references to the menopause, hormones, and related topics.

1451   PODOLSKY, EDWARD. Young Women Past Forty: A Modern Sex and
        Health Primer of the Critical Years. New York: National
        Library Press, 1934. 245 pp.
            Typical of Podolsky's many contributions to popular sex and
        health literature, Young Women Past Forty includes recommendations
        for diet and exercise. The focus of the book, however, is menopause
        and its impact on sexual behavior. Podolsky even includes a chapter
        on premenopausal sex, where he observes that woman's sexual nature
        is often misunderstood. He agrees with Havelock Ellis that it is
        more diffuse, but certainly not inferior to man's. Podolsky adopts
        the view that not only does sexual desire in women persist after
        menopause but it may increase or be channeled into "abnormal" di-
        rections, such as lesbianism, kleptomania, or exhibitionism. He
        suggests sublimation as one means of successfully dealing with
        sexual urges at this time and also offers suggestions for increas-
        ing sexual desire. The concluding chapter is, oddly, entitled "The
        New Woman in the Soviet Union."

1452   RETY, JOSEPH. The Change of Life. London: Pearson, 1939.
        158 pp.
            Rety believed that fear, anxiety, and worry based on lack of
        knowledge were responsible for a large percentage of the difficul-
        ties experienced by women during menopause. Blaming the churches
        for fostering the belief that sex is for impregnation only and that
        cessation of this possibility means an end to sexual activity as
        well, Rety recommended a positive outlook: "In the vast majority
        of cases a woman's sexual appetite remains the same during the
        'change' as it was before." Much of the book is devoted to a dis-
        cussion of the physiology of menstruation and menopause, including
        demographic and constitutional factors. Rety believed that women
        could be divided into five types--picnica, leptosomes, athletic,
        infantile, and intersexual--each of which had a characteristic re-
        action to menopause. In addition to Dr. Rety's narrative, the book
        included an advertisement for Menopax Tablets, a patent medicine
        alleged to "banish all the unpleasant symptoms."

1453   STARR, BERNARD D., and MARCELLA BAKUR WEINER. The Starr-Weiner
        Report on Sex and Sexuality in the Mature Years. New York:
        Stein and Day, 1981. 302 pp.
            Stereotyped, ageist views of older people usually deny their
        sexual lives. In an effort to gather data on actual attitudes and
        behavior in this group, Starr and Weiner distributed over 5,700
        questionnaires to various seniors' groups and other contacts. This
        report is based on the 800 returns they received from people rang-
        ing in age from sixty to ninety-one. Of these, 518 were from women
        and the remainder from men. Obviously, given the authors' discus-
        sion of this sample's composition, it could never be construed as
        representing older Americans as a whole. Nevertheless, with the
        paucity of information in this area, the study provides at least
        a beginning for future work. Among the authors' findings: a
        strong, continuing interest in sex exists after sixty; most of the

women are orgasmic and always have been; and for a majority, living together without marriage is acceptable. Starr and Weiner present verbatim comments from the open-ended questionnaire responses, as well as statistical tables, suggestions for improving sexuality in the older years, and predictions for the future. Readers should note especially their comments on the negative attitudes of some specialists and administrators of programs for older people to the study of such a topic as well as administration of the questionnaire itself.

1454   TILT, EDWARD JOHN. The Change of Life in Health and Disease: A Practical Treatise on the Nervous and Other Affections Incidental to Women at the Decline of Life. 2d ed. London: John Churchill, 1857. 307 pp.

Women called it "the dodging time," and E.J. Tilt adopted this phrase to indicate that part of a woman's life when the symptoms of menopause made their first appearance. Tilt was convinced, largely on the basis of his own observations at the Farringdon General Dispensary and Lying-In Charity and other London institutions, that menopause was a critical period of life, one that could lead to a marked improvement of health. Therefore, women's symptoms at this time should be taken especially seriously. Although his primary concern was with physiology and pathology, Tilt also observed certain characteristics of women's sexuality during this period, especially in chapter 5 on the so-called hygiene of the change of life.

Sexual intercourse at this time could cause uterine disorders, and the general atrophy of the organs should discourage entering into matrimony: "I believe sexual impulse at the c. of life to be generally an anomalous if not a morbid impulse, depending upon either neuralgic or inflammatory affections of the genital organs." Tilt also defined nymphomania as "the almost irresistible desire to relieve the irritation of the pudenda by friction," but distinguished it from erotomania, which was caused when "the mind is viciously inclined," distinctions not commonly made in the literature. Details of fifty-seven cases are presented.

1455   CHRISTENSON, CORNELIA V., and ALAN BLAINE JOHNSON. "Sexual Patterns in a Group of Older Never-married Women." Journal of Geriatric Psychiatry 6, no. 1 (1973):80-98.

1456   CHRISTENSON, CORNELIA V., and JOHN H. GAGNON. "Sexual Behavior in a Group of Older Women." Journal of Gerontology 20, no. 3 (July 1965):351-56.

1457   COLLISI, HARRISON S. "Marriage after Forty." Journal of the Michigan State Medical Society 40, no. 12 (December 1941):965-69.

1458   DALY, MICHAEL JOSEPH. "Sexual Attitudes in Menopausal and Post-menopausal Women." Medical Aspects of Human Sexuality 2, no. 5 (May 1968):48-53.

1459   DENBER, HERMAN C.B. "Sexual Problems in the Mature Female." Psychosomatics 9, no. 4 (July-August 1968):40-43.

1460   GAITZ, CHARLES M.   "Brief Guide to Office Counseling: Sexual
       Activity During Menopause." Medical Aspects of Human Sexuality
       8, no. 12 (December 1974):67-68.

1461   KAUFMAN, SHERWIN A.   "Menopause and Sex." Sexual Behavior 1,
       no. 2 (May 1971):58-63.

1462   LANER, MARY RIEGE.   "Growing Older Female: Heterosexual and
       Homosexual." Journal of Homosexuality 4, no. 3 (Spring 1979):
       267-75.

1463   MINNIGERODE, FRED A., and MARCY R. ADELMAN.   "Elderly Homosexual
       Women and Men: Report on a Pilot Study." Family Coordinator
       27, no. 4 (October 1978):451-56.

1464   MOZLEY, PAUL D.   "Woman's Capacity for Orgasm after Menopause."
       Medical Aspects of Human Sexuality 9, no. 8 (August 1975):104-5+.

1465   NEWMAN, GUSTAVE, and CLAUDE R. NICHOLS.   "Sexual Activities and
       Attitudes in Older Persons." Journal of the American Medical
       Association 173, no. 1 (7 May 1960):33-35.

1466   PFEIFFER, ERIC.   "Geriatric Sex Behavior." Medical Aspects of
       Human Sexuality 3, no. 7 (July 1969):19-28.

1467   PREVEN, DAVID W.   "Brief Guide to Office Counseling: Sexual
       Problems of the Widowed." Medical Aspects of Human Sexuality
       9, no. 2 (February 1975):135-36.

1468   RENSHAW, DOMEENA.   "Sexuality and Depression in Adults and the
       Elderly." Medical Aspects of Human Sexuality 9, no. 9 (September
       1975):40-62.

1469   SORG, DAVID A., and MARGARET B. SORG.   "Sexual Satisfaction in
       Maturing Women." Medical Aspects of Human Sexuality 9, no. 2
       (February 1975):62-79.

1470   TAVRIS, CAROL.   "The Sexual Lives of Women over 60." MS. 6,
       no. 1 (July 1977):62-65.

1471   TAYLOR, J. MADISON.   "The Sex Impulse after Maturity." Medical
       Review of Reviews 24, no. 11 (November 1918):665-71.

1472   THEWLIS, MALFORD W.   "Love in Old Age." Medical Review of
       Reviews 28, no. 6 (June 1922):279-86.

1473   WEINBERG, JACK.   "Sexuality in Later Life." Medical Aspects of
       Human Sexuality 5, no. 4 (April 1971):216-27.

DISABLED WOMEN

1474   BINDER, DONALD P. <u>Sex, Courtship and the Single Ostomate</u>. Los
        Angeles: United Ostomy Association, 1973. 20 pp. ISR.
            One of the pamphlets prepared by the United Ostomy Association
        to assist ostomates in adapting to their life situation, <u>Sex,</u>
        <u>Courtship and the Single Ostomate</u> urges flexibility in approaching
        the question of sexual technique: "Working out methods may take
        some research of books on alternate ways, a bit of practice, some
        extra patience, and most of all, understanding by both parties."
        Particular emphasis is placed on how ostomates should tell prospec-
        tive sexual partners about their condition.

1475   KEMPTON, WINIFRED. <u>Sex Education for Persons with Disabilities</u>
        <u>That Hinder Learning: A Teacher's Guide</u>. North Scituate, Mass.:
        Duxbury Press, 1975. 162 pp.
            Kempton, who is associated with the Planned Parenthood League
        of Pennsylvania, uses real-life experiences as well as material from
        her earlier publications and audiovisual productions in this manual
        for teachers of persons with learning disabilities. Emphasis is
        placed on developing responsible, well-informed patterns of sexual
        behavior. Much of the book is concerned with teaching techniques
        and consciousness raising in order to make teachers more effective.
        The resource list at the end of the book is especially complete,
        although, regrettably, the book list does not reflect much of the
        new research on sexuality, especially that relating to women.

1476   LANDIS, CARNEY, and M. MARJORIE BOLIS. <u>Personality and Sexuality</u>
        <u>of the Physically Handicapped Woman</u>. New York: Paul B. Hoeber,
        1942. 171 pp.
            Continuing the study of psychosexual development begun by
        Landis in <u>Sex in Development</u> (entry 977), Landis and Bolis turn
        their attention in this work to women with four types of physical
        disability: chronic heart disease, spastic paralysis, epilepsy,
        and orthopedic disabilities. One hundred women, twenty-five from
        each disability group, were selected, with controlled interviews,
        medical histories, and Rorschach Ink Blot tests serving as data
        sources. All the women had been disabled at or before thirteen
        years of age.
            The disabled group was compared with the 295 women studied
        in the earlier project. Landis and Bolis found that although the
        different physical disabilities did not yield equivalently differ-
        ent personality types, the simple fact of being disabled could be
        linked to hyposexuality and psychological immaturity. Overall, how-
        ever, psychosexuality was not found to be an important factor in
        personality formation. Statistical tables are included in an ap-
        pendix.

1477   NORRIS, CAROL, and ED GAMBRELL. <u>Sex, Pregnancy and the Female</u>
        <u>Ostomate</u>. Los Angeles: United Ostomy Association, 1972. 20
        pp. ISR.

311

The United Ostomy Association has prepared a series of educational materials in order to assist individuals undergoing or performing radical surgery to remove the bladder or intestines. Two of their pamphlets deal with sexual concerns. Sex, Pregnancy and the Female Ostomate discusses the impact that the various types of ostomies may have on sexual functioning and pregnancy, always keeping the two questions separate. Written with good humor, albeit with a bit of gender stereotyping, the pamphlet urges individual adaptations to situations. Doctors' negative attitudes toward ostomate pregnancy are shown to be based on subjective perceptions rather than medical facts.

1478 PATTULLO, ANN. Puberty in the Girl Who Is Retarded. New York: National Association for Retarded Children, 1969. 37 pp. NLM.
Written for the mothers of retarded girls, this pamphlet contains information on such subjects as sexual behavior, marriage, and especially menstruation and menstrual hygiene, where emphasis is placed on practical methods of teaching. Masturbation is seen as inevitable; Pattullo stresses how it can be managed so that it becomes a private rather than public activity. Heterosexual activity is treated somewhat gingerly, and although the author suggests some behavior rules to minimize the possibility of unwanted pregnancy, more information and suggestions are needed on how to explain sexual feelings to retarded daughters. The "Where Can I Go for Help" section mentions only nurses, physicians, and the PTA.

1479 Sexuality and Disability. Human Sciences Press, 1978-.
Sexuality and Disability, which began publication in the spring of 1978, is a journal "devoted to the study of sex in physical and mental illness." Running the gamut from diabetes to drug addiction, this wide-ranging periodical includes clinical practice reports, case studies, practice guidelines, news of developments in sex education and counseling for the disabled, and similar material.

1480 BREGMAN, SUE. "Sexual Adjustment of Spinal Cord Injured Women." Sexuality and Disability 1, no. 2 (Summer 1978):85-92.

1481 COLE, THEODORE M. "Sexuality and Physical Disabilities." Archives of Sexual Behavior 4, no. 4 (July 1975):389-403.

1482 COLE, THEODORE M., and MAUREEN R. STEVENS. "Rehabilitation Professionals and Sexual Counseling for Spinal Cord Injured Adults." Archives of Sexual Behavior 4, no. 6 (November 1975): 631-38.

1483 FITTING, MELINDA, et al. "Self-concept and Sexuality of Spinal Cord Injured Women." Archives of Sexual Behavior 7, no. 2 (March 1978):143-56.

1484 FLOOR, LUCRETIA, et al. "Socio-sexual Problems in Mentally

Handicapped Females." Training School Bulletin 68, no. 2 (August 1971):106–12.

1485   FRANK, DEBORAH, et al. "Mastectomy and Sexual Behavior: A Pilot Study." Sexuality and Disability 1, no. 1 (Spring 1978): 16–26.

1486   GRIFFITH, ERNEST R., and ROBERTA B. TRIESCHMANN. "Sexual Functioning in Women with Spinal Cord Injury." Archives of Physical Medicine and Rehabilitation 56, no. 1 (January 1975): 18–21.

1487   LYONS, ALBERT S. "Brief Guide to Office Counseling: Sex after Ileostomy and Colostomy." Medical Aspects of Human Sexuality 9, no. 1 (January 1975):107–8.

1488   MONEY, JOHN. "Phantom Orgasm in the Dreams of Paraplegic Men and Women." Archives of General Psychiatry 3, no. 4 (October 1960):373–82.

1489   MOONEY, THOMAS O.; THEODORE M. COLE, and RICHARD A. CHILGREN. Sexual Options for Paraplegics and Quadraplegics. Boston: Little, Brown, 1975. 111 pp.

1490   MOURAD, MAHMOUD, and WU SHUNG CHIU. "Marital-Sexual Adjustment of Amputees." Medical Aspects of Human Sexuality 8, no. 2 (February 1974):47–57.

1491   ROMANO, MARY D. "Sexuality and the Disabled Female." Sexuality and Disability 1, no. 1 (Spring 1978):27–33.

WOMEN PRISONERS AND GIRL DELINQUENTS

1492   BRECKINRIDGE, SOPHONISBA P., and EDITH ABBOTT. The Delinquent Child and the Home. New York: Russell Sage Foundation, Charities Publication Committee, 1912. 355 pp.
       There is no clearer evidence of the working of the double standard than this study of juvenile offenders in Cook County (Chicago), Illinois, between 1899 and 1909. Of the youth brought before the court, 31 percent of the girls but only 1.6 percent of the boys were charged with sexual immorality, and the evidence clearly shows that other charges (such as incorrigibility) were often closely linked to a girl's sexual attitudes or behavior. Moreover, girl offenders were sentenced to institutionalization (as compared to fines or probation) at a rate more than twice that of boys. Despite Breckinridge and Abbott's feminist background, they seemed unable to engage in the creative analysis that would have explored this and related issues (such as economic incentives to prostitution), contenting themselves with bemoaning the "perils besetting their [the girls'] virtue." This reluctance may have

stemmed from an underlying prudery such as we see in this note appended to the sample printed forms used in their study: "It has been thought best not to publish copies of two schedules dealing with the Delinquent Girl where Delinquency Involves Sex Relationship. Anyone engaged in a similar inquiry may obtain copies of these schedules from the Chicago School of Civics and Philanthropy."

There is much valuable information in this study on the economic and social conditions of juvenile offenders' lives, as well as an abstract of juvenile court laws in the United States, narrative descriptions of fifty typical girl offenders and their families, and statistics on a wide range of subjects. The authors' lack of analysis of certain issues, while regrettable, is only a minor deficiency in what is in other respects a pioneering piece of work.

1493   FERNALD, MABEL R., et al. A Study of Women Delinquents in New York State. New York: Century Co., 1920. 542 pp.
This study, a publication of the Bureau of Social Hygiene, analyzes characteristics of several groups of incarcerated women in New York, as well as a group of probation cases. One chapter, "History of Sex Irregularities," relates directly to sexual behavior, and focuses on prostitution and promiscuity. It reaches beyond these topics, however, and provides information on age at first sex offense, manner of sex education received by the offender, racial differences in offense patterns, venereal disease, and other social factors. This is not a study of prison conditions, but of those factors that led to the women being incarcerated. There are over two hundred statistical tables in the book, as well as a bibliography.

1494   GIALLOMBARDO, ROSE. The Social World of Imprisoned Girls: A Comparative Study of Institutions for Juvenile Delinquents. New York: John Wiley & Sons, 1974. 317 pp.
Between 1968 and 1973, Giallombardo studied three correctional institutions for juvenile girls in three states. Her goal was to understand the nature and structure of social relationships of these young female offenders within the institution and how these related to the culture outside, as well as to official institutional goals.

Giallombardo concluded that the social system was remarkably similar to that found in adult female prisons, involving elaborate family units and sex- and gender-role differentiation in a lesbian context. A separate chapter for each institution is devoted to an analysis of how the system operates.

1495   _____. Society of Women: A Study of a Women's Prison. New York: John Wiley & Sons, 1966. 248 pp.
Data for this study of a women's prison community was gathered during 1962-63 at the Federal Reformatory for Women in Alderson, West Virginia. Giallombardo focuses on the prison as a system of roles and functions. The development of lesbian relationships as

a substitute for heterosexual behavior receives detailed treatment: "The uniqueness of the situation compels the inmate to redefine and attach new meanings to homosexual behavior within the prison structure." Included is material on butch/femme role playing and the importance of romantic love, highlighted by reprints of "kites," or prison love letters. Also useful are a glossary of prison terms and the author's description of her methodology and ways of approaching and gaining the confidence of the study population.

1496   GLIGOR, ALYCE MAPP. "Incest and Sexual Delinquency: A Comparative Analysis of Two Forms of Sexual Behavior in Minor Females." Ph.D. dissertation, Western Reserve University, 1966. 299 pp. ISR, LC.

This very interesting dissertation examines and compares psychological, social, and educational characteristics of two groups, minor female incest victims and minor female sexual delinquents, in Cuyahoga County (Cleveland), Ohio. Gligor begins with a thorough review of historical, literary, psychological, and case literature on incest. She then examines a test population based on court cases occurring primarily between 1949 and 1965. She concludes that "fewer significant differences between the incest and nonincest groups emerged than would have been expected on the basis of the literature regarding incest." Incidentally, this study provides information on the use of court and other public records for historical and sociological research, including sampling techniques and records-keeping policies.

1497   GOLDBERG, JACOB A., and ROSAMOND W. GOLDBERG. Girls on City Streets: A Study of 1400 Cases of Rape. New York: Foundation Books, 1940. 358 pp.

This study of 1,400 cases of rape and attempted rape of girls aged sixteen and younger was based on New York City records "covering several years." The authors are not more specific than this about the source of their information, and the text of the numerous case histories gives no firm indication that these were based on court or social service agency materials. The Goldbergs found that the rape situations fell into two categories: those where the victims were forced and those where the girls were more or less willing. A variety of types of case groupings are described: runaways, broken homes, crowded homes, and bad environment. The authors also deal with offenses against younger children and incest. A summary chapter presents statistical material. The authors call for more active efforts on the part of parents, the community, and schools in promoting sex education aimed at preventing such sexual incidents from occurring.

1498   KAGAN, HERMAN. "Prostitution and Sexual Promiscuity among Adolescent Female Offenders." Ph.D. dissertation, University of Arizona, 1969. 167 pp. ISR, LC.

Human behavior can be seen either as a product of conditions and forces or as a symbolic expression. Kagan uses these two models to examine prostitution and sexual promiscuity among teenage female offenders. Four groups of forty girls each were studied. The groups were categorized as (a) prostitutes, (b) sexually promiscuous females, (c) nonpromiscuous delinquents, and (d) nonpromiscuous normals. Kagan concludes that neither the symptomatic (behavior as product) nor the symbolic view of prostitution or promiscuity serves as useful predictor of the results he achieved from tests of his subjects. He argues for a new synthesis of psychological models combining elements of both theories. His ideas are rather abstract, but should be of interest, especially to historians trying to develop theoretical historical models for the study of sexuality.

1499   KARPMAN, BENJAMIN. The Sexual Offender and His Offenses. New
       York: Julian Press, 1954. 744 pp.
       Karpman, who was chief psychotherapist at St. Elizabeth's
Hospital in Washington, D.C., includes only a small amount of material on women. The first section of the book, which is a synopsis of previously published research and case descriptions, would seem to indicate either that women sex offenders were not a common subject for research or, as Karpman suggests, that they were simply not present in significant numbers when compared with men. Karpman includes homosexuality among his categories of sex offenses, with almost all of his discussion focusing on male homosexuals. Convoluted organization makes this a difficult book to use.

1500   LION, ERNEST G., et al. An Experiment in the Psychiatric
       Treatment of Promiscuous Girls. San Francisco: City and County
       of San Francisco Department of Public Health, 1945. 68 pp.
       This pamphlet reports on a study conducted between January
1943 and June 1944 in San Francisco. Its overall objective was to determine the motivations for promiscuity in young women (age twenty five and under) in order to curb this promiscuity as one step in halting the spread of venereal disease, especially among defense workers and male members of the armed forces. For a number of reasons, including inconsistent research methodology, the conclusions of the study are of perhaps less interest than some of its basic assumptions. One, of course, was that women should be held responsible for venereal disease infection and that men needed to be protected from them. More significant, however, were the definitions of promiscuity used in selecting women for the study. This labeling selected (1) married women who had engaged in any extramarital sex within the six months prior to selection, (2) any single woman who had had sexual relations with more than one man within that six-month period, and (3) any single woman who had engaged in sexual relations more than twice with only one man during the same time frame. These women had been referred to the study by the San Francisco City Clinic, to which they were summoned after having been named by former partners as probable carriers of venereal disease (i.e., they were allegedly women who had infected men). Three-quarters of them were indeed diseased, but what effect did

such labeling have on the others, especially those in category three? There is a lot of rich material here, regarding both actual behavior and attitudes of public agencies and professional groups. A black/white racial division is maintained in the statistics and interview samples. The "criminalization" of the women is implicit.

1501   POLLAK, OTTO, and ALFRED S. FRIEDMAN, eds. Family Dynamics and Female Sexual Delinquency. Palo Alto, Calif.: Science and Behavior Books, 1969. 210 pp.
        This collection of essays consists, in part, of revised papers presented at a seminar on the role of the family system in influencing the personality and behavior of sexually active adolescent girls. The seminar was part of a larger project on family counseling for adolescent girls with sexual behavior problems. Other independently prepared papers were added to the seminar materials.
        The chapters move from a discussion of family dynamics to material on socioeconomic and cultural factors, psychology, family interaction, and methods of therapy. A variety of perspectives— psychiatric, psychological, sociological, and social work—are represented by the authors, but the editors do not present any final summary or conclusions that might integrate the presentation.

1502   PROPPER, ALICE M. Prison Homosexuality: Myth and Reality. Lexington, Mass.: Lexington Books, 1981. 237 pp.
        Propper begins by summarizing previous writing on prison homosexuality, much of which she finds to be unsatisfactory. Her immediate purpose in this study is to test the theoretical controversy regarding the importance of preprison and prison variables by comparing data from three coed and four all-female juvenile correctional institutions. She found that crushes were popular and incorporated male/female gender roles, accompanied by assumed "family" patterns. Institution officials regarded this so-called homosexuality as a social problem, and "considerable time and energy was spent in devising and maintaining rules to prevent it." Propper concludes that prison homosexuality among young women is associated with a rejection of the traditional female role and a desire for power and dominance. She also found that participation in quasi families was not usually a prelude to homosexuality or related to it. Critical of the Giallombardo prison studies (entries 1494, 1495), Propper includes an extensive bibliography and examples of her questionnaires and other research tools.

1503   VEDDER, CLYDE B., and PATRICIA G. KING. Problems of Homosexuality in Corrections. Springfield, Ill.: Charles C. Thomas, 1967. 63 pp.
        This short overview includes one chapter on female homosexuality in prisons. Documentation for generalizations is often absent, while other sources cited are of questionable validity (cf., Jess Stearn's The Grapevine: A Report on the Secret World of the Lesbian). It should be noted that King was on the staff of the

Federal Reformatory for Women at Alderson, West Virginia, while Vedder was a professor of sociology and anthropology at Northern Illinois University. Despite their credentials, they produced only a cursory report.

1504   WARD, DAVID A., and GENE G. KASSEBAUM. Women's Prison: Sex and Social Structure. Chicago: Aldine, 1965. 269 pp.
       Ward and Kassebaum did not intend to focus this study on lesbian relationships in prison when they began, but made this decision when they realized that the homosexual/heterosexual distinction was the key to understanding female prisoner types. Interacting with the population of the California Institution for Women at Frontera, they collected interviews with forty-five women, worked with a smaller group of "experienced, articulate, and perceptive women," and submitted questionnaires to both inmates and staff. Their research methods in some respects are questionable, for example, their admission that "we sacrificed statistical representativeness of the sample in favor of respondents with prison experience and the ability to communicate." Equally suspect is their use of staff and inmate estimates as if they were facts writ in stone.
       The authors view lesbian experiences in prison in a negative light and as a problem that prison staff needs to confront and eliminate. Despite their conclusion that prison lesbianism is temporary and situational and that it provides the inmates with a much needed sense of identity and self, they refuse to see it as a necessary survival mechanism and something that provides much positive good during the inmates' prison experience. Moreover, their generalization that lesbianism is a matter of "official" concern only in prison—not in society at large—is naive and displays a lack of awareness and sensitivity in an area with which they should have been more familiar.

1505   WULFFEN, ERICH. Woman as a Sexual Criminal. Translated by David Berger. New York: American Ethnological Press, 1934. 528 pp.
       Originally published in Berlin in 1923, this work of German criminologist Erich Wulffen is rooted in the concept that criminal tendencies in woman stand in a fixed, biologically determined relation to her sex life. Drawing on the work of various European writers on crime and sexuality, Wulffen exalts in wild generalizations, such as this typical one: "The old woman, robbed of all her sexuality, and often of an unpleasant or even witch-like appearance, shows marked traits of cold egotism, sordid greed and mean cruelty, probably adducible to the final extinction of her sexual life: so intimately tied, physically and spiritually is woman with her sex." There is a decidedly sensational cast to Wulffen's discussion of specific types of female sexual crime—"immoral commerce with children," prostitution, adultery, and so on—and he goes to great lengths to prove the sexual origins of such crimes as shoplifting, poisoning, and suicide. Several pathetic photographs (one of an

318

eighty-seven-year-old female transvestite) accompany the text.
This translation was apparently made from the third, revised German
edition, published in 1931, since case citations run up through
1930.

1506   BALL, JOHN C., and NELL LOGAN. "Early Sexual Behavior of Lower-
       class Delinquent Girls." Journal of Criminal Law, Criminology
       and Police Science 51, no. 2 (July-August 1960):209-14.

1507   BINGHAM, ANNE T. "Determinants of Sex Delinquency in Adolescent
       Girls Based on Intensive Studies of 500 Cases." Journal of the
       American Institute of Criminal Law and Criminology 13, no. 4
       (February 1923):494-586.

1508   BURNET, ANNE. "A Study of Delinquent Girls." Institution
       Quarterly 3, no. 2 (30 June 1912):47-53.

1509   "Causes of Sex-delinquency in Girls." Journal of Social Hygiene
       13, no. 2 (February 1927):109-14.

1510   FROST, CARRIE A. "The Degenerate Girl." Wisconsin Medical
       Journal 12, no. 9 (February 1914):287-89.

1511   HALLECK, SEYMOUR, and MARVIN HERSKO. "Homosexual Behavior in
       a Correctional Institution for Adolescent Girls." American
       Journal of Orthopsychiatry 32, no. 5 (October 1962):911-17.

1512   HAMILTON, ALICE. "Venereal Diseases in Institutions for Women
       and Girls." Proceedings of the National Conference of Charities
       and Corrections 37 (1910):53-56.

1513   HAMMER, MAX. "Hypersexuality in Reformatory Women." Corrective
       Psychiatry and Journal of Social Therapy 15, no. 4 (Winter 1969):
       20-26.

1514   McCORD, CLINTON P. "One Hundred Female Offenders, a Study of
       the Mentality of Prostitutes and 'Wayward' Girls." Journal of
       the American Institute of Criminal Law and Criminology 6 (May
       1915-March 1916):385-407.

1515   MACY, MARY SUTTON. "Criminal Tendencies of Adolescence in
       Girls." Woman's Medical Journal 20, no. 6 (June 1910):115-18.

1516   MINER, MAUDE E. "Reformatory Girls; a Study of Girls Paroled
       from the New York State Industrial School and the House of
       Refuge on Randall's Island." Charities and the Commons 17, no.
       20 (February 1907):903-19.

1517   MORSE, FANNIE F. "Delinquent Girls." Institution Quarterly 3,
       no. 1 (31 March 1912):115-18.

1518   NORRIS, LINDA. "Comparison of Two Groups in a Southern State
       Women's Prison: Homosexual Behavior versus Nonhomosexual Be-
       havior." Psychological Reports 34, no. 1 (February 1974):75-78.

1519   OTIS, MARGARET. "A Study in the Borderland of Morality."
       Psychological Clinic 8, no. 7 (15 December 1914):201-7.

1520   PURCELL-GUILD, JUNE. "Study of One Hundred and Thirty-One
       Delinquent Girls Held at the Juvenile Detention House in
       Chicago, 1917." Journal of the American Institute of Criminal
       Law and Criminology 10, no. 3 (November 1919):441-76.

1521   PYLE, W.H. "A Study of Delinquent Girls." Psychological Clinic
       8, no. 5 (15 October 1914):143-48.

1522   ROBERTS, ROBERT E.; LAURENCE ABRAMS, and JOHN FINCH. "'Delin-
       quent' Sexual Behavior among Adolescents." Medical Aspects of
       Human Sexuality 7, no. 1 (January 1973):162-83.

1523   SEARS, FREDERICK W. "The Wayward Girl." Vermont Medical Monthly
       18, no. 1 (15 January 1912):7-9.

1524   SULLIVAN, ELIZABETH A., and EDITH R. SPAULDING. "The Extent and
       Significance of Gonorrhea in a Reformatory for Women." Journal
       of the American Medical Association 66, no. 2 (8 January 1916):
       95-102.

1525   TALBOT, EUGENE S. "Juvenile Female Delinquents." Alienist and
       Neurologist 22, no. 4 (October 1901):689-94; 23, no. 1 (January
       1902):21-26; no. 2 (April 1902):163-75.

1526   TALLANT, ALICE WELD. "A Medical Study of Delinquent Girls."
       Bulletin of the American Academy of Medicine 13, no. 5 (October
       1912):283-93.

       TRANSSEXUALS AND PEOPLE WITH SEXUAL IDENTITY PROBLEMS

1527   BENJAMIN, HARRY. The Transsexual Phenomenon. New York: Julian
       Press, 1966. 286 pp.
          This is perhaps the first book-length account of transsexual-
       ism to be written by a member of the medical profession. Benjamin,
       a New York physician specializing in the treatment of transsexuals
       (he did not, however, perform transsexual surgery), focuses here
       on male transsexuals, men who wish to become women. Female trans-
       sexuals, whose numbers are far smaller, receive only one chapter.
          Benjamin discusses such topics as the etiology of trans-
       sexualism, its relationship to transvestism and homosexuality, and
       the results of operations on fifty-one cases. There are also some
       related essays by Gobind B. Lal, Richard Green, and R.E.L. Masters
       and an extensive bibliography complied by Green. Copies of the

book prepared for medical distribution include a sixteen-page photo supplement.

1528   BOGDAN, ROBERT, comp. and ed. Being Different: The Autobiography of Jane Fry. New York: John Wiley, 1974. 235 pp.
       One of the undercurrents of feminist thinking about sexuality is the quandary over male-female transsexuals, genetic males who believe they are women and who voluntarily dress and live as women, usually to the point of having sex-change surgery. Janice Raymond's The Transsexual Empire (entry 1535) provides an analytical basis for approaching this problem, but autobiographical accounts, such as this one done in the tradition of the Chicago School of Sociology, are valuable for their depiction of the transsexual's own perception of male and female sex and gender roles, as well as the expectations of those medical people who ultimately control the transsexual's destiny. Being Different is especially good in its depiction of institutional attitudes toward deviance.

1529   Clinics in Plastic Surgery--An International Quarterly 1, no. 2 (April 1974). Special issue on sex assignment and reassignment; intersex and gender identity disorders.
       Edited by Jon K. Meyer, this special issue of Clinics in Plastic Surgery focuses on the treatment of transsexuals and individuals who, because of sex and gender assignment disorders, require surgical and psychological procedures leading to a more definite sex assignment. Essays by such authors as Donald W. Hastings and John Money discuss subjects ranging from surgical construction of genitalia to psychological adjustment of postsurgical transsexuals. There is also material on embryologic and genetic factors and an assessment of the psychology of sex assignment. Some of the chapters appeared elsewhere in different form. Each is fully documented and is usually accompanied by photographs, medical illustrations, and technical charts. Much of the material on transsexuals is oriented toward the male-to-female transsexual.

1530   GREEN, RICHARD. Sexual Identity Conflict in Children and Adults. New York: Basic Books, 1974. 327 pp.
       A student of both John Money and Robert Stoller, Green adopts a somewhat more cautious attitude than his mentors toward generalizing about the etiology of sexual identity problems, frankly admitting that in the end it remains a "mystery." Nevertheless, in this eminently readable book, Green is concerned with testing theories of sex- and gender-role development, as well as allied questions, such as how hypotheses in the field are best constructed. He reviews psychologic theories of sex and gender identity as well as biological studies. Most of the book, however, consists of verbatim transcripts of clinical interview data with male and female transsexuals, children with gender identity problems, and their families. Roughly equal attention is given to men and women, although Green notes that they are not equivalent in etiology or treatment strategies. A concluding chapter poses problems for future research.

1531   KANDO, THOMAS. <u>Sex Change: The Achievement of Gender Identity</u>
        <u>among Feminized Transsexuals</u>. Springfield, Ill.: Charles C.
        Thomas, 1973. 159 pp.
        This is a unique sociological study of the postoperative
adjustment of seventeen male-to-female transsexuals, all of them
participants in an experimental program at the University of
Minnesota in the late 1960s. Examining the social relations of
individuals who have already undergone surgical sex change, Kando
discusses such topics as attitudes toward sex roles, masculinity,
femininity, gender self-concept, sex definitions, and sex-role
problems. He found that several distinct patterns of adjustment
could be discerned. These included the housewife type (the transsexual "who seeks to marry, settle down, establish middle-class
respectability and passage as a natural female"), the show business
type, the aspiring housewife, and the career woman. Kando concluded
that transsexuals are extremely conservative in their support of
traditional sex and gender roles. This is a skillful analysis and
utilizes such concepts as passing and stigma in its explication of
transsexual behavior.

1532   MARTINO, MARIO, with HARRIETT. <u>Emergence: A Transsexual</u>
        <u>Autobiography</u>. New York: Crown, 1977. 273 pp.
        This is perhaps the only autobiography of a female-to-male
transsexual and illustrates well the transsexual's dilemma over
both sex assignment and gender role. <u>Emergence</u> is especially interesting because Martino attempts to deal with the difference between his feelings toward women and lesbian identity; self-labeling
and self-perception appear to be crucial here. Although much of
the book relates to Martino's experiences in childhood and as a
nun and a nurse, he also comments on the transsexual situation in
general, surgical techniques, legal difficulties, and perceived
differences between male-to-female and female-to-male transsexuals.

1533   MONEY, JOHN, and ANKE A. EHRHARDT. <u>Man & Woman, Boy & Girl:</u>
        <u>The Differentiation and Dimorphism of Gender Identity from</u>
        <u>Conception to Maturity</u>. Baltimore: Johns Hopkins University
        Press, 1972. 311 pp.
        This technical monograph is based on clinical work done at
Johns Hopkins Hospital and School of Medicine as well as on other
investigators' research on sex- and gender-role identity differentiation. Money and Ehrhardt are especially concerned with the interaction between prenatal and postnatal determinants of psychosexual differentiation and include material on such topics as fetal
hormones and the brain and the impact of pubertal hormones on libido and erotic behavior. The chapter "Erotic Dimorphism of Brain
and Behavior" discusses sexual behavior differences between males
and females, such as responses to visual and erotic stimuli.
Readers will want to compare Money and Ehrhardt's views with those
of other workers in this field, such as Robert J. Stoller, since
this is an area of research that apparently thrives on controversy.
Money and Ehrhardt include an extensive bibliography and a glossary
for the neophyte reader.

1534   MONEY, JOHN, and PATRICIA TUCKER. Sexual Signatures: On Being
       a Man or a Woman. Boston: Little, Brown, 1975.   250 pp.
          This is a popular narrative on gender identity and gender
       role and is an obvious spin-off from Money and Anke Ehrhardt's
       1973 work Man & Woman, Boy & Girl (entry 1533).   Unfortunately, the
       translation is too frequently given to unsupported generalizations
       and skewing.   Money and Ehrhardt's 1973 definitions of gender iden-
       tity and gender role are presented to the reader as "official defi-
       nitions" (the authors's term!), and much of the presentation deals
       with problems of transsexuals and other ambiguously sexed individ-
       uals.   A section on homosexuality mentions Sappho but otherwise
       totally ignores women, while a brief summary of transsexualism deals
       only with male-to-female examples.   The authors' primary goal is to
       show how gender identity and gender role are learned and how these
       concepts, once firmly established in an individual, are not sus-
       ceptible to change.   Money and Tucker support a broadening of male
       and female role options, but still maintain the inevitability of
       sex-based roles and identity.

1535   RAYMOND, JANICE G.   The Transsexual Empire: The Making of the
       She-Male.   Boston: Beacon Press, 1979.   220 pp.
          In a feminist critique clearly inspired by the work of such
       theorists as Mary Daly and Adrienne Rich, Janice Raymond views
       transsexualism as a threat to feminism.   Fostered by the medical
       establishment, its ethos is the exchange of one gender stereotype
       for another.   "Transsexualism at this point constitutes a 'socio-
       political program' that is undercutting the movement to eradicate
       sex-role stereotyping and oppression in this culture."   Raymond re-
       views the work of John Money as well as other researchers and prac-
       titioners of transsexualism and concludes that transcendent feminist
       consciousness raising must be offered to potential transsexuals as
       an alternative preferable to that of surgical and hormonal altera-
       tion.   The Transsexual Empire contains much useful insight into the
       relationship between sexual appearance/behavior and gender role as
       well as the role of the male-dominated medical establishment in
       creating the transsexual empire and the ideology of transsexualism.

1536   STOLLER, ROBERT J.   Sex and Gender: On the Development of
       Masculinity and Femininity.   New York: Science House, 1968.
       383 pp.
          Some material in this book, an outgrowth of Stoller's work
       at the Gender Identity Research Clinic at UCLA, appeared earlier
       as journal articles.   Stoller is concerned here with gender iden-
       tity, which he concludes is culturally determined, although influ-
       enced by certain biological forces.   Describing individual cases
       in detail, he does not attempt any statistical validation of his
       findings, but uses a psychoanalytic perspective.   Although he
       maintains that sex and gender are not the same and that gender
       should not be confused with sexual activity and behavior, he vio-
       lates his own precepts more than once, as in chapter 9, where he
       labels one woman's affectation of so-called male gender behavior

as "bisexuality." Stoller's plea for the adoption of more scientific methodology by the psychoanalytic community might well have been heeded by him as he prepared this study.

1537   BARCLAY, DAVID L., and WILLIAM H. STERNBERG. "Women with Male Sex Chromosomes: The Syndromes of Testicular Feminization and XY Gonadal Dygenesis." Journal of the American Medical Women's Association 22, no. 11 (November 1967):885-93.

1538   BENJAMIN, HARRY. "Transvestism and Transsexualism in the Male and Female." Journal of Sex Research 3, no. 2 (May 1967):107-27.

1539   CROSSEN, H.S. "A Study of a Pseudohermaphrodite." Transactions of the American Association of Obstetricians and Gynecologists, 1911 24 (1912):137-52.

1540   DAVENPORT, CHARLES W., and SAUL I. HARRISON. "Gender Identity Change in a Female Adolescent Transsexual." Archives of Sexual Behavior 6, no. 4 (July 1977):327-40.

1541   EHRHARDT, ANKE A.; GUDRUN GRISANTI, and ELIZABETH A. McCAULEY. "Female-to-Male Transsexuals Compared to Lesbians: Behavioral Patterns of Childhood and Adolescence." Archives of Sexual Behavior 8, no. 6 (November 1979):481-90.

1542   EHRHARDT, ANKE A., and JOHN MONEY. "Progestin-induced Hermaphroditism: IQ and Psychosexual Identity in a Study of Ten Girls." Journal of Sex Research 3, no. 1 (February 1967):83-100.

1543   GREEN, FRANK K., and Q.W. HUNTER. "Anent So-called Androgynism." International Journal of Surgery 26, no. 11 (November 1913): 392-99.

1544   HAMBURGER, CHRISTIAN. "The Desire for Change of Sex as Shown by Personal Letters from 465 Men and Women." Acta Endocrinologica 14, no. 4 (1953):361-75.

1545   HAMPSON, JOAN G. "Hermaphroditic Genital Appearance, Rearing and Eroticism in Hyperadrenocortism." Johns Hopkins Hospital Bulletin 96, no. 6 (June 1955):265-73.

1546   HINCHEY, F. "Hermaphroditism, Pseudo-hermaphroditism and Differentiation of Sex." Medical Council 17, no. 5 (May 1912): 172-75.

1547   JACOBI, MARY PUTNAM. "Case of Absent Uterus; with Considerations on the Significance of Hermaphroditism." American Journal of Obstetrics and Diseases of Women and Children 32, no. 4 (October 1895):510-42.

1548 LANGEVIN, R.; D. PAITICH, and B. STEINER. "The Clinical Profile of Male Transsexuals Living as Females Vs. Those Living as Males." Archives of Sexual Behavior 6, no. 2 (March 1977): 143-55.

1549 LEFF, DAVID N. "Genes, Gender, and Genital Reversal." Medical World News 18 (18 April 1977):45-58.

1550 MANNING, JOHN B.; SAMUEL ROBINSON, and NATHANIEL H. BRUSH. "Pseudohermaphroditism (Female Type Predominating)." American Journal of Diseases of Children 35, no. 5 (May 1928):862-65.

1551 MONEY, JOHN; JOAN G. HAMPSON, and JOHN L. HAMPSON. "Hermaphroditism: Recommendations Concerning Assignment of Sex, Change of Sex, and Psychologic Management." Johns Hopkins Hospital Bulletin 97, no. 4 (October 1955):284-300.

1552 _____. "Sexual Incongruities and Psychopathology: The Evidence of Human Hermaphroditism." Johns Hopkins Hospital Bulletin 98, no. 1 (January 1956):43-57.

1553 NEWMAN, LAWRENCE E., and ROBERT J. STOLLER. "Gender Identity Disturbances in Intersexed Patients." American Journal of Psychiatry 124, no. 9 (March 1968):1262-66.

1554 OLES, MIRIAM N. "A Discussion of Transsexualism and Issues in Psychotherapy." American Journal of Orthopsychiatry 47, no. 1 (January 1977):66-74.

1555 PAULY, IRA B. "Female Transsexualism." Archives of Sexual Behavior 3, no. 6 (November 1974):487-526.

1556 PERSON, ETHEL SPECTOR, and LIONEL OVESEY. "The Transsexual Syndrome in Males, Part I." American Journal of Psychotherapy 28, no. 1 (January 1974):4-20.

1557 _____. "The Transsexual Syndrome in Males, Part II." American Journal of Psychotherapy 28, no. 2 (April 1974):174-93.

1558 ROESKE, NANCY A., and ANTHONY G. BANET. "Gender Identity; The Problem of a True Hermaphrodite." Journal of the American Academy of Child Psychiatry 11, no. 1 (January 1972):132-56.

1559 ROHEIM, GEZA. "Aphrodite or the Woman with a Penis." Psychoanalytic Quarterly 14, no. 3 (July 1945):350-90.

1560 ROLLINS, PAUL R. "Female Pseudohermaphroditism." Northwest Medicine 39, no. 5 (May 1940):181-82.

1561 SIMON, ROBERT I. "A Case of Female Transsexualism." American Journal of Psychiatry 123, no. 12 (June 1967):1598-1601.

1562 STOLLER, ROBERT J. "Etiological Factors in Female Transsexualism: A First Approximation." Archives of Sexual Behavior 2, no. 1 (June 1972):47-64.

1563 YARDLEY, KRYSIA M. "Training in Feminine Skills in a Male Transsexual: A Preoperative Procedure." British Journal of Medical Psychology 49, pt. 4 (December 1976):329-40.

Sexual Dysfunction and Related Problems

Sexual dysfunction has come into general use comparatively recently as the term for those conditions, both organic and psychological, that inhibit sexual functioning. Historically, terminology in this area was loosely applied. Frigidity, for example, the most common word used in relation to sexual dysfunction in women, has meant everything from general lack of sexual desire to the inability to achieve a vaginal orgasm. One of the achievements of contemporary sex therapy and research has been the replacement of such vague language with more scientifically precise, or at least less pejorative, definitions.

The lack of agreement over the basic use of terms is paralleled in the literature by diverse views regarding the causes and treatment of sexual dysfunction in women. Bernard Talmey in Neurasthenia Sexualis (entry 1590), published in 1912, maintained that all forms of nonvaginal erotic stimulation should be discouraged because they inhibited women's ability to achieve vaginal orgasm (Talmey agreed with Freud that vaginal orgasm was superior to the clitoral variety). Other early writers, such as Arthur Edis (entry 1572), recommended remedies, such as lubricants and douches, to relieve actual physical discomfort, but paid little attention to orgasm.

Marie Nyswander Robinson's The Power of Sexual Surrender (entry 1586) claimed that frigidity was a neurosis characterized by any form of sexual response short of vaginal orgasm. For her, the cure was psychoanalysis, but for Ronald M. Deutsch (entry 1570), writing just nine years later in 1968, it was conditioning of the pubococcygeus and other pelvic floor muscles.

General discrediting of the Freudian concept of the superiority of the so-called vaginal orgasm followed in the wake of Masters and Johnson's research into the physiology of sexual response. Feminists were quick to seize upon the myth of vaginal orgasm as just one more example of how men had devised theories of women's "normal" sexuality that served their own, rather than women's, desires and needs. Much of the new sex therapy of the 1970s had an implicit feminist component, as women were taught by Lonnie Barbach (entry 1565) and others to achieve independently their own sexual satisfaction. Other therapists,

however, felt that sexual dysfunction was usually a problem involving
two individuals and sought to involve both partners in a relationship
in the therapy process. Whatever the individual point of view, it is
clear that contemporary research in sexual and orgasmic physiology, as
well as women's own perception of their right to experience sexual
pleasure, have revolutionized the way professional and lay individuals
alike approach problems of sexual dysfunction in women.

1564   BAISDEN, MAJOR J., Jr. The World of Rosaphrenia: The Sexual
       Psychology of the Female. Sacramento, Calif.: Allied Research
       Society, 1971. 223 pp.
            Baisden, who has a Ph.D. in educational psychology and a
       California license as a marriage, family, and child counselor,
       claims to have identified a condition, Rosaphrenia (named for his
       late wife, Rosa), that afflicts 87 percent of the United States fe-
       male population. According to Baisden, this condition, which is
       caused by rape or "maternal osmosis," is characterized by "(1) the
       lack of self-realization sexually, (2) a poorly developed concept
       of the sexual role of the female, (3) frequent inert sexual rela-
       tionships, and (4) negative responses to the male whom she loves
       or with whom she feels closely associated." The whole book is full
       of wild assertions and unsound, unproved theories. Because of its
       various unique qualities, this work may be of some interest to
       students of unconventional sexuality theory and personality develop-
       ment.

1565   BARBACH, LONNIE GARFIELD. For Yourself: The Fulfillment of
       Female Sexuality. Garden City, N.Y.: Doubleday, 1975. 217 pp.
            This self-help book was written primarily for women who have
       difficulty in having orgasms. It is based on Lonnie Barbach's ex-
       perience as a psychologist and sex therapist at the University of
       California Medical Center in San Francisco, but incorporates tech-
       niques developed by others, such as Dr. Joseph LoPiccolo's scheme
       of progressive exercises. Unlike many sex therapy programs, which
       are designed to be engaged in by heterosexual couples, Barbach's
       is intended for women alone, although therapeutic self-stimulation
       techniques are supplemented by pair exercises. Most of the book
       is concerned with providing instructions for self-therapy, although
       Barbach includes additional material on such topics as sex and ag-
       ing and sex education.

1566   _____. Women Discover Orgasm: A Therapist's Guide to a New
       Treatment Approach. New York: Free Press, 1980. 237 pp.
            Lonnie Barbach first began using the group method for treat-
       ment of orgasmic dysfunction in 1972 at the University of California,
       Berkeley, health service. This book, written particularly for pro-
       fessional sex therapists, expands upon her 1975 self-help book for
       nonorgasmic women, For Yourself. Barbach, whose underlying philoso-
       phy is that women have responsibility for their own sexual satis-
       faction, describes the step-by-step process of organizing and

running a women's orgasmic therapy group. There is also a chapter on ethical issues of group treatment, a short review of causes of and modes of treatment for orgasmic dysfunction, and a bibliography.

1567   BERGLER, EDMUND. <u>Neurotic Counterfiet-Sex: Impotence, Frigidity, "Mechanical" and Pseudosexuality, Homosexuality</u>. New York: Grune & Stratton, 1951. 360 pp.

Bergler, a Freudian psychoanalyst, defined counterfeit-sex as sexual behavior in which tenderness, love, and concentration of feelings on one person are absent or rejected. Such behavior characterized many neurotics, and Bergler even went so far as to claim that it was the predominant form of sexuality of the time.

The book is divided into two sections, the first dealing with male impotence, the second with female frigidity. Defining frigidity as absence of vaginal orgasm, Bergler states that 90 percent of all women are vaginally frigid. Since frigidity is a symptom of neurosis, these women would be neurotic as well. A believer in the mature woman's transference of sexual sensation from the clitoris to the vagina, Bergler also claims that women "must inwardly accept passivity without resentment and grievances." Women who seek and enjoy cunnilingus "belong either in the group of pseudoaggressive 'castrating' females, in their conscious fantasies humiliating the male, or in the group of frigid women who are able to achieve clitoric orgasm in that way." Lesbians, all of whom fall into the frigid category, are branded as orally regressed and neurotic. Bergler's primary sources for this monograph are his previous publications and case histories, some of which are duplicated here.

1567   CAPRIO, FRANK S. <u>The Sexually Adequate Female</u>. New York: Citadel, 1953. 223 pp.

Caprio's primary concern in <u>The Sexually Adequate Female</u> is frigidity, a condition he finds to be rampant in women and a leading cause of divorce. His definition of the term is somewhat loose --at one point he calls it sexual inadequacy, specifically the inability to achieve a vaginal orgasm, while elsewhere he says it is simply difficulty in achieving vaginal orgasm. His emphasis on vaginal orgasm and conventional intercourse as the only normal sexual conditions for women is made clear in this passage regarding variations in sexual expression: "If the variation in expression serves as foreplay to the sex act, it is included within the range of normality. But if the particular deviation (fellatio, cunnilingus, stimulation of the clitoris, rectal intercourse, etc.) becomes an end in itself, then it . . . is not considered normal."

Caprio makes a great many undocumented assertions: frigid wives often become unfaithful, most women alcoholics are frigid, frigid women create neurotic, philandering husbands. He describes in great detail types of frigidity and frigid personalities, including the "anti-male" type. "Nature intended a woman to be feminine, affectionate, and passive. She can be helpfully persuasive. But when her aggressiveness far exceeds this, she becomes a 'personality freak.'" Incorporating case histories and dream analyses from his own psychiatric practice, Caprio recommends sex education, premarital surgical defloration, and psychotherapy as ways of avoiding and combating sexual frigidity.

1569   COPELAN, RACHEL. The Sexually Fulfilled Woman. New York: Information, Inc., 1971. 314 pp.

By "sexually fulfilled," Copelan means women who can achieve full orgasm, or vaginal orgasm. It is not clear why Copelan, who is obviously familiar with Masters and Johnson's work, makes this distinction, but she does, even maintaining that one full orgasm per love-making session is enough and that women who want more "can only be experiencing the clitoral type."

Copelan believes that women's psychological and emotional conditioning, as well as some physical inadequacies, prevent them from achieving orgasm, and in order to allay this inadequacy, she prescribes seven stages of mental and physical techniques, including autosuggestion and body relaxation.

1570   DEUTSCH, RONALD M. The Key to Feminine Response in Marriage. New York: Random House, 1968. 172 pp.

Deutsch, a popular medical writer, wrote this book chiefly to explain the use of Kegel exercises for conditioning of the pubococcygeus and other pelvic floor muscles. Believing that most American women suffer from some degree of sexual failure, he equates this with failure to respond to vaginal stimulation during intercourse. Thus, he perpetuates the idea of two kinds of orgasm, failing to see that the pelvic floor muscles may also play a major role in the achievement of a clitorally induced orgasm. Deutsch is cautious, however, in claiming too much for Kegel's discovery and discusses other causes of sexual inhibition and dissatisfaction lying outside simple lack of muscle tone.

1571   DEVENSKY, I. How to Overcome Sex Frigidity in Women: A Guide to Proper Sex Behaviour. New York: William-Frederick, 1952. 36 pp.

This pamphlet is described on the frontispiece as being an excerpt from a work entitled Sexual Incompatibility Prevented and Corrected, but there is no evidence in the National Union Catalog that such a book was ever published. Devensky, a self-styled sexologist, discusses differences in male and female sexual response and behavior which may lead to maladjustment. He discusses such questions of female sexuality as periodicity of desire, but his primary focus is frigidity, which he equates with lack of sexual satisfaction. They are, of course, technically different phenomena, since the latter may be due to no more than bungled efforts by the partner, whereas the former implies a physical or psychological state of the woman alone. Devensky was not the only writer to confuse the two. His advice on technique shows clear knowledge of female sexual response, although some of his conclusions may have to be taken with a grain of salt: "To a great extent the physical and mental health of a woman is regulated by the clitoris. . . . Remember, it takes two persons to make one frigid woman."

330

1572 EDIS, ARTHUR W. Sterility in Women, Including Its Causation and
      Treatment. London: H.K. Lewis, 1890. 112 pp.
          Edis's treatise on sterility in women was an expansion of a
      section of his 1881 Manual of Diseases of Women and was simulta-
      neously published in London and Philadelphia. Edis clearly distin-
      guished between frigidity and sterility, unlike such contemporaries
      of his as Hammond: "Numbers of wives become mothers who have even
      a positive aversion to the sexual act, and where not the remotest
      sensation of pleasure is experienced at those times, there being a
      complete absense of sexual feeling." Clearly, however, a condition
      such as vaginismus or dyspareunia could be aggravated, if not
      caused, by a woman's psychological anticipation of discomfort. Al-
      though Edis was not loathe to recommend heroic or surgical measures
      in persistent cases, his simple prescription of rest and constitu-
      tional healing, followed by the use of a lubricant to facilitate
      intromission, was probably effective in many cases. It is interest-
      ing to note that Edis practiced in Wimpole Street, and therefore his
      cases, many of which are described, were drawn from social and eco-
      nomic groups not usually seen in the hospitals that furnished the
      case evidence cited by many of his colleagues. This is apparent in
      his descriptions.

1573 GALLICHAN, WALTER MATTHEW. Sexual Apathy and Coldness in Women.
      Boston: Stratford, 1928. 183 pp.
          A lot of unfounded nonsense characterizes this book, which
      was originally published in London in 1927. One example: "The
      cold-natured [sexually frigid] woman is often an active supporter
      of reformative organizations, female emancipation crusades, purity
      campaigns, and societies for the suppression of vice." Not only
      does Gallichan equate "masculine" appearance and interests with
      frigidity, but he also claims that "a vast number of prudish women,
      who affect a horror of sex, are constant masturbators." Constipa-
      tion is also blamed. Although Gallichan cites many contemporary
      writers on sexual psychology, especially psychoanalysis, he is of
      a decidedly unscientific train of mind and has great difficulty
      discriminating between fact and fancy.

1574 HASTINGS, DONALD W. Impotence and Frigidity. Boston: Little,
      Brown, 1963. 144 pp.
          Psychiatrist Donald W. Hastings has been a key figure asso-
      ciated with several innovative programs relating to human sexuality
      at the University of Minnesota Medical School. Recognizing the
      dearth of knowledge in this field felt by many practitioners, he
      prepared this nontechnical book for physicians, counselors, and
      even lay readers. Topics discussed here relating to women include
      "normal" sexual intercourse, frigidity, and homosexuality. Hastings
      is especially sensitive to individual differences and variations
      from so-called norms as well as to the vagaries and misconceptions
      of past research and writing in the field. His generalizations are
      well documented and incorporate the latest (for that time) research.
      His dismissal of Freud's vaginal orgasm theory is brief and to the

point: "One is forced to regard the theory as the unsupported opinion of a very gifted man, but unsupported nevertheless."

1575   HIRSCH, EDWIN WALTER. Impotence and Frigidity. New York: Citadel Press, 1966. 284 pp.
    Frigidity is dealt with in the final hundred pages of this rather peculiar book. Hirsch presents short chapters, usually in the form of a case history or a dialogue, on specific topics-- masturbation neurosis, pseudofrigidity, and so on--relating to the general theme. Generally rejecting psychoanalytic theory, Hirsch denied that frigidity was a neurosis and took particular exception to the concept of vaginal orgasm. "Pay no heed to the Freudian ideas about physiologic clitorine autoerotism being a perversion. Too many people in America are neurotic because Freud had a neurosis and did not know how to cure himself." Hirsch believed that sexual success was simply a matter of physical technique. However, his glib presentation with lack of documented evidence makes him just as guilty of "unscientific" method as was Freud.

1576   HITSCHMANN, EDWARD, and EDMUND BERGLER. Frigidity in Women: Its Characteristics and Treatment. Translated by Polly Leeds Weil. Washington, D.C., and New York: Nervous and Mental Disease Publishing Co., 1936. 76 pp.
    Works such as this one by Viennese Freudians Hitschmann and Bergler helped to cement and perpetuate the myth of the vaginal orgasm among the English-language audience. Equating frigidity with the absence of a vaginal orgasm, they specifically discount the validity of the clitoral orgasm. Their ideas about woman's normal role are revealed by statements like these: "Woman's destiny to be complete must also include [in addition to the orgasm] child-bearing and suckling," and, if this were achieved, "ridiculous manifestations of the woman's movement would disappear." Of a case study, they remark, "Born with a female body, she should have found her destiny in passive surrender." As always, one must marvel at the Freudians' ability not only to elaborate theories based on not one whit of empirical evidence but to take "evidence" drawn from exceptional or extreme cases and extrapolate from it to the so-called normal. Perhaps the only good thing about this work is that it does provide a clear, concise summary of Freud's theory of the development of female sexuality.

1577   KANT, FRITZ. Frigidity: Dynamics and Treatment. Springfield, Ill.: Charles C. Thomas, 1969. 61 pp.
    No psychosexual term has had such a variety of definitions and interpretations as frigidity. In this somewhat superficial account, Kant defines frigidity as "absence of an orgastic reaction as a response to a male partner," allowing that its manifestations and causes are diverse and complex. He argues that impotence in men is not an equivalent condition. Although many of Kant's remarks indicate his support for conventional female gender roles, he does discard the Freudian concept of vaginal orgasm.

1578   KAPLAN, HELEN SINGER. The New Sex Therapy: Active Treatment
       of Sexual Dysfunctions. New York: Brunner/Mazel and Quadrangle,
       1974. 544 pp.
            One of the United States' best-known sex therapists, Helen
       Singer Kaplan is head of the sex therapy and education program of
       the Payne Whitney Clinic at New York Hospital. The New Sex Therapy
       summarizes contemporary research and technique in the field of treat-
       ment of sexual dysfunction. Kaplan includes general material on the
       determinants of sexual response, as well as extensive sections on
       biological and physiological causes of sexual dysfunction, treatment
       options, characteristics of specific dysfunctions (in the case of
       women's frigidity, orgastic dysfunction and vaginismus), sex thera-
       py results, and special problems, such as psychiatric disorders.
       Case histories and some illustrations amplify the points in Kaplan's
       narrative. This work is also significant in its attempt to relate
       technical material on sexual dysfunction to theories of psychopath-
       ology and psychiatric treatment. Although the book is extremely
       well written, it would have been more useful as a base for further
       study if the author's references and bibliographic citations had
       been more extensive.

1579   KLINE-GRABER, GEORGIA, and BENJAMIN GRABER. Woman's Orgasm: A
       Guide to Sexual Satisfaction. Indianapolis: Bobbs-Merrill,
       1975. 188 pp.
            Sex therapists Kline-Graber and Graber firmly believe that
       sex and orgasm are learned behaviors and that lack of knowledge,
       not psychiatric problems, is at the root of most women's orgasm
       problems. The first half of the book is devoted to a discussion
       of theories of and research on female sexuality and sexual response
       physiology as well as medical/physical problems that can cause or-
       gasmic dysfunction. Then, utilizing the work of Joseph LoPiccolo,
       the authors outline two step-by-step programs by which their read-
       ers can achieve orgasm—one by self-stimulation and the other uti-
       lizing heterosexual intercourse. Kline-Graber and Graber comment:
       "It is true that many women prefer sexual activity with a [male]
       partner and find orgasm with intercourse more emotionally satisfy-
       ing than one without, particularly within the context of a love
       relationship. However, the orgasm that occurs without the penis
       inside feels more distinct on a physical basis because it is physi-
       cally more intense."

1580   LEVINE, LENA, and MILDRED GILMAN. Frigidity. New York:
       Planned Parenthood Federation of America, 1952. 12 pp.
            Although Levine and Gilman define frigidity as "the complete
       lack of sex desire with a resulting inability to respond to stimu-
       lation and arousal," this pamphlet is focused more on factors re-
       lating to women's inability to achieve orgasm, such as differences
       between men and women, psychological factors, and physical factors.
       The authors suggest education and communication as the best means
       for overcoming "frigidity."

1581   LEVINE, LENA, and DAVID LOTH. The Frigid Wife: Her Way to
       Sexual Fulfillment. New York: Julian Messner, 1962. 256 pp.
         Levine and Loth believe that the term frigidity should be
       applied only to those women who have no sexual desire at all. In
       this book, however, they defer to popular usage and define it as
       women's failure to attain what they or their partners regard as
       adequate sexual desire and response. They subscribe to Freud's
       theory of vaginal orgasm and transference of sexual pleasure from
       the clitoris, but unlike Marie Robinson, do not seize upon this as
       a means of determining woman's sexual maturity and mental health.
       "There are many women who cannot go beyond clitoral orgasm. They
       are no less womanly, no less adequate as sex partners, no colder
       than women who have the same feeling with penetration." Causes of
       frigidity are discussed, as are methods for overcoming this dysfunc-
       tion.

1582   LYDSTON, GEORGE FRANK. Impotence and Sterility, with Aberrations
       of the Sexual Function and Sex-gland Implantation. Chicago:
       Riverton Press, 1917. 333 pp.
         Lydston's description of his experiments on human subjects
       (including himself!) in transplanting ovaries and testes and his
       advocacy of such procedures as a treatment for dementia praecox
       set this book apart from others on the topics of impotence and
       sterility. "In implantation of sex glands we have the most logical
       method for the administration of probably the most important of
       all the internal secretions in the field of psychiatry." Lydston
       did not stop at dementia praecox, however, in his advocacy of sexu-
       al surgery. He advocated ovariotomy and clitoridectomy as treat-
       ments for nymphomania, and sterilization "in all intractable cases
       of sexual psychosis." Sewing machines were condemned for producing
       "uterine congestion and irritation, with coincident sexual excite-
       ment," as were boarding schools, "sources of especial danger to
       both sexes."

1583   MARTIN, EDWARD. Impotence and Sexual Weakness in the Male and
       Female. Detroit: G.S. Davis, 1893. 102 pp.
         Martin, who was clinical professor of genito-urinary surgery
       at the University of Pennsylvania, devoted only six pages to women,
       including failure to achieve orgasm as a form of impotence in women.
       Martin emphasized the role of congenital or pathological abnormali-
       ties and also alluded to a connection between hysteria and unwanted
       sexual relations. He observed that many women never experience
       orgasms: "The sexual act is for them merely an expression of con-
       jugal obedience or a means of bearing children, . . . in itself the
       whole process is unpleasant or even positively revolting." Martin
       did not, however, consider this to be a problem: "Since sexual
       desire is dead, pleasure in the sexual act is not to be excited;
       nor is this to be regretted, since such women make good wives,
       loving mothers, and are not tempted to stray in the paths which
       the comparatively small number of their more amorous sisters at
       times find too alluring."

1584 MASTERS, WILLIAM H., and VIRGINIA E. JOHNSON. <u>Human Sexual</u>
<u>Inadequacy</u>. Boston: Little, Brown, 1970. 467 pp.
This natural sequel to <u>Human Sexual Response</u> (entry 580) describes the rapid-treatment programs for sexual dysfunction developed at the Reproductive Biology Research Foundation. One basic
premise of the therapy techniques developed by Masters and Johnson
is the necessity for involving the partner in any treatment program.
Moreover, treatment is undertaken by a therapy team with a member
from each sex. This contrasts with the approach taken by some other
therapists, such as Lonnie Barbach, who ulitize an individual approach.
Specific female sexual dysfunctions included in the book are
orgasmic dysfunction (the word <u>frigidity</u> does not appear), vaginismus, dyspareunia, and sexual inadequacy in aging women. Some case
history information is presented, and the authors reprint case
history forms, questionnaires, and other material used in diagnosing cases. One of the interesting aspects of this work is the five-
year followup and evaluation of the effectiveness of the therapy
program. There are also some candid remarks about the relationship
of this particular program of therapy to psychotherapeutic techniques. An extensive bibliography concludes the work.

1585 MORSE, BENJAMIN. <u>Sexual Surrender in Women: A Penetrating</u>
<u>Inquiry into Frigidity, Its Causes, Manifestations and Cures</u>.
Derby, Conn.: Monarch, 1962. 155 pp.
Unlike more serious authors, who assay a narrow definition
of frigidity, even though their discussion may entail a broader
area of sexual response, Morse, writing for the sexploitation market, offers this sweeping, sexist one: "Frigidity is a condition
in which a woman is unable to surrender herself sexually to her
mate." Such a definition, of course, admits a wide realm of possibilities, albeit always ones in which the "normal" state is one
where the male dominates the surrendering female. Morse exploits
his opportunities to the full, offering simplistic psychiatric
analysis of his cases: "The significant factors were not Gloria's
lesbianism, but the forces responsible for its existence in the
first place. A good examination and excavation of those forces
would cure her latent lesbianism, her frigidity, and all attendant
complications in one fell swoop." It isn't clear whether this is
fiction or fact. One hopes the former as it is depressing to consider that this kind of drivel may have been based on real-life
situations and cases.

1586 ROBINSON, MARIE NYSWANDER. <u>The Power of Sexual Surrender</u>.
Garden City, N.Y.: Doubleday, 1959. 263 pp.
There is perhaps no better introduction to stereotypes about
so-called vaginal orgasms than this popular work by New York psychiatrist Marie Robinson. Claiming that sexual frigidity is suffered by 40 percent of all married women, she describes that condition as any response short of a "true" vaginal orgasm. "Frigidity
is an expression of neurosis, a disturbance of the unconscious life

of the individual destructive to personal relationships." Needless to say, clitoral responsiveness is a form of frigidity.

Robinson firmly believes that a woman's lack of sexual responsiveness is never the male's fault, and, indeed, "caressing or manipulating the genitalia or secondary erotic zones . . . could deepen or encourage immature methods of gratification." The true, mature woman defers to men's wishes regarding whether or how they will make love.

There is more here, however, than just concern about orgasm, and Robinson reveals her underlying views of woman in her comments on gender role. The ideal woman does not get excited about a career or personal ambitions. "Her joy and satisfaction in the fulfillment of her own biological destiny [marriage and children] make all other personal achievements pale for her, any other considerable use for her energies almost a waste." Robinson recommends Marie Bonaparte and Helene Deutsch to her readers. Kinsey and Karen Horney are, predictably, absent from her suggested reading list.

1587 ROBINSON, WILLIAM JOSEPHUS. A Practical Treatise on the Causes, Symptoms, and Treatment of Sexual Impotence and Other Sexual Disorders in Men and Women. New York: Critic and Guide Co., 1913. 422 pp.

Since Robinson's works usually display a progressive sensitivity to questions relating to women, as well as an enlightened attitude toward such topics as abortion and birth control, it comes as a shock to read certain portions of this book that demonstrate a different side of Robinson's sexual and social philosophy. Not only does he fully subscribe to the idea of masturbation as a vice leading to a wide range of undesirable symptoms, but he recommends the most repressive measures to treat it, including restraint and the application of red hot wires to children's genitals (a case involving a seven-year-old girl is described). Prolonging intercourse so that women can achieve orgasm is condemned because of the alleged harm it causes men: "The woman who insists upon such methods of gratification should be gently but firmly repressed. If she persists, she should be gotten rid of as soon as possible--whether wife or mistress."

1588 SMITH, CAROLYN; TONI AYRES, and MAGGIE RUBENSTEIN. Getting in Touch: Self Sexuality for Women. San Francisco: Multi Media Resource Center, 1972. Unpaged. ISR.

Part of the Yes Book of Sex Series designed by the National Sex Forum, Getting in Touch encourages women to learn about their own sexuality in order to lead healthy and fulfilling sex lives. Typical of feminists of the early 1970s, the authors propose masturbation as the method for learning. Using simple, direct, positive language, the book offers suggestions and instructions and is illustrated with photographs.

1589 STEKEL, WILHELM. Frigidity in Woman in Relation to Her Love Life. Translated by James S. Van Teslaar. 2 vols. New York: Boni and Liveright, 1926. 304; 314 pp.

Stekel is concerned here with far more than frigidity in the usual sense. For while he builds his analysis around that problem, he is concerned with women's general psychosexual development as well. Although he incorporated psychoanalytic theories into his work, Stekel believed that frigidity was also a product of social forces and human evolution. Its prevalence in the early twentieth century could be linked to woman's renunciation of her earlier sexually defined role. Now, asserting herself against male domination, "woman rebels against her former role of a sexual creature. She abstains from responding so as not to yield."

Much of Frigidity consists of case records, including several lengthy reports in volume 2. Stekel notes the difficulty of obtaining reliable statistical data on frigidity and, unlike many psychoanalytically oriented observers, seems to be aware of the potential problem of drawing general conclusions about health from the observation of a patient population. He also cautions that each woman should be dealt with as a particular case; generalizations about women or attempts at pigeonholing are not appropriate here. His concluding remarks demonstrate his optimism and belief in the power of love: "If lovers were inspired by true love there would be no dyspareunia and perhaps there would be no neurotics in our midst."

1590 TALMEY, BERNARD SIMON. Neurasthenia Sexualis: A Treatise on Sexual Impotence in Men and in Women. New York: Practitioners' Publishing Co., 1912. 196 pp.

Talmey, author of the highly successful Woman: A Treatise on the Normal and Pathological Emotions of Feminine Love, turned his attention here to what he termed impotence, but which really embraced such diverse problems as frigidity and sterility. Talmey was one of many early followers of Freud who adopted his idea of the vaginal orgasm's superiority and necessity for sexual health. In fact, he linked masturbation, as well as other forms of nonvaginal erotic stimulation in women, to their inability to achieve such an orgasm. He was especially concerned not only because of Freud's convictions but because he believed that a vaginal orgasm with uterine contractions was necessary to suck sperm into the cervix and uterus in order to facilitate fertilization. His methods of treatment were, sadly, just as erroneous: electrical shocks to the reproductive and sexual organs, water cures, and drugs such as strychnine and cannabis indica. Also recommended to combat overstimulation were chastity and self-control.

1591 Unresponsive Wives. Sex Education Library, vol. 3. New York: Health Publications, 1960. 16 pp. ISR.

This is a reprint of four articles that originally appeared in Sexology magazine: Edward Dengrove, "Frigidity--Fact and Fiction"; Olivier Loras, "Frigidity and Marital Conflict"; Sarah R. Riedman, "Heightening Sex Satisfaction"; and Helen K. Branson, "Frigidity Is a Mutual Fault."

1592   WRIGHT, HELENA. Sex Fulfilment in Married Women: A Sequel to "The Sex Factor in Marriage". London: Williams & Norgate, 1947. 96 pp.
     Wright estimates that 50 percent of all wives fail to achieve sexual satisfaction in marriage. There are three main reasons for this: failure to understand the difference between an orgasm and generalized sexual response in the erogenous zones; lack of understanding of the role of the clitoris in orgasm; and adherence to misconceptions, usually based on a male model, of what a woman ought to feel in sexual intercourse. Wright describes techniques for correcting dysfunction and includes a historical survey of ideas on female sexuality and orgasm. There is also a bibliography and international list of societies concerned with sex, health, and education.

1593   AARON, RUTH. "Male Contributions to Female Frigidity." Medical Aspects of Human Sexuality 5, no. 5 (May 1971):42-57.

1594   BAKER, SMITH. "The Neuro-psychical Element in Conjugal Aversion." Journal of Nervous and Mental Disease 19, no. 9 (September 1892):669-81.

1595   BEIGEL, HUGO G. "The Use of Hypnosis in Female Sexual Anesthesia." Journal of the American Society of Psychosomatic Dentistry and Medicine 19, no. 1 (1972):4-14.

1596   BERNARDY, EUGENE P. "Report of Cases of Aneroticism in Women." Medical Council 1, no. 2 (April 1896):51-52.

1597   BEYME, F. "Archetypal Dreams and Frigidity." Journal of Analytical Psychology 12, no. 1 (1967):3-22.

1598   BOAS, CONRAD Van EMDE. "Group Therapy of Anorgastic Women." International Journal of Sexology 4, no. 1 (August 1950):1-6.

1599   BRADY, JOHN PAUL. "Brevital-Relaxation Treatment of Frigidity." Behaviour Research and Therapy 4, no. 2 (May 1966):71-77.

1600   BROWN, WARBURTON. "Some Disorders of the Female Sexual Function of Mental Origin." American Journal of Obstetrics and Gynecology 15, no. 4 (April 1928):528-33.

1601   BYCHOWSKI, GUSTAV. "Frigidity and Object Relationship." International Journal of Psycho-analysis 44, no. 1 (January 1963):57-62.

1602   COOPER, ALAN J. "Frigidity, Treatment and Short-term Prognosis." Journal of Psychosomatic Research 14, no. 2 (June 1970):133-47.

1603   DAVIDSON, SAMAI, and ROSA YFTACH. "The Therapy of the Unconsummated Marriage." Psychotherapy: Theory, Research and Practice 13, no. 4 (Winter 1976):418-19.

1604   DEARBORN, T.F. "Impotence in Women." Massachusetts Medical
        Journal 24, no. 11 (November 1904):481-91.

1605   De MOOR, W. "Vaginismus: Etiology and Treatment." American
        Journal of Psychotherapy 26, no. 2 (April 1972):207-15.

1606   DEUTCH, JAMES A. "Toward a Better Understanding of Female Sexual
        Inadequacy." Bulletin, National Guild of Catholic Psychiatrists
        16, no. 2 (May 1969):87-102.

1607   EASLEY, ELEANOR. "Atrophic Vaginitis and Sexual Relations."
        Medical Aspects of Human Sexuality 8, no. 11 (November 1974):
        32-58.

1608   EDWARDS, JOHN N., and ALAN BOOTH. "Cessation of Marital Inter-
        course." American Journal of Psychiatry 133, no. 11 (November
        1976):1333-36.

1609   ELLISON, CARICE. "Vaginismus." Medical Aspects of Human
        Sexuality 6, no. 8 (August 1972):34-54.

1610   FAULK, MALCOLM. "'Frigidity': A Critical Review." Archives
        of Sexual Behavior 2, no. 3 (June 1973):257-66.

1611   FINK, PAUL JAY. "Dyspareunia: Current Concepts." Medical
        Aspects of Human Sexuality 6, no. 12 (December 1972):28-47.

1612   _____. "When a Woman Does Not Climax." Sexual Behavior 3, no.
        1 (January 1973):22-25.

1613   FRANK, ELLEN; CAROL ANDERSON, and DEBRA RUBENSTEIN. "Frequency
        of Sexual Dysfunction in 'Normal' Couples." New England Journal
        of Medicine 299 (20 July 1978):111-15.

1614   FUCHS, KARL, et al. "Vaginismus--the Hypno-Therapeutic Approach."
        Journal of Sex Research 11, no. 1 (February 1975):39-45.

1615   "Furor over Vaginal Surgery for Anorgasmy." Medical World News
        19, no. 8 (17 April 1978):15-16.

1616   GILLET, MYRTLE MANN. "Normal Frigidity in Woman: A Plea to the
        Family Physician." International Journal of Sexology 5, no. 1
        (August 1951):34-35.

1617   GILLETTE, WALTER R. "A Postural Method of Copulation for Cure
        of Some Forms of Sterility in the Female." Archives of Medicine
        3, no. 1 (February 1880):57-64.

1618   GREER, BENJAMIN E. "Painful Coitus Due to Hymenal Problems."
        Medical Aspects of Human Sexuality 9, no. 2 (February 1975):
        160-69.

1619   GUNNING, JOSEPHUS HENRY. "Vaginismus; Its Causes and Treatment."
       American Gynaecological and Obstetrical Journal 7 (December 1895):
       613-19; 664-66.

1620   HAMILTON, EUGENE G. "Frigidity in the Female." Missouri
       Medicine 58, no. 10 (October 1961):1040-51.

1621   HITSCHMANN, EDWARD, and EDMUND BERGLER. "Frigidity in Women--
       Restatement and Renewed Experience." Psychoanalytic Review 36,
       no. 1 (January 1949):45-53.

1622   HUHNER, MAX. "Absence of Pleasure in the Female During Sexual
       Intercourse." American Medicine 39, no. 11 (November 1933):
       522-28.

1623   JOSEPH, EDWARD D. "An Aspect of Female Frigidity." Journal of
       the American Psychoanalytic Association 22, no. 1 (1974):116-22.

1624   KAPLAN, HELEN SINGER. "The Classification of the Female Sexual
       Dysfunctions." Journal of Sex and Marital Therapy 1, no. 2
       (Winter 1974):124-38.

1625   KAUFMAN, SHERWIN A. "Physical Clues to Sexual Maladjustment in
       Women." Medical Aspects of Human Sexuality 4, no. 6 (June 1970):
       38-46.

1626   KIEV, ARI, and ELIZABETH HACKETT. "The Chemotherapy of Impotence
       and Frigidity." Journal of Sex Research 4, no. 3 (August 1968):
       220-24.

1627   KINCH, R.A.H. "Painful Coitus." Medical Aspects of Human
       Sexuality 1, no. 2 (October 1967):6-12.

1628   KLEEGMAN, SOPHIA J. "Frigidity in Women." Quarterly Review of
       Surgery, Obstetrics and Gynecology 16, no. 4 (December 1959):
       243-48.

1629   KLUMPP, JAMES S. "Marital Maladjustments as They Affect the
       Physician." West Virginia Medical Journal 29, no. 2 (February
       1933):64-67.

1630   KNIGHT, ROBERT P. "Functional Disturbances in the Sexual Life
       of Women: Frigidity and Related Disorders." Bulletin of the
       Menninger Clinic 7, no. 1 (January 1943):25-35.

1631   KOLISCHER, G. "Sexual Frigidity in Women." American Journal
       of Obstetrics and Diseases of Women and Children 52, no. 3
       (September 1905):414-16.

1632   KOLODNY, ROBERT C. "Sexual Dysfunction in Diabetic Females."
       Medical Aspects of Human Sexuality 6, no. 4 (April 1972):98-106.

1633   KRAFT, THOMAS, and IHSAN AL-ISSA. "Behavior Therapy and the Treatment of Frigidity." American Journal of Psychotherapy 21, no. 1 (January 1967):116-20.

1634   KROGER, WILLIAM S., and CHARLES S. FREED. "Psychosomatic Aspects of Frigidity." Journal of the American Medical Association 143, no. 6 (10 June 1950):526-32.

1635   La BERT, JULES. "Vaginal Spasms--Vaginismus." Sexology 1, no. 10 (June 1934):689-91.

1636   LAMSON, HERBERT D. "Are American Women Frigid?" International Journal of Sexology 3, no. 3 (February 1950):162-67.

1637   LAZARUS, ARNOLD A. "The Treatment of Chronic Frigidity by Systematic Desensitization." Journal of Nervous and Mental Disease 136, no. 3 (March 1963):272-78.

1638   LING, THOMAS M., and JOHN BUCKMAN. "The Treatment of Frigidity with LSD and Ritalin." In The Psychedelic Reader: Selected from the Psychedelic Review, edited by Gunther Weil, Ralph Metzner, and Timothy Leary, 231-39. New York: University Books, 1965.

1639   LoPICCOLO, JOSEPH, and W. CHARLES LOBITZ. "The Role of Masturbation in the Treatment of Orgasmic Dysfunction." Archives of Sexual Behavior 2, no. 2 (December 1972):163-71.

1640   LOWRIE, ROBERT J. "Frigidity in Women." Western Journal of Surgery, Obstetrics and Gynecology 60, no. 9 (September 1952): 458-62.

1641   McGUIRE, TERENCE F., and RICHARD M. STEINHILBER. "Frigidity, the Primary Female Sexual Dysfunction." Medical Asepcts of Human Sexuality 4, no. 10 (October 1970):108-23.

1642   MAYER, MAX. "Classification and Treatment of Dyspareunia." American Journal of Obstetrics and Gynecology 24, no. 5 (November 1932):751-55.

1643   MOORE, BURNESS EVANS. "Frigidity: A Review of Psychoanalytic Literature." Psychoanalytic Quarterly 33, no. 3 (1964):323-49.

1644   _____. "Frigidity in Women." Journal of the American Psychoanalytic Association 9, no. 3 (July 1961):571-84.

1645   MUNJACK, DENNIS, and PAMELA KANNO. "An Overview of Outcome on Frigidity: Treatment Effects and Effectiveness." Comprehensive Psychiatry 17, no. 3 (May-June 1976):401-14.

1646   OFFIR, CAROLE WADE. "Women's Orgasm: Getting There Alone." Psychology Today 10, no. 6 (November 1976):94-97.

1647   OWENSBY, NEWDIGATE M. "Sexual Frigidity." Urologic and
       Cutaneous Review 33, no. 8 (August 1929):534-37.

1648   OYSTRAGH, PHILIP M.B. "Hypnosis and Frigidity." Journal of the
       American Society of Psychosomatic Dentistry and Medicine 21, no.
       1 (1974):10-18.

1649   PAULSON, MORRIS J., and TIEN TEH LIN. "Frigidity: A Factor
       Analytic Study of a Psychosomatic Theory." Psychosomatics 11,
       no. 2 (March-April 1970):112-19.

1650   PAYKEL, EUGENE S., and MYRNA M. WEISSMAN. "Marital and Sexual
       Dysfunction in Depressed Women." Medical Aspects of Human
       Sexuality 6, no. 6 (June 1972):73-101.

1651   PHILLIPS, G.M. "Sexual Infelicity." General Practitioner 2,
       no. 5 (May 1896):155-59; no. 6 (June 1896):194-99.

1652   POLATIN, PHILLIP. "The Frigid Woman." Medical Aspects of Human
       Sexuality 4, no. 8 (August 1970):8-25.

1653   POPE, CURRAN. "Virginity of Twenty Years Standing in a Married
       Woman Suffering from Neurasthenia." American Journal of Urology,
       Venereal and Sexual Diseases 11, no. 6 (June 1915):250-60.

1654   POPENOE, PAUL. "Marital Counselling, with Special Reference to
       Frigidity." Western Journal of Surgery, Obstetrics and Gynecology
       45, no. 1 (January 1937):27-35.

1655   REDMOND, ANNE C. "Brief Guide to Office Counseling: When a
       Wife's Desire Exceeds Her Husband's." Medical Aspects of Human
       Sexuality 9, no. 1 (January 1975):97-98.

1656   RICHARDSON, T.A. "Hypnotherapy in Frigidity and Parafrigidity
       Problems." Journal of the American Society of Psychosomatic
       Dentistry and Medicine 15, no. 3 (July 1968):88-96.

1657   ROSE, A. "Female Frigidity; Its Rational Treatment." Medical
       Council 15, no. 12 (December 1910):419-23.

1658   ROSENTHAL, SAUL H. "Brief Guide to Office Counseling: Frigidity
       in Women." Medical Aspects of Human Sexuality 8, no. 11 (November
       1974):81-82.

1659   ROSENTHAL, SAUL H., and CHAUNCEY F. ROSENTHAL. "Types of Fri-
       gidity." Medical Aspects of Human Sexuality 9, no. 5 (May 1975):
       116-25.

1660   SADOUGHI, W., and IRVING M. BUSH. "Urologic Symptoms as a
       Psychological Crutch for Underlying Sex Problems." Medical
       Aspects of Human Sexuality 8, no. 7 (July 1974):130-51.

1661   SCHAETZING, EBERHARD. "Female Impotence." International Journal of Sexology 8, no. 1 (August 1954):16-19.

1662   SCHNECK, JEROME M. "Hynotherapy for Vaginismus." International Journal of Clinical and Experimental Hypnosis 13, no. 2 (April 1965):92-95.

1663   SCHNELLER, M.R. "Sex Maladjustments of Life and Marriage." Sexology 1, no. 1 (Summer 1933):28-30.

1664   SETTLAGE, DIANE S. FORDNEY. "Brief Guide to Office Counseling: Clitoral Abnormalities." Medical Aspects of Human Sexuality 9, no. 5 (May 1975):183-84.

1665   SHUFELDT, R.W. "Frigiditas Uxoris, Sociologically and Medically Considered." Pacific Medical Journal 50, no. 11 (November 1907): 696-704.

1666   SMITH, A. LAPTHORN. "A Case in Which Sexual Feeling First Appeared after Removal of Both Ovaries." American Journal of Obstetrics and Diseases of Women and Children 42, no. 6 (December 1900):839-42.

1667   SMITH, ELAINE P., and JON K. MEYER. "Attitudes and Temperaments of Nonorgastic Women." Medical Aspects of Human Sexuality 12, no. 6 (June 1978):66-79.

1668   SONNE, JOHN C. "Women Who Fear Orgasm." Medical Aspects of Human Sexuality 7, no. 10 (October 1973):128-38.

1669   SOTILE, WAYNE M., and PETER R. KILMANN. "Treatments of Psychogenic Female Sexual Dysfunctions." Psychological Bulletin 84, no. 4 (July 1977):619-33.

1670   STOKES, WALTER R. "Sexual Frigidity in Women." Medical Annals of the District of Columbia 2, no. 11 (November 1933):264-71.

1671   STONE, HANNAH M., and ABRAHAM STONE. "Genital Spasm as a Cause of Sexual Disharmony." Medical Journal and Record 138, no. 10 (15 November 1933):350-53.

1672   STRONG, C.M. "Frigidity from the Sociological and Gynecological Viewpoint." Virginia Medical Semi-Monthly 14, no. 8 (23 July 1909):180-82.

1673   STURGIS, FREDERICK R. "Sexual Incompetence; Causes and Treatment." Medical Council 12, no. 2 (February 1907):61-63; no. 3 (March 1907):101-3; no. 4 (April 1907):125-29; no. 5 (May 1907): 163-65; no. 7 (July 1907):233-36; no. 8 (August 1907):269-71; no. 9 (September 1907):307-9; no. 10 (October 1907):345-46; no. 11 (November 1907):388-89; no. 12 (December 1907):422-25; 13, no. 1 (January 1908):8–12; no. 2 (February 1908):42–44; no. 3 (March 1908):80–83.

1674   TALMEY, BERNARD SIMON. "Frigidity and Sterility in the Female." Medical Record 100, no. 15 (8 October 1921):631–33.

1675   TERHUNE, WILLIAM B. "Marital Maladjustments." Yale Journal of Biology and Medicine 4 (December 1931):149–65.

1676   TOLAND, OWEN JONES. "Unsatisfactory Intercourse, Its Treatment." Medical Clinics of North America 19, no. 1 (July 1935):267–71.

1677   UDDENBERG, NILS. "Psychological Aspects of Sexual Inadequacy in Women." Journal of Psychosomatic Research 18, no. 1 (February 1974):33–47.

1678   Van de WARKER, ELY. "Impotency in Women." American Journal of Obstetrics and Diseases of Women and Children 11, no. 1 (January 1878):36–47.

1679   VECKI, VICTOR G. "Sexual Frigidity and Impotence; a New Endemic." Urologic and Cutaneous Review 25, no. 1 (January 1921):33.

1680   VINCENT, CLARK E. "Social and Interpersonal Sources of Symptomatic Frigidity." Marriage and Family Living 18, no. 4 (November 1956):355–60.

1681   WILLIAMS, P.H. "Psychic Vaginismus, with a Report of Two Cases." American Journal of Obstetrics and Diseases of Women and Children 74, no. 2 (August 1916):226–32.

1682   WINCZE, JOHN P.; EMILY FRANCK HOON, and PETER W. HOON. "Physiological Responsivity of Normal and Sexually Dysfunctional Women During Erotic Stimulus Exposure." Journal of Psychosomatic Research 20, no. 5 (1976):445–52.

1683   WORTIS, S. BERNARD, et al. "Unsuccessful Sex Adjustment in Marriage." Journal of Contraception 4, no. 10 (December 1939):227–35.

1684   ZEISS, ANTONETTE M.; GERALD M. ROSEN, and ROBERT A. ZEISS. "Orgasm During Intercourse: A Treatment Strategy for Women." Journal of Consulting and Clinical Psychology 45, no. 5 (October 1977):891–95.

Author/Title Index

Subject Index

Jenkins, W.O., 948

Johns Hoplins University, Hospital and School of Medicine, 1533

Johnson, Virginia E., 70, 133, 147, 164, 175, 178, 202, 349, 568, 584, 657, 668, 705, 867, 935, 943, 975, 1569

Jones, Ernest, 321

Journal of the American Psycho-Analytic Association, 318, 349

Joy of Sex, The, 923, 1354

Julian Press, 896

Jung, Carl Gustav, 341, 1081

Jung, Emma, 351

Jurisprudence, 155, 270, 273, 274, 293, 296, 298, 304, 307, 308, 464, 920, 1413

Juvenile delinquency, 76, 285, 1201, 1418, 1492, 1494, 1496, 1497, 1498, 1501, 1502, 1506, 1507, 1508, 1509, 1510, 1511, 1512, 1514, 1515, 1516, 1517, 1519, 1520, 1521, 1522, 1523, 1525, 1526. See also Criminal justice, administration of; Sex crimes

Kaplan, Eugene H., 339

Kaplan, Helen Singer, 173

Karezza. See Male continence

Kegel exercises, 812, 1570

Kellogg, John Harvey, 42

Kelly, Howard A., 402, 1105

Kerr, R.B., 156

Kestenberg, Judith S., 339

Kinsey, Alfred C., 55, 60, 68, 70, 169, 175, 568, 580, 584, 917, 934, 935, 962, 963, 964, 986, 994, 998, 1017, 1021, 1106, 1113, 1211

Kinsey Institute for Sex Research. See Institute for Sex Research

Kissing, 525, 781, 902, 1093

Kleeman, James A., 1212

Klein, Melanie, 321

Kleptomania, 311, 443, 481, 764, 1451, 1505

Know Thyself, 806

Kobelt, George Ludwig, 61

Koedt, Ann, 568

Krafft-Ebing, Richard von, 92, 184, 207, 273, 333, 407, 409, 410, 796, 837, 864, 1296, 1329, 1336

Krantz, Kermit E., 61

Labeling theory, 1345

Ladies' Home Journal, 78

Lady Chatterley's Lover, 144

Laing, R.D., 343

Lal, Gobind B., 1527

Lamballe, Princess, 1320

L'Amour, 319

Language: psychoanalytic theory, 343; sex and sex-related terminology, 61, 248, 362, 364, 578, 671, 859, 872, 919, 999, 1089, 1096, 1495, 1533

Lasch, Christopher, 1089

Lawrence, D.H., 191

Lectures to Ladies on Anatomy and Physiology, 1098

Legislation: birth control, ⌐ ¬; cohabitation, 260; Comstock laws, 77, 778, 780; protective, 211; sex crimes, 214, 252, 253, 258, 260, 262, 270, 273, 275, 284, 288, 309, 896, 1499; sex-related, 214, 252, 253, 258, 260, 262, 266, 270, 271, 273, 274, 275, 283, 288, 567, 577, 802, 899, 918, 969, 1492, 1532

Legitimité des actes sexuels, La, 256

Lesbianism, 158, 207, 271, 273, 274, 321, 341, 796, 839, 845, 872, 896, 920, 937, 944, 951, 952, 953, 957, 960, 965, 971, 975, 980, 981, 983, 1054, 1082, 1215, 1219, 1298, 1451, 1532, 1541, 1567; adolescents, 1156, 1174, 1198, 1216, 1402, 1418, 1494, 1502, 1511, 1519; bibliography, 11, 24, 49; definition, 40, 47, 73, 75, 80, 82, 104, 142, 144, 205, 330, 336, 823, 953, 1336, 1346, 1347, 1353, 1357; history, 38, 40, 47, 49, 56, 73, 75, 82, 100, 102, 104, 151, 1336; literature, 49, 73, 86, 91, 103, 119, 1336;